Civil Society

Civil Society

Theory, History, Comparison

Edited by
John A. Hall

Polity Press

First published in 1995 by Polity Press
in association with Blackwell Publishers.

Editorial office:
Polity Press
65 Bridge Street
Cambridge CB2 1UR, UK

Marketing and production:
Blackwell Publishers, the publishing imprint of Basil Blackwell Ltd
108 Cowley Road
Oxford OX4 1JF, UK

238 Main Street
Cambridge, MA 02142, USA

ISBN 0 7456 1061 7
ISBN 0 7456 1456 6 (pbk)

A CIP catalogue record for this book is available from the British Library
and the Library of Congress.

Typeset in Stempel Garamond on 11/12 pt
by Best-set Typesetter Ltd., Hong Kong
Printed in Great Britain by TJ Press Ltd Padstow, Cornwall

This book is printed on acid-free paper.

Contents

vi   *Contents*

Notes on Contributors

John A. Hall is Professor of Sociology at McGill University. His books include *Powers and Liberties*, *Liberalism* and, most recently, *Coercion and Consent*.

Ernest Gellner is Director of the Centre for the Study of Nationalism at the Central European University in Prague. His *Conditions of Liberty* has just appeared.

David L. Wank is Lecturer in Sociology in the Faculty of Comparature Culture at Sophia University in Tokyo.

Victor Pérez-Díaz is Professor of Sociology at the Complutense University of Madrid. His analysis of *The Return of Civil Society* has appeared recently.

Wlodzimierz Wesolowski is Professor at the Institute of Philosophy and Sociology, the Polish Academy of Sciences. Recently he co-authored with J. Wasilewski *The Beginnings of the Parliamentary Elite* (in Polish).

Christopher G. A. Bryant is Professor of Sociology at Salford University. His books include *Sociology in Action* and, most recently, *The New Great Transformation?* (co-edited with E. Mokrzycki).

Chris Hann is Professor of Social Anthropology at Kent University. His books include *Tázlár* and, as editor, *Market Economy and Civil Society in Hungary*.

Hudson Meadwell is the Chair of Political Science at McGill University. His analysis of 'The Politics of Nationalism in Quebec' appeared in *World Politics* in 1993.

Adam B. Seligman is Assistant Professor at the Department of Sociology, University of Colorado, Boulder. He is the author of *The Idea of Civil Society* and *Inner Worldly Individualism*.

Nicos Mouzelis is Professor of Sociology at the London School of Economics. His books include *Politics in the Semi-Periphery* and *Sociological Theory: What Went Wrong?*

Philip Oxhorn is Associate Professor of Political Science at McGill University. His *Organising Civil Society* is in press.

Şerif Mardin is the Chair of Islamic Studies at the American University in Washington. His many books include *The Genesis of Young Ottoman Thought*.

Salvador Giner is Director of the Institute for Advanced Social Studies, Spanish Higher Council for Scientific Research. He has written widely on corporatism and governability, and is the author of *Mass Society*.

1

In Search of Civil Society

John A. Hall

Civil society was placed at the forefront of public attention by attempts to establish decency in societies where it had most conspicuously been absent. If the term was invoked initially by Solidarity as part of its struggle against the Polish party-state, it soon became a rallying cry for many, on both sides of the Iron Curtain, who were opposed to statist socialism. John Keane's important 1988 collection on *Civil Society and the State* both captured and codified the spirit of civil society as it was understood in the 1980s.[1] Civil society was seen as the opposite of despotism, a space in which social groups could exist and move – something which exemplified and would ensure softer, more tolerable conditions of existence.

Whilst there is a core of sense in this definition that is of continuing relevance, many expectations implicit in Keane's volume were not realized. For one thing, communism did not fall, as many expected and some still believe, because of pressure from below, that is, from the forces of civil society; nor does that stunningly complete collapse ensure that the society that emerges will be civil. For another thing, the banner of civil society has been raised in very different social worlds. In February 1994, for example, José Alvarez Icaza told a demonstration held in Mexico City to support the Zapatista rebels of Chiapas that civil society should seize the political initiative and fight to open spaces for political participation.[2] The geographical extension in usage of the term points to a vital issue. Bluntly, the amount of diversity within the 'third wave' of democratization is very great.[3] Just as there are differential chances of consolidating civil society within the postcommunist world, so too are there major differences between this world as a whole and that in which societies seek to exit from authoritarian capitalism. The need for sociological precision about such matters is rein-forced by the discovery that hopes for the creation and spread of civil society in fact rested on entirely different social forces – East-ern Europeans favouring the advent of capitalism, whilst Western post-Marxists privileged 'new' social movements that served as functional equivalents to the proletariat within their conceptual system.

These social complexities led some scholars – understandably irritated by the confusion, at times licentious, of description and prescription – to attack the usefulness of the term altogether. Little would be lost by abandoning the notion, such critics suggested, since its key meanings are effectively present in the more familiar concepts of democracy and liberalism.[4] The present volume rep-resents current debate in containing papers – particularly that by Hann but with powerful reservations also coming from Wank and Wesolowski – written from this critical perspective. However, the character of the volume as a whole is positive. The response of most authors to the fuzziness of the term has been that of attempting to specify and delineate with greater care, to go beyond the essentially negative view of civil society as societal self-organization in oppo-sition to the state – and to do so by analysing particular societies rather than, as had previously been the case, with reference to figures in intellectual history such as Ferguson, Hegel and Gramsci. Certainly, this introductory chapter offers a positive characteriz-ation of civil society in the belief that the sociological usefulness of the term can thereby be established. Definition is achieved in stages. A 'thick description' of the concept is offered to begin with by considering both the European origins and the enemies of civil society. This makes it then possible to correct the received definition of the concept. Once that has been done, attention turns to establishing the sociological foundations that explain the origin, maintenance and potential expansion of civil society. The principal reason for the argument taking this route is that civil society *is* complicated, most notably in being at one and the same time a social value and a set of social institutions. Some immediate comments about such a 'package deal' may prevent misunderstandings.

Whilst social values are very definitely a part of social reality, they have to make their way in the midst of economic and political forces possessed of logics of their own; if social developments can be held back by the absence of ideological codification, so too can ideological advance be stymied when lacking institutional support.

No a priori or empirically based general law allows us to specify the exact relations between cultural and structural forces throughout history.[5] One generalization that can be made about civil society – a generalization, it should be stressed, that goes against the implicit and optimistic determinism of most scholars' social evolutionary viewpoints – is that the value has weak or incomplete sociological moorings. My own endorsement of the value of civil society makes me regret this situation; that is, I would gladly embrace social tendencies sure to establish civil society even though this would diminish any conception of social agency and human responsibility.[6] Now it is important to underscore what is involved in the recognition that civil society has weak sociological roots, that its establishment everywhere is by no means inevitable. Putting matters in this way is in effect to keep analysis separate from hope, to conceptualize social processes in their own terms rather than in those of mere political desire. Further to that end, the argument turns clearly from description to prescription only at the end of the chapter. In summary, the analysis of civil society offered should stand separate from judgements to be made about it. Such cogency the analysis possesses, in other words, should be of use to those who dislike the value, its institutional support or the package deal as a whole.

EUROPEAN ORIGINS

Gore Vidal once suggested that the deepest meaning of *Creation*, his magnificent novel about the origins of the world religions and ethics, was that agrarian civilizations before the advent of the great monotheistic creeds were the most tolerant in the history of mankind.[7] There is some justification for this view. On the one hand, the logistics of agrarian civilizations meant that they had no capacity to penetrate, let alone to police, the thoughts of the very varied pastoral tribes and peasant communities over which they ruled.[8] On the other hand, monotheism did bring in its train the potential for – and, with Christianity once Constantine had converted, the enthusiastic and vicious practice of – intolerance, for all that the principle of universal salvation envisaged and allowed the incorporation of all human beings into society for the first time. Nonetheless, the classical agrarian civilizations were not civil societies. The inability of the state to penetrate social life is not at all the same thing as the creation of social practices which make state-society interactions civilized. Differently put, civil society has everything to do with the modern world in which such interaction is necessary. As the origins of that modernity lie within Europe, and within Europe alone, it accordingly makes sense to turn to it immediately.[9]

The deepest roots of civil society in Europe result from the way in which the removal of the centralized authority of Rome placed power in several sets of hands. What is most striking in comparative perspective is the separation between ideological and political power. Christianity had always refused to provide ideological justification for Rome, and it found thereafter that it could survive and prosper without benefit of an imperial polity. If this pattern was strikingly different from that of China and Byzantium, it came to differ quite as much as from Islam. By this is meant less the failure of the papal attempt to establish theocracy than the way in which ideological power came to underwrite mundane political rule – an attitude absent from Islam to this day. Fear of concentration of power in the hands of a secular emperor led the church to encourage kings, whom it made more than *primus inter pares* by ritual anointing and the singing of the *Laudes regiae*. But it would be a mistake to imagine that royal power thereby became unfettered. Rather, state-building took place within a field of pre-existent social forces. Kings were faced with feudal nobilities whose property rights were firmly established, as of course were those of the church. In these circumstances kings sought to enhance their powers by granting autonomy to towns; these became islands within the feudal sea in which new ideas and practices could develop.[10] All in all, this was an acephalous world in which liberties were both widespread and firmly codified in a legal system that privileged corporate rights.

This vesting of power into separate bodies might have led to a static society, in which different sources of power merely blocked any common enterprise. This did not happen, with European society in consequence gaining a restless dynamism that changed the pattern of world history. Trust and cooperation was initially made possible by the sense of unity provided by Christian norms; shared membership in a civilization certainly helped to revive and deepen economic interaction even within the medieval period.[11] However, cooperative relations *within* states became of ever greater importance. European rulers did not, as was the case elsewhere, conquer a society which they then had little real interest in organizing. On the contrary, state–society interaction necessarily became ever more intense due to endless competition in war consequent on multipolarity; given the pre-existence of social relations, royal activism necessarily depended upon cooperation and coaxing quite as much as upon sheer coercion. The need for monies for war led to the practice of calling assemblies of the estates of the realm, that is, of church, nobility and townsmen – to whom were even added in Sweden and Norway representatives of the peasantry![12] Such assemblies took over tags of canon law – 'what touches all must be agreed by all' and 'no taxation without representation' – that made European states essentially rule bound. Of course, the fact that there were several such states was of enormous importance. A measure of internal decency was encouraged once it was realized that foul treatment to key social elements might encourage them to move and thereby to enrich a rival state, as clearly happened when the Huguenots were expelled from France. The presence of avenues of escape supported both economic and political liberties.

This account is slightly exaggerated. Central and Eastern European history took a turn away from social diversity in the fifteenth and sixteenth centuries, as nobles and kings allied against towns and independent peasantries.[13] In north-west Europe, by contrast, states remained rule bound even during absolutist rule in the seventeenth and eighteenth centuries; equally, multipolar pluralism was sufficiently well entrenched as to rule out all attempts – whether by popes, emperors or monarchs – at recreating imperial unity. Nonetheless, it is crucial for my argument to note that civil society gained in self-consciousness from the experience of fighting against politico-religious unification drives. What mattered most of all was the rise of toleration. Attempts at suppression of the religious diversity created by the Reformation failed because Charles V's imperial pretensions were destroyed by balance of power politics. The principle of *cuius regio, eius religio*, enshrined in 1555 at the Treaty of Augsburg, seemingly allowed for diversity and difference, at least between states. But the principle was not really accepted and internalized, as the brutality of the Thirty Years' War so decisively demonstrated. The Westphalian settlement of 1648 is a better marker of development in European attitudes, since it went beyond affirming the principle enshrined at Augsburg to the attempt to take religion out of geopolitics altogether, one mechanism towards which was the insistence that existing religious groups within states should be allowed to worship as they saw fit. As it happens, this marker too was incompletely observed, as is obvious once we remember that Locke's advocacy of toleration was written a generation later, with Montesquieu's chapters in *The Spirit of the Laws* accepting religion as long as it was not allied to fanaticism coming a full century later.[14] But even if there is no absolutely decisive single marker, the change itself remains obvious. The long religious wars of Europe could not be won by either side, as Gellner stresses in his chapter, for the forces of pluralism could always defeat any drive to politico-religious unification. In the face of endlessly destructive stalemate, an extraordinary switch in attitudes took place: if agreement on detailed matters of belief could neither be reached nor imposed, a background consensus, to tolerate religious difference, was a viable alternative. What is at issue can be characterized somewhat differently. If toleration was at first merely accepted as a sour-grapes philosophy, that is, one imposed by circumstances beyond one's control, it came to be valued in itself. Civil society is thus a complex balance of consensus and conflict, the valuation of as much difference as is compatible with the bare minimum of consensus necessary for settled existence.

If civil society gained a degree of self-consciousness in this way, its role was vastly amplified by changes in means of communication. Social self-organization was enhanced by the spread of literacy and the creation of a mass print culture. Horizontal linkages in society free from state control grew enormously in the eighteenth century, and are properly symbolized by those varied institutions, from coffee shops to wig-makers', in which journals could be read and discussed. This infrastructure made it possible, to use Anderson's now famous phrase, to imagine new communities.[15] Sources of this increased interaction varied. At one end of the spectrum was the Anglo-Saxon route in which the growth of commercial society enabled and encouraged lateral social communication. The other end of the same spectrum was represented by the more statist version of infrastructural development pioneered in Prussia, a world in which the ability to read drill manuals did more that anything else to spread literacy.[16]

Significant claims have been made about the nature of civil society on the basis of this revolution in communicative technique. The most dramatic is Habermas's claim that rational will formation was encouraged by the emergence of what he terms 'the public sphere'.[17] Some excesses in Habermas's account – both the idealized portrait of democratic openness in the eighteenth century, particularly the failure to see how the definition of the public was increasingly such as to exclude women, and the picture of its destruction by industrial capitalism – have become generally obvious.[18] Less remarked upon is the fact that the construction of new identities in civil society emerged in very large part for political reasons. Struggles for citizenship, whether internal to a state or separatist in character, were occasioned by the impact of an enormous jump in fiscal extraction on the part of late eighteenth-century states.[19] A claim closer to the spirit of the time is that civility in society is increased by an elective affinity between commerce and liberty.[20] Whilst money-making was rarely admired in itself, it was endorsed in very subtle argument: a world marked by interests would be one in which harsher passions, above all that of the desire to dominate, would lose their sway. More attention will be given later to the sociological links between capitalism and civil society, at that time and afterwards, and as a source of the maintenance of civil society as much as of its creation. But a final claim about eighteenth-century civil society must be noted first. An element of civil society as present in the mind of Montesquieu as in those of the Scottish moralists was that of fashion and refinement. These years saw the emergence of the first consumer society and of the modern novel: both forms exemplified a new form of individualism, in which people could try out, at first or second hand, different social roles.[21] Civil society was seen, in a nutshell, as a lively sphere marked by the spread of new codes of manners.

ENEMIES

Knowing one's enemies helps self-awareness because the acuteness of critique forces clarity in the conceptualization of one's own self-image. This principle distinctively applies here: five enemies of civil society are considered because of the power of their views and so as to better understand, by means of contrast, the nature of civil society.

The best-known enemy of civil society is despotism, whose greatest analysts are surely Montesquieu and Tocqueville. One element of Montesquieu's picture of despotism can be seen in the early *Persian Letters*. This has at its centre a subtle and shifting analysis of Usbek, a Persian visitor able to see the foibles of France but entirely deluded about his own situation as ruler of a seraglio. More particularly, Montesquieu anticipates Hegel's famous master–slave paradox in demonstrating the self-defeating quality of despotic rule. The women in the harem are right when they tell

Usbek that he is both lonely and unhappy. But the most acute
analysis of the psychological consequence of despotism is made by
his friend Rica who notes 'that being so firmly in possession leaves
us nothing to desire'.[22] Rica tells his master that it is the freedom of
French women that enables them to speak in such a way as to make
it possible to learn about real feelings:

> I knew nothing about women until I came here. I have learnt more
> about them in a month than I should have done in thirty years inside
> a seraglio. With us everyone's character is uniformly the same, be-
> cause they are forced. People do not seem what they are, but what
> they are obliged to be. Because of this enslavement of heart and mind,
> nothing is heard but the voice of fear, which has only one language,
> instead of nature, which expresses itself so diversely and appears in so
> many different forms.[23]

The emphasis on fear pervades the more formalized picture of
despotism in *The Spirit of the Laws*. Fear is humiliating for every
human being; it is a visceral and physical reaction, one that literally
makes the skin creep. It may be that Montesquieu's ideal-typical
portrait of oriental despotism is overdone, may further be that the
stereotype that it created has much to answer for, but this should
not distract in the twentieth century from the relevance of a politics
directed against fear. Whilst it is difficult to establish any shared
human conception of the good, a measure of universalism can be
guaranteed negatively along the lines suggested by Montesquieu,
that is, in terms of the prevention of fear.[24] If Montesquieu's intention was clear, the precise details of the character of the social and
political arrangements that would achieve his goal remain a little
murky. Whilst it is obvious that he advocated social pluralism so as
to check the state, the relative importance he assigned to lawyers
and nobles is by no means certain; equally, the extent to which
a liberal polity depended on Germanic roots as compared to
the beneficent effects of modern commerce was never finally
elucidated.[25]

Writing with an eye on the excesses of the French Revolution,
Tocqueville's initial hunch was that the people were politically
dangerous. The unleashing of their envy looked set to lead to a
tyranny of the majority. His favourable report on the United
States, that is, his discovery that it was able to combine social
equality with political liberty, did not finally change this viewpoint:
America had been blessed by so many special circumstances that
the full logic of popular sovereignty was held in check. But

Tocqueville did change his presupposition in his masterpiece, *The Old Regime and the French Revolution*.[26] One element in his portrait of the old regime, namely his analysis of centralization, is famed, and of great relevance here:

> Any independent group, however small, which seemed desirous of taking action otherwise than under the aegis of the old administration filled it with alarm, and the tiniest free association of citizens, however harmless its aims, was regarded as a nuisance. The only corporate bodies tolerated were those whose members had been hand-picked by the administration and which were under its control. Even big industrial concerns were frowned upon. In a word, our administration resented the idea of private citizens' having any say in the control of their own enterprises, and preferred sterility to competition.[27]

But still more important for Tocqueville was the discovery that envy had been created and social trust and cooperation destroyed by the regime's habitual playing of divide-and-rule politics.[28] In one sense, the discovery that kings were more to blame than were the people for France's subsequent difficulty in combining liberty with equal social conditions led to optimism: different groups and classes could, in a condition of liberty, be able to cooperate in common tasks, thereby obviating the danger of any popular tyranny. But at a deeper level, Tocqueville was driven to pessimism. The legacy of the destruction of trust was disastrous:

> It was no easy task bringing together fellow citizens who had lived for many centuries aloof from, or even hostile to, each other and teaching them to co-operate in the management of their own affairs. It had been far easier to estrange them than it now was to reunite them, and in so doing France gave the world a memorable example. Yet, when sixty years ago the various classes which under the old order had been isolated units in the social system came once again in touch, it was on their sore spots that they made contact and their first gesture was to fly at each other's throats. Indeed, even today, though class distinctions are no more, the jealousies and antipathies they caused have not died out.[29]

This is to suggest a sort of historical determinism: societies with a history of social trust are likely to maintain it through changing social conditions, whilst those without it are unlikely to be able to achieve freedom in modern conditions. Such societies may be faced with the following scenario, a nightmare for Tocqueville, given his complete love of liberty:

John A. Hall

The segregation of classes, which was the crime of the late monarchy, became at a late stage a justification for it, since when the wealthy and enlightened classes were no longer able to act in concert and to take part in the government, the country became, to all intents and purposes, incapable of administering itself and it was needful that a master should step in.[30]

There is far less understanding of the second enemy faced by civil society. In recent years, some political theorists attracted to the idea of civil society have also served as spokesmen for the revival of the tradition of republican civic virtue. This is a frightful *mésalliance*, as Seligman and Meadwell make clear, since the views at the heart of the two positions stand utterly opposed to each other. We can see this particularly clearly by considering some eighteenth-century thinkers.

Many of the Enlightenment thinkers who championed the idea of civil society, in fact if not always in name, were clearly opposed to the tradition of civic virtue, however much they admired some of its moral qualities. This was certainly true of Hume and Smith who preferred the world of wealth to that of virtue on the ground that the Greek experience should not be taken as our founding moment because it had been based on slavery.[31] It is equally true of Montesquieu. His *Considerations on the Causes of the Greatness of the Romans and their Decline* made clear that ancient virtue had been allied to militarism, and he made much of the spartan rigour of the regime that was necessary for its sustenance. In *The Spirit of the Laws* his preference was clearly for a liberal and commercial order in which social cohesion could be maintained by asking rather less of human beings. A commercial order, Montesquieu noted, was one in which 'happily, men are in a situation such that, though their passions inspire in them the thought of being wicked, they nevertheless have an interest in not being so.'[32] Further, he felt that fashion had a part to play in driving the economic mechanism of society, and he clearly endorsed the vigour that seemed to be part and parcel of commercial society. This was not to say that he naively assumed that an increase in money would ensure happiness. On the contrary, his remarks on suicide show him to have been well aware of the terrors that can haunt human beings. But here too his attitude is characteristically civil. It was irrational to make suicide an act calling for general opprobrium: the act should be decriminalized, a matter for private sorrow rather than public outrage. And this is but a single example of a consistent drive in

Montesquieu to make the law softer and more reliable, that is, to revise laws that were not needed or which were gratuitously cruel.[33]

There is then a world of difference between this view and that of Rousseau, the high apostle of virtue.[34] Rousseau's concern was less that the new commercial world would lack cohesion than that it would alienate human beings from their true selves – something which would, however, eventually lead to social collapse. Above all, Rousseau loathed everything to do with the world of manners. In his *Letter to M. D'Alembert on the Theatre*, he made crystal clear his dislike of the theatre, and of fashion and the city more generally, on the grounds that anything that allowed or encouraged the individual to imagine himself or herself as different would cause unhappiness.[35] Instead of encouraging the trying on of different personalities, it was rather necessary for humans to be anchored in a stage of simplicity, free from the diversion and complexity that he held to be the cause of psychic discomfort.[36] At this point a paradox positively jumps out at us. Rousseau portrayed himself as an honest soul, revealing his heart in a new spirit of authenticity, and thereby sought to condemn the superficial and false world of conventional social appearance.[37] What is striking then is that Rousseau's adulation of authenticity goes hand in hand with a low opinion of his fellows, seen as weak, easily distracted and incapable of handling complexity by themselves. Hence it is absolutely apparent that coercion is required to solve the problem of being: people really must be 'forced to be free', not least by the retention of social simplicity, that is, the downplaying of commerce and fashion in favour of a return to a world of considerable rigour. It is entirely appropriate to stress the elective affinity between Rousseau's implicitly authoritarian ideas and the actual violence perpetrated by revolutionaries seeking to establish a modern citizens' republic.[38] This stands in marked contrast to the legacy of Montesquieu, most famously used by the founding fathers of the United States to ensure a constitution of balance and moderation.[39]

The concern for moral unity based on the belief that the individual was incapable of handling complexity remained a perennial theme in social thought. This is clearly true of Durkheim, to whose ideas we shall return, as can be seen in the way in which his very first work admired Rousseau whilst signally mistaking Montesquieu's central purpose.[40] But the desire for moral unity marks the thought of Karl Marx quite as much. Durkheim's criticism of socialism – that it sought merely to enhance egoism rather than to establish genuine moral regulation – was wildly wrong.[41] At the deepest level, Marx resembled Rousseau in having an equal dislike for any splitting of human faculties. This is clearly seen in his early essays, a key theme of which is that the gap between civil and political society had to be overcome.[42] This concern with unity may well have Aristotelian roots.[43] Whatever the case, there is no doubt but that Marx's theory, despite its essential humanism and voluntarism, was used to justify the imposition of a coercive ideological tyranny.

The third enemy of civil society is one form of nationalism. By this is meant those varied practices – mass population transfers, forced integration, ethnic cleansing, genocide – by means of which complete social homogeneity is created. This version of nationalism can be seen as the linking of a single nation, whether real or constructed, to its own state. Such nationalism can strengthen, create or subvert states; whatever the case, its characteristic practices make it opposed to civil society.[44] Nonetheless, this is only one way in which to look at this form of nationalism. Gellner's chapter sees nationalism in general as an occasional friend rather than an eternal foe of civil society.[45] The most obvious consideration here is that nationalists can stand close to liberalism when they are part of a struggle against a despotic regime. More strikingly, Gellner stresses that modern industrial society depends upon homogeneity. There is a sense in which he averts his gaze – knowingly, hating the suffering involved – from the processes by which such homogeneity is established, whilst telling us that it is a background condition for civil as much as for industrial society. The implication of this position is, for example, that Slovenia and the Czech Republic – and Poland and Hungary, thanks to the depredations of Hitler and Stalin – have a better chance at establishing a civil society than does the Ukraine or Russia.

One problem with Gellner's position is that it tends to functionalism in seeing nationalism as being *caused* by the needs of industrialism. Whilst that notion can be given sense and reference, it remains the case that early European nationalism is best explained in political rather than in socioeconomic terms.[46] Nationalist feelings were evident, *pace* Gellner, before industrialization, and they resulted from states seeking to rationalize their societies so as to prosper in war.[47] But in a sense that is a detail. It is much more important to cast light on the vexed question of the causal patterning involved in different types of nationalism.

Bryant notes in his chapter that nations can be imagined in civic as well as in ethnic terms. This is an important distinction. Most obviously, ethnic imagining *even in combination with social homogeneity* can lead to continuing incivility in society. This finding raises the question as to whether the civic form of imagining might create – rather than, as Gellner has it, be the consequence of – the social homogeneity necessary for civil society. Differently put, do we in fact possess some principles that allow us to handle and direct nationalism, rather than merely to be at its mercy? One should not be too optimistic here. The very first civic nationalism, that of the United States, sought to exclude the loyalists, and it thereafter insisted on rather complete social homogenization, on being a 'melting pot' rather than, as in Canada, a 'salad bowl'. The second great civic nationalism, that of the French Revolution, felt so possessed of the truth that it became imperialistic, a process which did more to spread a nationalism stressing the need for a unitary societal will in nineteenth-century Europe than did industrialization. Nonetheless, some descriptive force as well as prescriptive hope does reside in the more civic style of imagining. For one thing, contemporary naturalization rates in 'civic' France are far higher than those in 'ethnic' Germany.[48] In terms of more general liberal principles, it is clear that nationalist movements have much to do with the desire to exit from authoritarian regimes. Austria-Hungary might have survived the nationalities problem had it been prepared to embrace political liberalism: most peoples sought to preserve their historic rights, their national identities, and would have been happy without their own state – so long, that is, as their voice could be heard within a liberal empire. The failure to adopt a more liberal option ranks as an historic tragedy because the option was a genuine possibility. The option was defeated by the arrogance of the emperor, the desire to continue to play great power politics and the belief that imperial possessions were necessary for economic well-being – all of which were held to demand a unitary state and to rule out more liberal, confederal solutions to the nationalities problem. But the optimism that this engenders needs to be qualified. What might have taken place in Austria-Hungary may not be at all possible elsewhere. There is a world of difference between building a nation, whether civic or ethnic, within previously established state boundaries and the creation of state and nation at the same time – with a clear relationship existing between an excluded group gaining democratic rights and political intolerance. Differently put, a measure of homogeneity existed within Austria-Hungary that lay behind and made possible a liberal and civic option. The complete absence of any such background vastly increases the chances of nationalism being opposed to civil society. But even here one should be cautious, given the remarkable and continuing success of the liberal and secular national identity created by the founding fathers of modern India.[49]

Ideologies have consequences, and both Marxism and nationalism have been used as strategies of forced development. The background assumption of Mouzelis's chapter is that late development tends to be an enemy of civil society. Such statist development concentrates economic and political power massively, and is normally undertaken under the aegis of total ideologies of varying sorts. Mouzelis shows how clientelism and populism served in Latin America as regime strategies designed to replace social self-organization. His general picture is reinforced by a consideration of the Soviet model of industrialization. Here the concentration of power was so great that it ruined any balancing of the state by social forces, with social self-organization being explicitly excluded along the lines noted by Tocqueville. Both these cases should be seen in the light of a further principle of Tocqueville's political sociology, namely that revolutions often reinforce existing social patterns. Certainly, the strategy adopted in Latin America, for all that it reinforced concentrations of power, reflected the interests of a highly inegalitarian society; further, the social atomization of Soviet rule in Russia merely perfected a strategy already present under the tsars.[50] In contrast, late development of Denmark and Finland, for all the trauma that it involved, was not such as to undermine pre-existing social pluralism.[51]

A final enemy of civil society is cultural. The desire to balance the state and to respect individualism is not inscribed in the historic process, an acorn somehow ready in every culture to turn into an oak tree. The emphasis on caste in Indian civilization emphatically condemns people to a status order. Further, current history makes it absolutely apparent that Islam possesses a civilizational vision of its own, radically opposed to that of the West. The logical clarity enshrined in Islam – the monistic and puritanical scripturalism of its monotheism – obviated any equivalent to occidental 'liberties': possession of the truth was so complete that the culture was radically contractualist rather than corporatist.[52] In addition, its social institutions did not allow for the autonomy of cities, that is, the shell within which many of the practices of civility have been born. But Mardin's brilliant chapter suggests that the force of this cultural ideal may be changing, certainly in Turkey and perhaps more generally. The impact of external cultural and institutional forces seems still more powerful on East Asian societies – in any case possessed of a cultural pattern with marked resonance to that inherent in the ideal of civil society.

ESCAPING SOCIAL CAGES

To this point, the account of the nature of civil society has sought to be suggestive by being descriptive. The principal point has been that living with difference is as important to the notion of civil society as is the control of despotism. But it is now time to change tempo by making the argument more directly analytic. The best way of doing so is to make use of the material presented in order formally to go beyond the traditional definition of civil society as the self-organization of strong and autonomous groups that balance the state.

That definition must be qualified to prevent it encouraging error. The fundamental argument made by Gellner's chapter is that not every set of autonomous groups creates a civil society. He illustrates this claim with reference to the ancient world and to the classical heartland of Islam, in both of which the individual is caged by kinship groups.[53] This analysis of the potential for cousins to be as tyrannical as the state is surely correct. Civil society must depend upon the ability to escape any particular cage; membership of autonomous groups needs to be both voluntary and overlapping if society is to become civil. This is to make individualism a core component of civil society – with the provision of social space for human experimentation being, *pace* Rousseau, necessary to that end. A corollary of this point about the sort of groups that suit civil society concerns relativism. Gore Vidal was wrong to stress the 'tolerance' of the world before monotheism because of the intolerance within the social segments of that world. Similarly, any modern version of multiculturalism which completely caged its members would be opposed, as Seligman properly insists in his chapter, to the spirit of civil society. Diversity is attractive only within a shared framework which values the worth of the individual.

If Gellner's point marks a real advance, we can improve analytically upon the received notion of civil society still further by correcting a prejudice that seems to remain at the back of his mind. The notion that groups, albeit of the right type, should balance the state is subtly wrong. This manner of conceptualizing state–society relations leaves much to be desired because it tends to see the state exclusively as a threat. In Eastern Europe in recent years, this led many reformers to seek virtually to abolish the state, in the belief that civil society would work best in its absence. The current situation of Russia, bereft of the rule of law, demonstrates the weakness of this view. The state is needed by civil society for protection and so as to ensure basic social conditions, such as, in recent years, the protection of women inside the household. It is important to stress that strength is not given to the state by its sitting autonomously above society, detached from the key groups of society. On the contrary, the image of the state that suits civil society is that of eighteenth-century Britain in which state and society interacted continuously, with state capacity being increased by the ability to work through notables who accepted this because they trusted an institution – *their* institution – that they could control. The expression that catches this notion best is that applied by Samuels to the contemporary Japanese state, that is, that it amounts to being a 'politics of reciprocal consent'.[54]

No discussion of social caging would be complete without reference to the future of our own principal cage, namely that of the nation-state. It is often claimed that the era of the nation-state is now over, that its autonomy has been undermined by the globalization of capital and of culture.[55] This usefully points to the fact that states exist in larger societies, albeit the fact that they have done so for a very long time diminishes the power and the originality of this claim. How should this social pattern, whose salience has certainly increased – that is, the fact that we have multiple and overlapping identities because we belong to different societies[56] – be seen by analysts and adherents of the notion of civil society? Does it represent a loss of the ability to control a state, or is it something altogether more positive, an extension of international links allowing for the emergence of an international civil society? There is some truth to both sides of the equation without absolute clarity being yet available as to which will prove to be the more important. The fact that civil society has been gained through nation-states must cause hesitation. It is at least possible that the members of a more international society will gain advantages at the expense of those who remain nationally caged within a state less and less capable of providing decent social conditions. But the form that international society takes in the future remains open. Against this vision of the increasing salience of capitalist society can be set that of the European Union: this larger shell decidedly increases civility, of Great Britain as much as of states in Eastern Europe wishing to join, because of its insistence on democracy allied to minority rights. But if national social caging brought citizenship, it equally proved capable of causing disaster. When the leaders of nation-states are tightly caged by nationalist pressure groups, they may no longer be able to play the game of realism – that is, they are forced to place 'national interest' above the norms of international society. German leaders became caged in this manner in the years before 1914, and this was one factor that led to the onset of world war.[57] The safety of the world thus depends upon what can usefully be called sophisticated realism, that is, a realism that stresses the society of states rather than a crude Hobbesian realism based on a view of mere international anarchy.[58] The growth of international society, the fact that the leaders of the G7 countries understand each other and, literally, speak the same language, is thus something to be welcomed by the adherents of civil society.

It is as well to own up to an ambivalence on my own part at this point. Peace between nations rests on two different and potentially opposed foundations. To this point emphasis has been placed on the ability of statesmen to inhabit a single international society. The conduct of realism certainly depends upon a shared appreciation of its rules, mechanisms and signalling devices; to this base of international relations is sometimes added the sharing of other norms – as between Anglo-Saxon powers in the past and between liberal states in the European Union. But it is always dangerous to leave the conduct of international affairs completely to statesmen; more particularly, statesmen are often saved from making mistakes by public scrutiny of their policies. There is a clear tension here, between international elite understandings and national popular control. In the long run, the only way in which that tension could be resolved would be for the spread of international society to be such as to involve popular forces rather than elite segments. If that is desirable, it does not as yet look sociologically likely, given that very many remain nationally caged – and thereby potential fodder for nationalist political agitation.[59]

DEVELOPMENT, REGIME, TRAUMA

Perhaps the most difficult aspect of civil society concerns its sociological moorings, that is, the nature of the social processes that cause and support it. A key matter here is whether the processes of the first birth of civil society are, so to speak, universal, so that we can look forward to a spread of civil society in consequence. Any easy universalism will have to be rejected. This makes the chances for an extension of civil society at one and the same time worse and better. Obviously, the balanced social portfolio of European history is missing in many areas of the world, not least because of the pressure of forced nation-building and industrialization. Against this negative consideration can be set, however, other factors pointing in the opposite direction. For one thing, the contours of civil society are recognized and sought for, in large part because the notion is associated with economic development and softer political rule; differently put, the popularity of the concept helps corrode some of the certainty of the ideological visions still powerful in the modern world. For another thing, the modern world political economy is blessed with an international order of sorts, making both protectionism and geopolitical conflict, at least between major powers, less likely; this may allow nationalism to be slightly less fundamentalist in some places, that is, it may permit confederal experiments, given that unitary states are less necessary.

Before seeing how these factors play out in different regions of the world, it is important to begin analysis with the social evolutionary optimism noted at the start of the chapter. Such social determinism is quite widespread in classical social thought. Marx is an exemplar in holding that the bourgeoisie was fated to attack feudalism, and thus serve as the carrier, at least for a period, of liberal ideals. From this sort of general view came the optimistic notion that economic development will lead to greater social differentiation, and that this raw material will become organized so as to create a decent polity.[60] The pioneering role of a capitalist bourgeoisie was held to be particularly significant in accounting for the emergence of civil society in the West; the potential of the same class for demanding and maintaining civil society has equally formed the basis of most theories which hope for or expect civil society in the East and in the South.[61] But the idea that social differentiation would create civil society has not rested only on the bourgeoisie. Particular attention to the contribution made by working classes has recently been given by Rueschemeyer, Stephens and Stephens.[62] The core of their case rests as clearly upon economic interest as had that of Marxist and other social evolutionist accounts, with a difference in interpretation following from the insistence that bourgeoisies will find it in their interests to oppose and workers in theirs to demand social change. Beyond such economistic views, however, stand accounts, particularly of the last days of the Soviet bloc, which make much of the role played by pressures from church and environmental groups in causing the collapse of communism.

Whilst developmentalist views are not bereft of all sense, above all because a wide diffusion of property does help to *maintain* civil society, scepticism should be shown with regard to the *causal* pattern identified. Most obviously, little pressure for change in communist society came from below, with the *annus mirabilis* of 1989 rather seeing social forces suddenly occupying political space hurriedly vacated by party-states.[63] More generally, the origins of civil society in Europe go back, as noted, well before the social differentiation induced by economic development; differently put, social differentiation was clearly present, *pace* Durkheim, before the modern division of labour. Putnam's important book on traditions of government within Italy recognizes this, and adds to it a virtually complete historical determinism: civil society is seen as being very old, and, against received wisdom, as the condition rather than the consequence of economic development.[64] But if we bracket this consideration for a moment, further analysis undermines the view that classes are bound to demand an extension of civil society.

It is indeed true that the bourgeoisie in European history was at times an opponent of the state. One background factor making it so was relative pacification; differently put, the fact that urban middle classes in the classical heartland of Islam faced continuing incursions of nomadic tribesmen necessarily made them friends of the state.[65] Nonetheless, capitalists and other middle-class fragments in the West have often made vertical connections to the state, not least in the important case of Wilhelmine Germany, and this is always likely to be so when such actors are in fear of challenges from below.[66] Wank's chapter demonstrates the opportunistic behaviour of Chinese capitalists in 1989, and to this could be added the sorry fact that some privatizations in the former Soviet bloc are in effect piratizations, in which *nomenklatura* connections matter as much as ever.[67] Whilst it is true that the record of working classes in connection with the defence of civil society is strikingly good, essentialist definitions of class work no better here than they did for the middle classes. Those few working-class movements that have been – or that have seemed to be – genuinely radical have bred an intransigence on the part of their opponents that has helped block the emergence of civil society. In Latin America liberalizations from below, in contrast to decompressions initiated from above, have tended to fail.[68]

If all of this suggests caution about any easy and automatic triumph of civil society, it also calls for more constructive analysis and explanation. Something must first be said about the way in which working classes gain differential characters from the regimes with which they interact.[69] This analysis will in turn push back the causal chain from popular forces to the political elite, that is, towards explanation of regime character. Attention will first be focused on the birth of civil society in the West before then examining the chances that it might be extended elsewhere.

There has been very great variation in levels of class consciousness amongst different working classes.[70] At one end of a scale of militancy in the years before 1914 can be placed the accommodationist working class of the United States and at the other the revolutionary workers of St Petersburg, with British labour loyalty and German socialist militancy standing between these poles. Such variation is best explained in political terms. Liberalism diffuses social conflict, whereas autocracy and authoritarianism concentrates it. There is everything to be said, in other words, for Dahrendorf's observation that conflict becomes intense when different types of conflict are imposed on top of each other.[71] Russian workers had no choice but to 'take on' the state since it prevented them organizing their own trade unions; by contrast, American workers organized their class conflict at the industrial level, whilst remaining loyal to a political system which had given all white males the vote by the 1830s.

This analysis reinforces a point made earlier, that pure exclusion from power does not produce civility. Russian workers were revolutionary and, still more importantly, served as a vehicle by means of which an utterly illiberal political intelligentsia came to power. Equally, however, one can again doubt the extent to which the United States deserves to be considered a civil society. Mann has recently shown that the complete domestication of the American working class owed as much to a stick employed by liberalism as to its more familiar carrots – as much to vicious repression of socialist ideals as to easy acceptance of business unionism and economic growth.[72] Differently put, there is in the United States a single culture, essentially capitalist in spirit, rather than a civil society based on the coexistence of competing political traditions. If at times the presence of such traditions has led to stalemate in Europe, at best it has represented that genuine difference – not to mention the material achievements of the welfare state – which stands as the core of civil society.

If the causal link between workers and civil society is less than perfect, what can be said about the sociology of more middling groups? More particularly, the analysis demands that attention be given to a prior question. Why were some states blessed with regimes sufficiently liberal to produce moderate working classes which could be relatively easily incorporated into the polity? In the English case, such liberalism was not always present; on the contrary, it was a historical achievement. Seventeenth-century England had been prey to civil war, treason trials, regicide, conspiracy and the sundering of families. The very sudden move to political stability between 1675 and 1725 seems to be best explained by this traumatic experience. In a condition of continuing stalemate, in which neither side was capable of outright victory, it suddenly began to make sense, as it had to those divided by religion in early modern Europe, to try to live together – the successful accomplishment of which then fostered a culture of civility.[73] For all that this political achievement was genuinely autonomous, it was nonetheless aided by economic factors. For one thing, the stalemate itself resulted from negative resisting power in society being widely spread. For another thing, the acceptance of party alternation in government was eased by the presence of a growing economy, that is, of a source of remuneration other than that derived from political power. Differently put, separate patterns of power reinforced each other, making any full account of the creation of civil society necessarily multi-causal in character.

Let us reflect on what has been said by distinguishing between three analytic categories. Putnam may be right, firstly, to say that the civility of some societies is virtually shrouded in the mists of time. But his case is exaggerated, given the existence of a second category, that in which civil society may (or may not) be *achieved*. This category is one in which a proto civil society is in existence, that is, social differentiation is available on the basis of which civil society could be consolidated. It may be that industrialization increases the number of societies of this type. Nonetheless, what remains striking is that political skill is required to make the breakthrough to civil society. Britain achieved this in the early eighteenth century and Spain in recent years. In contrast, Germany was unable to make this transition autonomously. Factors that explain this failure are not hard to find: divide-and-rule politics were encouraged by the lack of social homogeneity in the country, above all by

religious division, and this in turn created such social distrust that
different groups were thereafter unable to cooperate with each
other. All the same, structural conditions were not so overwhelm-
ingly unfavourable as to make an autonomous transition impossible to envisage. Max Weber was right, for example, to argue the
liberal Machiavellian case just made, namely, that the working class
could have been accommodated within the nation, and would have
responded to such an offer with an increase in loyalty and a diminution of radicalism.[74] In consequence, the disastrous failure to
move towards civil society becomes ascribable to political irrespon-
sibility. This judgement is much reinforced when noting the existence of a third category, that in which structural factors are so
massively unfavourable as to make the chances of achieving civil
society very slim indeed. Societies facing rapid industrialization
and, still more, nation-building often find themselves with politics
of such total societal novelty – a situation in which, unfortunately,
everything is up for grabs – as almost to rule out the possibility of
civil society.

Let us turn from – or, rather, put flesh on – these abstract
considerations by straightforward analysis of the chances of extending civil society in the different political economies of the
modern world. Let us begin with the east, and then turn to the
south.

Hindsight makes us realize that communist power systems
rested, so to speak, on feet of clay. Lenin had once remarked that
the absence of self-organizations under tsarism would make it hard
really to penetrate society. The prescience of this insight was most
spectacularly seen in the manner in which this historical project
came to an end. Civil society had been so destroyed – by bolshe-
vism still more than by tsarism – that a reforming elite could find no
partner with whom to make pacts, so as to conduct a controlled
decompression of political life.[75] In consequence, the name of the
game in this part of the world is now democratization rather than
liberalization. Many scholars accordingly suggest that the reform
plans of most elites are likely to be blocked by instant democratic
pressures.[76] Such reform is of course desperately needed since all of
this world is involved in a double transition, to democracy and the
market – to which some must add basic nation-building as well.[77]
The chances for the emergence of a civil society look dim in the face
of such a historical agenda.

Pessimism can be overdone. Depoliticization has resulted from
absolute disenchantment with the past, leaving a good deal of steer-

ing room for elites to push through economic reforms. There may be little to fear from movements from below:

> it also follows that it is entirely possible to have pluralism and a wide variety of small groups competing for influence without ever pulling large numbers of people into political life . . . if states remain strictly liberal and do not grant organisational advantages to large groups, it may well be possible to maintain pluralism without extensive mass movements. If, for example, workers are free not to join unions, many will simply not join.[78]

Further, postcommunist societies have no equivalent of Latin America's intact and powerful landed elite. Revolution destroyed the old classes, whilst those *nomenklatura* members who did not enter business are now very clearly defeated – except, of course, for those who have retained power by changing their colours, that is, by moving from communism to nationalism. All in all, the amount of resistance from within the elite to radical change is historically abnormally low. Most important of all, however, is something that has nothing to do with the legacy of communism, namely geography. Many East and Central European states are extremely happy to have policies directed by experts associated with the European Union. The desire to return to Europe means that there is considerable resistance to the reintroduction of authoritarian incivilities.

If these factors lend advantage, it remains important to stress that depoliticization is not the same thing as the consolidation of civil society. The absence of positive faith in a regime can lead at any time to the emergence of symbolic politics, and in particular to trust in one's ethnic group – a situation especially likely to block moves to civil society, given the large number of ethnic Russians resident in the former peripheral republics. More generally, a country is only strong when an orderly civil society works with the state. At present, most states in former communist countries may have autonomy but this scarcely makes up for the absence of linkages with society. The lack of self-organization of society may be impeded, interestingly enough, by the legacy of excessive egalitarianism: differently put, the striking of bargains – that is, the practice of normal, civil politics – only becomes possible once interests have become conscious and organised.

It is already apparent that there will be diverse national outcomes to these postcommunist dilemmas. Societies which broke firmly with the communist past, which are physically close to the European Union, which have civil traditions and histories of social self-organization and which have already undertaken basic nation-building may well be able to establish civil societies. Against the hopes that can be entertained for the Czech Republic, Hungary, Poland, Estonia and Slovenia, however, have to be set the fears and pessimism that inevitably rise up when one looks further east. In this connection it is well worth noting the contrast between the post-Soviet Russian situation and that which is developing in the remaining great communist power. China's reversal of Soviet policy, that is, its emphasis on *perestroika before glasnost*, looks set to create a proto civil society, that is, a socially differentiated society in which interests are well articulated. If elite skill can engineer a political opening, civil society may thereby have a good chance of being consolidated.

The picture of Latin America revealed by the chapters of Mouzelis and Oxhorn suggests a social world whose chances of achieving civil society are poised on a knife edge. For all that the transition to civil society is far less complicated than it is in postcommunism, the fundamental difficulty that remains is recognizable from that world. The legacy of populism and clientelism is such that societal self-organization is very far from yet forming a proto civil society. In addition, redistributive policies – which, given gross social inequality, are needed if civil society is to have meaning – may lead to resistance on the part of the established elite. Against the obvious pessimism engendered by these considerations can be set three factors which point in the opposite direction. Firstly, fights within the elite of many countries have become moderated and civil as the result of brutal trauma. The determination to keep conflict within bounds in countries such as Argentina and Chile, where memories of the vicious consequences of extremes are sufficiently fresh, is such as to induce considerable self-discipline. Secondly, the chances for civil society are on balance improved by the historic rejection of import-substituting industrialization. The possibility of a rise in levels of economic growth and an increase in connections to the external world will both lend support to civil society. What is most exciting, thirdly, is Oxhorn's picture of the creation of genuine movements from below, designed to ensure that economic liberalization will not be at their expense. As yet, it is too early to be certain that such new movements will remain free from state interference. What remains desperately needed is the creation of a modern party system, that is, of parties at once independent of the state apparatus and under the control of well-articulated interests in society. It is worth noting in this connection that East Asian societies, whose marked economic growth has given them both wealth and sufficient social differentiation to support a civil society, suffer quite as much from the absence of a party system. Trust within the political elite is limited, with the current president of South Korea seemingly seeking legitimacy by means of open populism.

If one can hope, with more or less conviction, for the spread of civil society in the social worlds considered, foreboding seems natural when considering other political economies. Adherence to the ideal of civil society in modern India, amongst popular sectors as well as within the elite, is very remarkable; but this exists within the social context of caste, which still cages huge numbers with awful efficiency. The situation in Islam is probably more threatening. Whilst Mardin may be right to say that the dream of Islam can be diluted in favour of that of civil society, the process he notes in modern Turkey is far from general at the moment. One reason for this is that social and economic modernization can be aided by Islamic 'fundamentalism', that is, by stressing that high tradition of the belief system favouring literacy and puritanism. Another reason is that many Islamic countries are almost swamped by enormous social problems: this is most obviously true of Egypt, whose political system, anyway far from liberal, looks as it will have the greatest difficulty dealing with an immense demographic revolution. A similar point must be made about Africa. Whilst one can hope that consociational deals of one sort or another can promote civic imaginings and so limit ethnic conflict, there is much to be said for the view that the nation-state has been a curse for Africa. This point is made with unrivalled force by Basil Davidson. Unfortunately, his hopes that 'ethos of African community' might replace the nation-state seem terribly vague.[79] To that extent, Africa seems so condemned to harsh nation-building as to rule out many hopes for civil society.

FROM DESCRIPTION TO PRESCRIPTION

Civil society is a particular form of society, appreciating social diversity and able to limit the depredations of political power, that was born in Europe; it may, with luck, skill and imagination, spread to some other regions of the world. If this central claim is clear, an ambivalence at work in the argument can usefully be highlighted once again. The presence of difference, of varied identities, has been seen as a benefit, but an emphasis has equally been placed on the capacity and right to move between – even shop around for – such identities; diversity is valued within certain bounds. The European tone to the argument, including critical comments made about the monolithic nature of American culture, should certainly not be accepted too easily. European society bred two world wars – which is to say that its civility has been far from stable.

It is well worth moving away from this definition towards endorsing it. The best way to start doing so is to stress that the concept of civil society is *not* equivalent, as some would have it, to more familiar and valued notions. Democracy can be decidedly incivil, as Tocqueville realized and as ethnic cleansing often demonstrates; differently put, we value democracy in large part because we expect it to be married to civil practices. More controversially, liberalism is not quite the same thing as civil society. In this matter, I differ from Seligman whose chapter can best be seen as a call for civil society to be held in the spirit of civic virtue.[80] One can easily see that he has in mind the need for a strong *conscience collective*, which he believes was present in seventeenth-century New England, so that difference will not lead to disaster. I agree that some background sense of unity is needed, but am troubled by the Durkheimian tone of his demand for an extensive shared social identity – and am far from convinced of the civil nature of early America. More importantly, Durkheim should be seen in the last analyis as an illiberal thinker, wishing to cage individuals morally because convinced that they could not manage their lives on their own. A more limited shared identity is surely proper to liberalism, as is the insistence, derived from Montesquieu and Tocqueville, that the people can be trusted to rule themselves.[81]

It is not hard to mount a defence of the desirability of this sort of morally complex society. Meadwell's chapter suggests that the privileging of diversity has a great deal to do with the workings of modern science, and interestingly criticizes Habermas, as I have criticized Seligman, for wishing for more unity than is proper to liberalism. A more general way to support the notion of moral diversity is by returning to the question of authenticity. It is quite true that many social practices of civil society project a false front for the individual. There is a very great deal to be said in favour of such good manners, that is, of such moderated hypocrisy. Human beings need the privacy of social roles in order that they can experiment with who they are and what they wish to become. The trouble with Rousseau, and with his intellectual descendant Sartre, is the belief that we have a fixed personality.[82] Life is not quite like that. We suffer, as Proust put it, from the 'intermittences of the heart', from varied longings, many of which make us unhappy. Still the response of Proust to this situation seems to me the only one that makes sense for the maturity of mankind. At the end of his great novel, the narrator sees a young boy gazing longingly at an aristocratic house. He looks set to go down the false trails of adulation for society and for art, and the author accordingly wonders whether he should warn him that he might waste his life. He decides not to do so, in the belief that every human being must find his or her way in life. If civil society can liberate, this is not to say that life suddenly becomes easy. The establishment of a personal identity is difficult.

If this is straightforward but cautious endorsement, this chapter can usefully finish on a more immediately prescriptive note. One can detect something of a difference between authors such as Habermas, who see civil society as deeply threatened and comprised by late capitalism,[83] and others – represented here by Giner and Pérez-Díaz – who characterize modern society rather differently and stress the presence of social trends that may help the consolidation of civil society. But this is a difference between friends. Civil society is fragile, and it needs to be extended.

NOTES

1 J. Keane, ed., *Civil Society and the State: New European Perspectives*, Verso, London, 1988. Although Keane's contribution to the revival of the concept in the West was critical, many of his views had been anticipated by J. Cohen, *Class and Civil Society: The Limits of Marxian Critical Theory*, University of Massachusetts Press, Amherst, Mass., 1983.

2 I am indebted to Patricia Foxen for this reference.

3 S. P. Huntington, *The Third Wave*, University of Oklahoma Press, Norman, Okla., 1991.

4 K. Kumar, 'Civil Society: An Inquiry into the Usefulness of an Historical Term', *British Journal of Sociology*, vol. 44, 1993. The usefulness of the term has been interestingly defended by C. G. A. Bryant, 'Social Self-Organisation, Civility and Sociology: A Comment on Kumar's "Civil Society"', *British Journal of Sociology*, vol. 44, 1993. This debate was continued by the same authors in the *British Journal of Sociology*, vol. 45, 1994.

5 J. A. Hall, 'Ideas and the Social Sciences', in J. Goldstein and R. Keohane, eds, *Ideas and Foreign Policy*, Cornell University Press, Ithaca, N.Y., 1993.

6 In this I differ from Pérez-Díaz's argument, despite agreement as to the weak institutional bases of civil society.

7 G. Vidal, *Creation*, Heinemann, London, 1981. The comment in question was made in a BBC interview shortly after the publication of the novel.

8 E. Gellner, *Nations and Nationalism*, Blackwell, Oxford, 1983, ch. 2; P. Crone, *Pre-Industrial Societies*, Blackwell, Oxford, 1989.

9 J. A. Hall, *Powers and Liberties*, Blackwell, 1985, part I.

10 P. Burke, 'City States', in J. A. Hall, *States in History*, Blackwell, Oxford, 1986.

11 M. Mann, *Sources of Social Power. Volume One: From the Beginning to 1760 AD*, Cambridge University Press, Cambridge, 1986, ch. 10.

12 A. R. Myers, *Parliaments and Estates in Europe to 1789*, Thames and Hudson, London, 1975.

13 P. Anderson, *Lineages of the Absolutist State*, New Left Books, London, 1974; J. Szúcs, 'Three Historical Regions of Europe', in Keane, *Civil Society and the State*; G. Schöpflin, 'The Political Traditions of Eastern Europe', *Daedalus*, vol. 119, 1990; D. Chirot, ed., *The Origins of Backwardness in Eastern Europe*, University of California Press, Berkeley, Cal., 1989.

14 J. Locke, *A Letter concerning Toleration*, M. Nijhoff, The Hague, 1963; Montesquieu, *The Spirit of the Laws*, trans. A. M. Cohler, B. C. Miller and H. S. Stone, Cambridge University Press, Cambridge, 1989, books 25–6. Cf. H. Kamen, *The Rise of Toleration*, Weidenfeld and Nicolson, London, 1967.

15 B. Anderson, *Imagined Communities*, Verso, London, 1983. Cf. M. Warner, *The Letters of the Republic*, Harvard University Press, Cambridge, Mass., 1990.

16 M. Mann, *Sources of Social Power. Volume Two: The Rise of Classes and Nation-States, 1760–1914*, Cambridge University Press, Cambridge, 1993.

17 J. Habermas, *The Structural Transformation of the Public Sphere*, trans. T. Burger and F. Lawrence, MIT Press, Cambridge, Mass., 1989; C. Calhoun, ed., *Habermas and the Public Sphere*, MIT Press, Cambridge, Mass., 1992.

18 For the position with regard to women see: N. Fraser, 'Rethinking the Public Sphere: A Contribution to Actually Existing Democracy', M. P. Ryan, 'Gender and Public Access: Women's Politics in the Nineteenth Century' and G. Eley, 'Nations, Publics and Political Cultures: Placing Habermas in the Nineteenth Century', all in Calhoun, *Habermas and the Public Sphere*; C. Pateman, 'The Fraternal Social Contract', in Keane, *Civil Society and the State*; C. Hall, 'Private Persons versus Public Someones: Class, Gender and Politics in England, 1780–1850', in C. Steedman, C. Urwin and V. Walkerdine, eds, *Language, Gender and Childhood*, Routledge and Kegan Paul, London, 1985. For Habermas's view on capitalism, see the chapter by Pérez-Díaz in this volume.

19 Mann, *Sources of Social Power. Volume Two*, chs 7 and 10.

20 A. O. Hirschman, *The Passions and the Interests*, Princeton University Press, Princeton, N.J., 1977.

21 N. McKendrick, J. Brewer and J. H. Plumb, *The Birth of a Consumer Society*, Europa Press, London, 1982; I. Watt, *The Rise of the Novel*, Penguin, London, 1963.

22 Montesquieu, *The Persian Letters*, trans. C. J. Betts, London, Penguin, 1973, letter 38.
23 Montesquieu, *The Persian Letters*, letter 63.
24 In this matter I follow the last, deeply moving work of Judith Shklar, especially 'The Liberalism of Fear', in N. Rosenblum, *Liberalism and the Moral Life*, Harvard University Press, Cambridge, Mass., 1989. Shklar's indebtedness to Montesquieu is made apparent in that essay, but her full appreciation is in her *Montesquieu*, Oxford University Press, Oxford, 1987.
25 R. Kingston, 'Montesquieu and the Parlement of Bordeaux', unpublished PhD thesis, McGill University, 1994.
26 J. A. Hall, 'Trust in Tocqueville', *Policy Organisation and Society*, no. 5, 1992.
27 A. de Tocqueville, *The Old Regime and the French Revolution*, trans. S. Gilbert, Anchor Books, New York, 1955, p. 64.
28 Tocqueville, *The Old Regime and the French Revolution*, p. 136.
29 Tocqueville, *The Old Regime and the French Revolution*, p. 107.
30 Tocqueville, *The Old Regime and the French Revolution*, p. 107.
31 M. Hont and M. Ignatieff, eds, *Wealth and Virtue*, Cambridge University Press, Cambridge, 1983.
32 Montesquieu, *The Spirit of the Laws*, pp. 389–90. Attention was drawn to this by Hirschman, *The Passions and the Interests*, especially pp. 70–80.
33 Shklar, *Montesquieu*.
34 The contrast between Montesquieu and Rousseau was particularly clearly drawn by R. Aron, 'De la Liberté politique: Montesquieu et Jean-Jacques Rousseau', *La France Libre*, vol. 3, 1942. Philippe Couton and I are presently working on the contrast between the thinkers, in the light of E. Durkheim, *Montesquieu and Rousseau*, University of Michigan Press, Ann Arbor, Mich., 1965.
35 J. J. Rousseau, *Politics and the Arts: Letter to M. D'Alembert on the Theatre*, trans. A. Bloom, Cornell University Press, Ithaca, N.Y., 1977.
36 J. Shklar, *Men and Citizens*, Cambridge University Press, Cambridge, 1969; M. Berman, *The Politics of Authenticity*, Atheneum, New York, 1970.
37 L. Trilling, *Sincerity and Authenticity*, Oxford University Press, Oxford, 1977.
38 C. Blum, *Rousseau and the Republic of Virtue*, Cornell University Press, Ithaca, N.Y., 1986; S. Schama, *Citizens*, Knopf, New York, 1989.
39 J. Shklar, 'Montesquieu and the New Republicanism', in G. Bock, Q. Skinner and M. Viroli, eds, *Machiavelli and Republicanism*, Cambridge University Press, Cambridge, 1990.
40 Durkheim, *Montesquieu and Rousseau*.
41 E. Durkheim, *Socialism*, trans. C. Sattler, Collier Books, New York, 1962.
42 L. Kolakowski, 'The Myth of Human Self-Identity: Unity of Civil and Political Society in Socialist Thought', in L. Kolakowski and S. Hampshire, eds, *The Socialist Idea: A Reappraisal*, Weidenfeld and Nicolson, London, 1974.
43 J. Booth, *Households: On the Moral Architecture of the Economy*, Cornell University Press, Ithaca, N.Y., 1993.
44 Mann, *Sources of Social Power. Volume Two*, chs 7 and 20.
45 Cf. E. Gellner, *Nations and Nationalism*, Blackwell, Oxford, 1983.

46 J. A. Hall, 'Nationalisms, Classified and Explained', *Daedalus*, vol. 122, 1993.
47 M. Mann, 'The Emergence of Modern European Nationalism', in J. A. Hall and I. C. Jarvie, eds, *Transition to Modernity*, Cambridge University Press, Cambridge, 1992.
48 R. Brubaker, *Citizenship and Nationhood in France and Germany*, Harvard University Press, Cambridge, Mass., 1992.
49 A. Varshney, 'Contested Meanings: India's National Identity, Hindu Nationalism, and the Politics of Anxiety', *Daedalus*, vol. 122, 1993.
50 T. McDaniel, *Autocracy, Capitalism and Revolution in Russia*, University of California Press, Berkeley, Cal., 1988.
51 D. Senghaas, *The European Experience*, Berg, Leamington Spa, 1985.
52 M. Hodgson, *The Venture of Islam*, vol. 2, Chicago University Press, Chicago, Ill., 1974, ch. 7.
53 The concept of 'caging' is drawn from the work of Mann, *Sources of Social Power, passim.*
54 R. Samuels, *The Business of the Japanese State*, Cornell University Press, Ithaca, N.Y., 1987.
55 For a criticism of this view see M. Mann, 'Nation-States in Europe and Other Continents: Diversifying, Developing, Not Dying', *Daedalus*, vol. 122, 1993.
56 Cf. M. Mann, *Sources of Social Power. Volume One*, ch. 1.
57 Mann, *Sources of Social Power. Volume Two*, ch. 21.
58 H. Bull, *The Anarchical Society*, Macmillan, London, 1977; H. Bull and A. Watson, eds, *The Expansion of International Society*, Oxford University Press, Oxford, 1984.
59 For a full development of this argument see J. A. Hall, *International Orders*, Polity Press, Cambridge, forthcoming.
60 The most recent review of this literature is by one of its originators: S. M. Lipset, 'The Social Requisites of Democracy Revisited', *American Sociological Review*, vol. 59, 1994.
61 B. Moore, *Social Origins of Dictatorship and Democracy*, Beacon Press, Boston, Mass., 1966; I. Szelenyi, *Socialist Entrepreneurs*, University of Wisconsin Press, Madison, Wis., 1988.
62 D. Rueschemeyer, E. Stephens and J. Stephens, *Capitalist Development and Democracy*, Polity Press, Cambridge, 1992.
63 Of course, there is an exception to this generalization: Solidarity was a genuine movement from below, and the eventual opening of the archives in Moscow may show that this crucially affected social rule as a whole – as was claimed by L. Kolakowski in 'Amidst Moving Ruins', *Daedalus*, vol. 121, 1992.
64 R. Putnam, *Making Democracy Work: Civic Traditions in Modern Italy*, Princeton University Press, Princeton, N.J., 1993.
65 E. Gellner, *Muslim Society*, Cambridge University Press, Cambridge, 1981, p. 15.
66 D. Blackbourn and G. Eley, *The Peculiarities of German History*, Oxford University Press, Oxford, 1984.
67 J. Staniszkis, *Dynamics of the Breakthrough in Eastern Europe*, University of California Press, Berkeley, Cal., 1991, part I.

68 T. Karl, 'Dilemmas of Democratisation in Latin America', *Comparative Politics*, vol. 22, 1990.
69 It is worth stressing what should anyway be apparent from the discussion as a whole, namely that the character of political regime affects varied types of movements.
70 There is a large literature here: see *inter alia* C. Waisman, *Modernisation and the Working Class*, University of Texas Press, Austin, Tex., 1982; D. Geary, *European Labour Protest, 1848–1945*, Methuen, London, 1984; R. McKibbin, *The Ideologies of Class*, Oxford University Press, Oxford, 1990; I. Katznelson and A. Zolberg, eds, *Working Class Formation*, Princeton University Press, Princeton, N.J., 1987; McDaniel, *Capitalism, Autocracy and Revolution in Russia*; Mann, *Sources of Social Power. Volume Two*, especially chs 15, 17–18.
71 R. Dahrendorf, *Class and Class Conflict in Industrial Society*, Stanford University Press, Stanford, Cal., 1959.
72 Mann, *Sources of Social Power. Volume Two*, ch. 18.
73 J. H. Plumb, *The Growth of Political Stability in England, 1675–1725*, Penguin, London, 1969.
74 Weber made his views particularly clear in his wartime reflections on the historical sociology of Wilhelmine Germany. See M. Weber, 'Parliament and Government in a Reconstructed Germany', in *Economy and Society*, trans. G. Roth and C. Wittich, University of California Press, Berkeley, Cal., 1978, p. 1391.
75 R. Bova, 'Political Dynamics of the Post-Communist Transition: A Comparative Perspective', *World Politics*, vol. 44, 1991.
76 The most sustained analysis is that of A. Przeworski, *Democracy and the Market*, Cambridge University Press, Cambridge, 1991, but see too J. Elster, 'When Communism Dissolves', *London Review of Books*, 24 January 1990, and C. Offe, 'Capitalism by Democratic Design? Democratic Theory Facing the Triple Transition in East Central Europe', *Social Research*, vol. 58, 1991.
77 Offe, 'Capitalism by Democratic Design?'.
78 E. Comisso, 'Property Rights, Liberalism and the Transition from "Actually Existing Socialism"', *East European Politics and Society*, vol. 5, 1991.
79 B. Davidson, *The Search for Africa*, Random House, New York, 1994.
80 See too A. Seligman, *The Idea of Civil Society*, Free Press, New York, 1992.
81 It is worth noting here that one recent bestseller, R. Bellah, R. Madsen, W. Sullivan, A. Swidler and S. Tipton, *Habits of the Heart*, University of California Press, Berkeley, Cal., 1985, misinterprets Tocqueville, in effect through reading him with Durkheimian eyes. Striking negative comments on this book in line with my difference with Seligman were made by A. Greeley in his review in *Sociology and Social Research*, vol. 70, 1985, as was noticed by S. Lieberson, 'Einstein, Renoir, and Greeley: Evidence in Sociology', *American Sociological Review*, vol. 57, 1992.
82 For a full justification of this claim, see J. A. Hall, 'Politics and Sincerity: the "Existentialists" vs Goffman and Proust', *Sociological Review*, vol. 25, 1977.
83 J. Habermas, 'Further Reflections on the Public Sphere', in Calhoun, *Habermas and the Public Sphere*.

2

The Importance of Being Modular

Ernest Gellner

WHAT IS CIVIL SOCIETY REALLY?

The simplest, immediate and intuitively obvious definition, which also has a certain amount of merit, is: civil society is that set of diverse non-governmental institutions, which is strong enough to counterbalance the state, and, whilst not preventing the state from fulfilling its role of keeper of the peace and arbitrator between major interests, can nevertheless prevent the state from dominating and atomizing the rest of society.

Such a definition conveys the idea contained in the phrase, and also highlights the reason for the newly emerged attractiveness of the slogan in Eastern Europe. Nonetheless, from the viewpoint of a sustained and serious, historically comparative investigation, this definition has a grave deficiency. It is good as far as it goes, but it does not go far enough. The trouble is simple: such a definition would include under the notion of 'civil society' many forms of social order which in fact would not satisfy us, or those who have in recent years felt inspired by this slogan.

The point is this: historically, mankind has not *always* suffered under centralized despotisms. Quite frequently, it has not. The imposition of a despotism is not always an easy matter. Pre-modern polities lack the equipment for first pulverizing and then running the societies they control. They are interested in extracting as much surplus as possible, but frequently, the best way of doing this is to allow local communities to administer themselves, and merely oblige them to supply produce – or labour – on pain of punishment. In favourable circumstances, such as those conducive to mobile pastoralism, or in difficult mountainous terrain, local communities can even become fully independent and resist demands for taxation.

The centralizing logic of successive elimination of power centres, till one only is left, only operates in conditions which favour it, such as river valleys. What all this amounts to is that the traditional agrarian world, though its polities are most often monarchical, is nevertheless very well endowed in highly structured and partly or wholly autonomous communities.

These, however, maintain their cohesion, internal discipline and solidarity by a heavy ritual underscoring of social roles and obligations. The roles are generally conceived and defined in kin terms, and may in fact frequently be filled in terms of the kin positions of their occupants. Political, economic, ritual, kin and any other kinds of obligations are superimposed on each other, and their visibility and authority strengthened by a plethora of ritual reminders: as in a military organization, discipline is enforced by a proliferation of minor punishable transgressions, the avoidance of which puts a burden on each individual and keeps him in awe of the social order as a whole.

So, traditional man can sometimes escape the tyranny of kings, but only at the cost of falling under the tyranny of cousins. The kin-defined, ritually orchestrated, demanding and life-pervading systems of the 'ancient city', in Fustel de Coulanges's sense, do indeed succeed in avoiding tyrannical centralization, but only at the cost of a demanding culture which modern man would find intolerably stifling. The general sociological law of agrarian society runs, roughly, man must be subject to either kings or cousins, though quite often he is subject to both at once. Kings generally dominate societies through the intermediary of local institutions and communities.

So, if we are to define *our* notion of 'civil society' effectively, we must first of all exclude from it something which may be in itself attractive or repulsive, or perhaps both, but which is radically distinct from it. Fustel de Coulanges in *The Ancient City* perhaps did more than anyone else to establish this distinction. His aim was to disabuse his fellow French citizens, who had for some time been eager to invoke the alleged liberties of the ancients as precedents for the liberties they were eager to acquire or to fortify in their own society. But this was a total misunderstanding, Fustel claimed:

> The ideas which the moderns have had of Greece and Rome have often been in their way. Having imperfectly observed the institutions of the ancient city, men have dreamed of reviving them among us.

They have deceived themselves about the liberty of the ancients, and on this very account the liberty of the moderns has been put in peril.[1]

Fustel was eager to cure his compatriots of their illusions and thereby guard against the dangers inherent in them.

This particular danger may not be serious in our time: the rhetoric of the recent converts to the idea of civil society does not contain much, if indeed it contains any, invocations of the ancient liberties of the Greeks and Romans. Nevertheless, a proper understanding of what the ideal really means now must refrain from an uncritical invocation of any and every plural society, in which well-established institutions counterbalance the state. Such an equation is not merely in error sociologically, it also has practical misleading consequences which, even if they are not the same as those of the French contemporaries and predecessors of Fustel, are nonetheless important, and must be guarded against.

Fustel is exceedingly eloquent on the matter of how much real individual liberty, in the modern sense, there was in the ancient city:

> The city had been founded upon a religion and constituted like a church. Hence its strength; hence, also, its omnipotence and the absolute empire which it exercised over its members. In a society established on such principles, individual liberty could not exist. The citizen was subordinate in everything, and without any reserve to the city ... Private life did not escape the omnipotence of the state ... It exercised its tyranny in the smallest things ... [2]

Fustel was concerned to show how this kind of plural, non-centralized, but socially oppressive society, which for all its political pluralism would not satisfy a modern craving for civil society, was replaced by a new order in which the Christian separation of religion and polity made individual liberty thinkable. In this way, Fustel was not merely the ancestor of those who, like Louis Dumont, seek the religious origins of Western individualism, but also of those who seek to analyse the societies based on principles he had laid bare, and which in due course were to be called 'segmentary'.[3]

Fustel was interested in the disappearance and replacement of such societies, but in fact they had not disappeared from the earth, or even from the Mediterranean. Fustel and his ideas have also become the inspiration of those many investigators, who have since come to be called social anthropologists, who are eager to understand societies which still function in the way which Fustel credited to Mediterranean antiquity. In his own time, Emile Masqueray rediscovered the ancient city, under Muslim camouflage, in the Berber hills of Algeria.[4] More recently, an American scholar has used Fustel, directly rather than mediated by Durkheim as is customary, in studying a long-urbanized Asian population. After summarizing Fustel's segmentary account of society and the way in which each level of segments was sustained by its deities and rites, Levy goes on to comment:

> Fustel's portrait contained a deeply felt myth, that of an earthly paradise of orderly, family-based unities prior to a transformation into a larger, impersonal and conflict-ridden state organisation.[5]

Unquestionably, Fustel's materials were used to help foster such a myth, though Fustel himself was rather concerned, as we have seen, to counter an earlier myth, that of the ancient city as a kind of precursor of the French Revolution.

What concerns us now is that the situation is, at the very least, triangular: there are the segmentary communities, cousin-ridden and ritual-ridden, free perhaps of central tyranny, but not free in a sense that would satisfy us; there is centralization which grinds into the dust all subsidiary social institutions or sub-communities, whether ritually stifling or not; and there is the third alternative which is the one we seek. A proper definition must take all this into account: it has at least two contrasts, its essence cannot be seized with the help of a merely bi-polar opposition between pluralism and monocentrism.

DAVID HUME ON RELIGION, OR, CIVIL SOCIETY A FAILED *UMMA*?

There is a fascinating contradiction in the thought of David Hume on this topic, a contradiction which is probably more revealing and illuminating than the consistencies of lesser men. In *The Natural History of Religion*, Hume works out a sociology of religion which is, at the same time, a sociology of the emergence of liberty. His views resemble those of Gibbon and those of the great latter-day follower of both Hume and Gibbon, namely Frazer. They are well in the style and spirit of the Enlightenment, manifesting admiration for the virtues of classical antiquity, and distaste for the monotheist scripturalist and egotistical ethos which has replaced it. Hume does not yet have the sophistication of Fustel de Coulanges or Benjamin Constant, and he fails to appreciate that the liberties of the ancient would not be altogether to modern taste. The contrast in terms of which he argues is basically one which opposes classical religion – social, civic, this-worldly, communal, traditional, tolerant – to the world religion which replaced it, which by contrast is egotistic, other-worldly, doctrinal and intolerant. His code word for the former is *superstition*, and for the latter, *enthusiasm*. His conclusions are clear:

> The tolerating spirit of idolaters, both in ancient and modern times, is very obvious to any one . . .
>
> The intolerance of almost all religions, which have maintained the unity of God, is as remarkable as the contrary principle of polytheists.[6]

The contrast drawn is obvious, and the reasoning persuasive. The priests administering the rites of civic religion inculcate civic virtues, and are not concerned with doctrinal orthodoxy, barely possessing any doctrine or the means for fixing and codifying it. By contrast, the zealots of individual salvation through adherence to doctrine, on the one hand encourage their followers to place the salvation of their own private souls above all else, and, on the other, define members of the community of the saved in terms of commitment to formally defined *conviction*, deviation from which defines heresy, which in turn calls for exemplary punishment.

It follows that mankind was much better off under the regime of the ancients, and that the adoption of revealed, doctrinal, scriptural, universalistic religion was a disaster. The argument is persuasive, and evidence supports it. Yet something is not quite right. Even in *The Natural History of Religion*, which in the main is devoted to expounding the Augustan theme of the excellence of the ancients and the corruption of the moderns, he comments on the counter-example:

> And if, among CHRISTIANS, the ENGLISH and DUTCH have embraced the principles of toleration, this singularity has proceeded from the steady resolution of the civil magistrate, in opposition to the continued efforts of priests and bigots.[7]

The greater liberty of the English and the Dutch clearly contradicts the Augustan thesis, and Hume invokes the not really very adequate *Hilfshypothese* of the civil magistrate and his steady resolution to overcome the difficulty. This won't really do, and elsewhere Hume does rather better. His remarkable essay 'Of Superstition and Enthusiasm' deserves to be counted as one of the earliest, and most perceptive, contributions to the debate concerning the role of protestantism in the emergence of the modern world. In it, he puts forward three propositions:

> that superstition is favourable to priestly power, and enthusiasm not less or rather more contrary to it, than sound reason and philosophy.

> that religions, which partake of enthusiasm are, on their first rise, more furious and violent than those which partake of superstition; but in a little time become more gentle and moderate.

> that superstition is an enemy to civil liberty, and enthusiasm a friend to it.[8]

Here we are no longer in the pre-Fustel world of Gibbon, committed to the equation of the good social condition with the best to be found in antiquity, but rather, in the world of Max Weber, pervaded by the awareness that something very distinctive indeed had happened in the modern world, and that it is connected with the Reformation.

The last of the three propositions sums it all up: the other two offers attempts at explanation of this strange phenomenon, so contrary to the plausible reasoning of *The Natural History of Religion*. The explanation offered resembles what Max Weber was later due to call 'routinization': the religions addicted to 'enthusiasm', that is to firm commitment to abstract doctrine and its serious implementation, though uncompromising initially and thereby inimical to liberty, eventually soften and become tolerant. They make a double (at least) contribution to freedom: first, they destroy the priests, in part by universalizing priesthood and thus terminating the existence of a distinct priestly caste, and, secondly, by being directly inclined to liberty during the period of diminution of zeal. This diminution is further aided by the absence amongst these erstwhile enthusiasts of a special category of people charged with maintaining the flame of faith. That very equalization of the religious condition, which had made the puritans such formidable enemies of liberty at the time of maximum fervour, also made them more tolerant during the time of diminution of enthusiasm.

All this is excellent, and immeasurably superior to Hume's attempt at explaining the liberal potential of enthusiasm in *The*

Natural History of Religion. The balance of power in society, as
between the enthusiasts and the addicts of superstition, must surely
also be taken into consideration. Perhaps the full story could
run something like this: the enthusiasts made great inroads on the
society, and in fact were, for a time, victorious. Nonetheless, in the
end, they were defeated but not crushed. The society as a whole
favoured a compromise, a retention of superstition, priestly power
and ritual and all, but with limited power and a toleration of the
extremists/enthusiasts, who, obliged to renounce their ambition
of imposing the rule of righteousness on earth, if necessary by
political force, turn instead to pacifism and tolerance. The priests
concentrate on combating the enthusiasm of the zealots, and
quietly tolerate disbelief provided it is discreet and ambiguous; the
zealots turn inwards, to the worldly asceticism of *disinterested*
accumulation.

So the coming of civil society, a society liberal in the modern and
not in the ancient, non-liberal, cousinly and ritualized though
plural sense, presupposed two things: a political stalemate between
the rival contestants, such as in fact occurred in seventeenth-century England, leading to a compromise consisting of a watered-
down ritualism and mediation at the centre, and a so-to-speak
privatized *Umma* at home among the minoritarian enthusiasts; and,
prior to all this, the kind of balance between mediation-cum-ritual-
ism (the left-over from communal religion) and universalistic-
doctrinal elements, which in fact is found in Christianity.

When doctrinal, soteriological, omnibus world religions partially
replaced communal religions in the 'Axial Age', they seldom if ever
replaced them completely. The doctrinal, individualist, universalist
element was introduced, and the doctrine or illumination offered to
any questing and anguished individual was added to the com-
munity-defining ritual and its guardian priesthood; but the second
element did remain. Henceforth, the religious life of mankind in the
more complex societies was due to be the interaction of these two
major elements, sometimes fusing harmoniously, something in
overt confrontation. The manner in which these two elements met
in Christianity and in Islam is interesting: the two cases are almost
mirror images of each other.

In Islam, the scripturalist, puritan, universalist, individualist
variant prevailed at the centre. Not always endowed with political
power, it was generally credited with a kind of normative authority.
The ritualistic, mediation-addicted, ecstasy-seeking, hierarchical
variants were fragmented, peripheral, popular, and often a little

shame-faced. So we have *Umma* at the centre, community at the periphery and in the lower levels of the social hierarchy. Periodically, conflict erupts between the two: the enthusiasts at the centre for a time prevail over the superstition at the margins, but social factors eventually restore the balance, and the circle repeats itself; in the traditional world, this goes on for ever, it would seem.

Or should one say rather, *because* the circle repeats itself for ever, Islam never breaks out of the traditional world. This is the cyclical, non-progressive dynamic of Islam, analysed by Ibn Khaldun and rather contemptuously noted by Friedrich Engels, in fact echoing Ibn Khaldun without actually citing his name.[9] Come the modern world, however – imposed by extraneous forces rather than produced indigenously – and the new balance of power, favouring the urban centre against rural communities, causes the central faith to prevail, and we face a successful *Umma* at long last. This is the explanation of the secularization-resistant nature of Islam.

In Christianity, the mix of the two religious elements was quite different. Hierarchy, organized mediation, bureaucratized ritual and magic, prevailed in the very central and single Organization, claiming a monopolistic link to the Founder of the religion and the coming of the unique Revelation. The scripturalist, puritan, individualistic, symmetrical, ecstasy-spurning and mediation-repudiating enthusiasts were at the margin. *They* were disunited, the Organization was unique and united (at least most of the time).

It was this mix which in fact engendered, by some internal chemistry, the modern world. Whether only it could have done so, as a very great sociologist claimed, we shall probably never know: we cannot rerun the experiment in order to find out. This mix, plus the fact that the great confrontation between superstitious centre and enthusiastic periphery ended in a draw and in a deadlock, meant that the modern world was produced, and when produced, the compromise led to no general *Umma*, nor even to a series of ghetto-*Ummas*, but to a widespread secularization. And also, and this is what concerns us in the present argument, to a pluralism free of the imposition of the *Umma*, but not resembling the cousinly ritualism of communities either.

We have at least three situations to consider: the Muslim *Umma* which succeeded, the Christian one which failed but engendered civil society and the would-be secular *Umma* of the immanentist, formally materialist socio-historical religion, which signally failed as an *Umma* but has not yet demonstrated its capacity to produce a civil society either. All that the latter has achieved is to generate,

at least amongst a significant proportion of its citizens, an evidently
sincere and ardent *desire* for civil society.

MODULAR MAN

There are firms which produce, sell and advertise modular furniture. The point about such furniture is that it comes in bits which
are so to speak agglutinative: you can buy one bit, which will
function on its own, but when your needs or your income or the
space available to you augment, you can buy another bit and it
will fit in with the first bit, and the whole thing will still have a
coherence, aesthetically and technically. You can combine and
recombine the bits at will. This makes modular furniture quite
different from the ordinary kind: with that, if you want coherence,
you have to buy it all at once, in one go, which means that you have
to make a kind of irrevocable commitment, or at any rate, a commitment which it will be rather costly to revoke. If you add a new
bit of non-modular furniture to an old bit, you end with an eclectic,
incoherent mess. You must then either resign yourself to such
messiness, or scrap the old and start altogether anew, which is
costly.

We are investigating the notion of civil society partly by means of
contrasting it with its alternatives, and our point is that not one, but
more than one important contrast is involved. We are concerned
not merely by the opposition between liberal civil society and an
ideological *Umma* (whether the dismally failed secular *Umma* of
Marxism, or the strangely successful *Umma* of Islam), but also with
the contrast between it and the as-it-were Durkheimian society
of ritual-based and communal, rather than doctrine-based and
soteriological society. What really marks this distinction is that
genuine civil society requires, not modular furniture, but modular
man.

The main point of Durkheimian sociology, and perhaps of the
organicist or communalist tradition in social thought generally, is
that man is markedly un-modular. He cannot be bonded into a
social organism easily or at will. The Social Contract theorists had
thought the opposite, and supposed that a society could be set up as
easily as modern man can buy a washing machine on hire purchase.
The trouble with them was not merely that their position was
logically circular – if it is contracts which bind men, then a meta-
contract is required to make the first one binding, and so on forever

– but above all, they were illegitimately generalizing from one kind of man, who takes his own promises and commitments seriously, to man in general.

But man in general is not modular, his individual isolated acts and affirmations are not to be taken seriously or to be relied on, his only real commitment is to a kind of interdependent and ritually orchestrated totality. Before you can trust his promise, it has to be made with trumpets and drama, with witnesses and presentations, dancing and music. By laying on the solemnity, preferably with a sacrifice, by linking the act to all kinds of other social relationships and symbolically fusing it with a whole network of solemn occasions, you can get it to be taken seriously. A traditional wedding involves two entire clans, great expense, much sound and fury; it is modern man who can get married in a quick sober procedure with a couple of witnesses and yet incur legally and socially serious consequences.

Non-modularity is as it were the normal human condition, which can be assumed to obtain unless some very special circumstances make for modularity. But the political and economic consequences of non-modularity are tremendous. The political ones are, above all: the only effective social groups, which alone can engender a social balance of power and counteract arbitrary centralized tyranny, are heavily ritualized, socially pervasive, deeply demanding, stifling social segments. The only alternative to the tyranny of kings is the tyranny of cousins (though of course, you *can* have *both*). The economic consequences of non-modularity are simple and obvious: rigidity, conservatism, stagnation. The bonding of practices and procedures to ritual and to kin group means the freezing of technique. Technical innovation means social disruption and the de-stabilization of that essential social segment, which alone offers protection, and 'life meaning', to man. It obviates the possibility of choosing techniques simply in terms of clearly defined criteria of efficiency, and of nothing else. It imposes instead the need to judge practices, if indeed they are to be subject to critical scrutiny at all, in terms of the multiple, imponderable, complex considerations of their participation in an indivisible, 'organic', cultural totality.

It is the political consequences of modularity which are really important. Modular man can combine into effective associations and institutions, without these being total, many-stranded, underwritten by ritual, and made stable through being linked to a whole set of relationships, all of these then being tied in with each other

and so immobilized. He can combine into specific-purpose, *ad hoc*,
limited associations, without binding himself by some blood ritual.
He can leave an association when he comes to disagree with its
policy without being open to the charge of treason. A properly
terminated contract is not an act of treachery, and is not seen as
such. A tenant who gives due notice and pays the recognized rent,
acquires no stigma if he move to a new tenancy. Yet these highly
specific, unsanctified, instrumental, revocable links or bonds are
effective! *This* is civil society: the forging of links which are effective even though they are flexible, specific, instrumental. Society is
a structure, it is not atomized, helpless and supine, and yet the
structure is readily adjustable and responds to rational criteria of
improvement.

MODULAR MAN IS A NATIONALIST

The modularity of modern man was probably a precondition of the
industrial miracle, and is certainly – by definition – a precondition
of civil society: civil society is a cluster of institutions and associations strong enough to prevent tyranny, but which are, nevertheless, entered freely rather than imposed either by birth or by
awesome ritual.

But the modularity has a price, or at any rate, a precondition,
which in turn is liable to raise problems. So far, we have focused on
certain moral and intellectual qualities which are presupposed by
modularity: what is required is that a man should be capable of
undertaking and honouring, deeply internalizing, commitments
and obligations by a single and sober act. He will honour his debts
and obligations without prolonged and fearful rituals, without
involving the honour of all his kin and so forth. It is not so much
that his word is his bond, but that his word is his word even when
spoken softly, without emphasis, in ordinary circumstances, without artificial heightening of the atmosphere, so to speak. And he
must also be capable of lucid, Cartesian thought, which separates
issues rather than conflates them and takes them one at a time: the
non-conflation of issues, the separation out of the social strands,
which makes society non-rigid, presupposes not merely a moral
willingness, but also an intellectual capacity. Clear thought is not
a birthright but an accomplishment, and somehow it had to be
taught and its principles internalized: it is an acquired taste, and the
acquisition had to be fostered.

But the modularity, the flexibility of institutions, requires the substitutability of men for each other: one man must be able to fill the slot previously occupied by another. To do this, they need not be identical in all respects: were that so, nothing would be accomplished by the substitution. The substitution or replacement of one man by another only has point if, precisely, they do differ, and the substitution effects an improvement in the totality within which it occurs. But, nevertheless, if it is to be possible and workable as well as constituting an improvement, the connections between the occupant of the slot and his neighbours must be standard, so that communication, interaction, can continue at least at the previous level. The communication symbols employed by the new occupant of the slot must be culture-compatible with those of his new neighbours.

This is indeed one of the most important general traits of a modern society: cultural homogeneity. The old segmentary societies of various kinds highlighted and fortified the boundaries between the segments by cultural differentiation: people spoke, ate, dressed, etc., differently, according to their precise location in a complex, intricate social structure. They had to speak and generally comport themselves as their station required, and to speak in any different manner would have been offensive presumption, if not violation of legal or ritual prescription. There was, in these conditions, not merely no incentive for, but plenty of reasons against, defining political units in terms of identity of culture. This idea, which is the very essence of nationalism, goes against the grain of traditional society. If ever it does exemplify any degree of correlation between political and cultural boundaries, it does so by accident, and not from any kind of inner compulsion.

But not so in the new realm of modular man. It requires men to be modular, for it requires them to be mobile as between social positions in an inherently unstable social structure. It cannot tolerate idiosyncrasies of communication, which would only inhibit the shifting of one social pawn from a given position to another. It cannot tolerate locally idiosyncratic idioms of communication, which, when taken from one position to another where the neighbours are no longer familiar with them, would immediately lead to unintelligibility and the inhibition of the easy flow and comprehension of messages.

The standardization of idiom is in any case imposed on this kind of society by the nature of work, which has ceased to be physical and has become predominantly semantic: work is now the passing and reception of messages, largely between anonymous individuals in a mass society, who cannot normally be familiar with their interlocutors. Located as is the partner in the exchange of messages at the other end of a telephone or a fax, his identity normally is not even known, let alone familiar. But this being so, it is no longer acceptable that the partner's facial expression, body posture, past history and habits should enter into the determination of the meaning of the message, as a kind of additional but essential phoneme. In the old intimate, closed peasant communities, in which all speakers and listeners were intimately familiar with each other, these as it were personal, privatized phonemes were not merely tolerable, they were, very nearly, the only ones tolerated. Explicitness of speech, which detaches the meaning from these elements and makes it a function exclusively of standardized phonetic elements, independent of context and identity of speaker and listener, is something reserved for, at most, a few scholastics and lawyers. Its practice by others is unthinkable.

All that changes in the society of universal and anonymous communication. Modularity, with its moral and intellectual preconditions, makes civil society, and the existence of non-suffocating yet effective segments, possible; but it makes not only for civil, but also for nationalist society. Modular man is not *universally* substitutable: he is substitutable within the cultural boundaries of the idiom in which he has been trained to communicate, to emit and to receive messages. He has had to be *trained* for this, for the capacity to observe a standardized code cannot be acquired through the informal procedures of daily living, which is the way in which old, folk, popular traditions were, by definition, transmitted. It can only be done by means of formal education, transmitting to its wards the standardized, codified rules of a culture which, precisely in virtue of this codification and its inherent links to a specialized educational institutions, is a *High* Culture. In these circumstances, for the first time in world history, a High Culture, in this sense, becomes the pervasive and operational culture of an entire society, rather than being the privilege and badge of a restricted social stratum.

But it also means, of course, that the territorial or social limits of the use of any one such High Culture at the same time also sets the limits of the substitutability, the possible deployment and social insertion, of the given modular individual who had received his training in that particular culture. For the average person, the limits of his culture are the limits of his employability, social acceptability, effective participation and citizenship. His educationally acquired culture is by far his most important possession and investment, for it alone gives him access to all else; and the existence of a secure, preferably extensive political unit identified with that culture, and therefore automatically conferring full status on him as a bearer of it, is his most pressing and powerful political concern. He is not a nationalist out of atavism (quite the reverse), but rather, from a perfectly sound, though seldom lucid and conscious, appreciation of his own true interests.

As indicated, the previous agrarian world was enormously rich in cultural nuance, having used it to indicate and highlight and confirm and sacralize an enormous multiplicity of social distinctions. For the same reasons, it could not use cultural boundaries to indicate and highlight political ones. Now, the reverse is the case. *Inside* political units, cultural differentiation and nuance are to a large extent wiped out, in the interests of furthering that invaluable modularity. But at the same time, as the limits of substitutability are the limits of commitment, political boundaries will tend to converge with boundaries of High Cultures, and indeed, High Cultures will generally displace Low ones.

At the beginning of the social transformation which brought about the new state of affairs, the world was full of political units of all sizes, and of cultural nuances, and hence of men whose own culture did not converge with the one used by the political unit they inhabited. Under the new social regime, this became increasingly uncomfortable. They then had two options, if they were to diminish the discomfort: they could change their culture, or they could change the nature of the political unit, either by changing its boundaries, or by changing its cultural identification. Men generally adopted one or the other of these strategies, sometimes both, whether in succession or simultaneously. The surface result of all this was the nationalist turbulence of the nineteenth and twentieth centuries.

FRIEND OR FOE?

The same, or largely overlapping, forces have produced both human modularity and nationalism. Modularity is the precondition of civil society and, according to the most famous and most influential sociological theory, it is itself the fruit of protestantism. It was protestantism which, on this theory, had taught men to stand alone, to be bound by their word without the benefit of reinforcing ritual and communal context. Protestantism, by making the absence of ritual into its own most potent ritual, and the absence of graven images into its most suggestive fetish, liberated mankind, or rather, a segment of mankind, from that addiction to audio-visual and socio-contextual reinforcement which is so characteristic of most of humanity, and which had prevented the emergence of that modern world to which we are now committed, and whose most valued political features are associated with the notion of civil society.

If civil society and nationalism are both the offspring of the same forces, does this kinship turn them into political allies or enemies?

At the start, they tended to be allies. For one thing, early nationalism was modest and timid, the Herderian defence of the charms of folk cultures against the imperialism of the French court or of British commercialism or the bloodless universalism of abstract man of the Enlightenment. (Later, the philosophical anthropology of nationalism was to become more aggressive, not to say ferocious, but that was yet to come.) But above all, initially liberalism and nationalism had the same enemy, the baroque absolutist state which was indifferent to the folk culture of its subjects, and in any case disinclined to allow them too many liberties or too much participation. So, the claim for greater liberties for the individual, the ratification of that which was to become the normal comportment of modular man, and the claim for greater equality of cultures, could be presented together, and even endowed with an elective affinity with each other, as jointly seeking greater human fulfilment.

But in due course, their paths diverged. The individualism inherent in the condition of modular man, if pushed to its logical conclusion, was hostile to the cult of community. The position was indeed pushed to its extreme logical conclusion by those whose own social situation impelled them in that direction. Nationalism, on the other hand, went in a different direction. Notwithstanding the fact that its real social roots lay in the emergence of a mass anonymous society destined to use a shared and standardized culture, it adopted the pretence (held in all sincerity by its protagonists and propagandists) that it was defending and perpetuating a village, folk culture. Rooted in an emerging *Gesellschaft*, it preached *Gemeinschaft*. In Central and Eastern Europe, it was forced into this stance partly by the fact that new High Cultures had to be forged on the basis of peasant cultures. But the nationalists were hostile not merely to rival cultures, but also, and perhaps with special venom, hostile to bloodless cosmopolitanism, perhaps because they sensed in it an ally of political centralism, a support for the attempt to maintain the old transnational empires against neo-ethnic irredentism. (They were right: in the end, the liberals, committed to an open market in goods, men and ideas, were the last supporters of centralism, remaining faithful to it, even when the old baroque absolutism and the partisans of the *ancien régime* had given up the struggle.)

So, in the later stages, the push towards an individualist civil society, and the nationalist striving, tended to come in collision with each other. The ambiguity of this relationship was very visible in the Habsburg empire, and the pattern was due in the end to be replayed in the terminal stage of the tsarist-bolshevik empire.

THE TIME ZONES OF EUROPE

The manner in which the nationalist aspect of modular humanity manifested itself in Europe varied from region to region, and the differences are both inherently interesting, and important for the understanding of subsequent developments. Roughly speaking, and allowing for certain complications which will be specified later, Europe falls into four time zones, resembling a little those global maps one sometimes sees at airports, which indicate the different times in the various vertically defined stretches of the globe.

It is perhaps useful, if contrary to nature, to proceed from West to East, as in this matter the West is less problematical than the East. The westernmost time zone is that of the Atlantic coast of Europe. The point about this area is that from the late Middle Ages onwards if not earlier, it was occupied by strong dynastic states, which roughly, even if only roughly, correlated with cultural areas. This meant that when, with the coming of nationalism, political units had to adjust themselves to cultural boundaries, no very great changes were required here. History had made a present to nationalism of a broad region, where the nationalist imperative was already, at least in some measure, satisfied before the event. Some turbulence there was, of course, even within this zone: to this day, there is violence in Bilbao and Belfast. One major adjustment of the political map did take place, namely the establishment of the Republic of Ireland. But all in all, the map of this part of Europe in the age of nationalism does not look so very different from what it had been in the age when dynasty, religion and local community had been the determinants of boundaries. The dynastic states, finding themselves in charge of an area correlating with a culture, tended to identify with that culture, even before nationalism had turned culture into the most potent political symbol. There was no need for very widespread ethnic irredentism when the new order arrived. New cultures did not need to be created, and the attempt to revive one in Ireland failed. The cultures which exist did not need to acquire new political roofs: the roof was ready, waiting for them.

The next zone to the east was different. Far from possessing ready-made dynastic states, it was an area of quite exceptional political fragmentation, endowed with effective political units much smaller than the geographical extension of the two locally dominant High Cultures. The major political meta-unit of the area, the Holy Roman empire, had lost effective reality and, by the time of the coming of the age of nationalism, had ceased to exist even in name. But if the region lacked pre-existing political units ready for the nationalist requirements, it was well equipped with pre-existing, codified, normative High Cultures. Both Italian and German were well codified, ever since the Renaissance and the Reformation respectively, at the very latest.

So here there was a need for polity-building, but not for culture-building. There was no need for schoolteachers, ethnographers, folklorists, and national 'Awakeners' generally, to go out to the villages and construct a national culture from the chaos of regional dialectal variety. It had all been done, before nationalism. Whereas in the westernmost zone, all that needed to be done was to transform peasants sunk in local cultural particularism into properly educated members of the national culture, here (though perhaps this had to be done too), the main thing required was a political change. An existing High Culture had to be endowed with a political roof worthy of it. It took a certain amount of military and diplomatic activity, but not a great deal else. By the latter part of the nineteenth century, the task had largely been accomplished.

It was the next time zone to the east which presented the greatest problems, from the viewpoint of the implementation of the nationalist principle of *one culture, one state*. Here there was an appallingly complex patchwork of diverse cultures, intermixed both geographically and in the social structure, with political, cultural and religious boundaries devoid of any coherence or overlap. Many of the cultures were not clearly endowed with a normative High Culture and educational institutions capable of protecting, perpetuating and disseminating it in a world in which a High Culture had to become co-extensive with an entire society, rather than defining a narrow minority. Here both cultures and polities had to be created, an arduous task indeed. If the eventual units were to be compact and reasonably homogeneous, more had to be done: many, many people had to be either assimilated, or expelled, or killed. All these methods were eventually employed in the implementation of the nationalist political principle.

Finally, there is Europe's fourth time zone, corresponding more or less to the territories of the erstwhile tsarist empire. The pattern here corresponded fairly closely to that of the third zone – until the end of the First World War. Till then poly-ethnic empires, with a dynastic-religious foundation, managed to survive the pressure generated by nationalist irredentism. But in each case the empire was defeated in the war and disintegrated. But thereafter, the two paths diverge. The tsarist empire was re-established rather quickly, under entirely new management and in the name of a uniquely new, formally secular ideology, though one endowed with all the zeal and messianism of a salvation religion, which in fact it was.

The new faith was imposed with conviction and ruthlessness, and in fact generated a secular *Umma*, a charismatic community which saw its task on earth as the implementation of absolute righteousness, and saw itself as being in possession of the recipe for that righteousness. The faith which was being implemented had undergone, under the leadership and inspiration of Lenin, a kind of inverse Reformation: initially, the faith possessed no clauses which would entail an internal stratification of the faithful. All mankind eventually, and in the meantime at any rate all the oppressed and dispossessed, were granted an equal and symmetrical access and relationship to the truth which was to save humanity. Lenin, however, had come to the conclusion that ordinary humanity was incapable of rising to the perception of the truth (i.e. the unaided working class would merely be reformist rather than revolutionary, would concentrate on improving its position within the existing social order, rather than grasp that its role was to usher in a wholly different new order). This being so, a special dedicated and highly disciplined Order was required, capable of understanding and appreciating the great Message. When, rather surprisingly, the revolution succeeded and, even more surprisingly, survived despite the absence of external aid from fraternal revolutions elsewhere, this Order naturally inherited the governance of all the Russias, and performed the task which had thus fallen to it in a manner befitting the possessor of an absolute and supremely important revelation. As Lenin observed, the teaching of Marx was all-powerful because it was *true*. A red banner with this quotation continued to hang in the entrance hall of the Institute of Philosophy of the Academy of Sciences of the USSR well into the late 1980s, by which time however it was impossible to draw the attention of any passing Soviet citizen or scholar to it without provoking a wry smile.

Anyway, the new secular *Umma*, under this dedicated and determined leadership, had even less difficulty in containing nationalist irredentism, than had the empires of the erstwhile Holy Alliance during the century which stretched from 1815 to 1918. The new ideocracy, and the institutions it spawned, controlled the entire territory with ease, and obliged its inhabitants to proclaim that their nationalist aspirations were satisfied. A complication of importance, which must be noted, is that as a result of its military victory in 1945, the socialist *Umma* pushed the boundary of the fourth zone westwards, and incorporated large areas which had, between 1918 and the second war, belonged to the third zone. Moscow time, ideologically and politically speaking, now extended to the Adriatic and the Elbe.

For reasons which are of the greatest importance, which have not been adequately elucidated, the world's first secular ideocracy collapsed in the late 1980s, making plain that the faith in this particular salvation creed at any rate had disappeared almost completely in those lands in which its implementation had been attempted. It is of course this very collapse which engendered that craving for civil society, and the revival of the phrase and its elevation to a potent political symbol. The interaction between this aspiration, and the sudden release of nationalist irredentism following the end of dictatorship, calls for further discussion. But this must be preceded by a kind of typology or timetable of the successive forms of nationalism.

THE VARIETIES OF NATIONALIST EXPERIENCE

There is a sense in which the *third* time zone is most typical of the human condition: the transition from the situation in which culture underwrites status but not political boundaries, to the condition in which it does the very reverse, is most manifest in it, and least disturbed by contingent intrusions – by the contingent presence of dynastic states which just happen to correspond, roughly, to future national ones, or by the contingent presence of a well-codified High Culture, or by the Second Coming of Soteriology or Ideocracy in a secular guise. It is the third zone which proceeded from a blatantly ethnicity-defying, dynastic-religious order to a rabid nationalism, and did so relatively undisturbed by other factors. In this sense, the stages through which it passed can be considered 'normal': they are what one would expect, if no unusual additional factors are operative.

There is the first stage in which the old dynastic-religious system is still operative, as it was at the Congresses of Vienna in 1815. There is the second stage of sustained but, all in all, ineffective nationalist irredentism: the new principle of culture-based states is operative, but cannot prevail against the established order, unless the established order is particularly weak. This was the state of affairs between 1815 and 1918, except for the Balkans, where the unusual weakness of the Ottoman empire permitted the creation of five or six national buffer states. Stage three is interesting: it could be called the Age of Nationalism Triumphant and Self-defeating. It lasted from 1918 till the domination of Europe by Hitler and Stalin in the course of the Second World War. It was characterized by a political system consisting of fairly small states, overtly and proudly self-defined as national states, which had succeeded the old poly-ethnic, religiously validated empires. These new states had all the weaknesses of the old empires: they were just as haunted by minorities as they had been, if not more so. In addition, they had a whole series of additional weaknesses of their own. They were small; they were, in the main, new, and were not hallowed by age; they often had inexperienced, greedy and uncautious ruling classes, more eager to make hay while the sun shone, without expectation of or much concern with stability; and they had, amongst their minorities, members of the erstwhile dominant ethno-linguistic groups, unhabituated to submission and minority status, resentful of it and endowed with external support, in their 'home' national state, which helped and encouraged them to struggle against their newly attributed subordinate status. The consequences of these manifold weaknesses soon became manifest: the system offered virtually no resistance, and in any case no effective resistance (except for Finland), when the two great dictators of the century agreed to carve it up between themselves. The system of supposedly national states, set up in the name of national self-determination in 1918 and 1919, collapsed like a house of cards.

The time when it collapsed was also the period of an unprecedentedly large-scale and total war, in the course of which both the flow of information and the strength of moral susceptibilities were markedly diminished. A century of ineffective national striving, followed by a quarter of a century during which the role of oppressor and oppressed was in part inverted, left the region as a seething mass of ethnic resentments. On top of all that, the dominant power, Hitler's Germany, was committed to a mixture of a communalist and biological ideology, which singled out certain ethnic minorities without a territorial or peasant base as specially noxious and deserving of extermination. The interstitial position with which the most important of such minorities was endowed had in any case made it an object of hatred amongst the 'host' populations.

The hatred and resentments were there, and so was the ideological rationale, and as it happens, so was the political will and the organizational machinery. Wartime secrecy made it all easier. The consequence is known. The Jews, but not only they, were objects of a massive, well-organized and efficient campaign of extermination. But other populations suffered as well, and during the immediate postwar period, though information now flowed more easily, indignation and the desire for retaliation permitted the employment of methods – above all, forcible transplantation of population in disregard of normal principles of justice – as a result of which, in some but not all regions, the previously complex ethnic map was brought into closer relationship with the newly imposed political boundaries, thus satisfying the requirements of nationalism more closely than had been feasible in days of moral restraint.

So much for stage four. Thanks to the crimes of Hitler and Stalin, some but not all areas of Eastern Europe now satisfied the nationalist imperative. At the same time, being subjected to the extended area of domination of the new secular ideocracy, it did not matter too much whether or not they did satisfy that imperative, in as far as the new empire had the will and the means to impose its authority in any case, both in areas in which murder and transplantation had produced ethnic homogeneity, and in areas in which the old complexity continued to prevail.

Eventually, during the second half of the 1980s, the secular soteriological ideocracy collapsed, in some measure because of internal opposition, but in the main because of a loss of conviction and nerve at its centre. The leaders, faced with sustained defeat in both the consumerist and the arms races, turned to liberalization in the hope of a quick – or only – remedy, and found themselves incapable of arresting its course once it had gathered momentum, or at any rate, unwilling to adopt the extreme measures which would have been required to arrest it. Their predecessors, in the days of faith, would not have hesitated to use them, but ruthlessness on such a scale no longer seems to come easily (to their credit) to members of this political culture.

So the authoritarian system collapsed, sufficiently to reveal both the yearning for civil society *and* the powerful ethnic passions. It is the interaction and the relative strength of these two newly liberated forces which concern us here. At present, their interaction makes up much of the great political drama of Eastern Europe, and the outcome is far from clear, and will presumably remain unclear for quite some time yet. But it is already possible to make a certain number of observations.

Both the economic and the political aspects of civil society are rather difficult to erect, or to stimulate into emergence. Initial political parties tend to be ephemeral clubs of intellectuals, without effective grass roots. It is easy enough to stimulate certain kinds of enterprise, notably the kind of service industry which tends to exist in semi-legal form anyway, in all but the most repressive of dictatorships. A small restaurant required little space, not a great deal of entrepreneurial talent or imagination, little more than a certain amount of gastronomic and visual taste and fastidiousness. But a genuine open market, as opposed to mere networks, and an entrepreneurial class and institutions – it does not seem easy to set these up by fiat. Much the same goes for political institutions.

By contrast, ethnically based and defined associations appear to be capable of almost immediate formation and so to speak crystallization. Solid organization with local branches, shared symbols and sentiments, recognized and respected leadership – it seems to be possible to create these on a nationalist basis with amazing speed and effectiveness. This may be regrettable: one might wish that the other aspects of modular man, other than his eagerness to identify with the social category within which he is, in virtue of his cultural traits and training, substitutable, should make as ready an appearance. The fact is, they do not. We may or may not like this, but we have to recognize it. The sleeping beauty of ethnicity can be awakened with the gentlest and most tender of kisses. The sleeping beauty of civil society may be more desirable, at least to those sharing our taste, but to wake her up is the devil's own job.

Once again, are nationalism and liberalism allies? At first, certainly: both were oppressed by an authority which combined dogmatism with centralism, and those who long for free thought, and those who long for autonomy for their own cultural totem pole, will naturally be in alliance against the centre. Given the speed with which ethnicity can be mobilized, and the slowness with which anything else can be roused, it is probably a good thing to use ethnic bases as fortresses against centralist reaction. This had been, for instance, Boris Yeltsin's strategy in his confrontation with Gorbachov. Some of us doubted the wisdom of such indiscriminate encouragement of ethnic particularism, a weakening of the centre at any cost, but when, in August 1991, both Yeltsin and Gorbachov had to be saved from a would-be violent reaction by the centrists, it was Yeltsin's capacity to fall back on such a base which saved the day . . .

One can sum it all up as follows: the modularity of man, so intimately tied up with an industrial and growth-oriented society, has two aspects, two principal social corollaries: it makes *possible* civil society, the existence of plural political associations and economic institutions; and it makes *mandatory* the strength of ethnic identity, arising from the fact that man is no longer tied to a social niche, but to a culturally defined pool. The one potentiality is a mere possibility, essential in the long term if the society is to be capable of competing with its rivals, but dispensable in the short run; the other, however, is an immediately felt imperative. This is something one must recognize and take into account, whether or not one likes it.

NOTES

1 F. de Coulanges, *The Ancient City: A Study on the Religion, Laws and Institutions of Greece and Rome* [1864], Anchor Books, New York, 1970, p. 11. It is sometimes claimed that Benjamin Constant had anticipated Fustel on this point in his famous address of 1819 on 'The Liberty of the Ancients compared with that of the Moderns' (Constant, *Political Writings*, ed. B. Fontana, Cambridge University Press, Cambridge, 1988, pp. 309–28). But Constant only stressed that ancient liberty was not *individual* liberty, and in fact opposed such liberty; but he did not specify the role of social sub-groups and their heavy ritualization in the process *both* of depriving the individual of freedom *and* of maintaining social order in the absence of a strong coercive centre. It is *this* perception which makes Fustel the ancestor of modern 'segmentary' theory, of the understanding of a society which *is* plural but *not*, in our required sense, 'civil'.

2 Coulanges, *The Ancient City*, pp. 219–20.
3 L. Dumont, *From Mandeville to Marx: The Genesis and Triumph of Economic Ideology*, Chicago University Press, Chicago, Ill., 1977. The theory of segmentary society begins, of course, with the first major book of one of Fustel de Coulanges's students, namely E. Durkheim, *The Division of Labour in Society*, trans. W. D. Halls, Free Press, New York, 1984. The theory was used by such scholars as Emile Masqueray, Robert Montagne, Edward Evans-Pritchard and Jacques Berque, all of whose work is discussed in and stands at the back of E. Gellner, *Muslim Society*, Cambridge University Press, Cambridge, 1981.
4 E. Masqueray, *Formation des cites chez les populations sedentaires de l'Algerie* [1886], new edn, ed. F. Colonna, Edisud, Aix-en-Provence, 1983.
5 R. I. Levy, *Mesocosm*, University of California Press, Berkeley, Cal., 1990, p. 21.
6 D. Hume, *The Natural History of Religion* [1757], Stanford University Press, Stanford, Cal., 1956, pp. 49, 50.
7 Hume, *The Natural History of Religion*, p. 50.
8 'Of Superstition and Enthusiasm' [1741], in D. Hume, *Essays, Moral, Political, and Literary*, Liberty Classics, Indianapolis, Ind., 1985, pp. 75, 76, 78.
9 Ibn Khaldun, *The Muqaddimah*, trans. F. Rosenthal, Routledge and Kegan Paul, London, 1958; F. Engels, *Die Neue Zeit*, winter, 1894/5.

3

Civil Society in Communist China?
Private Business and Political
Alliance, 1989

David L. Wank

In a view forged by East Central European dissident intellectuals in the late 1970s, civil society opposes the communist party-state. The former is market-based, horizontally organized voluntary associations such as political parties, schools, professional and religious groups and the media – all of which have some autonomy from the state. The latter is the bureaucratically based and hierarchically organized administrative, policing, military, productive and distributive organs of the state.[1] This opposition of society and party-state is said to create historical processes of political change. As one Polish intellectual writes: 'It is here [civil society] that ideas and values inimical to the system of state and economy domination incubate and develop, and eventually lead to the creation of a new "historic bloc" . . . which challenges the old "bloc".'[2]

In this view, the popular upheavals in 1989 that toppled communist states throughout Eastern Europe are an evolutionary outcome of the emergence of civil society during the preceding decade.[3] In some countries this followed a political course, as in Poland where Solidarity emerged as a popular movement that demanded concessions from the state. In other countries it followed a more economic course, as in Hungary where revived private business gave individuals independence from state control. In all these countries, the emergence of autonomous institutions is said to have stimulated popular demands for autonomy; this placed great pressures on party-states, creating a snowball process culminating in the popular upheavals of 1989.

For this view, events in China are highly ironic. During the 1980s, China was widely held to be at the forefront of the wave of liberalization sweeping the communist world. China's emerging market economy was second to none in the communist world and its private business included capitalist firms. There was an expanding associational life of religious and professional groups, private schools and colleges, private scientific research and polling institutions and think tanks, and even budding independent media.[4] According to one sociological observer, China's civil society in the late 1980s compared favourably with those in Eastern Europe. While weaker than Poland's, it was only slightly less robust than Hungary's and East Germany's and was equivalent to the Soviet Union's and Czechoslovakia's.[5] Yet despite the relative robustness of its civil society, China is the only country where a communist state suppressed popular upheaval in 1989 and survives into the 1990s. How can this lack of fit between the East European view of civil society and the Chinese situation be explained?

This paper considers the relevance of the East European view as a framework for understanding the Chinese situation in the late 1980s and beyond. The aim is two-fold. The first is to consider the usefulness of the East European view for the empirical analysis of shifting state–society boundaries during departures from state socialism.[6] The second is to discern the actual configuration of party-state and civil society in China by testing hypotheses derived from the assumptions of the East European view.[7] The empirical focus is on private capitalist business, perhaps the most distinctive aspect of China's civil society in the 1980s. The paper has five sections in addition to the introduction and conclusion. The first section traces the re-emergence of private capitalist business in China. The second section examines the causal argument of the East European view concerning the link between private business and political change. For the argument to be valid, the processes it highlights should be visible in concrete situations. Therefore, in the third section several hypotheses derived from the East European view are tested by examining the actions of entrepreneurs in a local urban setting during China's 1989 crises. The fourth section examines several competing explanations as to why the actions of the entrepreneurs do not support the hypotheses. Explanations derived from the East European view are contrasted with an institutional explanation that emphasizes the competition among actors for resources in the organizational context of the emerging market economy.[8] The fifth section generalizes from the preceding analysis to sketch the *actually existing* configuration of China's state and civil society.

After more than two decades of state suppression, private business was revived in 1979 'from above' in order to supplement the planned economy in the production and circulation of consumer goods and services and in the creation of employment. It has grown rapidly through two distinct policy streams, one reviving the licensed private sector and the other innovating within the collective sector.[9]

Private sector revival began with the Individual Business Family (*Getihu*) policy. This permitted petty private enterprises limited to seven employees, non-mechanized production and transport and a narrow business range. Restrictions on equipment and some business were subsequently removed in 1983. However, the limit on employees, a sensitive matter because of the opposition to wage labour in socialist ideology, was not removed until the 1988 Private Enterprise Law (*Siying qiye fa*) which permitted private enterprises with eight or more employees. The other stream of private business revival, innovations in the collective sector, occurred through policies in the early 1980s that let groups of four or more unemployed individuals pool private capital to set up collective enterprise. The 'public' status of these privately run collectives – hereafter referred to as cooperatives – enabled entrepreneurs to bypass restrictions on the licensed private sector and enjoy public enterprise advantages such as lower taxes and easier access to bank loans. Although cooperatives are formally 'owned' by local bureaux and production units, they are considered 'private' by entrepreneurs and the officials who regulate them.

The growth of private business has been rapid. Within a decade the number of petty private enterprises had grown from 150,000 in 1978 to 14 million in 1988. By 1988, according to official figures there were also 225,000 larger private firms including 50,000 cooperatives.[10] However, official figures for the larger firms are only an estimate and their actual number is much greater. This is because many larger firms in the licensed private sector conceal their size, while many cooperatives are counted only in collective sector statistics, practices that reduce the official number of larger private firms. By 1988, the licensed private sector accounted for 20 per cent

of all retail sales, up from 2.1 per cent in 1978.[11] Furthermore, much
of the dynamism of the collective sector in the 1980s is attributed to
cooperatives. The number of employees in urban collective enterprise grew from 20 million in 1978 to 35 million in 1989.[12] By 1988,
the collective sector accounted for 38 per cent of all retail sales, up
from 7.4 per cent in 1978.[13]

The local development of business varies regionally due to differences in history, geography and policies. The situation of Xiamen
city, the fieldsite for this study, reflects its rapid growth along the
southeast coast, a region enjoying liberal economic policies and
easy access to financial capital and trade networks through Taiwan,
Hong Kong and overseas Chinese connections. Xiamen is a former
British treaty port and the commercial hub of Fujian province. It
had a registered urban population of 579,510 in 1988.[14] Its dialect is
similar to Taiwan's, a hundred miles away across the Taiwan
Straits, and it is in the ancestral region for one-fifth of the world's
overseas Chinese. These favourable conditions led to the city's
designation in 1980 as one of China's five Special Economic Zones
designed to take the lead in creating a market economy and attracting foreign investment. In contrast to other local governments
which restrict private wholesale trade in order to control local
circulation of commodities, Xiamen is one of the few localities to
license general trading companies in the private sector. This is
because the main concern of the local government is to hasten the
circulation of commodities between domestic and international
markets through Xiamen in order to spur the Special Economic
Zone economy.

Private business in Xiamen has grown rapidly. By 1988 there
were 15,254 petty private enterprises, mostly in commerce and
trading in consumer commodities. There were also 621 private
capitalist trading firms by 1989, with 180 in the licensed private
sector and 441 cooperatives.[15] The entrepreneurs who run these
capitalist firms have no formal position in the bureaucracy. They
hire from eight to several hundred employees, provide their own
start-up capital, keep account books and reinvest profits for expansion. They are forging national and international networks for trade
in such consumer commodities as home appliances, car parts and
designer clothing and in such producer commodities as chemicals,
minerals and construction materials. A number of firms are diversified into such manufacturing ventures as textiles, foodstuffs,
handicrafts and assembly of imported computers and medical
equipment, and into such service ventures as restaurants, automo-
tive garages and computer software development institutes. Many

have also formed partnerships with bureaux and public units through arrangements such as urban cooperatives, rural village and township enterprises, public-private joint ventures and leased and contracted concerns. A small number are also in partnerships with Chinese businesses from Taiwan, Hong Kong and overseas and with foreign businesses.

THE EAST EUROPEAN VIEW OF CIVIL SOCIETY: THE QUESTION OF ALLIANCE

In the East European view, private business is a force for political change by horizontally integrating civil society, empowering it *vis-à-vis* the state. In this section I will examine the causal logic of this argument.

The East European view distinguishes between civil society in the economic sense and in the political sense.[16] The former refers to the egoistic interests of individuals and households expressed through private business. The latter refers to the collective interests of groups expressed through voluntary associations. Civil society challenges party-state domination, it is maintained, when collective popular movements emerge in political civil society. Therefore, the key question regarding economic civil society is how the egoistic economic interests of individuals become the collective group interests of political civil society. This is precisely the question Vajda asks of the Hungarian situation: 'Could these scattered individual autonomies lead to a relatively autonomous global society with genuine trade unions, independent interest groups, and a free and open cultural life, an independent judiciary?'[17]

One of the most elaborated answers thus far is Szelenyi's study of the re-emergence of the private business class in rural Hungary during the 1970s. According to Szelenyi, individuals become entrepreneurs in order to gain independence and freedom of choice denied them in public employment. Therefore entrepreneurship is by definition an active 'strategy of resistance' to state control.[18] Entrepreneurs will, Szelenyi concludes, eventually enter into horizontal alliances with other 'subordinated' groups (i.e. intellectuals, workers, etc.), thereby enhancing the capacity of civil society to extract further concessions from the state.[19] Although Szelenyi does not explicitly say so, it seems implicit in this scenario that the alliance would stem from the mutual interests of these groups to safeguard and expand their autonomy.

To interpret the political consequences of China's economic reforms, numerous analysts have drawn on the East European view of civil society. For example, Gold sees 'the resurgence of Chinese civil society, flourishing in the fertile soil of autonomous economic activity'.[20] In another example, Yang deploys the distinction between economic and political civil society to interpret the initial consequences of market reforms.[21] She further argues that:

> as they gain greater autonomy from the state, relations of exchange between economic groups increasingly tend to take place without the vertical mediation of hierarchical administrative channels. Thus the horizontal integration of civil society is enhanced in the economic sphere, and civil society begins to detach itself from the state.[22]

Analysts have documented several instances of entrepreneurial actions during the 1989 student movement that support this view. For example, young private entrepreneurs formed a motorcycle squad called the Flying Tigers to convey messages and act as scouts for the students. The information they provided on troop movements enabled citizens to mobilize at key street intersections and block the initial attempts by troops to enter the capital. Another often cited example is the Stone Corporation, a private computer company whose members counselled students on political strategy and gave access to communications equipment. The thrust of the above observations supports the view of private business as a force for integrating civil society.[23]

The argument that the market economy in general, and private business in particular, promotes the horizontal integration of civil society can be restated as hypotheses in order to test it against a local situation. Two hypotheses can be derived regarding the orientation of entrepreneurs towards horizontal alliances:

1. Entrepreneurs seek alliance with other entrepreneurs, thereby enhancing their collective representation as a political interest group.
2. Entrepreneurs seek alliance with other subordinated social groups, thereby enhancing the collective capacity of civil society *vis-à-vis* the state.

The first hypothesis will be tested by the behaviour of entrepreneurs regarding an independent business association established to represent them. The second will be tested by the attitudes of entrepreneurs towards the 1989 student movement. Should entrepreneurs actually seek or enter into relations with civil society actors, horizontal alliance can be said to exist and the conception of political change in the East European view is supported. Should entrepreneurs not enter into or spurn such relations, no such alliance can be said to exist, necessitating an alternative account of the link between private business and political change.

The data were obtained during research on the re-emergence of Chinese private business in a local situation. Fieldwork was conducted in Xiamen for 18 months over a two-year period from June 1988 to June 1990. During this time, I interviewed in Mandarin Chinese 100 entrepreneurs running private capitalist firms and socialized intensively with some of them. I also interviewed entrepreneurs running private petty shops, officers in the Xiamen Chamber of Commerce, officials in relevant government bureaux and students and teachers involved in the local student movement. During the fieldwork two events occurred that my informants regarded as the biggest crises for private business in the decade since its revival in 1979; the Economic Rectification Campaign launched in September 1988 and the student movement in mid-1989. The former was a bureaucratic campaign initiated by the central state against problems in the market economy that had defied routine administrative solutions. It targeted activities that complicated central state regulation of the market economy by blurring the boundaries of public and private, a target that included cooperatives. It merged with the crackdown following the student movement and did not run its course until the early 1990s. The student movement occurred in the spring of 1989, reaching its climax on 4 June. A severe political crackdown ensued in its aftermath which included a campaign against corruption in private business. The heightened political tension spurred my entrepreneurial informants on to more extreme behaviour and attitudes, putting their orientation to alliances into sharper relief than would have been the case in less troubled times.

AN EMPIRICAL TEST OF THE ALLIANCES
OF ENTREPRENEURS

*Entrepreneurial Behaviour towards the Union
of Private Industry and Commerce*

The first modern business associations were established by the imperial Qing dynasty in the early twentieth century.[24] They were important intermediaries between business and government, giving business communities autonomy through self-regulation. In 1953 the chambers were amalgamated into the National Federation of Industry and Commerce. The Federation was active in the criticism and re-education of former capitalist businessmen during the nationalization of private business in the 1950s.[25] The Federation ceased functioning altogether during the Cultural Revolution. Revived in 1979, its first task was to rehabilitate the reputations of businesspeople who had been persecuted during the Cultural Revolution. Local Federation branches have gradually begun to help the new businesses created since 1979. The revival of the Xiamen branch has been especially noteworthy. The first local branch to adopt its pre-revolutionary name, it is now once again called the Xiamen Chamber of Commerce. It has financial autonomy to run its own commercial establishments and sponsors a number of specialized business associations. In an even more radical move, the Xiamen Chamber of Commerce housed a business association from 1988 to 1990 that sought to lobby the city government on behalf of local private entrepreneurs.

The formation of the business association was stimulated by the 1988 Private Enterprise Law which stipulated that any locality with 30 or more larger private enterprises could establish a Union of Private Industry and Commerce. However, the regulations did not stipulate which bureau should sponsor it. Xiamen's private entrepreneurial elite, those running the largest cooperative and licensed private firms as well as those running some of the oldest private petty shops, saw this as a chance to establish a Union to represent them. The following account is based primarily on interviews and conversations with 17 of the original 23 members, Xiamen Chamber of Commerce officials and Bureau of Industry and Commerce officials.

The entrepreneurs sought a sponsoring agency for the Union that would actively represent them. They especially wanted to avoid sponsorship by the Bureau of Industry and Commerce. The Bureau issues private-sector business licences, regulates private enterprise in matters such as ensuring entrepreneurial compliance with family planning policies and cooperates with other bureaux in tax collection, confiscating counterfeit goods and other matters. To support these regulatory activities, the Bureau established the Self-Employed Labourers Association in the early 1980s for petty private businesses licensed under the Individual Business Family. Entrepreneurs were justifiably fearful that a Bureau-sponsored Union would also serve a regulatory function rather than actively

64 *David L. Wank*

represent them. They turned instead to sympathetic officials in the Xiamen Chamber of Commerce. The Chamber has no regulatory functions regarding private enterprise and was therefore preferable as a sponsor to the Bureau.

A Chamber-sponsored Union, hereafter referred to as the 'independent Union', was established in early 1988 and formally affiliated as a specialized business association of the Chamber. Its stated purpose was to help entrepreneurs acquire management skills, establish business contacts, obtain information, protect their legal rights and represent them in dealings with government bureaux. The entrepreneurs elected officers from among themselves and hired their own staff. The independent Union moved quickly on their behalf. It effectively lobbied the city government to reduce taxes for licensed private firms from the national rate of a 55 per cent business profits tax to the lower 15 per cent rate enjoyed by public enterprises in the Special Economic Zone. The independent Union also lobbied on behalf of individual members. In one case, one of the independent Union's four elected officers ran a joint venture firm with a rural township government. A township official absconded with the firm's cash and the entrepreneur was unable to pay back bank loans. When the city procuratorate placed a lien on the firm's assets, the entrepreneur sought the intervention of the independent Union to make the township government rather than the firm responsible for the loss.

From the start, the independent Union was the focus of intra-bureaucratic conflict. On the one hand, the Chamber officials considered themselves the rightful sponsors because their national organization, the National Federation of Industry and Commerce, had supervised businessmen as a social group since the 1950s. On the other hand, Bureau officials considered themselves the rightful sponsors because they issued private business licences. Bureau officials saw the independent Union as a challenge to their regulatory authority. This was a well-grounded concern as entrepreneurs frequently expressed anger with BIC regulatory practices such as the arbitrary fees for annual licence renewal which were manipulated to punish uncooperative entrepreneurs.[26] The matter of licensing fees also points to a key concern in the conflict: the sponsoring agency could obtain income from the entrepreneurs through fees, donations and sundry charges.

The Bureau moved to suppress the independent Union. It harassed members by summoning them for meetings at short notice and raising their licensing fees, and warned non-members against joining. The leading officer of the independent Union was the first local target of the 1988 Economic Rectification Campaign. The son of a stevedore and formerly unemployed, he had by 1989 built a small grocery stall founded in 1979 into a diversified enterprise group that conducted a national trade in car parts and construction materials. His widely publicized arrest on charges of bribing officials and smuggling goods out of the Special Economic Zone fuelled the image of the independent Union as a motley collection of corrupt businessmen. In early 1990, the Bureau established its own Union of Private Industry and Commerce. The leading entrepreneur of the Bureau-sponsored Union was the offspring of a city government official. His polished manner, easy projection of authority and high level of education, which included graduate study in the USA, contrasted with the more roughhewn personal styles of the independent Union's officers. His business activities also attested to his excellent bureaucratic connections; his firm exported scarce raw materials and chemicals and was among the first licensed private firms in China in line to receive direct import-export authority.[27] When I left Xiamen in the summer of 1990, the independent Union had stopped all activity, its fate sealed by a central state decision supporting the Bureau-sponsored Union.

I found much variation in the reaction of member entrepreneurs to the suppression of the independent Union. Those running smaller enterprises, little more than shops licensed under the Individual Family Business policy, showed little concern. They mostly did retail trade within the private sector and had no problems requiring independent Union representation. To my surprise, entrepreneurs running the largest enterprises, diversified firms and enterprise groups, also showed little regret at its suppression. They rapidly dissociated from the independent Union as it became embroiled in intra-bureaucratic conflict. The entrepreneurs most upset by its suppression ran medium-size firms licensed under the 1988 Private Enterprise Law that were expanding into wholesale trade. They hung on to the independent Union hoping for a favourable resolution to the question of its sponsorship.

Entrepreneurial Attitudes towards the Student Movement

Student demonstrations have played a highly visible role in twentieth-century Chinese politics.[28] Although specific goals have varied, the demonstrations have always been directed at perceived wrongdoing by the state elite. A main focus of demonstrations in the 1980s was the bureaucratic corruption and windfall economic gains to state elite families engendered by market reform.

The 1989 student movement emerged as a student eulogy to Hu Yaobang, a central leader who advocated rapid reform, was sympathetic to intellectuals and who died on 15 April. In Beijing it swelled into a broad popular movement joined by workers, journalists and other citizens. The students occupied Tiananmen Square for two months. Events in the capital were widely publicized in the media and emulated by university students across the country. Under 'Democracy' and other slogans, the movement's leaders called for an end to government corruption, free media and a meeting with national leaders. By late May, state elite tolerance of the students in Tiananmen Square waned and the military was dispatched to oust them. The first attempts by troops to enter the city were peacefully repulsed by a spontaneous outpouring of the citizenry who blocked the streets. Finally on the night of 3 June, the troops violently removed the students from the square, killing at least several hundred civilians.[29]

During April and May students at Xiamen University, the locally based national university, boycotted classes, occupied dormitories and sent representatives to Beijing. They kept abreast of events in the capital through radio broadcasts and phone calls from the representatives in Beijing. The timing of marches and even the content of slogans emulated those in Beijing. The largest march occurred on 17 April with students from a number of local colleges and technical institutes participating. Marches were peaceful, lasting about five hours as they traversed the entire city while police redirected traffic away from the route. In another form of visible protest, students organized a hunger strike in the city centre. When news of violence in Beijing on 3 and 4 June reached Xiamen, a small number of students made a short, quick march to the city centre and back. Despite rumours to the contrary, there was no apparent movement of troops against the students at Xiamen University. The semester was cancelled and students dispersed to their homes throughout the country.

The students in Xiamen lacked the visible outpouring of popular support evident in the capital. Whereas workers, journalists and office workers marched under their own banners in Beijing, the only non-student marchers in Xiamen were Xiamen University teachers. Students from other local institutions marched only in the 17 April demonstration. Citizens lining the march route were curious but impassive, while merchants shuttered their stores, fearful of unrest. Attempts to encourage worker participation in the marches were fruitless.[30] The few visible instances that occurred were of ambiguous significance in determining the degree of local popular support. In May students stood with collection boxes in the city and collected several thousand yuan daily.[31] However, they stood at key transportation junctions and shopping areas, places frequented by overseas Chinese tourists who were the largest donors. While students told me of instances of support from the local populace, on closer inquiry these turned out to be hearsay rather than the direct experiences of the students. For example, a member of the movement's local student coordinating committee told me that sympathetic workers in the city power plant had refused an order from the city government to cut off electricity to dormitories occupied by the students. However, a teacher told me that it was the university president who had intervened to maintain power out of concern that a blackout might cause panic and injury among the students. In short, it proved impossible to determine whether reports of local popular support that circulated among students had actually occurred or were rumours (that nevertheless boosted student morale).

What were the actions of the entrepreneurs regarding the student movement locally? From its beginning in April through its aftermath in the late summer, the student movement came up frequently in my conversations with them. Only two of the 29 entrepreneurs I spoke with acknowledged any actions in support of the students. One had given money to a student, the daughter of a close friend, soliciting contributions to send student representatives to Beijing. Another let a student he employed as a part-time translator use the firm's telephone to call local colleges in organizing the April demonstration. In both cases entrepreneurial support was forthcoming in the context of a pre-existing personal relationship. It is thus questionable as to whether these actions indicate support for the Democracy Movement or the pull of personal ties.

The attitudes of the entrepreneurs as expressed in conversations are less ambiguous and are notable for their lack of support of the movement. One commonly voiced attitude was that the students demanded too much, too quickly. Political change should be gradual and initiated by policies from above in an orderly reform (*gaige*) rather than forced by popular pressure from below in a potentially chaotic transformation (*gaizao*). As one entrepreneur said, 'We must go slowly generation by generation . . . A country's stability is connected with its order. Only by having normal order can people have a normal life' (Informant no. 22).

In the eyes of many entrepreneurs, student demands for change through concessions from the leaders, while based on pure and noble sentiments, were politically naive. As expressed by one entrepreneur:

> The students don't understand reality. They have a high political consciousness but little understanding of politics in practice. The more you tell the Communist Party to do something, the less it is willing to do so. It feels that it set up the country and knows what is best.

Entrepreneurs were also concerned that the students were being manipulated. One entrepreneur saw it as a plot:

> Two organizations appeared during the movement, the Students' Autonomous Union and the Workers' Autonomous Union. We don't really understand what these two organizations are. According to official reports, the burning of cars, the fighting and other violence was done by these two organizations. It is clear they orchestrated the violence. As soon as they set things off in Beijing, they ran off to stir people up elsewhere.

Some entrepreneurs saw the state elite as the behind-the-scene manipulators who were using the students as pawns in their factional politics. Others saw foreign elements as manipulators, a perception heightened by the movement's use of foreign symbols such as a replica of the Statue of Liberty (renamed the Goddess of Democracy) and the subsequent flight abroad of many student leaders after 4 June.

A fourth prominent attitude was simply that the students' goal of democracy is incompatible with Chinese political culture. Representative government only burdens leaders with a cacophony of voices and undermines strong, decisive leadership. Some entrepreneurs used the word 'anarchy' interchangeably with 'democracy' during conversations. The following comment expresses this attitude.

> Chinese want a good emperor, not a democratic environment. Chinese always think that things will be better if they change the emperor. At the founding of each dynasty, the emperor gives a little, improving people's lives. For a while people are content but then become dissatisfied. Everybody welcomed Deng Xiaoping

when he came to power because he opened things up. But after a few years, people again became dissatisfied and wanted to change the emperor.

Another entrepreneur said that, while democracy should be a long-term goal, it does not suit China's current level of development because it requires a literate, well-informed populace to debate issues, a condition not yet met in China.

In sum, the entrepreneurs showed little tendency to forge horizontal alliances with the participants of the student movement. Their articulated attitudes towards the movement's goals ranged from unease to hostility. They were concerned that the students were being manipulated, that democracy was alien to Chinese tradition, and that social chaos would result. Even when I pushed the entrepreneurs by pointing out that one of the movement's goals, an end to bureaucratic corruption and nepotism in the market economy, could improve their business environment, they were still, to my surprise, unsympathetic. Many, especially those running the largest firms, felt that bureaucratic corruption could not be solved by policy measures and that problems between an entrepreneur and officials should be worked out on a personal basis. To the extent that the entrepreneurs desired political change at all, it should be initiated from above in an evolutionary fashion.

CONTRASTING EXPLANATIONS OF ENTREPRENEURIAL ALLIANCES

The situation of private business in a Chinese city does not support the two hypotheses derived from the East European view that entrepreneurs forge horizontal alliances that integrate civil society. How can this be explained? This section considers two explanatory routes. One extends the causal logic of the East European view, the analytic task therefore being to explain why entrepreneurs did not forge horizontal alliances when there was a clear opportunity to do so. The other route is to explain what kinds of alliances the entrepreneurs did, in fact, forge.

Explanations Derived from the East European View

Several possible factors can be derived from the East European view to explain why horizontal alliances did not occur. One factor could be the strength of traditional political attitudes that militate against interest-based politics. For example, Whyte attributes the general weakness of interest-group-based popular movements in China in 1989 to the traditional view that interest-based associations are selfish.[32] This could explain why the Xiamen entrepreneurs showed a weak attachment to the independent Union. Another barrier could be the low political consciousness of the entrepreneurs. The strong egoism of entrepreneurship precludes entrepreneurs from seeing beyond self-gain to group interests. Such an explanation is foreshadowed in Gold's insight, made several years before 1989, into the consequences of market reform for personal relations. He sees commercialization bringing about an 'individualization of consumption' that intensifies competition between people and leads them to withdraw from public movements into the personal bonds of the family. This insight could account for the egoism of entrepreneurs that prevented their identification with the student movement.[33]

Another factor could be that the state is still strong enough to prevent horizontal alliances. Entrepreneurs are still very dependent on the bureaucracy regarding licences, fines, taxation and other matters, and it could be argued that they did not support the student movement for fear of administrative repercussions. In this scenario, private entrepreneurs in the late 1980s were still too tentative and weak *vis-à-vis* the state to develop into a political interest group or to seek broader alliances in civil society. While no China analyst working with the East European view has made this argument specifically about private entrepreneurs, Yang offers a compatible scenario. The emergence of new economic groups, she writes, is the 'first step' in the emergence of civil society but that its 'full strength ... will not be realized, however, until the state mono-organizational structure is further dissolved ...'[34]

The above explanatory route is problematic on two counts. First, while it provides compelling reasons for why entrepreneurs *did not* forge horizontal alliances, it gives no account of the alliances that their economic activity *did* lead them to forge. Secondly, it cannot explain variation among entrepreneurial behavior and attitudes towards horizontal alliances. Why, for example, did the entrepreneurs running the largest firms so actively dissociate themselves from the independent Union and show the greatest antipathy to the student movement's anti-corruption goals? To answer these questions requires a closer look at the social relations that entrepreneurs actually forge in the market economy. The conspicuous lack of horizontal alliances between entrepreneurs and 'subordinated' groups is in marked contrast to the dense web of relations between entrepreneurs and the officials staffing the lower levels of bureaucracy. These relations cannot be attributed to the 'false consciousness' of entrepreneurs or to the power of the state to prey on private enterprise. Instead, they are mutually beneficial and desired and cultivated by entrepreneurs and officials alike. The reason for this is rooted in the organization of the emerging market economy and the place of private business within it.

An Institutional Explanation

One of the distinguishing characteristics of the pre-reform economy was the state monopoly over goods and services through the planned economy. With reform, the emerging market economy has become intertwined with the planned economy. Specifically, officials have been able to turn their bureaucratic control over the allocation of public assets into commercial advantage and profit and have greatly benefited. The clearest example is the two-tier price system. Beginning in 1980, commodities have circulated at two prices, a lower administrative price set by the state and a higher market price determined by supply and demand. Officials who control the allocation of or access to commodities at lower administrative prices can profit if they dispose of them at market prices.[35] There are numerous other examples. Officials can profit by control of licences, real estate, bank loans and host of other unpriced and underpriced public assets which have become commodified by market reform. They can profit by controlling access to direct foreign trade because only state foreign trade corporations are authorized to conduct import and export. Officials staffing the bureaux that regulate private business can profit by their discretionary control over fines, licences, fees and taxes.

Entrepreneurs running private enterprise pursue one of two strategies with regard to the bureaucratic power that pervades the market economy. One is a strategy of avoidance which sees bureaucracy as an obstacle. It is widespread among entrepreneurs running private petty shops licensed under the Individual Business Family policy. They perceive the demands by officials for cash pay-offs over taxes, fines and licences as highly arbitrary and perdatory. Through avoidance they seek to minimize contact with officials in order to reduce bureaucratic interference in their business. The other strategy is one of alliance which sees bureaucracy as a source of opportunity. It is pursued by entrepreneurs running the larger private firms that are licensed under the Private Enterprise Law or that are cooperatives. Through connections with the bureaucracy, they benefit from the discretionary control of officials. For example, larger firms form business partnerships with state and collective enterprises and local government bureaux. These partnerships give entrepreneurs access to administratively (low-) priced commodities and real estate as well as bureaucratic protection from policy fluctuations, central state campaigns and harassment by officials in other bureaux. For officials, these partnerships create institutional channels to the market economy through which they can turn discretionary control of public assets into a cash profit.[36] As the scale of private enterprise expands, connections with the bureaucracy proliferate, blurring the boundaries of 'public' and 'private'.

The different ways by which private business strategies are linked to different policies and enterprise scales helps explain entrepreneurial variation in behaviour regarding the independent Union. The independent Union's strongest supporters were entrepreneurs running medium-sized firms. They were from petty business or working-class families and had started out with private petty shops in the early 1980s. Their enterprises grew and were reregistered as firms under the 1988 Private Enterprise Law in order to facilitate more rapid expansion. Yet while their enterprise scale was no longer petty, these entrepreneurs lacked institutionalized bureaucratic connections for profit and protection. Because of their low social backgrounds, they had few personal ties with officials and their firms were not yet large enough to form significant partnerships with bureaux and public units. For these entrepreneurs, the independent Union provided some protection and the chance to develop contacts with officials for profit opportunities. In contrast, entrepreneurs running the smallest enterprises did not need bureaucratic support because they conducted retail trade largely through the strategy of avoiding bureaucratic power. Entrepreneurs running the larger firms already enjoyed institutionalized bureaucratic support through cooperatives and other business partnerships with the bureaucracy, and through personal ties, as many were the offspring of officials. Therefore, they did not need the independent Union for developing bureaucratic profit and protection.

Variation in entrepreneurial attitudes towards the student movement are also linked to different scales of private business. Entrepreneurs running the larger firms wanted to maintain the stability of the bureaucratic support that constituted profit and protection. They worried that the student movement would result in a state crackdown that would disrupt this support. They particularly opposed policy measures to halt corruption because these would target precisely the kinds of personal ties that they were so assiduously cultivating with officials. Entrepreneurs also suspected, correctly as it turned out, that such measures would not affect the largest transgressors, the entrepreneurial offspring of the central state elite, but would fall hardest on entrepreneurs at more local levels who lacked high-level patrons to shield them. As for nepotism, some of the larger firms were run by the offspring of high city government officials, parental relationships that had been commercially valuable. Naturally, these entrepreneurs did not support a crackdown on nepotism.

The Role of Private Entrepreneurs in the 1989 Crises

Although the entrepreneurs did not develop horizontal ties, they were centrally involved in the crises of 1989. However, this involvement did not involve contact with other participants in the student movement – as was the case for some Beijing entrepreneurs. Many of the entrepreneurs I interviewed in Xiamen seem to have been conducting a larger scale of business than the Beijing entrepreneurs, who appear to have run petty shops licensed under the Individual Business Family policy. As the situation in Xiamen indicates, entrepreneurs running larger enterprises are more likely to seek alliances with officials in the bureaucracy and have little need for horizontal alliances in civil society. The role of the capitalist entrepreneurs in the 1989 crises lies in the long-term consequences of these bureaucratic alliances rather than any actions towards civil society groups during the course of the student movement from April to June.

The connections between entrepreneurs and officials helped fuel the perception among the state elite of diminished central control. During the 1980s, some visible manifestations of diminished control had been rampant corruption among lower-level officials and inflation. Officials circumvent central policies not in their interests, while bureaucratic corruption causes incalculable amounts of money to circulate in concealed economic activity, exacerbating inflation and derailing state monetary policy. Central attempts to assert control has been an ongoing theme since the beginning of market reform. The launching of the Economic Rectification Campaign in late 1988 indicates mounting state elite concern over diminished central control in the months preceding the student movement. This rising concern contributed to the state elite's decision to use military force to suppress popular upheaval in June 1989, whatever the cost.

RETHINKING STATE–SOCIETY RELATIONS
IN CHINA

The above empirical study suggests a configuration of communist state, civil society and private enterprise that diverges considerably from the East European view. First, entrepreneurs have little coherent identity as an 'interest group' stemming from the common 'private' nature of their enterprise. Instead their interests are fashioned by the organizational logics of a market economy emerging out of a planned economy. Variations in social background, business scale, economic policies and bureaucratic support split the entrepreneurs into distinct groups, each facing discrete opportunities and constraints and oriented to specific alliances. Entrepreneurs running pettier forms of private enterprise are more oriented to horizontal alliances, in part because their business strategy is to reduce economic uncertainties by avoiding bureaucratic power. However, entrepreneurs running larger firms are oriented to alliance with officials as their business strategies seek to 'maximize' profit and protection through stable connections with the bureaucracy. As the scale of enterprise expands, entrepreneurial orientation to alliances with officials intensifies.

Second, entrepreneurial alliances with the bureaucracy are neither market nor plan relationships.[37] They are not horizontal market connections because they are not between legally equal individuals but rather involve power asymmetries between individuals and institutions inside and outside the state structure. Nor are they hierarchical plan linkages because exchanges are not through authority relations between superiors and subordinates but involve cash and can be exited by either actor. Instead, they are networks between actors inside and outside the state structure in discrete organizations who forge alliances for mutual benefit. This benefit is embedded in bureaucratic discretion over public assets and much of the resulting economic activity is considered 'bureaucratic corruption' and 'economic crime' by the central state. Therefore, alliances are embedded in personal ties between entrepreneurs and officials who know and trust each other.

Third, the state is not a unitary structure but rather beset by cleavages between the lower levels of the bureaucracy and the centre. Lower-level officials have experienced uncertainties and problems during the course of market reforms such as the eroding value of public subsidies and wages due to inflation and state austerity policies. As these officials often interact with private businesspeople during the course of duty, they can seek solutions for their problems in the local society under their jurisdiction. More specifically, they have increasingly sought rewards and opportunities through alliances with entrepreneurs, which reduces their responsiveness to the wishes and inducements of bureaucratic superiors. In short, the stratum of lower-level officials, standing between the central state and civil society, is an independent component of the overall political configuration.

Fourth, changes in the power distribution are not zero-sum.[38] Expansion of the market economy and its institutions such as private enterprise does not necessarily empower civil society at the expense of the state. Indeed, in some key respects it is the power of the local bureaucracy that is most enhanced by the emergence of private capitalist business. Through discretionary control over regulatory levers, officials can extract an income from private enterprises that enables them to commercialize their authority over local society, thereby reducing their financial dependence on the central state.[39] The emergence of 'autonomy' in the overall political configuration, therefore, is less the growing autonomy of society *vis-à-vis* the state but rather the heightened autonomy of locales composed of alliances between local state and society actors *vis-à-vis* the central state.

CONCLUSION

Critical refection on the usefulness of the East European view should be tempered by acknowledgement of the context of its creation. One of the original participants in Solidarity characterized the view of civil society deployed by the Polish opposition in 1980 as a 'projection into the future of a vision'.[40] This, I think, is an apt characterization. East central European intellectuals in the 1980s rediscovered the concept of civil society – a realm of voluntary associations enjoying some autonomy from the state – to fashion a counter-discourse of history to that of the communist state in their struggle for greater liberty. In a mirror image of that state ideology, this counter-discourse also contains a structural view of change towards a 'utopia'. History is a continuum with the state socialist order at one end and a democratic capitalist order at the other. Although the current situation does not yet conform to either end, it is moving along the continuum towards democratic capitalism.

This teleological view of history, economy and politics no doubt galvanized opposition to communist states, but it appears less effective for understanding local transformations of state–society relations during departures from state socialism. By its programmatic thrust, the East European view conflates the analysis of *what is* with the 'vision' of *what should be*. Events and phenomena are explained in terms of how they propel the situation towards an assumed outcome – the 'vision' – while analysis of institutionalized political processes in specific organizational contexts is downplayed.[41] The preceding analysis of political shifts at the local borders of the communist state and civil society suggests that directly applying the East European view as a frame of understanding obfuscates as much, if not more, than it clarifies. However, this analysis also points to a fruitful use of the East European view; it is fertile ground for testable hypotheses.

NOTES

Research in China was supported by the Committee on Scholarly Communications with the People's Republic of China. My host institution in Xiamen, Lujiang College, provided much support, including arranging interviews in bureaux. An early draft of this paper was written while I was an Academy Scholar at the Harvard Academy for International and Area Studies. I am grateful to Anita Chan, John A. Hall, Jon Unger and Susan Young for comments on this paper.

1 See the essays in J. Keane, ed., *Civil Society and the State*, Verso, London, 1988.
2 Z. A. Pelczynski, 'Solidarity and the "Rebirth of Civil Society" in Poland', in Keane, *Civil Society and the State*, p. 368.
3 Examples include T. G. Ash, *The Magic Lantern*, Vintage, New York, 1990; I. Banac, ed., *Eastern Europe in Revolution*, Cornell University Press, Ithaca, N.Y., 1992.

4 See for example T. B. Gold, 'The Resurgence of Civil Society in China', *Journal of Democracy*, vol. 1, 1990; D. Strand, 'Protest in Beijing: Civil Society and Public Sphere in China', *Problems of Communism*, vol. 39, 1990; M. Whyte, 'Urban China: A Civil Society in the Making?', in A. Rosenbaum, ed., *State and Society in China: The Consequences of Reform*, Westview, Boulder, Col., 1992; M. M. Yang, 'Between State and Society: The Construction of Corporateness in a Chinese Socialist Factory', *Australian Journal of Chinese Affairs*, no. 22, 1989.

5 Whyte, 'Urban China', p. 94.

6 For a critical discussion of the East European view see K. Kumar, 'Civil society: an inquiry into the usefulness of an historical concept', *British Journal of Sociology*, vol. 44, 1993.

7 Another example of hypothesis testing is G. White, 'Prospects for Civil Society in China: A Case Study of Xiaoshan City', *Australian Journal of Chinese Affairs*, no. 29, 1993. For a consideration of contrasting views of civil society to China's 'floating population' see D. J. Solinger, 'China's Transients and the State: A Form of Civil Society?', in Rosenbaum, *State and Society in China*. For an example of hypothesis testing in Hungary see R. Manchin, 'Individual Economic Strategies and Social Consciousness', *Social Research*, vol. 55, 1988.

8 For a sustained institutional analysis of market reform in China's state sector see S. Shirk, *The Political Logic of Economic Reform in China*, University of California Press, Berkeley, Cal., 1993.

9 The formal sectors of the economy are defined by ownership and are private, collective and state. The latter two are public: collective enterprises are owned by lower government levels and state enterprises are owned by higher levels.

10 H. Y. Zhang and S. X. Qin, 'Siying jingji zai dangdai Zhongguo de shijian' [The Practice of the Private Economy in Contemporary China], *Jingji cankao* [Economic Information], 14 November 1988, p. 4.

11 *Statistical Yearbook 1989*, Chinese Statistical Publishers, Beijing, p. 115.

12 *Statistical Yearbook 1990*, p. 115.

13 *Statistical Yearbook 1989*, p. 601.

14 Like other prosperous Chinese cities, Xiamen had an unregistered population in the late 1980s estimated at from one-quarter to one-third the size of the registered population.

15 All statistics were obtained through interviews with the Bureau of Industry and Commerce which issues business licences. The figure for cooperatives is a bureau estimate.

16 E. Hankiss, 'The "Second Society": Is There an Alternative Model Emerging in Hungary?', *Social Research*, vol. 55, 1988.

17 M. Vajda, 'East-Central European Perspectives', in Keane, *Civil Society and the State*, p. 358.

18 I. Szelenyi, *Socialist Entrepreneurs: Embourgeoisement in Rural Hungary*, University of Wisconsin Press, Madison, Wis., 1988, p. 64.

19 Szelenyi, *Socialist Entrepreneurs*, p. 218.

20 Gold, 'The Resurgence of Civil Society in China', p. 31.

21 Yang, 'Between State and Society', p. 37.

22 Yang, 'Between State and Society', p. 59.
23 For private petty entrepreneurs in the student movement see A. Chan and J. Unger, 'Voices from the Protest Movement, Chongqing, Sichuan', *Australian Journal of Chinese Affairs*, no. 24, July 1990; T. B. Gold, 'Urban Private Business and China's Reforms', in R. Baum, ed., *Reform and Reaction in Post-Mao China: The Road to Tiananmen*, London, Routledge, 1991.
24 For chambers of commerce see W. K. K. Chan, *Merchants, Mandarins and Modern Enterprise in Late Ch'ing China*, Harvard University Press, Cambridge, Mass., 1977, ch. 11.
25 For the dismantling of the business class see K. G. Lieberthal, *Revolution and Tradition in Tientsin, 1949–1952*, Stanford University Press, Stanford, Cal., 1980.
26 For example, the licensing fee of one entrepreneur doubled to 500 yuan after he joined the independent Union.
27 This plan was suspended by the 1988 Economic Rectification Campaign.
28 For overviews of the 1989 student movement see T. Saich, ed., *The Chinese Peoples Movement: Perspectives on Spring 1989*, M. E. Sharpe, Armonk, 1990, and M. Han, ed., *Cries for Democracy: Writings and Speeches from the 1989 Chinese Democracy Movement*, Princeton University Press, Princeton, N.J., 1990. For Fujian province see M. S. Erbaugh and R. C. Kraus, 'The 1989 Democracy Movement in Fujian and its Aftermath', *The Australian Journal of Chinese Affairs*, no. 23, 1990.
29 There is disparity between government and non-government casuality figures. On 4 June, the Chinese Red Cross Society put the casualities at 2,600. Initial government reports on 6 June put the number killed at 300 and 6,000 wounded, while a 30 June report put the number of civilians killed at 200, including 36 students, and the wounded at 3,000. See 'Chronology of the 1989 Student Demonstrations', in Saich, *The Chinese People's Movement*.
30 According to one informant, students attempted to seek support from workers in the export-processing factories established by foreign capital. However, the city government, concerned that labour unrest would discourage foreign investment, warned students to desist.
31 In mid-1989 1 yuan equalled $US0.27.
32 Whyte, 'Urban China', pp. 93–4.
33 T. B. Gold, 'After Comradeship: Personal Relations in China Since the Cultural Revolution', *China Quarterly*, no. 104, 1985, p. 670.
34 Yang, 'Between State and Society', p. 60.
35 Before 1980, the prices of commodities produced by public enterprises were set by administrative fiat. Scarce raw materials and commodities were also produced by and supplied to enterprises according to state plan and at administrative prices; public enterprises could not exchange or resell these commodities. Beginning in 1980, commodities were gradually released from regulation, and enterprises could sell or purchase them at market prices. Market prices are usually much higher than administrative prices, which do not reflect actual production costs or market demand. Thus any individual or enterprise that can obtain commodities at administrative prices can reap large profits by reselling

at market prices. Many officials obtain administratively priced commodities that they control to sell at market prices for their own gain. Goods change hands many times, reaching final market prices far above the administrative price. In one case fertilizer resold three times underwent a markup of 94.4 per cent (*China News Analysis*, no. 1399a, 15 August 1988, p. 4). Through relations with officials, entrepreneurs seek access to these scarce commodities.

36 For this argument see Y. Liu, 'Reform From Below: The Private Economy and Local Politics in the Rural Industrialization of Wenzhou', *China Quarterly*, vol. 130, 1992; D. J. Solinger, 'Urban Entrepreneurs and the State: the Merger of State and Society', in Rosenbaum, *State and Society in China*; D. L. Wank, 'Bureaucratic Patronage and Private Business: Changing Networks of Power in Urban China', in A. G. Walder, ed., *The Waning of the Communist State: Economic Origins of Political Change in China and Hungary*, University of California Press, Berkeley, Cal., 1995.

37 For the network as a form of economic organization distinct from market and hierarchy see W. Powell. 'Hybrid Organizational Arrangements', *California Management Review*, vol. 30, 1987.

38 Pelczynski's statement at the beginning of this paper suggests a zero-sum concept of power. For a more explicit statement see Keane, 'Introduction', *Civil Society and the State*, pp. 4–5.

39 See Liu, 'Reform From Below'.

40 B. Geremek, 'Civil Society Then and Now', *Journal of Democracy*, vol. 3, 1992, p. 12.

41 The continuum also consists of logically opposed dichotomies such as 'plan versus market', 'authoritarianism versus autonomy', 'social control versus social contract', etc. For a general critique of continuum theories of historical change see A. L. Stinchcombe, *Theoretical Methods in Social History*, Academic Press, New York, 1978, pp. 89–97. For a critique equating it with modernization theory see M. Burawoy, 'The End of Sovietology and the Renaissance of Modernization Theory', *Contemporary Sociology*, vol. 6, 1992.

4

The Possibility of Civil Society: Traditions, Character and Challenges

Víctor Pérez-Díaz

As we enter an age of increasing uncertainty and our nations face the challenges posed by the rise of plural societies and an international order in a state of flux, we may be well advised to reassess the cultural and institutional traditions of civil society and to trace those traditions back to their sources. We might then find a conception of polity and society and a basic attitude that were fairly well-balanced, hopeful yet demonstrating a full awareness of our cognitive and moral limits, which, in sum, could prove useful. This is what I shall be suggesting here, together with some refinements of the theory and an emphasis on the historical contingency of an ideal character of this nature, its eventual distortions and the loose fit existing between its different elements. I shall also be suggesting that we ground our hopes and, eventually, a guarded optimism about the future of civil society, not on any basic foundation, but on our own capacity to make prudent moral proposals, to understand their implications, to anchor them in the appropriate traditions and thus to help these proposals materialize through institutional experimentation. In other words, I shall be suggesting we trust in our own ability to choose the right tradition, to use our limited cognitive and moral resources the best we can and to take advantage of every local circumstance. There are neither firm trends to cling to, nor guarantees of any sort, but this may be the interesting part of it.

A COMPOSITE IDEAL, AND ITS HISTORICAL DISTORTIONS

'Civil society' refers to an attempt to theorize about a specific historical experience: an ongoing, uninterrupted tradition of a core of socioeconomic and political institutions (interconnected with some key cultural dispositions) in some North Atlantic nations dating back at least two to three centuries.[1] Other nations, notably in continental Europe, have joined in that tradition more recently and in a more fractured and discontinuous way. Of course, other countries have experimented with similar institutions at one time or another and, as there seems to be some agreement that these experiments have been successful, there is today a fairly strong worldwide trend towards achieving them. The institutional core consists of the following combination of political and socioeconomic arrangements: a government which is limited and accountable and operates under the rule of law; a market economy (implying a regime of private property); an array of free, voluntary associations (political, economic, social and cultural); and a sphere of free public debate. At the same time, real, historical civil societies have always been specific nations which have survived and eventually prospered within a framework of alliances and enmities with other nations, civilized or not. The common goal of survival as a nation was taken for granted in normal times, while eloquently stated in times of duress. There were national interests other than sheer survival which required the appropriate domestic and foreign policies. The inner dynamics of some of their societal components may have led those nations to take the world as the theatre for their operations: following in the wake of their expanding markets, propagating their ideas (their Christian faith, democratic ideals or scientific knowledge) or demanding the recognition of the entire world. Military and political factors preceded or accompanied such societal moves.

Civil societies, therefore, are hybrids, composite or secondary ideal characters, formed from a combination of what Oakeshott considered the two primary ideal characters of the 'modern European state': an association in the character of a 'civil association' and an association in the character of an 'association as enterprise', with, in my opinion, a bias in favor of the 'civil association'.[2] A 'civil association' is an association with no purpose of its own, exclusively oriented towards insuring the general, abstract and universalistic rules everyone could be obliged to follow while pursuing their own individual, egotistical or altruistic drives.[3] An 'association as enterprise' does pursue goals of its own and requires its members to contribute, and eventually to sacrifice themselves, to such common goals.[4] When saying that civil societies are hybrids of the two, albeit with a bias forwards the 'civil association', I should emphasize the point that their common goals are supposed to be kept within strict limits. There is no reason for the state corresponding to those societies to be a minimal one, but its goals and the scope of its operations should be maintained fairly close to those of providing a framework for individuals' endeavours in the pursuit of their own goals – or, in Kant's words, to ensure 'the greatest possible freedom of human individuals by framing the laws in such a way that the freedom of each can coexist with that of all the others'.[5]

Arrangements coinciding quite closely with that description were in operation by the mid/late eighteenth century in Great Britain and the old North American colonies and they still exist today, with some significant changes but no basic alteration of their institutional core. Historical experience seems to corroborate the tentative speculations of the Scottish philosophers of the eighteenth century to the effect that the proper functioning and persistence of those institutions rest on a combination of several strands of moral sentiment and dispositions.[6] These include sentiments which are associated with the pursuit of individual interest or happiness: the salvation of the soul, a sense of community, the search for truth, employment in active exertions or in sensual gratifications, beauty, the possession of wealth, power or status, or whatever. Nothing, however, in the nature of these moral preferences predetermines their contents in so far as they can be either 'egotistical' or 'altruistic' or any combination of the two depending on how interest or happiness is defined. In fact, the self-interested moral sentiments that individuals belonging to a civil society are supposed to feel are hard to disentangle from (a) other sentiments associated with the welfare of the immediate circle of their family and their soul mates, because it would be hard to understand their personal happiness disconnected from sexual love, friendship, intellectual conversation or family happiness, and because it would be unlikely for these individuals to feel the urge for personal wealth with no consideration for family inheritance; as well as from (b) sentiments of an altruistic character addressed to a much wider social circle, that of the nation, the defence of which, along with its cultural identity, welfare, prosperity and basic institutions, requires sentiments of patriotism and civic virtue, since civil societies are supposed to be civil, civilized or polished *nations*; as well as from (c) sentiments of social benevolence of a milder nature which are implicit in respect for the law and the rules of reciprocity, and in the toleration of diversity.

Civil societies, therefore, have been and are historical experiments of, and institutional attempts at, an accommodation between the two ideal characters of 'civil associations' and 'associations as enterprises', and they have reflected the tensions between them.[7] At the same time, they have combined moral sentiments that may be loosely associated with both characters. On the one hand, the morals of the family and of states/societies as enterprises are reminiscent of those appropriate to closed, tribe-like communities: they arise out of intense feelings of intra-solidarity and of a fair amount of animosity or potential hostility towards strangers and foreigners. On the other, the morals of economic markets, and of the quasi-markets of voluntary associations and conversational communities, with their implicit values of mutual toleration and respect for the procedural rules that regulate specific exchanges, belong in a world of abstract, open societies.[8] This duality of morals would match the two sets of moralities that Hayek suggests we have inherited from the past: on the one hand, moral sentiments corresponding to the experience of one million or more years in which mankind operated as a loose collection of tribes which owed their survival to the cultivation of the virtues of intra-group solidarity; on the other, moral traditions that have blurred the boundaries between the in-group and the out-group, that are of a more open and universal character, and that have tended to loosen the ties between individuals and their immediate communities and to reduce the constraints of these communities over their individual members.[9] We have to live with this composite legacy by living in two moral worlds, standing on the edge and shifting from one to another, making *ad hoc* compromises between both, and trying to reach a precarious equilibrium between conflicting moral demands and contrary dispositions.[10]

Societies fairly similar to the ideal character just described have existed in the Western world for extended periods of time, and it seems that, taken as a whole, the institutional experiment of a civil society has survived its own distortions and its own pathological developments, particularly those of the twentieth century, in relatively good shape. The distortions have been deep and durable, and have affected every political and social component of civil society.

Limited, accountable governments under the rule of law have
shown a tendency to expand the scope of their operations, to minimize the transparency of their actions and to put themselves above
the law. In engaging in these practices, such governments have
struck fairly stable alliances with economic, social and political
elites. Well-meant, sensible governmental attempts at policies to
reduce suffering and social misery have regularly been put to the
service of building up extraordinary concentrations of political and
economic power which, in turn, have distorted the functioning of
the markets and abused governments' regulatory and administrative powers under cover of pursuing (though in fact, at the expense
of) the common welfare. The state and interest groups (business,
the unions, the professions) have combined to create different
variants of corporatist arrangements intended to reduce the scope
of social pluralism and social spontaneity, and to recruit individuals
into quasi-obligatory organizations. Similar understandings between states, churches, political parties and large media organizations have resulted in the manipulation of public opinion and the
indoctrination of the public.

These institutional distortions developed gradually throughout
the nineteenth century and the beginning of the twentieth century.
They were furthered by different traditions belonging to the 'right'
and to the 'left': to the conservative as well as to the socialist
traditions. They were also furthered as a result of governments and
elites making a connection between their domestic and their foreign
policies when the latter realized that popular support could be
mustered for a foreign policy of nationalist self-assertion and impe-
rialist expansion. This was fully consistent with a policy of nationalization of the masses, military conscription, universal literacy and
the creation of a welfare state in which the unions and the socialist
parties would eventually develop a strong stake – a trend that,
incidentally, Max Weber was well aware of, and supported.[11] In this
way the public could be incorporated into the national fabric less as
a critically active and discriminating citizenry than as people tamed
by the mass parties they belonged to and trained in obedience to
their manipulative and charismatic leaders.

These distortions reinforced the ideal character of 'association as
enterprise', as well as the tribal morality associated with it. Thus,
gradually, the original bias of civil societies in favour of the 'civil
association' was replaced by the contrary bias in favour of 'association as enterprise', this evolution achieving momentary success in
the First World War and its aftermath. The totalitarian experiments

in fascism and communism that followed can be seen as pushing those distortions to the limits and beyond. Under these regimes the remnants of civil society as a civil association disappear altogether, and the state/society is construed as an (almost) all-encompassing 'association as enterprise', with the corresponding paroxysm of tribal morality.

PLURALISM AND INTERNATIONALISM

Only now, at the very end of the twentieth century, are we free from the totalitarian nightmare which has haunted our civil societies for almost one century; it grew from the very roots of those civil societies, and had to be understood and confronted ideologically, economically and militarily. As a result we might now expect to be witness to most people feeling wiser, relieved at having left those totalitarian horrors and delusions behind. Instead, a sense of malaise and of anxiety seem prevalent once again. It may be that many people have been so well trained in the practice of relentless criticism that they feel embarrassed to enjoy themselves. It may also be that, in some nations, people whose hopes are still attached to certain residual, collectivist, near-totalitarian forms of nostalgia are confused and project that confusion onto others; and that, being disproportionately present in cultural networks, churches, the media and academia, their confusion permeates national public opinion. This could be, however, a minor, local problem in the long run, since it may be just a matter of time for these strategically located individuals to get used to a post-totalitarian age, to see the point of it, to overcome their emotional routines and to find new objects for their moral indignation and new outlets for their trained capacities.

However, there is also reason to believe that the roots of the present malaise go beyond those residual confusions and provisional misadaptations. Civil societies of the Western type are facing new challenges that suggest we are entering an age of uncertainty. In fact, uncertainty may prove to be a better name than 'the end of history', which proclaims the final triumph of Western civilization, its expansion and its reforms being just a matter of time and patience: such a proclamation sounds premature, and unnecessary.[12] Uncertainty seems to express better the legacy of the twentieth century as an ironical counterpoint to this century's long-standing love affair with the paired idols of absolute certainty and absolute politics. Maybe that is why this *fin de siècle* seems a good time for returning to the more discrete, more genuine spirit of the Enlightenment.

In a sense, in the aftermath of what looked like being the final victory, with the fall of the Berlin wall and the demise of communist rule in the Soviet Union, we seem to be back to the quasi-familiar territory of the twentieth century, or at least prior to the First World War, and we cannot avoid having a sense of *déjà vu* when we confront, once again, the usual proclivities of governments and economic, social and cultural elites to combine in order to challenge the limited and accountable character of the state, to reduce the scope of the markets, of social and cultural pluralism and of the public sphere, to abuse their powers and to manipulate the public, and to incline towards nationalism both in policy and in political sentiment. In view of that, we may feel we have to be on the watch for any new combination of old and new forms of absolute politics and dogmatism that may come along, usually with the help of significant segments of the intelligentsia: in short, to be alert to any new avatar of totalitarianism, since we have learnt from the experience of the twentieth century to expect it to take root in any ground, including that of our civil societies.

The fact is that this new age looks like a new time of troubles where every civilized nation in the world is feeling the heat from a variety of sources: ethnic and national conflicts, migratory movements, environmental degradation, terrorism, AIDS, nuclear proliferation, fundamentalism, increasing economic competition, crisis of the welfare state and moral confusion. In the end, most of these problems can be reduced to two interrelated phenomena. First, civil societies which used to be quasi-homogeneous sociocultural nations are becoming plural societies, and this may or may not aggravate the potential for distortions of their basic institutions. Second, we are witness to what seems to be the birth pains of an international social configuration that may or may not become an international, cosmopolitan civil society. Arriving at orderly plural civil societies and an international civil society is far from certain. Just a few of these difficulties are listed below.

Today's increasing global economic competition seems a leap forwards in a secular trend towards a relatively unified world-wide economy. It has created a variety of counter-trends, however, since it requires continuous readjustments to national economies, a repositioning of social groupings, any number of organizational changes and drastic alterations in people's expectations almost from one day to the next. The discourse of social classes, territorial units or interest groups appears today to have fallen short of providing the necessary schema either for giving a semblance of order to what is going on, or for giving direction to efforts to reproduce the sentiments and social attachments needed to maintain the national social fabrics threatened by the changes. Trying to find a meaningful national interest that softens the impact of those changes, keeps the different segments of society together and helps them make necessary adjustments is an exceedingly complicated task, particularly in view of the fact that every nation seems to be caught in the same dilemma: either it tries to keep strong its links to the international community, and thus seems to lose control of its fate; or else it retreats into an even more dangerous pattern of protectionism and mercantilism.

Opening the national boundaries to international flows of capital and trade, migrants and tourists, media communication and cultural influences, military and political alliances, has profound consequences on the character of the recipient nations. Granted that in the past they were more or less homogeneous sociocultural societies, they are now moving along a road at some point of which they will become plural societies, possibly with significant ethnic, linguistic or religious minorities different from those that formed the original community. People living in such composite societies may or may not develop a sense of belonging to a community. They may do so only when and if a new cultural basis for such a sense is formed around a few common values and institutions that allow for diversity and experimentation with different individual and social life-styles, and for toleration of unceasing competition between different cultural traditions: this includes competition between historical narratives regarding the character of that plural society (or new versions of the original nation). This is a process that should reinforce the character of 'civil association' in civil societies, and the moral sentiments associated with that character, even if, in the process, a sense of community develops which has a character different from the one most nations were used to: a sense of community of individuals and/or an array of micro- or meso-communities that want to stay together for reasons not easy to articulate in full, maybe out of shared hopes, and of an increasingly shared liberal disposition.[13] For a long time, the United States has been an eloquent illustration of a plural society; the European Union may or may not become another version of it; and even the European nations which are part of that Union (such as France, the United

Kingdom or Germany) are already engaged in such a process. It is worth noticing, however, that the combination of being plural societies internally and of being increasingly exposed to, and interlinked with, the external world tends to challenge whatever identity these societies may have, or at least makes that identity look problematical, thus eroding the plausibility of domestic and foreign policies constructed around the notion of a national interest.

These processes, therefore, have generated an intensely emotional, defensive response within and without the Western world. Fundamentalism and (primordial) nationalism are powerful sociocultural and political movements on the rise that deeply challenge the links between particular nations and the international community. More to the point, they challenge the very notion that such an international community can ever be a real community. According to them, individuals' meaningful, deeply felt attachments can only be forged with primordial communities such as the family or family-like associations: communities of blood, or religious or near-religious faith, which have at their command magical or quasi-magical mechanisms by which individuals are induced to identify with them and by means of which the former are promised happiness or intense feelings (associated with martyrdom, sacred revenge, a sense of empowerment or similar experiences) that an international civil society seems unable to provide for. On the other hand, these emotional urges may (or may not) be tamed, and the evolution of various Christian churches from, say, the Middle Ages to the present shows that religious organizations which have been, at some point, fundamentalist to the core and quite inimical to values such as those built into markets, political liberties and cultural toleration, can end up finding ways to live with, and even to promote, civil society. This may perhaps give some clue about what could be expected from the religious fundamentalisms of today if they were allowed time to mature. In some cases this could take a few centuries (which should give some hope to those inclined to take an unusually long-term view of current events), but in others it can take just a few decades – as the evolution of the Spanish church during approximately the last 60 years illustrates.[14]

In any case, it seems that one of the clearest challenges of our time (for those attached to the institutions of civil society) consists of making the very powerful forces of nationalism compatible with the development of a variety of plural societies, and the emergence of a world-wide civil society. This is far from being an easy task since both the destructive and the constructive dimensions of nationalism have always been intimately intertwined: as Ferguson made clear a long time ago, patriotism is the result of love for one's community and hostility to aliens.[15] The use of rational arguments can be of only limited help, and the current difficulties can easily obfuscate people's reasoning. History shows that conflicts concerning boundaries between 'us' and 'them' and the identification of those belonging to one side of those boundaries or the other are often insoluble by appeal to rational argument, and that it is usually impossible to agree on any definitive, morally binding and authoritative judgement concerning the definition of any collective identity, much less so of a nation; this is a matter for *ad hoc* compromises, considerable toleration of ambiguities, evolving moral sentiment and prudential judgement. All we can possibly do is to deflate the arguments, so to speak, and blunt the sharpest edges of nationalistic enthusiasm by means of institutional and cultural mechanisms.

First, we can try to promote institutions and understandings that facilitate a procedural agreement on ways for settling disputes which would be aimed at minimizing the use of physical coercion. Second, we can preach the virtues of a historical understanding of our recent and more remote past that insists on the looseness of the links between nations and states, which will demonstrate that, contrary to common opinion, nation-states are the exception not the rule in recorded history, thus suggesting various possibilities for safeguarding a national identity that may be compatible with different configurations of political power. Third, we can try to focus the attention of policy-makers and public opinion on the practical matter of establishing and guaranteeing the rights of national or ethnic minorities whatever political systems they find themselves in. Fourth, we can persuade at least those people who do not feel the overwhelming urge to die for a cause, of the desirability of encouraging or tolerating institutional and cultural experimentation with dual and plural collective identities in the expectation that these experiments will become more and more common as plural societies as well as an international civil society develop. That these developments, particularly that of an international civil society, should proceed apace might, in turn, prove beneficial for the persuasiveness of the above arguments and the establishment and proper functioning of the institutional mechanisms. The fact is that, for all the present confusion, this is indeed the way things seem to be going.

International politics is still dominated by states and state-dominated (and/or bureaucracy-dominated) international organizations, which act as if nations, and not individuals, were their ultimate concern, and as if they aimed at a kind of world government not in terms of a 'civil association' but rather of that of world management.[16] However, international politics evolves within ever more dense networks of economic interdependence and communication and is contingent on a growing (though probably still superficial) awareness that we are dealing increasingly with non-local problems (human rights, famines, nuclear proliferation, terrorism, the environment) which concern all nations and require concerted action.[17]

The growth of an international civil society implies the growth of its various components. Markets and social networks are crucial. But the development of such an international civil society also requires the existence of an international public authority able to establish and implement a minimal operating body of international legislation concerning critical issues such as human rights, possibly the environment and control of weapons of mass destruction; furthermore, it requires an international public sphere where a continuous moral-political conversation can take place regarding those issues and regarding whatever rules or policies may come from such an international public authority to meet them: a conversation that would take place not only at the elite level, but also at that of an increasingly concerned, discriminating world citizenry.

Even allowing for the desirability of such an international civil society, and of the kind of soft, well-mannered, polished or civilized interaction it should bring with it, we have to reckon with the fact that the international social network is highly vulnerable, that the international public debate is in its infancy and that the aforementioned policy issues are extremely difficult to solve, while nothing on the record so far proves they can be handled by the international civil society-in-the-making that we have today. Western nations (which form the core of that international society) have demonstrated both their attachment to the fundamentals of a civil society and a remarkable ability to distort these central institutions and to live with these distortions for a quite long time. In so doing they have exhibited predatory and self-destructive capacities which should not be overlooked, particularly in view of the fact that many states/societies of today, including civil societies (both those which have a long liberal tradition behind them and those which do not), have acquired a frightening technical capacity to inflict immense harm on themselves, and possibly to destroy, or almost destroy, life on the planet. This is an irreversible development: a fact that our societies are doomed to live with for the rest of time and, so far, it is doubtful that we have acquired either the wisdom or the institutions to do so, and even more doubtful that, if having acquired them, they would be maintained.

Why then should we keep coming back to this conception of civil society? As a cue for understanding our disorderly and dangerous times? As an instrument to anchor any hope we may have (or as a magical device to make up for the hope we have lost) in the survival of a civilized way of life? As the answer to questions about our identity, troubled as we are with recent memories of the totalitarian period, and the current transformations of the societies we are part of? As a way of turning the clock back on the mixed heritage of the last two centuries, and retracing our steps to that hard, hopeful mid-eighteenth century in order to draw from it some inspiration to face our current challenges and assist an improbable international civil society in its birth-pangs? Whatever the reasons, if we are to return to that conception we must refine and develop it.

LIMITED FIT, HISTORICAL INDETERMINISM

The classical liberal theorists of the eighteenth century developed an analytically broad and historically specific definition of civil society which encompassed some peculiar societal arrangements and an apparatus of government close to present-day practice in a given set of nations at the time. As they distilled an ongoing, uninterrupted experience with limited governments, political liberties, free markets and voluntary associations in the North Atlantic countries for a relatively long period of time, the theorists of this tradition were inclined to take the view that these elements reinforced each other and that there was a fairly good fit, or degree of congruence, between the political and the societal components of the system: the fit was sufficiently good to maintain the system within a variety of states, even though tensions, difficulties and an unending sequence of challenges arose. Thus, the Scottish philosophers were well aware of the tensions existing between the market and the political system, as is particularly obvious in Ferguson.[18] Nevertheless, they argued that there could be no markets without the rule of law, the enforcement of contracts and private property guaranteed by the public authority; and that, in turn, the govern-

ment could not be expected to be limited unless free markets and
private property (as well as free associations) were able to circum-
scribe the government's capacity to intervene in the reserved do-
main of its citizens. Therefore, the so-called private sphere seemed
to be a precondition for the citizen to perform his/her public role.
From this viewpoint there might, of course, be trade-offs between
the energy or resources the citizen would put into his public and
private capacities; but there was no fundamental, insoluble contradiction between the two. The modern citizen was to be both *homo
oeconomicus* and *homo politicus*, and, what is more, he was to be the
one only because he was the other. This left many problems un-
answered such as that of the political capacity of a dispossessed
class; yet they were not problems of a theoretical aporia, but practical ones to be solved through practical reforms (the generalization
of ownership, the openness of the markets, the diffusion of intangi-
ble property like skills and information by means of education and
others).

This understanding of civil society as a secondary or composite
ideal does not deny, as noted, that real-life societies were merely
approximations to the ideal, nor that they could be distortions of
that character. These distortions, far from being exceptional, have
been periodic lapses, discontinuous yet relatively frequent occur-
rences in the history of the civil societies which have actually existed. By implication this means that the fit between the different
elements of the system must be considered a limited one. The
Scottish theorists knew very well that the commercial states of their
time were problematical approximations to a civilized society, since
even the governments of their time which were limited and operated, very broadly speaking, under the rule of law, were in the
hands of oligarchical groups and courts inclined to make use of
patronage and corruption as ways of dealing with problems of
policy and the distribution of power, and because the defence of the
country was entrusted to mercenary armies – possibly a prudent
arrangement, but hardly an invitation to civic virtue.[19] They also
knew that a specialization of function and an emphasis on material
prosperity could weaken the public's interest and ability to participate in political life. They saw, moreover, that private economic
interests, possibly in conjunction with the public authorities, could
easily conspire to defraud or abuse the public; yet there would still
be markets, and respect for private property. The multitude could
be inclined to follow the lead of popular demagogues (of any persuasion) and support tyranny, and in this way the public sphere

could easily be corrupted; yet there would still be room for free speech. All the components of civil society could be maintained, maybe in a mitigated but still recognizable way; and yet they would be parts in a different, distorted configuration.

One of the implications of a theory of the limited fit between the different components of civil society is that the maintenance of the system is far from guaranteed, and this applies even more so to the genesis of the system in the first place. Civil society is a contingent, indeterminate historical formation, and the search for some explanation of the historical sequence leading to it is not to be equated with a search for so-called historical laws. In fact, the Scottish philosophers' use of conjectural history was done more as an exercise of the imagination and as an intellectual game, than with the pomposity and in the *esprit de serieux* of a philosophy of history. The Scottish theorists viewed historical sequences as the result of an interplay of human actions and institutional inertias, and of the unintended consequences of both.[20] The implication of these views is that those historical processes may be (partly) corrected, channelled and understood by people. People's focus as it is applied to these experiences can be sharp or blurred, and they may or may not learn from them, since for people to learn from their mistakes they first have to recognize them, and there are plenty of ways for them to avoid doing so. As we know, human beings are driven by contrary passions, have a limited intelligence and are not too persevering, if for no other reason than that they are going to die, a fact that makes their ability to carry on the same tasks one generation after another quite problematic.

In these circumstances, trying to find some rational argument at work in the succession of ages, civilizations and periods of history makes sense only if by 'a rational argument at work' we mean a metaphor for a convenient game men play when trying to understand their own identity, their time and the tasks they choose to carry out in that time. We can perhaps understand people's activities and the situation they respond to when we can focus on them at relatively close range – activities and situations corresponding to our time or going back for two or three generations within a narrow cultural range. The rest we have to try to reconstruct applying professional assertiveness, even bravado, to inner uncertainties that can be handled but will never be conclusively decided. There are two reasons for this. First, most of the local knowledge needed for a satisfactory account of the phenomena will have been irrevocably lost. Second, we engage in this effort at a sensible reconstruc-

tion of the past by anchoring ourselves in particular points in time
and making distinct choices regarding the tradition we decide to
follow.

In this respect, we should understand the Scottish philosophers
as if their historical understanding was connected with the fact that
they had made a particular existential and intellectual choice of
tradition. In their time, Scotland was able to be either a significant
or peripheral part of British civil society, or to go her own way.
Most of the philosophers chose (for themselves and for their own
country) to play a central part in the emerging British domination
of the world.[21] This local choice was connected with, and influenced
by, a wider understanding of their times. Before their eyes stood the
results of a broad historical experiment which had taken place over
the previous two centuries, the contrast between two different
paths of development. On the one hand was the path followed by
the Netherlands and Great Britain, leading to limited government
checked by political representation, a substantial degree of religious
toleration and an ever-expanding market economy. On the other
hand was the historical path of a polity and society marked by
absolutism, religious uniformity and an economy that was closely
regulated, supervised and interfered with by the discretionary acts
of the state and by traditional practices, of which Spain provided
a clear example. France was often seen as an intermediate case
between the two opposing sociopolitical types.

By the middle of the eighteenth century the experiment had
run full course, and the results were plain for all to see. Spain, the
most important nation of the sixteenth century, had become a
second-rate world power, her cultural creativity exhausted and her
economy stagnant, a peripheral player on the world-historical
scene and the antithesis of the enlightened commercial state.[22] In
turn, England was successfully challenging France both in
continental Europe and overseas: she showed a superior capacity
for economic growth, scientific and philosophical innovation,
increasing social complexity and a lively public sphere, setting
standards that France could only hope to compete with by learning
from, and to a large degree imitating, the Anglo-Saxon and Dutch
experience.

For the generation of Scottish philosophers these results could be
read as proof of the superiority of the 'British' model over the
'Spanish' one. However, it could not be seen as the result of any
concerted action engaged in by successive generations of Britons
with any common purpose or historical project in mind. It was

rather the result of a happy combination of institutions which had proven successful in the long run, and certain cultural dispositions which had spread throughout strategically located segments of the public – above all, that of reasoning according to logic, and that of respect for facts and for proper moral sentiments. These sentiments had played a crucial role in the functioning of the civil societies of pre-modern times, in the Greek cities and in Rome, and were expected to play a similar role in those of the modern period: moral sentiments both of self-love and benevolence (of friendship as well as civic engagement). Though some communitarian writers draw a sharp contrast between a liberal-individualistic and a communitarian tradition, the truth is that most of the Scottish philosophers can be seen as belonging to both of them: they preached the virtues of energetic, self-assertive individuals acting out their own convictions and looking after their own interests, while at the same time they were well aware of those individuals' embeddedness in their communities, and praised their civic commitments.[23] The Scots were in search of a fully fledged community of free individuals in which a moral and emotional equilibrium would be reached through a conciliation of private and public pursuits.

Therefore, for these theorists, success in maintaining the historical experiment of civil society could not be trusted to any automatism or historical determinism: it depended on many contingencies and, among other factors, on the maintenance of moral traditions. Thus, their recourse to speculation about the different stages of mankind and their essays in conjectural history were ingenious meta-narratives which may or may not have prepared the ground for a better (more scientific, so to speak) account of past events, but whose main point was to illustrate their search for the institutional and cultural/moral conditions that enhanced the probability of a civil society. In this respect the Scots exhibited a guarded, qualified optimism regarding the real, though limited, capacity of the men of their time to reason and to stick to a balanced moral tradition of self-love and social benevolence.

This sense of limits was missing in Hegel, and in most of the other authors belonging to the statist/revolutionary tradition of the theories on civil society. In this tradition those limits are supposedly transcended by collective subjects which combine extraordinary theoretical and practical capacities, of reasoning, articulation and will-power. These subjects may be the bearers of tasks imposed upon them by some impersonal historical process following some inner logic. Such speculations can apparently be rendered plausible by some particular historical experiences. The cult of the state in France corresponded to the long-standing tradition of a fairly powerful state apparatus, over several centuries and under various guises, monarchical, revolutionary, Bonapartist and republican. Also, Hegel's theories were the distillation of human practice embedded in a society of a kind quite different from the one the Scottish philosophers were part of. Hegel's main frame of reference was the state-dominated Prussian society of the first quarter of the nineteenth century recovering from the shock of its defeat of Napoleon, and the circles closest to his mind and heart were those of the academic intelligentsia and civil servants. Hegel's theory showed a strong elective affinity with the dispositions of those circles as they had been shaped by their own peculiar history of one and a half centuries (encompassing three or four generations) in which a few energetic princes had used a relatively cohesive bureaucratic-military machine and an opportunistic *Realpolitik* to seize a large territory at the expense of their immediate neighbours, to regiment and extract as many resources as possible from their subjects in order to support that machine and in this way to become a respected continental European power. Hence their conviction that a well-ordered, civilized society was state-centred and consisted of a teleocratic order under strong political and bureaucratic leadership.[24] Hegel chose to embrace the Prussian historical and cultural tradition, and to make his own contribution to it.

This is why, though it may be argued that Hegel somehow attempted to combine what we know of as liberal individualism and civic republicanism, in the end the attempt was thwarted by his fundamental choice, and what emerged was the quite different conception of the state as a moral actor in the world-historical scenario.[25] Hegel tried to offer a reconciliation of 'subjective freedom' and 'objective freedom', of individual liberties and socioeconomic and political institutions, the institutions being understood as providing the basis for such subjective freedom. However, it is quite significant that Hegel referred to objective freedom by the name of 'the state', and not of 'civil society'.[26] Hegel's civil society (*sensu lato*) was still a combination of markets and so-called corporations, together with a public authority responsible for the tasks of 'policing' and 'justice'. But it is clear that, in Hegel's mind, such a construction belonged to the past, and was to be superseded, or had already been so, by a more modern and more rational sociopolitical configuration: one which retained some elements of the markets and corporations of 'civil society' (*sensu stricto*), but in which the public authority had become a much more complex and developed apparatus (the 'political state') with the bureaucracy playing the key role in that apparatus.[27]

The change of meaning of the term 'civil society' from Ferguson to Hegel came about from an altogether different understanding of historical explanation. Instead of engaging in conjectural history, Hegel pretended to develop a so-called philosophy of history. According to this, historical development was synonymous with the process of self-understanding of some supra-historical, absolute subject whose very identity was constructed through and *pari passu* with that process. In modern times, the key for the advance of mankind towards increasing 'freedom' and participation in that absolute subject lay in the activities of collective subjects and/or institutions of social coordination organized around a central agency: they would be the bearers of some universal principle destined to be fulfilled, as they had access to the true knowledge needed for such fulfilment.

The modern state was just such a collective subject and coordinating agency, with the bureaucratic group at its centre. Inferior forms of decentralized social coordination such as markets were allowed, though partly tamed by the existence of corporations, but only if both markets and corporations were under bureaucratic supervision.[28] Hegel moved well beyond the Scottish philosophers' guarded optimism. He attributed to such collective subjects and central coordinating agencies the most extraordinary cognitive and moral capacities. The state was 'God on earth', and the bureaucrats were a 'universal class' devoted to the public good, fully competent to envision and able to implement such public good; the obvious implication being that civil society lacked precisely these capacities, since their members only had access to tentative, local and dispersed knowledge which could never be fully articulated, and since they were driven fundamentally by private concerns.

So Hegel goes back to the point the Scots thought they had left behind. They had discovered, or so they thought, that a new society was emerging in a variety of places, in which kings, courtiers, civil servants and political factions would play a useful but rather limited role, because most of such a society's potential for cultural and material growth, and for social order, would lie in the initiative and the spontaneous self-coordination of the individuals that made it up: individuals able to contribute to the growth of knowledge and moved by moral sentiments of self-love and benevolence that balanced and reinforced each other. Those views were dismissed by Hegel and the statist/revolutionary tradition that followed.[29] In this tradition the macro-historical subject received several names: the working classes, the revolutionary party, the socialist state, social movements (in the left-wing tradition); or nations with a world-historical destiny or providential mission to fulfil (in the right-wing tradition). These could not be more different and yet they were all collective subjects and central coordinating agencies which demanded absolute loyalty and which periodically tested their followers' resolve in wars, in revolutions and counter-revolutions, and eventually in acts of terror and other death games. This tradition allowed for both mild and extreme forms. Totalitarianism both left and right has been just one of the most recent avatars of that tradition in its most extreme form, indeed pushed to paroxysm: where society was required to put all its trust in those central coordinating agencies, and where individuals became either instruments to be used, or obstacles to be removed, by them.

INSTITUTIONAL AND CULTURAL BASES
FOR PRECARIOUS HOPES

I have used a broad concept of civil society as an ideal character that covers political components (limited government) as well as social components (markets, associations, public sphere). But other concepts are possible. A narrower, stricter sense of the concept would refer only to the social components, in which case we would be interested in emphasizing the autonomy of society, and its differences from the state and the political class for the purpose of explaining some specific developments.[30] Some authors reduce the contents of the concept ever more and refer only to some particular social component or some combination of two of them. For some, it is the equivalent of a 'bourgeois society', the core of which is a market economy, in which market-like relations prevail among agents moved by self-interest. For others, it refers to a segment of society populated by voluntary associations (intermediary bodies, social movements, interest groups, political parties, ideological groupings) which pursue both their own particular interests, including the assertion of their identities, and their own version of the general interest, and which are, therefore, engaged in permanent debate. In this respect civil society becomes nearly synonymous with a public sphere.[31]

However, there are good reasons for holding to the broad, original conception to which I have referred, at least for some general purposes, particularly in view of the new challenges of building up civil societies in the context of plural societies and of an emerging international community. By doing so we facilitate the task of tracing our present position back to the sources of the classical liberal tradition, while emphasizing three points: the critical importance of the connections, and mutual dependence, between the different components of civil society, and particularly between the social and political ones, as opposed to stressing the boundaries between them; the centrality of the agents in each and every one of these components as they perform their interconnected roles as citizens, producers/consumers/taxpayers, members of associations and participants in the public debate; and the character of these components not as reified systems but as sets of activities carried out by, and interactions among, largely autonomous agents the end result of which is open and indeterminate. Also, by doing so we may be able to leave behind, or at least place within the limits of reason, some 'dangerous' nostalgias: nostalgia for a basic foundation for, or some faith in groups or institutions which would be considered the bearer of, a sequence of reforms equal to a historical project of human emancipation, the so-called project of the Enlightenment; nostalgia for building up a central, coordinating agency able to ensure the successful realization of that sequence of enlightened reforms, or, in default of this, nostalgia for a final moral/political consensus among the participants in a conversation regarding the nature of those reforms. This may lead us to argue with those who, like Habermas and others, tend to reduce the concept of civil society to the public sphere, who make the complementary move of constructing the state and the economy as an integrated field or system which would stand opposed to civil society, and who suggest a reified, machine-like character of the state and the economy (and by so doing, underline, and eventually overstress, the 'thickness' of political and economic institutions at the expense of human agents' capacity to play around with, alter and subvert those institutions).

Those nostalgias, and the theories associated with them, appear plausible due to the fact that they are part of a remarkable tradition of the last century and a half: that of the radical, critical intelligentsia. This tradition is rooted, at least in the West, in particular experiences which have developed in close, though ambivalent, connection with those of broad circles of civil servants, politicians and party (and union) officials, enlightened businessmen and journalists. A large part of that intelligentsia has allowed itself to become dependent not so much on a market of readers (that might have ensured them a modicum of independence, provided individual consumers bought their products) as on a new avatar of the system of patronage of kings, popes, merchants and other patrons of the past: the one that has been established by the apparatus of the welfare state, by parties (social democratic, communist, conservative, Christian democratic or others), unions and associated newspapers, foundations and similar organizations that might reward them with influence, power, money and reputation. Another alternative for the critical intelligentsia has been to find a niche in the academic communities, thus becoming (at least in continental Europe) civil servants of a rather peculiar kind and dependent on the state's largesse for a living.

The point is that these particular institutional practices have placed the Western intelligentsia in an apparently benign and protected environment. This has reinforced its disposition to keep alive and develop arguments in the statist/revolutionary tradition mentioned above, not just as a matter of theoretical argument for debate, but as a life form to be experienced and understood, the core of which is supposed to be positively evaluated and defended, even if its peripheral parts can be continuously improved upon and its so-called pathological deviations condemned. The tradition of a fundamental ideological rejection of the market economy has been maintained at minimal cost and risk, exercised so to speak from a safe haven, and requiring only a tangential familiarity with the subject, while there has been ample room for exploring ways to anchor that fundamental dissent in different variants of the Marxist tradition.

In turn, the Marxist intellectual tradition has gone through several metamorphoses which have been connected with the avatars of the practices and institutions of the various branches of Marxist parties, unions, newspapers, cultural circles, social movements and, last but not least, Marxist governments, either of a communist or a social democratic variety. But the experience of trying to build bridges between the intelligentsia's protected life in the benign environment it found in the West and the practice of the Marxist parties actually in existence once they got control of the state (both in the East and in the West) has been disconcerting. It is important to realize that living in the West, in the context of liberal democratic polities, a capitalist economy and plural societies, the various Marxist parties, unions and related associations have developed adaptive mechanisms, which have, in turn, facilitated an ambivalent disposition on the part of Marxist intellectuals (and, by implication, of the Marxist theoretical tradition they were responsible for) towards Western societies: a sort of reluctant appreciation of their liberal institutions and values. The key to this appreciation lies in the fact that these intellectuals could conduct their personal lives and follow their intellectual calling relatively free from coercion in these societies, while at the same time they could not avoid becoming gradually aware of the fact that they would not have been able to do so – would indeed barely have been able to survive – in the actual socialist societies of the East.

Marxist intellectuals of the West have been reluctant to face up to that 'recalcitrant experience' of being able to live in the capitalist societies they could not justify and being unable to live in the socialist societies they felt morally close to. This 'small fact of life' has eroded the persuasive force and the substance of their arguments.[32] They have tried to present their arguments as if they were in the process of deepening and radicalizing their basic proposals when in fact they have gradually been abandoning their original position, *pari passu* with the ever sharper and clearer contrast between the plausibility of Western societies (as proved by the fact that they could live with them) and the loss of plausibility of the socialist societies (as proved by the fact that they could not live in them). Another disturbing element of the equation is that, in reaching this conclusion, the critical intelligentsia could only give limited credit to the Western socialist/social democratic (originally Marxist) organizations. Since the intelligentsia believed that the capitalist core of the West was inimical to the project of human progress with which it identified itself, it could only contemplate the contribution of those organizations in supporting or even saving capitalism with the utmost reserve. Conversely, neither did the part that social democratic organizations had played in nurturing the gentler side of those societies, the welfare system and a liberal polity, provide grounds for unequivocal, enthusiastic support. Either the welfare state and the liberal polity were evaluated negatively, as part of a grand strategy legitimating a system which was fundamentally defined as exploitative and manipulative, as a device to consolidate the alliance of state and capital by coopting new elements to be part of it: which was nothing to be grateful for. Or, if they were evaluated positively, then it was doubtful that thanks for their existence should be given principally to the Marxist tradition, since responsibility for the welfare system rested on conservative and liberal governments at least as much (if not more) than on social democratic ones (with socialist parties and unions' responsibility for a liberal polity being thus considered as at best derivative and second to that of the liberal tradition).

Therefore, living in a capitalist polity has become an increasingly troubling, disquieting experience for the critical intelligentsia: it has had serious problems anchoring its dissent on the Marxist tradition (East or West) while lacking the disposition to accept the basic tenets of civil society (in the broad sense in which we use the term). Hence, its need to find a language for articulating this complex world of ambiguities and ambivalences; to locate this experience in a niche near to, but not within, the soft Marxist tradition of the social democratic parties of the West; to make a point of understanding but not supporting the communist experiences of the East; and to live off the wealth and opportunities of capitalism without enjoying the experience (like virtuous, joyless souls keen on using the 'system' for its reproductive utility not for the immediate gratification it may procure). This is where Habermas's discourse placing the 'economic-political system' in opposition to the 'lifeworld' comes in, together with a defensive, minimalist strategy that renounces control of the 'system' provided that the space of the 'lifeworld' is protected.[33] In this long march of the Western Marxist intellectuals back to a 'bourgeois' society, in this strategic retreat into honourable defeat, the case of Habermas is emblematic in that it shows the limits but also the residual 'rational kernel' of the Marxist tradition, as he points to challenges and questions that will not easily go away.

Without going into every aspect of Habermas's exceedingly complex (and changing) discourse, just a few notes on some of Habermas's relatively recent writings may help in furthering our discussion.[34] His thinking seems to evolve around a basic tension between an economic and political system and the 'lifeworld' (of which civil society in a very narrow sense would be a part). He thinks of 'the system' in terms of the state apparatus and the economy as systemically integrated action fields, having a bureaucratic and capitalist life of their own, and he further assumes that they can no longer be democratically transformed from within.[35] Though Habermas explicitly states that the evolution of his thinking has pushed him beyond the 'paradigm of subjectivity', we may infer, from both the contents of his statements and the rhetorical and practical context that these statements are part of, that his assessment of the 'system' is not much different from the semi-conspiratorial understanding of organized or monopoly capitalism that formed the background of his early work. This 'system' sounds like the institutional core (with a life of its own in the best tradition of the philosophy of the praxis and the theories of alienation or reification) of what is known in common parlance as 'the establishment', or some modern version of a combination of Court and Country, which would be the bearer of objective, impersonal interests, and whose influence would be overwhelming.

In turn, civil society in the Habermasian sense corresponds to the institutions of sociability and discourse of the 'lifeworld', and reappears in Habermas's writings as a sort of new impersonation of the public sphere that he analysed at the beginning of his career. This version of civil society refers to voluntary associations out-side the realm of the state and the economy: churches, cultural associations, academia, independent media, sports and leisure clubs, debating societies, groups of concerned citizens and grass-roots petitioning drive right through to occupational associations (that is, business and professional organizations), political parties, labor unions and – of greatest import to Habermas – *alternative institutions*.[36] Habermas places unions and even parties (with some reluctance[37]) and, above all, social movements in the 'lifeworld', hoping that they will be the bulwarks against its colonization by the 'system'. Given that the 'system' cannot be transformed, the moral-political goal of Habermas and the tradition he belongs to shifts from transformation to containment. Having came to the conclusion that the Eastern socialist societies were beyond repair, having lost faith in a social democratic strategy for the West, and having sensed the limits of what the social movements could achieve, Habermas's goal now is 'to erect a democratic dam against the colonializing encroachment of system imperatives on areas of the life-world'.[38] It may very well be, however, that Habermas is mistaken on both counts: neither is the 'system' what he believes it to be, its 'logic' being more defective and its power less than he thinks, nor are the bearers of the 'lifeworld' to be trusted in the way that he does to provide a firm basis for such a minimalist defence against the 'system'.

Habermas's 'system' refers to an integrated set of political and economic activities. In other words, he postulates a stable combination of economic and political institutions and organizations. It may be said, in passing, that it is highly unlikely that such a combination would be stable, and that Habermas overstates his case

for the probability of a concerted strategy and/or institutional fit
between two systems of activities which, first, can easily be shown
to 'follow different logics', and, second, neither of which follows
such logic that closely, though they may certainly be affected by
different institutional inertias. Habermas seems to imply that both
the economic and the political systems (or sub-systems) are 'reified'
structures, apparently meaning that they function according to
machine-like logic out of human control, much in the way Marx's
capital and Weber's bureaucratic machinery are supposed to do.
This means taking both Marx and Weber much too seriously. From
all we know, the economic system is an extremely complex and
open one, contingent on millions (or billions for that matter) of
unpredictable, ever-changing decisions made by large numbers of
autonomous units. We could attribute a moderate degree of rationality to the functioning of the system in that we would be able to
forecast tentatively the short-term evolution of some of its pattern
variables (but not the future state of the system with any degree of
precision) only if the other variables could be held stable for a
period of time, a very unlikely eventuality; and in that we could
possibly explain some actual developments after the fact only if we
were able to reconstruct all the relevant local knowledge, which is
hardly possible.

The open, indeterminate character of the market is rooted in the
open, indeterminate character of the decisions made by its basic
units: producers and consumers. Some, or many, of these units can
be hierarchical organizations. But one of the problems in
Habermas's oversystemic view of politics and the economy consists of his subscribing all too easily to Weber's understanding of
modern bureaucracies as impersonal, machine-like systems. As an
ideal type this theory has its uses. It is not useful, however, if it
implies a characterization of real modern bureaucracies, because
most of them are not, and do not work in that way. The modern
organization as a well-oiled machine working in accordance with a
carefully thought-out plan for a sustained period of time may be the
desideratum or utopia of an executive chief of a corporation, a
government agency or an organizational designer, but it does not
correspond to the bulk of actual, everyday experience in most real-
life organizations. Organizational decisions are a complicated,
messy business. They are based on so-called scientific predictions
and technical reports, which are commissioned, selected, read,
accepted in their entirety, in part or disregarded in frequently
baroque decision-making processes, which are intersected by

power conflicts between organizational cliques and in-fighting between changing coalitions, and where memories, personalities and all sorts of exogenous factors play an important part. Then, once the decisions have been made, comes the very risky and open-ended sequence of their implementation. In fact, most decisions are rarely implemented, and merely have a symbolic value. Once made and if implemented, they quite often have to coexist alongside institutional routines (parading as rational procedures) with which they may or may not fit in. Of course, there are both internal and external constraints that provide organizations with some continuity, giving them the appearance of strategic units whose trajectory would respond to goals or objectives. And it may be that organizations go through those strategic moments periodically; but they do not last for long, and new institutional inertias soon take over. This is why restructuring, *pace* Weber, is an endemic, everyday feature of our so-called modern, rational, predictable organizations. These considerations apply to capitalist firms and even more so to parties and to state bureaucracies. Far from being machine-like, state bureaucracies are unpredictable animals, though they do of course have some mechanical, routine-like dimensions too.

The point of these remarks is that economic and political systems persist and change as the result of a myriad of agents' decisions which are embedded in social forms and cultural frameworks. The 'system' does not determine the preferences of producers and consumers, politicians, bureaucrats or citizens. Choices are made by them all, and these choices are undetermined by economic and political conditions. They are contingent, among other factors, on implicit or explicit normative considerations. If 'lifeworld' is supposed to mean that part of human experience in which social forms and cultural dispositions combine to give a breathing space to moral communities of some kind, then we must recognize that 'lifeworld' spaces may be discovered everywhere, including at the very heart of the political and economic system. And this is so, because the very structure of such a system is contingent on choices made by those producers, consumers, politicians, bureaucrats and citizens, and because those choices are connected to, and rooted in, moral traditions.

We can move on from an analytical to a normative theory of 'lifeworlds' and decide to give a special value to moral communities of a particular kind: for instance, those organized around a morality of 'discourse ethics', composed of free individuals who engage in a reasonable and honest conversation, and who respect and care

for each other (and hopefully make some decent decisions too).[39]
But then we have to recognize that the kind of institutions and
associations of the historical, or existing 'lifeworlds' that Habermas
considers, may not contribute to creating that particular kind of
moral community. In fact, they may also have within them oligarchical components, routines and 'reified' structures, violence
(moral or otherwise) and deception in doses strong enough to cast
more than a reasonable doubt on the promise they hold for human
improvement. The stereotyped language, or *langage de bois*, of
revolutionary rhetoric of a party, a union, or a social movement
may be similar in nature to that of the language of the government
decrees that appear in the state's official publications, or the list of
commodity prices on the stock market that we read in the financial
pages of a newspaper, and this is so because it reflects similar power
games, ritual performances and institutional inertias. Social movements, for one, are just organizations of a fuzzy nature in which
there is a fairly large diffusion of power and relatively open
boundaries. But they may have a hard core of well-coordinated
militants who lead the movement, or who take control of it at
critical moments, make crucial choices, establish precedents that
decide the future course of events, create exemplars and myths and
narratives that dominate the discourse of the place, and who therefore shape memories and language, and marginalize anyone they
dislike, making them feel that they do not belong. The apparent
looseness of the organization of a social movement makes for a
sense of frailty or vulnerability *vis-à-vis* the outside world, and this
may generate, in turn, a search for compensatory mechanisms, one
of them being the intensity of the militants' belief in the legitimacy
of their moral authority, and another the emotional vehemence of
their discourse. Such vehemence may be a convenient device in
the task of building up stores of potential aggressiveness, that in
due time can be directed against internal dissenters and external
adversaries under cover of moral indignation.

The truth of the matter is that there are no ultimate foundations
anywhere from which to build those moral communities, while at
the same time work on them can start any- or everywhere in the
different spaces of civil society (in the broad sense in which I have
used the term: in the polity, economy, social life or the public
sphere) with varying chances of success. In this respect, looking for
the right institutional and cultural mechanisms needed to help those
moral communities develop is an endless affair in which we may be
well advised to engage, in the spirit of Diogenes' search for the right

man, with a lamp and looking all around. On the other hand, our
search is given some direction by the accumulated experience of
civil societies over several centuries and in a number of nations.
That should give us confidence in a basic institutional core, even if
we know these institutions need nurturing and developing, and can
be easily distorted. Hence, we need ever-renewed commitments to
those institutions to avoid their distortion. The historical indeterminism of the past, the limited fit of the present, the *fourmillement*
of agents' decisions that underlie the operations of organizations
and institutions, all give an open, precarious character to the state of
the system of our civil societies at any given time. This is not to be
taken as a minus, but as part of the normal, healthy uncertainties of
human life.

If we observe world history and life in some of the relatively free
and civilized fragments of today's Western societies we see precarious groupings of people who spend the few decades of their lives
doing what they consider to be decent and sensible things often
enough to produce a modicum of social trust in their social encoun-
ters; they evolve in a world that they are barely able to understand,
they cling to some crucial institutions, they come to reject some
dangerous delusions and they communicate with others, sometimes
in the spirit of conversation, sometimes preaching, but on the
whole with sufficient respect and curiosity to keep the conversation
going. All these people revere a few sacred texts, and they take
courage from the memories they rearrange periodically in the hope
they will leave some traces to the people they expect to follow
them. Thus, they develop loyalties to each other and to the people
who came before them and will come after them, and in so doing
they cling to several traditions: a variety of particular traditions
(national and local, religious and of political sentiment, and many
others) that support them in their search for their own identities,
and a liberal tradition that keeps them loosely connected to each
other while allowing for all those different identities to coexist,
compete with each other and thrive. This is something that people
belonging in the liberal tradition, whether by birth, adoption or
hard-won acquisition, do from within an institutional and cultural
context at least partially permeated by liberal principles and values.
We may as well call such an institutional and cultural context, as did
some of the founders of our liberal tradition, the Scottish philosophers, a civil society. If this is the case, then civil society may be at
the same time the ground for our choice of tradition, and one of the
names for it.

NOTES

1 M. Oakeshott, *On Human Conduct*, Oxford University Press, Oxford, 1990, pp. 1–30.

2 Oakeshott, *On Human Conduct*, p. 185.

3 Oakeshott, *On Human Conduct*, p. 185.

4 Oakeshott, *On Human Conduct*, pp. 144ff.

5 I. Kant, *The Critique of Pure Reason*, cited in K. R. Popper, *The Open Society and its Enemies*, vol. 1, Princeton University Press, Princeton, N.J., 1971, p. 247.

6 A. Smith, *The Theory of Moral Sentiments*, Liberty Classics, Indianapolis, Ind., 1982; A. Ferguson, *An Essay on the History of Civil Society*, Edinburgh University Press, Edinburgh, 1966.

7 Oakeshott, *On Human Conduct*, p. 326; A. Black, *Guilds and Civil Society*, Cornell University Press, Ithaca, N.Y., 1984.

8 Popper, *The Open Society and its Enemies*, vol. 1, p. 174.

9 F. A. Hayek, *New Studies in Philosophy, Politics, Economics and the History of Ideas*, Routledge and Kegan Paul, London, 1978, p. 61, and *The Fatal Conceit*, University of Chicago Press, Chicago, Ill., 1988, pp. 17, 70.

10 Oakeshott, *On Human Conduct*, p. 326; Hayek, *The Fatal Conceit*, p. 18.

11 G. L. Mosse, *The Nationalisation of the Masses*, Howard Fertig, New York, 1975; W. Mommsen, *Max Weber and German Politics, 1890–1920*, University of Chicago Press, Chicago, Ill., 1984.

12 F. Fukuyama, *The End of History and the Last Man*, The Free Press, New York, 1992.

13 R. Rorty, *Objectivity, Relativism and Truth*, Cambridge University Press, Cambridge, 1991; S. Macedo, *Liberal Virtues*, Oxford University Press, Oxford, 1991.

14 V. Pérez-Díaz, *The Return of Civil Society*, Harvard University Press, Cambridge, Mass., 1993, pp. 108–83.

15 Ferguson, *An Essay on the History of Civil Society*, pp. 21–5.

16 Popper, *The Open Society and its Enemies*, vol. 1, p. 288; Oakeshott, *On Human Conduct*, p. 313.

17 V. Pérez-Díaz (convener), H. M. Enzensberger, P. Hassner, W. Lepenies, R. Nozick, S. Williams and A. Sen, 'Conversations in Madrid on Freedom, Democracy and Values', November 1992.

18 Ferguson, *An Essay on the History of Civil Society*; J. G. A. Pocock, *The Machiavellian Moment*, Princeton University Press, Princeton, N.J., 1975, pp. 499ff; D. Kettler, *The Social and Political Thought of Adam Ferguson*, Ohio State University Press, Columbus, Ohio, 1965; D. Forbes, 'Introduction', in Ferguson, *An Essay on the History of Civil Society*; J. Keane, 'Despotism and Democracy: The Origins and Development of the Distinction between Civil Society and the State, 1750–1850', in J. Keane, ed., *Civil Society and the State*, Verso, London, 1988, pp. 39–45.

19 J. G. A. Pocock, *Virtue, Commerce and History*, Cambridge University Press,

Cambridge, 1985.

20 Ferguson, *An Essay on the History of Civil Society*, p. 122; Hayek, *New Studies in Philosophy, Politics, Economics and the History of Ideas*, p. 5.

21 Kettler, *The Social and Political Thought of Adam Ferguson*, pp. 16ff; A. MacIntyre, *Whose Justice? Which Rationality?*, University of Notre Dame Press, Notre Dame, Ind., 1988, pp. 219ff; Pocock, *Virtue, Commerce and History*.

22 A. Pagden, *Spanish Imperialism and the Political Imagination*, Yale University Press, New Haven, Conn., 1990, p. 9.

23 Macedo, *Liberal Virtues*, pp. 15ff.

24 F. L. Carsten, *The Origins of Prussia*, Oxford University Press, Oxford, 1954; H. Rosenberg, *Bureaucracy, Aristocracy and Autocracy*, Beacon Press, Cambridge, 1966.

25 Pérez-Díaz, *The Return of Civil Society*, pp. 66ff.

26 G. W. F. Hegel, *Hegel's Philosophy of Right*, ed. T. Knox, Oxford University Press, Oxford, 1967.

27 Hegel, *Hegel's Philosophy of Right*, paras 163, 267, 273, 276. Cf. V. Pérez-Díaz, *State, Bureaucracy and Civil Society*, MacMillan, London, 1978, pp. 6–24; Pérez-Díaz, *The Return of Civil Society*, pp. 70–3.

28 Hegel, *Hegel's Philosophy of Right* para. 252, addition to para. 255, para. 288.

29 Pérez-Díaz, *The Return of Civil Society*, pp. 69–75.

30 Pérez-Díaz, *The Return of Civil Society*, pp. 55ff.

31 J. Habermas, *The Structural Transformation of the Public Sphere*, MIT Press, Cambridge, Mass., 1989, and 'Further Reflections on the Public Sphere', in C. Calhoun, ed., *Habermas and the Public Sphere*, MIT Press, Cambridge, Mass., 1992; J. Cohen and A. Arato, 'Politics and the Reconstruction of the Public Sphere', in Calhoun, *Habermas and the Public Sphere*, and *Civil Society and Political Theory*, MIT Press, Cambridge, Mass., 1993.

32 M. White, *What Is and What Ought To Be Done*, Oxford University Press, Oxford, 1981; V. Pérez-Díaz, 'El proyecto moral de Marx, cien años después', in A. Rojo and V. Pérez-Díaz, eds, *Marx, Economia y Moral*, Allianza Editoral, Madrid, 1984.

33 C. Offe, 'Bindings, Shackles, Brakes: On Self-Limitation Strategies', in A. Honneth, T. McCarthy, C. Offe and A. Wellmer, eds, *Cultural-Political Interventions in the Unfinished Project of Enlightenment*, MIT Press, Cambridge, Mass., 1992, p. 69; Habermas, 'Further Reflections on the Public Sphere', p. 442.

34 J. Habermas, *The Theory of Communicative Action*, vol. 1, Beacon Press, Boston, 1984; *Moral Consciousness and Communicative Action*, MIT Press, Cambridge, Mass., 1991, and 'Further Reflections on the Public Sphere'.

35 Habermas, 'Further Reflections on the Public Sphere'.

36 Habermas, 'Further Reflections on the Public Sphere', pp. 453–4.

37 Habermas, 'Further Reflections on the Public Sphere', p. 454.

38 Habermas, 'Further Reflections on the Public Sphere', p. 444.

39 Habermas, *Moral Consciousness and Communicative Action*.

5

The Nature of Social Ties and the Future of Postcommunist Society: Poland after Solidarity

Wlodzimierz Wesolowski

Attempts to move from communism to democracy and a market economy in East central Europe are shaped by many local factors: by traditions, both old and new; by the different degrees of cultural proximity to Western societies; by the quality of leaders and political activists; and by the consequences, unintended as well as intended, of the initial protests. When the countries of the former Soviet Union and of the former Yugoslavia are included in comparisons, the range of differences grows. We see that at least two contrasting models of political systems may emerge in postcommunist countries. The first is a system of bureaucratic authoritarianism, exploiting both old communist structures and nationalist emotions. This system retains many features of a command economy. Countries that are moving in this direction include Ukraine, Russia, Serbia and Romania. Second, and typologically at the opposite extreme, are those countries – Hungary, Poland and the Czech Republic – which are becoming conventional liberal democratic states. Their constitutional state organs function acceptably, though not in an exemplary way. The political rights of the citizens are secured. The transformation of their economies into privately owned and market led seems assured.

Within this democratic type we see variations. Socio-historical context complicates the typological profile. Workers in Poland, for example, played a powerful role in the earliest stages of transition, and they may yet do so again. There are also peculiarities of mass psychology that will play a role in shaping specific features of each democracy within the region; I will refer to some of them when analysing the Polish case. What interests me most is a particular type of communitarian relationship.

My analysis depends on employing general concepts, hitherto not used, to analyse the changes in the former Soviet bloc. The concepts are not completely alien to sociologists since they are derived from the famous *Gemeinschaft/Gesellschaft* dichotomy introduced by Ferdinand Tönnies, and from the Weberian concepts of associative and communal relations.[1] Actually, I will use three concepts: 'associative ties', 'communal ties' and 'communitarian ties'. Associative and communal ties are, in a Weberian sense, ideal-typical constructs. They overemphasize certain sets of characteristics which in reality are rarely met in a complete constellation and with the full development of each characteristic. In contrast, communitarian ties have a wholly mixed character; further, there may be many sub-variants within this type. In pointing to the possible variants, I am again following Weber's methodological belief, that mixed types of social arrangements are closer to reality; they may also be more likely to survive and function successfully than 'pure' types.

Groups held together by associative ties show the following characteristics. They are freely joined and freely left. They usually rely on socio-political discourse to reach conclusions. They pursue interests and goals laid down by their members. They show a propensity for internal loyalty. Yet at the same time, when they negotiate with other groups, they treat them as equally valid social units. These associative characteristics create a framework for resolving conflicts between groups, and are typical of stable Western democracies. At the most abstract level, they can be seen as the generic features of civil society and the democratic state. Society organized in the state is a 'union of unions', to use the phrase of John Rawls.[2] If associative groups use established procedures of the democratic political game, they may have an integrative influence on the whole societal system.

Communal ties have a different character. The individual is born with them, or at least is considered by fellow members to be born with them. Individuals are integrated into the group by a set of symbols, values and beliefs that produce a high degree of loyalty and devotion to the group. At the same time communal groups display a tendency to separateness and closure. For all these reasons they are much more prone to generate conflicts than are associative groups. In extreme cases other groups seem not only alien but also fundamentally misguided in their values. They may see other groups as a threat. The communal group's high degree of internal cohesiveness is coupled with a high potential for divisiveness within the society as a whole. Ethnic groups as well as religious groups have a potential for becoming this type of group, which I will also refer to as 'spiritual communities'.[3]

Communitarian ties combine characteristics of associative and of communal bonds.[4] Freedom of access to the group is coupled with acceptance of some 'fundamental values'. Communitarian groups act to increase cooperation, both within the group and between groups. The procedures for resolving conflicts combine two elements. First, they refer to some basic human value, for example to the principle of Christian brotherhood. Second, they involve pragmatic principles which have developed over a long time of practice. There are two types of communitarian bonds; they have different intellectual roots, though their social results can be quite similar. The first sub-type deeply respects tradition and is guided by a belief in one's duties towards one's fellow human beings. Protestant and Catholic *social doctrines* are usually seen as pro-moters of communitarian ties. Where the Protestant version stresses the role of smaller communities of the faithful, and of egalitarian relations within such communities, the Catholic version promotes the spiritual bonds of the universal church and empha-sizes hierarchy within it. The second sub-type has its intellectual roots in social democratic principles and practices. Some versions of liberalism are also close to it. This school of thought insists that society is, or should be, bound together by the principles of coop-eration, mutual aid and the organized provision of basic goods for every member of the society. Social relations are both associative, in providing welfare, and communal, in producing social cohesion by affiliating members to such fundamental values as solidarity, liberty and democracy. The state is accepted as an agent acting on behalf of society; society is seen as the community of the highest order.

A society organized according to any of these three types of social bonds will experience both integrative and disintegrative tendencies. Further, the three types release very different social forces within postcommunist societies.

THE SOLIDARITY ETHOS

While Western movements since the 1960s have been single- or specific-issue movements, Solidarity was a general movement opposing communism. Its critique of the old system was holistic, and its principles and programme sought to organize society in a completely new way. The 'Solidarity ethos' focused on certain fundamental values in its social thinking. These included national independence, human dignity, societal solidarity and fair industrial relations. Nonetheless, Solidarity resembled Western European social movements in its reliance on demonstrations and its distrust of fixed internal structures. It was determined to avoid the distinction between leaders and led. Accordingly, workers reached decisions in their factories by means of direct democracy. Further, it was assumed that everyone viewed the situation in the same way and had the same goals. Personal contacts mattered a great deal. Leaders were treated simply as experts or organizers, to whom the body of the movement temporarily delegated some functions in pursuit of the common goal. Even Lech Walesa, though seen by many as a charismatic leader, was not an exception. He was just one of us, and nobody was prepared to give him any special powers or prerogatives. All these were strong communal features.[5]

The Solidarity ethos drew on elements of Polish culture, both popular and intellectual. This included Christian theology and the philosophy of Polish Romanticism, a movement which was as much literary as political, and which has been transmitted to this day through the literature taught in schools. Solidarity also had roots in living social memories of the Polish people's heroic and communal opposition to Germanization and Russification over the past 200 years. Further, a strong emphasis was placed on sacrifice and the devotion to human values. Self-government was considered to be important, whilst the 1981 Congress proposed to organize society by means of a network of self-government.

By elevating society over the state, Solidarity propagated very important aspects of the classical model of civil society, in particular the rule of law, individual freedom, freedom of communication and association and public debate.[6] However, one could say that Solidarity's emphases on 'deliberative democracy' and the 'humane control' of the market economy added up to a socialization of the classical view of civil society. Equally important were elements of communal ideology, drawn principally from nationalism and

Christianity. This amalgam of principles created a force which proved, in its confrontation with the dependent and oppressive party-state, to be indestructible.

THE SWITCH TO NEO-LIBERAL PRINCIPLES

After communism collapsed it became clear that the Solidarity ethos did not provide a workable set of principles for the future organization of society, or at least for such an organization as perceived by leaders who came to dominate the political arena. Entering the victorious stage of the anti-communist revolution, in other words becoming the ruling movement, seemed to demand a historical switch in the perception of goals and the principles of societal organization, putting more emphasis on its competitive structures and formal political organizations. The market economy, private property and representative democracy had to be brought into being. For that purpose, the Solidarity ethos, and Solidarity's internal organization and methods of acting, were inappropriate, in some aspects counter-productive. Intellectual circles came to realize that Solidarity itself was in a way the swan-song of Polish Romanticism.[7] Differently put, there has been a move away from the enriched, socialized idea of civil society toward the more limited classical notion emphasizing the rule of law, political citizenship and the freedom of economic action – all of them seen in terms of individual rather than group or community rights. The political climate amongst leaders has evolved in a direction opposed to such communal feelings formerly represented in Solidarity as respect for the dignity of labour, responsibility for the weak and defenceless, mutual help and an appreciation of basic human dignity.

Since 1989, the programme to reform the economy and to build a democratic state has been at the front of everyone's mind. On both fronts difficulties have emerged. The slow pace of economic reform and the split between the goals of politicians and popular sentiments became ever more obvious. Dissatisfaction with the state of the economy was particularly marked: government policies have led to high unemployment and a diminution in the standard of living. In these circumstances, society seemed to oscillate between apathy and rebellion. In factories that remained under public ownership, in hospitals and in schools, some groups of people withdrew from public life completely, while others organized militant strikes.

In July 1992 the accumulated dissatisfaction produced a big wave of strikes; further waves followed in the winter of 1992 and the spring of 1993. The rebellious workers refused to accept that they should pay a high price for their glorious victory over the communists. The most active wanted to take part in decisions determining the future shape of their factories and local communities. In contrast, those who were apathetic possibly saw no viable alternative to the path which had been chosen, the path leading to a society based on individual endeavour, risk and political bargaining, a society which was not envisaged in the Solidarity ethos.

In economics, all four successive Solidarity governments between 1989 and 1993 imposed neo-liberal discipline. Many of the results of this programme dissatisfied workers and led them to question the direction of reforms. In politics, on the other hand, the liberal programme of the leaders has been much more in accord with popular opinion. This is true, for example, regarding individual freedoms such as that of the press, of speech and of association. But public opinion, though unorganized, has shown clearly its disapproval of the political practices of the governing elite. The quarrels between leaders of the emerging parties, which have contributed to an inefficient party and government system, has been especially important in creating a negative image of government and of politics in general. In consequence, political participation has declined.

The failure of the neo-liberal programme for effectively transforming the economy, described below, has unexpectedly revitalized communal feelings and strategies. Those unable to participate in individualist strategies for arranging their own lives were returning to a modified version of the assumptions and modes of action of Solidarity in its earliest days. During the strikes, people voiced dissatisfaction with the method of privatization, which excludes them from negotiations and planning. They were still urging the government to represent them, and not to abandon them to impersonal market forces. They show no desire to become self-motivated individuals taking responsibility for their own lives. And in fact they have no resources to start their own businesses. Two sets of trades unions exemplify and favour these older communal attitudes. The first set, OPZZ, was made up of the unions of the former communist federation of unions. The second was the radical wing of former Solidarity, called Solidarity 80, which split with the core trade union movement because it perceived Solidarity's mainstream as too moderate in its fight against communism. The core of the

Solidarity trade union, NSZZ Solidarity, has been looking for a moderate position, whilst becoming ever more impatient with the government. Its programme could be seen as embracing elements of communitarianism, but the most striking feature of its position between 1989 and 1993 was the growing rift between it and subsequent governments on the one hand and the loss of membership on the other. The ordinary worker blames NSZZ Solidarity for inconsistency and for the inefficiency of its negotiations with the government.

From the rebellious factories and mines there emerges an interesting picture of how workers believe conflicts should be resolved and society should be governed. Workers urged Walesa as president to bypass the laws and to resolve industrial conflicts directly. The waves of strikes revealed three important elements in the outlook of militant Polish workers. First, they deliberately aimed to gain direct political influence in order to satisfy their economic interests. They wanted to circumvent NSZZ Solidarity so as to compel the government to change the laws covering industrial regulations instantly. Secondly, they were half-consciously recreating a sociopolitical identity, specific to workers, that had last been seen in 1980–81. They wanted to resurrect a political movement in defence of 'the common people'. They saw themselves as the avant-garde of the people, driven to oppose an incompetent and insensitive governmental elite. Thirdly, they were reactivating workers' communal ties through direct action. A strike creates a feeling of fellowship in the factory, of intimacy and of strong social cohesion. Workers across the country, including those who do not strike as well as those who do, tend to be hostile to all attempts to individualize their economic position, whether by management or by impersonal economic processes. They oppose processes selecting those who will stay at the job and those who will have to go. The threat of unemployment strengthens this anti-individualism. Among all their grievances, the one that filled them most with anger and despair was that they, the heroes of a revolution, seem to have become a forgotten class. So they were reactivating a kind of 'civic communal' attitude, this time disentangled somehow from the undifferentiated former Solidarity ethos.

What were the deepest causes of these developments? On the one hand, confusion reigned in the sphere of economic interests; on the other hand, politicians were unable to provide sound leadership. Let us consider these factors in turn.

THE DELAYED ARTICULATION OF
ECONOMIC INTERESTS

The pace and shape of the economic reforms since 1989 have not helped to strengthen an individualist, market-oriented capitalist mentality. Poland's basic economic structures have changed only very slowly. Large industries have not been privatized. The lack of domestic capital and the low interest shown by foreign capital in part account for this failure; but so too does the delay in implementing a 'popular privatization' scheme. Polish agriculture is actually in the same condition as it was before the revolution, divided into small and inefficient traditional farms. The government has had no money to help farmers to modernize. The only real change is in commerce, where a new class of small retail and wholesale traders has emerged. A thin stratum of people with large capital resources has been created; they mainly import goods from abroad and have little interest in domestic manufacturing. Governments have repeatedly announced their intention to transform services like health into semi-privatized undertakings, but this has not gone beyond mere words. All four Solidarity governments were slow to draw up programmes of change, and still slower to implement them.

It was assumed that with the introduction of a tough monetarist policy and the removal of state controls, a capitalist economy would establish itself smoothly and speedily. This was a belief in capitalism as a *deus ex machina*. Competition would press industrial structures to implement new technologies and to seek new foreign markets. Profit-seeking individuals and skilled managers would take a leading role in the whole process. Government involvement and the organized activities of groups of employees were not thought to be helpful to the process; the passive acquiescence of factory collectives was seen as desirable. Some social activists from the largest plants wanted to involve workers in the privatization process, by presenting them with detailed plans of changes; they were discouraged from this course of action.

As a result of these delays and discouragements, the Polish economy has only very slowly generated new ownership structures, new patterns of management and new economic strata typical of a private enterprise market economy. For more than three years, there was no organization to protect and promote the interests of middle-class businessmen and self-employed professionals. Small tradesmen have not been very keen to organize themselves, while the few larger capitalists have been more interested in setting up social clubs than business associations. Only recently have both groups of capitalists started creating official associations to contact government, so as to influence its decisions. Members of emerging business classes assume that government will not be much help in promoting their interests specifically, although overall its activities clearly benefit them.

The large majority of the working population was – and still is – employed in state-owned factories and state-run institutions. These employees cannot tell where their future interests lie. They are unable to answer questions like the following: What will my social position be in the future? In what way will that position determine my income? Where will it fit into the national economy? And what kind of national economic structure will best serve my future interests? Let me give one illustration. There are at least three ways of dealing with a big state-owned manufacturing enterprise. First, foreign capital may buy up the factory. Second, the factory may be kept under state ownership, but modernized to make it more efficient. Third, the factory may be sold to its own workers, to own and run it themselves. Each solution would shape the interests of the factory's workers in a completely different way. It is extremely difficult for an ordinary worker today to imagine which solution will be the best for him.

The situation in postcommunist countries shows how difficult it is for various strata to predict, let alone be able to control, their own economic destiny in an economy undergoing structural transformation. Differently put, a degree of certainty about how an economic system will develop is needed, not only for rational calculation, but also for embracing risky and innovative enterprises. After all, while the entrepreneur partly has the ability to shape his own destiny, he is at the same time at the mercy of larger social and economic forces. The same can be said about the trade union activist who organizes workers to take over an enterprise and create a cooperative. He also depends for success on the efforts of his fellow members, on the government's policy on cooperatives and on the effect of governmental policies more broadly on the economy.

This situation helps to explain why Polish workers and the employees of state institutions cling to their traditional view of industrial conflict. They still see the government as their adversary. The continuation of the old ownership structure drives them to press the government to satisfy their demands. They do not have the money to go into business on their own. This is another factor that prevents them from acting and becoming individualistic. So they are instead condemned to collective strategies of defending their own interests as they see them now. Alessandro Pizzorno has emphasized that there is always an element of group consciousness in calculating individual economic interest.[8] This is certainly true in a period of sustained change; uncertainty about future developments creates a climate favourable to sticking to collectively made perceptions of the situation. In his ability to grasp the situation, a person is assisted by those assumptions that are shared by the group. These perceptions may be right or wrong, but they nevertheless enhance the feeling of correctness in perceiving shared destiny. Those who did not strike themselves, but only sent signals of sympathy to the more combative sectors of the class, were also marked by this structure of sentiment.

The conflicts of 1989–93 were not inevitable. We can imagine a scenario in which intellectuals and politicians could see, even if only in outline, the shape workers' interests would take in the market economy and were able to propose ways of protecting those interests. There is a social democratic way of promoting workers' interests in a market economy. There is also a Christian democratic way. In Poland neither was considered in detail nor presented to workers as a feasible solution to the problems of moving from communism to democracy and to capitalism. Of course, it is possible to argue that, by their natures, neither doctrine would have been suitable for the period of transition. But nobody tried to prove this, or even simply to say it.

On the most general level, one can say that there were some possibilities of transforming the communal sentiments of Polish workers into communitarian ties. These chances were not seized by the Solidarity governments. As late as 1993 the coalition government led by the Democratic Union of Mrs Suchocka seemed to sense the possibility and necessity of an appeal to communitarian principles. Her government prepared the Social Pact which was then successfully negotiated and signed by the three main trade union organizations, OPZZ, NSZZ Solidarity and Solidarity 80. In this pact, workers were given a role in the privatization process at the factory level as well as a privileged proportion of the shares of newly privatized firms. The interests of those who would lose their jobs for longer periods, if not forever, were also taken into account. But this pact was negotiated too late; signing it did not prevent the collapse of the government in June 1993. It was ironic that the parliamentary motion to dismiss the government was put forward by NSZZ Solidarity. The fourth Solidarity government was brought down by fractions of historic Solidarity in alliance with the parties of the old order, that is, by the former communists of the Social Democracy of Respublica and the Polish Peasants' Party.

PARTIES IN CHAOS

In the situation I have described, the impulses from the structure of interests to political parties were very weak. Parties have emerged at the level of leadership, but not at the grass-roots level. The 'war at the top' waged by Walesa began the fragmentation of Solidarity, and this quickly accelerated. Just before the presidential and parliamentary elections in 1990–1, more than 100 would-be parties appeared on the Polish political scene. As a result, between 1991 and 1993 the Polish parliament was made up of 29 factions, only some of them with links with larger sections of the population. Most lacked real local branches. These political parties were not real parties because they served neither as an articulating channel nor as an organizational link between society at large and governmental bodies. They lacked definite political and economic programmes. What was missing on the Polish political scene in these years was any real responsiveness to the demands of the electorate and any responsibility for the country as a whole.

The structure of the party system clearly distinguishes Poland from Hungary. In Hungary there are four parties with relatively clear programmes, and these have maintained a stable relationship with each other. The system has produced a stable government which has lasted for more than three years, and which, despite many criticisms, has consistently pursued a programme of economic and constitutional reform. In contrast, Poland's four Solidarity governments jumbled programmes together out of elements suggested by various factions and by political personalities who happened to enter the coalition. Coalitions of leaders have changed constantly. Perhaps the situation is best typified by the government of Mrs Suchocka. After the government was first formed, it promised to present its political and economic programme within three weeks. This is the reverse of the order that we see in a Western parliamentary system, where accepting the main body of someone's programme is the precondition for electing them to lead the government.

Unlike Western societies, Poland's fragmented party system between 1989 and 1993 could not be mapped on a simple left-to-right political axis, as individual parties often combined elements from widely different parts of the spectrum. The many competing ideological divides in Polish politics also prevented the party system from coalescing into comprehensible larger units. There were six main ideological divisions cutting across the Polish party system (and they still exist, though several parties have started negotiations about unification). The first five divisions were between national and universal, confessional and secular, authoritarian and democratic, marketist and interventionist and populist and elitist. The sixth division is peculiar to former communist societies. It is between those demanding the purging of former communists from many or all areas of public life, and those who wish, in the phrase of Tadeusz Mazowiecki, to 'draw a thick line with the past'. I will call this divide that between communist-purging and communist-forgiving.

The national/universal divide separates parties by their approach to the nation's interests and icons. At one extreme we find parties warning that the national interest is in danger from foreign capital, from non-Poles (by which they tend to mean Jews) taking over Polish politics and from the Germans or the Russians, who are supposedly ready to take over some Polish territories once again. At the other extreme are parties which favour integrating Poland into Europe, which of course includes Germany, which seek to strengthen cultural ties with western Europe and which desire foreign capital to rescue the economy.

But each main divide is further complicated by subdivisions. Consider the nationalist position. Those on one side of a subdivision may simply urge caution in negotiating economic treaties with the European Union and want trade links with other countries on the best possible terms. On the other side are those who believe that Poland must defend herself from internal and external threats to her culture and her state, and who advocate keeping the Polish people in a permanent state of readiness against alleged enemies, even to the extent of creating paramilitary organizations.

One can find similar subdivisions within each main divide. Possibly the most important are the subdivisions within the confessional/secular opposition. It is widely accepted that in Poland

there is a growing conflict between secular politicians and politicians closely linked to the Catholic Church hierarchy; the latter
pushed for anti-abortion laws and for religion to be taught in
schools in a way that would discriminate against children from
non-believing families. However, there are many Catholics, from
prominent intellectuals to the rank and file, who oppose making
Poland a confessional state. They are for a moderate anti-abortion
law and argue against any discriminatory functions of religious
instruction in school. They are not traditional conservatives, but
rather progressive thinkers and activists, trying to bring the Catholic Church closer to Western thinking about the role of religion.
They are in open conflict with conservative Catholic politicians,
who insist on the need to place public life under the control of so-
called Christian values, or who combine a conservative obedience
to hierarchy with a nationalist hatred of 'alien people' threatening
Polish culture and faith.

There are even subdivisions within the divide between marketists
and interventionists. Among the marketists are those who propose
completely freeing the nascent forces of capitalism and the market
from any control, and those who accept the need for a governmental guiding hand in the transition to capitalism and the market
economy. Meanwhile, interventionists themselves are divided
between those who want society to maintain a safety net for the
disadvantaged and those who want to postpone it until better days.

The populist/elitist divide, though latently present in 1991–2,
fully crystallized during the electoral campaign of 1993. Populism
had been steadily strengthening in some quarters of NSZZ Solidarity since the strikes of 1991. It became visible with the open
pronouncements of some regional and factory leaders in 1993, including leaders from Warsaw and from the Katowice region. These
leaders introduced 'us' and 'them' terminology reminiscent of the
image of socio-political division that existed in communist times.
However, populism became an open and aggressive ideology in
another political entity, the 'Samobrona' movement that emerged
as the most combative force in 1993. Its leader, Mr Lepper, was the
most outspoken electoral compaigner. He pretended to defend
farmers and poor city-dwellers from the 'stupid', 'anti-people' and
'anti-national' economic policy of the elite. In contrast, the elitist
position was not well articulated, although it was present in the
unvoiced assumption that people had to be demobilised in order to
open the way for economic reforms; in parallel, the business of
politics should be left to politicians and the emerging class of big

capitalists. This was – and still is – the position of leaders of neo-liberal persuasion as well as of many influential journalists.

There is a very low degree of convergence between the main divides within the Polish party system. Let me give some examples. It is less common than is often thought that a politician who is very nationalistic will be strongly confessional and strongly authoritarian too. Somebody who fights for workers' interests will not necessarily oppose reforms to introduce capitalism. And a politician who wants to give the president more power, and even create a more authoritarian state, need not also favour restricting citizen's political rights, including that to free speech.

A further element of incongruence was that of factional divergences within several parties. Formalized factions were clearly present within Democratic Union: one of them is of left-liberal, another conservative and a third of Christian Democratic persuasion.[9] Within the Social Democracy of Respublica, there were at least two groups, one believing in the adequacy of neo-liberal economic policy (thereby making them similar to the neo-liberal Liberal Democratic Congress) whilst the other stressed egalitarianism. Within parties of the 'right', some groups emphasized anti-communism, others adherence to tradition and to the Catholic Church, whilst still others emphasized the importance of national virtue. The presence of such varied groups caused incessant splits and changing alliances, and the consequent creation of new factions and party constellations.

Another aspect which has to be emphasized because it is neglected by foreign observations of the Polish scene is the following. It seems that these ideological divides are much stronger between politicians themselves than amongst ordinary people. The virtual disconnection of the parliamentary parties from society at large keeps the interactions weak between leaders and led. It is true that leaders partly reflect confessionalism, nationalism and anti-Semitism which exist within the population. But their ability in turn to reinforce these emotions and prejudices in the population is limited. People are busy dealing with their everyday lives and problems; they are not very susceptible to manipulation by politicians because they do not pay very much attention to them. So the alienation of leaders from the masses, whilst not on the whole a positive feature of the political system, may here produce a positive result.

It is a negative aspect of Poland's present political situation that parties are weak in interacting with various strata, representing them and producing stable links to the electorate. There are only a few exceptions to this generalization, the most obvious being those of parties of the old order. The strongest link to a definite social stratum of the electorate was that of the Polish Peasants Party. It had represented the interests of private farmers under communism, to the extent that this was possible, and in the process had made many discreditable compromises. After 1989, it changed ideologically whilst maintaining most of its infrastructure of organization. Local chapters and activists continue party activity, organize elections and are bearers of 'continuity' and 'renewal'. The Social Democracy of Respublica also has organizational infrastructure at the grass-roots level, but its link to workers is not direct, being heavily dependent on OPZZ, its principal ally in government.

Political parties that branched out from Solidarity have not developed significant memberships nor have they created any body of local activists. The Democratic Union alone has some local chapters with active members, although the Confederation of Independent Poland is making efforts, especially in Silesia, to recruit and organize locally. It is worth noting, however, that NSZZ Solidarity has links to fellow workers in factories.

PARTIES OF CIVIL SOCIETY AND PARTIES OF SPIRITUAL COMMUNITIES

Standing back from the whole situation, it seems that, notwithstanding chaotic divisions, two general types of party are in the process of formation. The national/universal and confessional/secular divides belong to the category which produce parties unified by symbols rather than by interests. The same is true of the communist-purging/communist-forgiving divide. If a party puts in the front of its programme religious or nationalist ideology, it is a party of a spiritual community. It promotes communal ties and attitudes. At the centre of its ideology are values which cannot be renounced under the pressure of economic interests or particular circumstances. Values are not a subject of negotiation. A convinced patriot will not use national values as bargaining chips. The same is true of a Catholic and his or her religious beliefs. The marketist/interventionist divide produces parties of a completely different type. They are more prone to trade and bargain, to accommodate the interests of different strata. Their ideology does not consider membership of a social group to be exclusive, fixed for life either by birth or through any sort of ritual. This second group of parties is that of civil society.

Let me give some examples. The Liberal Democratic Congress favours neo-liberal economic policy and a secular polity. It clearly belongs to the civil society type of party, albeit of the 'right'. The Social Democracy of Respublica concentrates its pronouncements almost solely on economic issues, distancing itself from any general ideology. So it too is a party of civil society, but with an allegiance to the 'left'. The Labour Union and the Polish Peasants Party also deserve to be seen as 'leftist' parties of civil society; the 'rightist' Conservative Party falls within this camp as well, for its espousal of national and Christian values is moderate.

To the communal parties belong several nationalist and confessional parties. Amongst the former are the Confederation of Independent Poland and the Movement of the Third Respublica: both these parties consider all civil society parties to be traitors to the nation and an ever-present danger to the very identity of Poles. They fight also against the alleged domination of former communists in banking and industry, and are equally opposed to the 'cosmopolitan' attitudes of liberals. The National Christian Union has a strong confessional faction whose opinions tend to drown out all moderation. This faction promotes the active role of the Catholic Church in public life and fights for the establishment of Christian values in state law. The same policy is promoted by the Party of Christian Democrats and many other small parties claiming to be Catholic. Every party of spiritual community tends to loathe liberals, reform communists, socialists and social-liberals – for all are suspected of 'libertarianism', atheism, lack of patriotism and cosmopolitanism.

The Solidarity ethos, which was once considered to be a powerfully integrating force, clearly no longer exists. In its place have emerged conflicting ideological currents, with real potential for organizing society along different lines. It is accordingly vital to ask which type of party will dominate in the coming years. Will the crystallization of larger parties be dominated by the national/universalist divide, by the split between confessional and secular or by the opposition between market and intervention? Will the parties of civil society or those of spiritual community gain the upper hand?

LIBERALS, COMMUNITARIANS AND THE PROSPECTS
FOR POLAND

A prominent Catholic intellectual, Stefan Wilkanowicz, warned quite early on that Polish political culture was moving in a very dangerous direction.[10] The complex that he called Christian-National-Solidaristic was waning, and the more individualistic Utilitarian-Darwinist complex was waxing. He openly denounced the Darwinist component as glorifying ruthless competition and the survival of the fittest. Being Catholic, he believed that the rise of the Utilitarian-Darwinist complex held many dangers for society's future cohesion and moral standards.

In the light of recurring strikes, the strength of this individualistic complex, at least among the masses, looks doubtful. On the other hand, it seems impossible to go back to the complex he called Christian-National-Solidaristic. In fact, this complex – in effect, the Solidarity ethos – was also composed of elements drawn from the classical model of civil society. Anyway, the new situation demands reconsidering the various possible roads to the future democratic order.

Poland has a serious deficit in intermediate groups that link society and state organs in a democratic way. Those associative ties typical of Western civil societies are absent. The slow pace of economic reforms and chaotic politics have created a vacuum which produces rebels or sceptics rather than committed supporters and devoted activists. It seems that the economic and political doctrine of orthodox liberalism is not adequate to produce legitimacy for the emerging system. I believe that in the coming years doctrines with strong communitarian aspects have a greater potential for producing legitimating beliefs.

Allow me to refer to the debate currently going on between liberals and communitarians in political philosophy in England and the United States, as initiated by John Rawls and critically followed by Michael Walzer, Charles Taylor and Michael Sandel.[11] Such critics say that orthodox liberals locate the state's legitimacy in its ability to secure and promote individual freedoms. The fundamental freedom is the individual's right to choose and pursue his own individual idea of 'the good life'. But for individuals to have this freedom, they not only need to be free to choose their own concept of 'the good life'; they also need the resources to pursue it. The communitarian critique pointed out not only that there are shared ideas of 'the good life' woven into social life, but also that access to specific goods that people want in a given culture is unequal. This controversy is evidently linked to the concept of shared tradition, on the one hand, and to the contemporary role of the state, on the other. Liberals argue that the state should remain neutral, with respect for individual ideals. Communitarians, on the other hand, say that both voluntary associations and state agencies are obliged to help people in finding the resources for achieving decent lives and social citizenship.

Michael Walzer argues that one could read liberalism in a communitarian manner: 'A good liberal (or social democratic) state enhances the possibility for cooperative coping.'[12] He has in mind first of all the obligation of the state as a 'larger union' to arrange new institutions in order to help groups and communities to cope with their problems. For example, the state should, if the need emerges, redress the balance of power between employers and trade unions, as did the Wagner Act, or introduce tax exemptions to encourage donations which, in turn, allow schools, hospitals and churches to help the needy. On the most general level, Charles Taylor links the legitimation of the modern democratic system and the formation of modern individual identity with the shared perception of life as a supreme good:

> This (individual) identification exists where the common form of life is seen as a supremely important good, so that its continuance and flourishing matters to the citizens for its own sake and not just instrumentally to their several individual goods or as the sum total of these individual goods. The common life has a status of this kind when it is a crucial element in the members' identity, in the modern, Eriksonian sense of the term.[13]

This brief theoretical discussion allows me to analyse the socio-political situation in Poland. It seems that the legitimacy of the state in the coming years can be better secured by theoretical and practical reference to communitarian principles than to those of orthodox liberalism. People themselves, without the help of state policies, will not be able to pursue their own life plans. On top of liberty, they need decent housing, employment, just industrial relations, education for their children, health care and social support. A liberal economic order conceived in an orthodox way does not provide the mechanisms to translate political freedom into the socioeconomic means for each family to pursue its own definition of the good life. Moreover, people who have experienced the emotional arousal of the Solidarity days are longing for some cohe-

sive and justificatory ideology. To them the practical policy measures should have a reference to values which are socially accepted
and commonly cherished. The expectation of value transparency is
a legacy of Solidarity that lingers on. In the light of both older and
more recent Polish traditions, moving towards some version of
communitarian philosophy and socio-political practice may provide a more easily achieved accommodation of workers and employers to the capitalist economy. A communitarian arrangement
may also provide a more certain road to the legitimation of the new
democratic order.

The contemporary communitarian version of social thought has
some affinity to socialist ideas.[14] But, more importantly, it has also
been strongly articulated, and in an elaborated form, within the
modern Catholic doctrine of the social market economy and of
the social functions of the responsible state.[15] The affinity at the
theoretical level between the social teaching of the Catholic Church
and the social-democratic type of communitarian doctrine could
lead to intensive debate and mutual stimulation. But it could
also exert pressure 'from both sides' to put these communitarian
principles into practice. Such a development could find support
in genuine contributions to social philosophy by some Polish
thinkers.[16]

What are the implications of these remarks for the rearrangement
of the party structure? One can say that there exists in Poland an
opening for a strong and well-articulated party which would claim
to represent the spiritual community of Catholics, and yet not
necessarily be a party primarily of a conservative, confessional
orientation, but rather be a party of a social orientation, for which
both individual freedom and the social protection of the needy, are
vital. Both the 'centre' faction within the Democratic Union and
the 'moderate' faction within the National Christian Union may
claim to be such a party in embryo. However, both factions are
slow to articulate their fundamental premisses. In many smaller
Christian parties there is also a growing insistence on the introduction of the practical social programmes implemented by local
communities. On the whole, among the circles of progressive
Catholics there is growing support for the operation of free market
forces, however modified by the principles of social justice and by
the demand for employment and for the dignity of all kinds of
work. The inspiration of Vatican II has been distinctively
communitarian.

In contemporary Poland, there is also an opening for a party that
will invoke, firstly, secular traditions and, secondly, social memo-

ries of the associative actions of workers, doctors and teachers, in forming a modern social democratic programme. This I would call the revival of the communitarian approach which was woven into the Polish legacy by the so-called 'organic' work of the Polish intelligentsia in the nineteenth century, and by the Polish socialist movement at the beginning of this century. The socialist doctrine in its social democratic version is communitarian.

Some parties exist which try to link their programmes to the legacy of the pre-war socialist party (Polish Socialist Party) or to the employee-interest oriented tendencies within the Solidarity movement (Labour Union). These parties are haunted by the practices of 'real socialism' and have only a potential appeal to workers. The Social Democracy of Respublica has also signalled that it is accepting associative relationships and becoming 'communitarian' – but it is a party pulled in many different directions.

Communitarian aspects, under the name of the 'agrarist ideology', were rather strong in the pre-war Polish Peasants Party, allowing its leaders to call the party a social movement. Reassimilating these communitarian elements into the programme of the contemporary party, after years of unhappy compromise with the communists, is a vital and immediate necessity. However, the styles of thought of party activists and members has been changing only slowly. The immediate pressures of purely economic interests push the party to act rather as an 'interest group' than as a 'peasant movement' possessing broad social and cultural goals. Thus, there are forces which need to be balanced by a deliberate effort to reintroduce communitarian aspects in the ideology and practice of the peasant party.

On the whole, the potential for communitarian ties to develop seems greater than party leaders and activists imagine. The functioning of communitarian parties in the emerging political system may be amenable to social cohesion and responsibility in many spheres of life. Because of the nature of Polish history, they may give meaning to people's involvement in democracy. They may activate people to civic actions. Moreover, they may contribute to the development of beliefs bestowing civil legitimacy on the state.

LESSONS OF THE 1993 ELECTION

In September 1993 the Polish political elite received an important signal about popular perception of its leadership in the process of transformation. Alarmist interpretations of electoral results suggested the imminent return of communists to full power, abandoning capitalistic market reforms and forgetting about democratic institutions. Optimistic interpretations point to the defeat of the nationalist, confessional and populist parties. More moderate assessments point to two irrefutable facts: the shift of public opinion 'to the left' and the end of governments formed from the ranks of the once all-powerful Solidarity.

The two parties of the old regime won the election: 36 per cent of votes cast (20.4 per cent and 15.4 per cent respectively) gave them 66 per cent of the seats in the Lower Chamber. This was due both to the failure of several parties to pass the 5 per cent threshold and to the method of allocating seats in multi-member districts. This methodology was designed to make it easier for large parties to govern. The results of the 1991 elections based on proportional representation and those that resulted from the new electoral laws are contrasted in table 1.

The analysts of electoral behaviour and results agree on one point: the victory of the Social Democracy of Respublica and Polish Peasants Party was the result of a loss of trust in Solidarity government. This was confirmed by many public opinion polls. Today the same polls indicate a high level of confidence in Mr Pawlak's government.[17]

Contrary to the most gloomy predictions, the coalition government of the Social Democracy of Respublica and the Polish Peasants Party does not intend to abandon economic reform nor to curb democracy. The state budget prepared for 1994, and presented to the parliament on 29 December 1993, is informed by tough monetarist principles. It evoked the 'restrained' approval of neo-liberal economists.[18] As the new budget indicates, there will be more continuity than change in overall policy. There will be slightly more protection for farmers, a little bit more concern for industrial policy and several attempts to help pensioners, the unemployed and the poor. There will be many tasks to be considered and more to reconsider. Many of them have been delayed for too long.[19]

Here we arrive at a more general question: why is Poland entering a post-Solidarity period, that is, why is it abandoning the four-year period of rule by noble and economically competent democrats? Some partial answers to this complex question can be given immediately. They have been already formulated by some thoughtful leaders of the Democratic Union, the party which feels

Table 5.1 Polish popular elections, 1991 and 1993: number of seats in the Lower Chamber

Political Parties	1991	1993
UD (The Democratic Union)	62	74
SLD (The Democratic Left Alliance)*	58	171
PSL (Polish Peasants Party)	50	132
ZCnN (National Christian Union)	48	–
KPN (Confederation of Independent Poland)	46	22
KLD (Liberal Democratic Congress)	36	–
PC (Centre Alliance)	32	–
NSZZ Solidarity	26	–
HPL (Popular Agreement)	19	–
RdR (Movement for the Republic)	18	–
PPG (Polish Economic Programme)	12	–
SLCh (Popular Christian Party)	10	–
The German minority	7	4
UP (Labour Union)	7	41
PChD (Party of Christian Democrats)	6	–
ChD (Christian Democracy)	5	–
UPR (Union of Realistic Politics)	3	–
BBWR (Non-Party Bloc for Reforms)	0	16
Non-organized	15	–
Total	460	460

* The Democratic Left Alliance joins together Social Democracy of Respublica, OPZZ and some other minor organizations.

responsible for the failure of the Solidarity government. The explanations given have some affinity to the analyses contained in this essay. One may summarize them as follows. Instead of continuing the mobilization of groups and communities that had marked the post-revolutionary period, leaders chose to emphasize demobilization instead. Such leaders believed that individualist rather than group strategies were more appropriate for achieving economic reform as understood by neo-liberal theory. However, because few people had the resources and entrepreneurial spirit required by that theory, leaders of the state unintentionally started to rely ever more on adminstrative means in order to achieve reform. Now the key question concerning the transformation of the postcommunist economy lies precisely here. What method should be used? Which method suits this strange reality? What method will work with people deprived of individual resources, who have recently gone through an exciting collective experience – to say nothing of being the possessors of very particular historic traditions?

Jacek Kuron wrote a particularly penetrating analysis in the aftermath of Solidarity's demise. He argued that it was foolish of the Solidarity elite to give up the possibility of transforming the general movement into separate, highly motivated movements, aiming at reforming various speheres of life, from schools and industry to hospitals and recreation services. The author suggests that it is now time to return to group activity, so as to design and implement specific programmes. He sees the fusion of governmental inspiration and coordination with new citizens' movements:

> We have many specific programmes, some of which have already been elaborated in detail: the Social and Industrial Pact, the project for the reform of state and local administration, the plan to rearrange the health services, the new 'housing order', the plan to combat unemployment ... Without social movements, the transformation of the country will take decades, meanwhile pushing people into poverty, distress and revolt.[20]

This is a vision involving both government and people in a programme designed to create communitarian ties. This goal may be within reach today, provided that political leaders rethink their positions. Until recently they were more preoccupied with 'power politics' than with 'social politics'. The reduction in the number of parties at the recent election could exert a very positive impact on Polish development. But will small parties accept this fate?

Many sets of talks designed to unify the small parties have already begun. Out of the dozen small rightist nationalist and confessional parties may emerge three larger blocs. President Walesa has declared publicly that he wishes to help the 'right leg' become stronger. Such integration of the political scene is needed to make politics mature and healthy. Integration of the confessional and nationalistic parties poses the problem dealt with in this essay, that is, the role of potentially aggressive and divisive communal feelings. The 1993 elections brought a result that nobody had expected, namely the elimination of this type of party from parliament; the Confederation of Independent Poland is the sole party that now represents this position.

One could interpret the result as a sign of a profound historical transformation of the Polish nation. This would suggest that we had made a major step along a civilizational route leading towards 'civil society'. This conclusion seems to me to be premature. Conjunctural elements were powerfully favourable in this election. In September 1993, Poland was not threatened by Russia nor by Germany, making this the first time for centuries that the Polish people have not felt themselves to be in geopolitical peril. The victory of Zhirinovsky in Russia has since changed the geopolitical perceptions of the Polish people. Another relevant consideration in this respect are perceptions about the West. Nationalist sentiments may well be strengthened should the European Union maintain restrictions against Polish agricultural products and light industrial goods and NATO refuse to take new members. This last move might be perceived by Poles as a second Yalta. It is important always to remember that nationalism in Poland derives less from expansionist dreams than from the feeling of having been abandoned by trusted allies.

The weakness of confessional parties may prove to be equally short lived. The issues of abortion and religious instruction had been dealt with by the time of the election. But combative sentiments remain on both sides of the confessional/secular divide. They may yet resurface. In general, transitional politics remain volatile. Something that seems of marginal significance may suddenly become a major political issue. If the confessional and nationalist militants create viable parties, efficient in organizational matters and able to propagate ideas of seductive simplicity, the opposition and conflict between communal and civil projects for public (and so also for private) life may return. Any untoward events in international affairs would make this scenario all the more likely. All in all, efforts at developing communitarian attitudes are vital, and are the best way, in Polish circumstances, in which to consolidate civil society.

NOTES

1 F. Tönnies, *Community and Association*, Routledge and Kegan Paul, London, 1955; M. Weber, *Economy and Society*, University of California Press, Berkeley, Cal., 1968.

2 J. Rawls, *A Theory of Justice*, Harvard University Press, Cambridge, Mass., 1971.

3 My use of this term owes much to B. Anderson, *Imagined Communities*, Verso, London, 1983.

4 My conceptualization of communitarian ties has been influenced by the recent

Western debate between 'communitarians' and 'liberals'. For a helpful overview of the debate, see S. Mulhall and A. Swift, *Liberals and Communitarians*, Blackwell, Oxford, 1992.

5 S. Kowalski, *Krytyka solidarnosciowego rozumu* [A Critique of Soidarity Reason], Pen Publishers, Warsaw, 1990.

6 J. Habermas, *The Structural Transformation of the Public Sphere*, Polity Press, Cambridge, 1989; A. Arato, 'Civil Society Against the State: Poland, 1980–1', *Telos*, no. 47, 1981; E. Shils, 'The Virtue of Civil Society', *Government and Opposition*, vol. 26, 1991; Z. Pelczynski, 'Solidarity and the Rebirth of Civil Society', in J. Keane, ed., *Civil Society and the State*, Verso, London, 1988; M. Kennedy, 'The Intelligentsia in the Constitution of Civil Society and Postcommunist Regimes in Hungary and Poland', *Theory and Society*, vol. 21, 1992.

7 M. Janion, *Projekt krytyki fantazmatycznej* [The Project of a Phantasmatic Critique], Pen Publishers, Warsaw, 1991, and 'Koniec epoki?' [The End of an Epoch?], *Zycie Warszawy*, 7 and 9 December, 1991.

8 A. Pizzorno, 'On the Rationality of Democratic Choice', *Telos*, no. 63, 1985.

9 One of these factions (a conservative one) left the Democratic Union at the end of 1992.

10 S. Wilkanowicz, 'O nowy ksztalt wartosci' [For a new shape of values], *Znak*, no. 438, 1991.

11 Rawls, *A Theory of Justice*; M. Sandel, *Liberalism and the Limits of Justice*, Cambridge University Press, Cambridge, 1982; M. Walzer, *Spheres of Justice*, Basic Books, New York, 1983, and 'The Communitarian Critique of Liberalism', *Political Theory*, vol. 18, 1990; C. Taylor, 'Alternative Futures: Identity and Alienation in Twentieth-Century Canada', in A. Cairns and C. Williams, eds, *Constitutionalism, Citizenship and Society in Canada*, University of Toronto Press, Toronto, 1985, and *Sources of the Self*, Harvard University Press, Cambridge, 1990.

12 Walzer, 'The Communitarian Critique of Liberalism', p. 19.

13 Taylor, 'Alternative Futures', p. 213.

14 D. Miller, 'In What Sense Must Socialism Be Communitarian?', *Social Philosophy and Policy*, vol. 6, 1989; J. Israel, 'Sweden: The Rise and Decline of a Welfare State', *International Review of Sociology, Monographic Section. Advanced Societies at the Threshold of the Third Millennium: Status and Perspectives*, Borla, Rome, 1992.

15 John Paul II, *Laborem Exercens*, Lublin, Catholic University Press, 1986, and *Centisimus Annus*, Wroclaw Archdiocese Bookstore Press, Wroclaw, 1991.

16 T. Mazowiecki, 'Spotkania Chrzescijanstwa z ideami socjalistycznymi i kontrowersje miedzy nimi' [Encounters of Christianity with Socialist Ideas and the Controversies between Them], in W. Wesolowski, ed., *Losy idei socjalistycznych i wyzwania wspolczesnosci* [The Fate of Socialist Ideas and the Challenges of Modern Times], Polish Association of the Club of Rome, Warsaw, 1990; J. Strzelecki, *Kontynuacje (2)* [Continuations (2)], Panstwowy Instytut Wydawniczy, Warsaw, 1974.

17 L. Kolarska-Bobinska and M. Glowacki, ' "My" i "Oni" dwanascie lat pozniej'

["Us" and "Them" twelve years later], *Gazeta Wyborcza* [Electoral Gazette], 8 December 1993.

18 'Wystapienie premiera, ocena poslow' [Statement by the Prime Minister, Evaluation by Deputies], *Rzeczypospolita*, 30 December 1993.

19 W. Wesolowski, 'In Quest of Strategy', *Polish Sociological Bulletin*, no. 3/4, 1992.

20 J. Kuron, 'Rynek z ludzka twarza' [The Market with a Human Face], *Gazeta Wyborcza* [Electoral Gazette], 20–21 November 1993.

6

Civic Nation, Civil Society, Civil Religion

Christopher G. A. Bryant

Given their salience in nineteenth- and twentieth-century history and popular consciousness, nations, as distinct from nationalisms, have been surprisingly undertheorized. In terms of both individual identity and collective action, nations have figured at least as prominently as class – even if the much more voluminous social science literature on class would lead one to suppose otherwise. No doubt one reason for this is that the intellectual content of nationalist writings has seldom impressed social scientists of any political allegiance. Romantics, in particular, tend to leave rationalists cold; nationalisms are real enough but nations themselves often seem dubious entities. Gellner, for example, has written an erudite and judicious book on *Nations and Nationalism* which offers a typology of nationalisms but no clear conception of nation.[1] He skirts the issue entertainingly without ever quite deciding how to address it. Such diffidence is no longer tolerable. If men and women believe entities to be real, they have real consequences. Relative inattention to nation continues to cost us dear as we struggle to come to terms with the dissolution of the Soviet Union and the former Yugoslavia and the horrors of ethnic cleansing in the Caucasus and Bosnia-Hercegovina. Is any conception of nation at the heart of any claim for nationhood made by any political activist, intellectual or social scientist as defensible as any other?

In this essay I want to review and develop further some of the theorizing of nation that does exist. In particular, I want both to sharpen the analytical distinction between civic and ethnic nations and to commend the virtues of civility and an inclusive civil society which are features of a civic nation. In other words, I want to combine social science with political philosophy and embrace the double hermeneutic – that is, that mechanism which interconnects the world as constituted by social scientists and the world as constituted, in this case, by citizens. In the course of this exercise I will attempt to clarify the relationship between the concepts of civic nation, civil society and civil religion.

CIVIC AND ETHNIC NATIONS

According to Weber, a nation is a 'community of sentiment, which would find its adequate expression only in a state of its own, and which thus normally strives to create one'.[2] 'Objective' bases for such communities include race, language, religion, customs, political memory and experience, all of which Weber treats as components of 'culture'. In addition there is a 'subjective dimension' to nation which has to do with consciousness and lived experience; Weber refers to solidarity and pathos. Combining the objective and the subjective, Weber treats nations as constructions which some make successfully and others do not. Each is constructed in a unique way and has an identity of its own. A nation exists, then, where people succeed with a claim to be one by securing recognition of it from others; in this respect nations are relational. A nation is also a *Gemeinschaft* and intellectuals are important in forming the language of solidarity; whereas the state is a *Gesellschaft*, an instrument of politicians. Nations usually need a state to protect their integrity and interests; states usually need a nation if they are to command the allegiance of the individual. There speaks the German nationalist.

Weber is a good starting-point for a theoretical discussion of nation because he insists that nations are communities of sentiment, raises questions about the who and the how of their construction and connects them to states without suggesting that there is a one-to-one relationship. At the same time he does not make race or ethnicity a necessary element in the formation of a nation, even if it is a frequent one.

Of contemporary writers, Anderson is the one who most strikingly repeats the notion that nations are constructions, or, in his now celebrated term, 'imagined communities'. According to Anderson, a nation is 'an imagined political community' and it is 'imagined as both inherently limited and sovereign'.[3] It is imagined because no member ever meets most others, yet 'in the minds of each lives the image of their communion'.[4] It is a community because it is imagined as a horizontal comradeship, a fraternity, capable of eliciting love, selflessness, even, in some circumstances, a readiness to give one's life. There can be an altruism in nationalism. It is imagined as limited because the community has finite boundaries even where these are contested. In other words – and in contrast to, say, the self-conception of pre-Meiji Japan – a nation is one among others. Finally, it is imagined as sovereign 'because the concept was born in an age in which Enlightenment and Revolution were destroying the legitimacy of the divinely-ordained, hierarchical dynastic realm'.[5] The sovereign community is self-determining, and the 'gage and emblem' of its freedom is the sovereign state.[6]

It is not practical here to explore the contentious issue of how historically the nation came to be imaginable in Europe and elsewhere. Instead I want to raise other questions. Who imagines national community? Who responds? What materials enter into imaginings and their representation? What are the implications for democracy, statehood and pluralism?

One paradoxical answer to who imagines is 'nationalists', or as Gellner memorably put it, 'Nationalism is not the awakening of nations to self-consciousness: it invents nations where they do not exist'.[7] Nineteenth-century Italian nationalism is an obvious example. Anderson concurs but warns that the association of invention with fabrication could misleadingly imply falsity and forgery; there are no natural, authentic or true nations.[8] Another answer is the promoters of high culture, above all those who promote the literary, public and occupational use of erstwhile vernacular languages – in short, intellectuals – especially where, as Hroch stresses, the majority population is of a different ethnic community from the ruling minority.[9] Those who respond are those who have an interest in doing so whether in terms of opportunities for advancement in work and politics, or in terms of the publicly authenticated articulation of a culture which resonates with their own experience of land, labour and oppression and the tales of their forebears.

The factors Weber connects as 'culture' provide the potential material for national imaginings. I have space to make only two points about them. First, Anthony D. Smith has emphasized the ethnic origins of nations.[10] But, as Gellner has pointed out, there were and are more *ethnies*, or ethnic communities, than there are nations; of itself ethnicity does not explain how and why some claims to nationhood succeed, others fail and others that we might imagine were not even made.[11] The ethnic origins of some nations are also, by all accounts, complicated. The United States provides an obvious example, but Britain is another. Second, in their historical remembering and forgetting, nations are meta-narratives which connect past with present and present with future. Anderson has given the example of Switzerland: 'In 1891, amidst novel jubilees marking the 600th anniversary of the Confederacy of Schwyz, Obwalden and Nidwalden, the Swiss state "decided on" 1291 as the date of the "founding" of Switzerland.'[12] Mickiewicz and other nineteenth-century Polish romantics in exile from their partitioned homeland provide another example. Their messianic allegory in which Poland, the 'Christ among nations', suffered, is crucified but will rise again for Europe's redemption has given a particular slant to Polish history and understandings of national destiny. Indeed, it could well be that meta-narratives of nation retain their hold for many people even in a postmodern age in which so many other totalizing notions of reason and faith, politics and religion, have forfeited their dominion.

Weber expected most nations to seek a state to protect their interests and most states to promote a nation to enhance their legitimacy, but he allows the possibility of stateless nations and nationless (or multinational) states. Scotland is a stateless nation; Prussia was a nationless state and the Soviet Union a multinational one. Nineteenth-century nationalism, by contrast, identified nation and state in the nation-state. Similar thinking in the twentieth century has given us such misnomers as the League of Nations and the United Nations.

Surprisingly, there are social scientists who endorse the conflation of nation and state. Giddens is perhaps the most prominent contemporary example.

By a 'nation' I refer to a collectivity existing within a clearly demarcated territory, which is subject to a unitary administration, reflexively monitored both by the internal state apparatus and those of other states ... A 'nation' ... only exists when a state has a unified administrative reach over the territory over which sovereignty is claimed.[13]

This is, I think, a mistake. It disallows McCrone's careful account of Scotland as a stateless nation, and it requires that Yugoslavia be regarded as a nation until its fragmentation in 1991–2 despite the 1971 census returns in which only 1.3 per cent of the population gave their nationality as Yugoslav.[14] It also excludes the process of nation-building undertaken by newly independent states in Africa. It even distorts British history. As Colley points out, there was no British nation at the time of the Treaty of Union of England and Scotland in 1707; but a nation had been forged by the time Victoria acceded to the throne in 1837.[15] What Giddens properly highlights is the completion of a world state system – there can be no opting out as the invasion of Tibet by China indicated in 1953, or the creation of the United Arab Emirates confirmed in 1971 – but he wrongly presents it as a world *nation*-state system.

The conflation of nation and state is also politically contentious. It suggests that national interests can never be secured outside the formula of 'one nation–one state', thereby endorsing the fragmentation of multinational states, the claims of irredentists and the protestations of those who deny the possibility of being, for example, both English or Scottish and British. It underwrites both the ethnic conception of the nation-state and the use of political religion and other devices by the state to create the state-nation, regardless of evidence that the former can issue in ethnic cleansing and the latter in Soviet-style sacralization of representations of a state-imposed new order.

Is there, in any case, an alternative to the ethnic nation, with or without a state? Kohn has argued that the middle classes in Britain, France and America who came to power in the late eighteenth century generated a rational and associational 'western' (i.e. west of the Rhine) conception of the nation: an association of human beings living in a common territory under the same government and laws.[16] East of the Rhine, by contrast, the middle classes were relatively insignificant. Instead, intellectuals, who were excluded from power, promoted an 'eastern' conception of the nation, a seamless organic unity with a mystical 'soul' and 'mission' which only vernacular intellectuals could define. It is easy, as Smith has pointed out,[17] to identify exceptions to Kohn's western/eastern division – Irish nationalism usually favours an organic conception of the nation, whereas Masaryk and some other Czech nationalists inclined to the rational ideal – but recast as a distinction between the civic and the ethnic conception of the nation it throws light on many past and present disputes. Between 1871 and 1914, for example, the republicans in the French Third Republic subscribed to the civic version whilst their monarchist and Catholic opponents favoured the ethnic and organic.

Smith has developed Kohn into a typology of nationalisms. I shall shift the emphasis to conceptions of nation and give my own examples. First, Smith distinguishes two types of *territorial nationalism*, the pre-independence and the post-independence.

1(a) 'Pre-independence movements whose concept of the nation is mainly civic and territorial will seek first to eject foreign rulers and substitute a new state-nation for the old colonial territory; these are anti-colonial nationalisms.'[18] The revolt of the Netherlands provides an old example and the Congress movement in India a more recent one.

1(b) 'Post-independence movements whose concept of the nation remains basically civic and territorial will seek to bring together and integrate into a new political community often disparate ethnic populations and to create a new "territorial nation" out of the old colonial state; these are integral nationalisms.'[19] The United States offers an old example, and many African countries more recent ones. The ANC and the other parties to the Conference for a Democratic South Africa will have to try to accomplish a territorial nation after the elections based on universal suffrage in April 1994.

Second, Smith differentiates two types of *ethnic nationalism*, the pre-independence and the post-independence:

2(a) 'Pre-independence movements whose conception of the nation is basically ethnic and genealogical will seek to secede from a larger political unit (or secede and gather together in a designated ethnic homeland) and set up a new political "ethno-nation" in its place; these are secession and diaspora nationalisms.'[20] Polish nationalism in the nineteenth century supplies an example of the former, as does Croat nationalism today; Zionism is the classic example of the latter.

2(b) 'Post-independence movements whose concept of the nation is basically ethnic and genealogical will seek to expand by including ethnic "kinsmen" outside the present boundaries of the "ethno-nation" and the lands they inhabit or by forming a much larger "ethno-national" state through the union of culturally and ethnically similar ethno-national states; these are irredentist and "pan" nationalisms.'[21] Romanians interested in the incorporation of Moldova, and Hungarians who would like to recover Transylvania, are illustrations of the first; pan-Arabist references to the 'Arab nation' are an instance of the second.

I propose to combine Kohn's associational nation and Smith's territorial nationalism to constitute a civic nation, and Kohn's organic nation and Smith's ethnic nationalism to constitute an ethnic nation. Kohn's description of an associational nation as an association of human beings living in a common territory under the same government and laws may seem to perpetrate the very conflation of nation and state I wish to avoid, but the reference to association calls to mind not only the state but also civil society. Contrary to Weber's claim that all nations are *Gemeinschaften*, civic nations are more *gesellschaftlich*. But does this alignment of civil society with civic nation preclude any possible alignment of civil society with ethnic nation? There is a historical and a conceptual answer to this question. The historical answer given by Hroch is that the nationalist challenge to Russian, Austrian and Turkish oppression in the tsarist, Hapsburg and Ottoman empires came not from bourgeois but from vernacular intellectuals, and it did so in the absence of legitimate opportunities for the political articulation and representation of (emergent) differences of interest within the dominated community. 'In these circumstances, there was little room for more developed forms of political discourse or argument. On both sides of a given conflict,' Hroch continues, 'it was easier to articulate social contradictions or hostilities in national categories – as dangers to a common culture, or particular language or ethnic interest.'[22] Denied other possibilities, Bohemians, for example, expressed all discontent in terms of national opposition to Austria. But even if ethnic nations are often first constituted in circumstances which are not conducive to the formation of civil society, might they not develop a civil society subsequently – as in the Czech lands after 1918? The answer depends, in part at least, on what one means by civil society.

CIVILITY, CIVIL SOCIETY AND CIVIL ECONOMY

From the Greeks to Gramsci there are many variants on the notion of a civil society.[23] I want to make use of the 'sociological' variant which stretches back from Gouldner to Tocqueville and, arguably, to the Scottish moralists.[24]

Until the late eighteenth century 'civilization' and 'civility' were used interchangeably by English and Scottish writers, but 'civilization' always included what was subsequently distinguished as civility – the civil treatment of others. Differentiation between civil society and the state begins, somewhat equivocally, with the Scottish Enlightenment. For Ferguson, Hutcheson, Smith, Millar, Hume and others, civil society refers to a civilized or polished society in contrast to a rude, barbarous or savage society. What makes a society civil? Civility for the Scots has to do with manners, education and cultivation which enjoin respect for the sensibilities of others. What the Scottish moralists imply, but never quite say, is that the constitutional state is not synonymous with civil society but rather complements it by guaranteeing civil and property rights and equality before the law.

In *Democracy in America*, Tocqueville distinguishes between the state, or more often government, and civil life.[25] The state or government includes assemblies, ministries, courts, police and armed forces. Civil life refers to the public life of citizens, that is, their life outside the household. Civil life in America, according to Tocqueville, is notable for the proliferation of associations, the coming together of citizens for common purposes. Associations are of many kinds, but a basic distinction between civil and political association recurs. Civil associations have to do with private economic interests, with commerce and industry. Political associations have to do with 'the public and formal support of specific doctrines by a certain number of individuals who have undertaken to cooperate in a stated way in order to make these doctrines prevail'.[26] Tocqueville marvels at their range and vitality.

> Americans combine to give fêtes, found seminaries, build churches, distribute books, and send missionaries to the antipodes. Hospitals, prisons and schools take shape that way ... if they want to proclaim a truth or propagate some feeling by the encouragement of great example, they form an association.[27]

Political associations are free schools for democracy; they provide lessons in the art of association. Citizens learn to exchange views, to organize, to guard their autonomy and to keep an independent eye on government – for all of which the free dissemination of news and views through newspapers and other outlets is crucial. It is worth noting, too, that Tocqueville mixes private bodies, like churches and literary associations, and public bodies, like town councils, in his political associations. Autonomous local public bodies provide one of the means whereby citizens both achieve common purposes and maintain their independence of (state and federal) government.

Gouldner argues that it is precisely this area of political association which sociology has made its object and its historical mission. Saint-Simon, Comte, Tocqueville, Durkheim, Tönnies, Simmel and Parsons, for example, all try to find a middle way between 'unbridled individualism' and 'the atomization of competitive market society' on the one hand, and 'a state-dominated existence' on the other.[28] In the aftermath of the French and Industrial Revolutions such concerns were often, Gouldner says, conservative. In the face of the over-mighty state in capitalist as well as socialist societies, however, contemporary sociology's interest in 'the infrastructure of the public sphere' has a liberative potential.[29]

Although he does not so call it, it is this sociological variant of civil society that Keane has done so much to revive.[30] It affirms the self-organization of society, rejects the state-dependency of citizens and treats civil society as an entity in its own right which is irreducible to economic structures. It thereby connects with left disillusionment with the state as an instrument for the delivery of socialism and social justice. There is a danger in critiques of the state, however, that the decoupling of civil society and the state will go too far. In Western Europe, new social movements have prompted much debate about relations between civil society and the state. In Eastern Europe, Solidarity and the Polish case in the 1980s all too easily prompted the notion of 'civil society against the state' which made sense as an oppositional strategy to the party-state, but is unhelpful in conditions of democratic reconstruction.[31] Frentzel-Zagórska avoids this by treating civil society 'as a structure of the self organisation of society, located outside, though not disconnected from, the institutional framework of the state'.[32] Within the sociological variant, it is always important not to lose sight of the Tocquevillean line on the art of association and citizenship.

The sociological variant of civil society also embraces Habermas's public sphere[33] as developed by, for example, Nancy Fraser. She argues that this sphere:

> designates a theater in modern societies in which political participation is enacted through the medium of talk. It is the space in which citizens deliberate about their common affairs, hence an institutionalized arena of discursive interaction. This arena is conceptually distinct from the state; it is a site for the production of discourses which can in principle be critical of the state.[34]

Civic Nation, Civil Society, Civil Religion 145

In short, civil society refers to social relations and communications between citizens. These may sometimes be informed by the law and by state policy but even then they are not dependent on them.

It is also necessary, I believe, to add to the sociological variant the civility of the Scottish moralists and, indeed, of long-standing English usage. In the eighteenth century civility may have degenerated into a snobbish disdain for the unlettered but it remains a fundamentally democratic idea. Courtesy was for the court; gentility was for the gentry; civility is for all citizens. Civility bespeaks a common standard within which a multiplicity of ways of living, working and associating are tolerated. It demands that in all life outside the home we afford each other certain decencies and comforts as fellow citizens, regardless of other differences between us. It is, it should be noted, a cool concept. It does not require us to like those we deal with civilly, and as such it contrasts strongly with the warmth of communal, religious or national enthusiasms.

As a society of citizens, civil society can be inclusive and tolerant of pluralism (as in the Netherlands) or inclusive and assimilationist (as in France), or it can be exclusive and suspicious of pluralism (as in Germany). The alignment I referred to between civic nation and civil society is thus more accurately an alignment of civic nation with an inclusive civil society. All nations imagine their past, connect it to their present and lay claim to a homeland. Civic nations may attribute a leading role in their formation to one or more particular ethnies but they also extend citizenship to all who permanently and lawfully reside within their territory and who join in the national imagining or at least refrain from contesting it. By definition they are pluralist and/or assimilationist.[35] Ethnic nations, by contrast, relate citizenship and full participation in society to ethnicity and descent. They can and do develop civil societies but these are exclusive; residents of other ethnic origins, even of long standing, are denied citizenship. There is a suspicion of difference and a rejection of pluralism.

Civic and ethnic nations, as such, are ideal-types. In practice many nations combine elements of the civic and the ethnic nation. The proportions vary greatly not only between nations but also sometimes within a nation over time. Having entered these qualifications, examples spring easily to mind. In some ways America is the classic civic nation with an inclusive civil society, although the huge incidence of violent crime is a vivid reminder of the limits to civility. Shooting each other is uncivil. Britain approximates a civic nation as does France, though in each the integration of black citizens is incomplete. Significantly, the British National Party and the National Front in France, both subscribe to an ethnic conception of nation. Poland, on the other hand, is an ethnic nation in which non Pole-Catholics are vulnerable and in which the transition from society against the party-state to a civil society which affords the crystallization, accommodation and mediation of social differences is proving difficult.

The differences between France and Germany, recently examined brilliantly by Brubaker, are particularly striking.[36] France is a civic nation willing since the revolution to bestow the honour and benefit of being French to all who were born there and to many who migrate there, in the expectation that they will acknowledge the honour and the benefit. Civil society is inclusive and assimilationist (though dual citizenship is permitted). Difficulties have arisen in the 1980s, however, with those second-generation Algerian immigrants born in France after Algerian independence who have had a French citizenship imposed on them at 18 which they do not want and with some other Mahgrebians who view their French citizenship instrumentally, as a convenience, but who do not identify with France. This desacralization of citizenship, to use Brubaker's term, has offended many other French men and women and has prompted the rejoinder from the far right that to be French you have to deserve it ('L'être français, cela se mérite').[37]

Germany by contrast is an ethnic nation. Whereas in France the *jus sanguini* is complemented by a *jus soli*, in Germany it is not. German nationhood is vested in the *Volk*, a community of descent, which affords instant citizenship to returnees from Eastern Europe (whose forebears settled there in the nineteenth century or earlier and who may no longer be proficient in German) but denies it even to second-generation migrant workers who were born in Germany. Germany also demands renunciation of other citizenships by those who are naturalized – a problem for long-settled Turks who would like German citizenship but who are unwilling to renounce their Turkish citizenship. Civil society is exclusive and suspicious of pluralism. It is thus only to be expected that naturalization rates are but a quarter or a fifth what they are in France, and that the overall rate of civic incorporation for immigrants is but a tenth of what it is in France.[38]

Civil society cannot be taken for granted. It is a project which makes demands on all citizens. Openness to difference and civility have to be continuously taught and learned; they have to be worked at. But this presumes, contrary to Tester's recent book, that civil society is still worthy of our imagination. Tester suggests that it is 'inappropriate to talk any longer about the possibility of civil society';[39] the very notion of a civil society is anachronistic. It was an appropriate way for Locke and others to imagine relations with strangers at the beginning of the modern era but it is inappropriate today when the modern is dissolving into the postmodern. Civil society involves similitude and difference. Within defined boundaries it treats (some) strangers with different interests and sensibilities as all the same, as citizens with the rights that all citizens possess, as persons worthy of our consideration because they are human beings, or whatever. In other words it promotes some universal principle of inclusion, even as it marks itself off from outsiders beyond its boundaries and from outsiders in its midst who do not satisfy its principle of inclusion, thereby particularizing in practice as it universalizes in principle. Today, however, contradictions render the notion of civil society untenable. No principle of liberty, equality, fraternity or whatever has the authority to bear universal application, and if it had it would transcend the boundaries of each and every civil society anyway. Civil society is thus now a pretence, something imagined in bad faith.

Tester's mistake is to place the emphasis in civil society on similitude, or as he prefers, homogeneity, rather than on difference. Civil societies are bounded and they do have principles of inclusion and exclusion – as the histories of property and gender immediately reveal – but within their parameters they accommodate differences of interest and sensibility and that is their virtue. Postmodernity does not reduce differences of interest and sensibility – on the contrary it threatens to multiply them – and the accommodation of differences remains as vital a task as ever.

Tester says of civil society:

> it could explain, as safe and pleasant, normal and indeed natural, a symmetric reciprocity between people who knew nothing whatsoever about each other, and who probably cared about each other rather less. Civil society tied these disconnected strangers into communities of mutual responsibility which were expressed in mutual connections of trust, consideration and, for that matter, embarrassment.[40]

The impression he gives is one of distaste. Social relations in civil society are superficial and inauthentic.

It did not really matter if the reciprocity was as empty as the hat-doffing described by Jean-Paul Sartre in *Nausea* just so long as individuals continued to prove themselves to be tied to each other as morally identical citizens of the community. Indeed, in the work of Norbert Elias, the very emptiness and formality of civilization is taken as an indication of the tightening of reciprocity.[41]

But what Sartre treats as malign, Goffman views as benign. For Goffman the courtesies – I would prefer civilities – of everyday life, such as using a title with a surname or holding a door back for someone, are 'interaction rituals' which confirm the humanity of others and their right to proper treatment. For Goffman, as Gregory Smith has argued, 'individuals are little islands of sacredness.'[42] Tester also complains that civil society, precisely because it does accommodate difference, ends up endorsing what MacIntyre has called secondary values – pragmatism, cooperation and compromise, fair play and tolerance, all of which are about means – instead of attempting to secure universal commitment to the realization of primary values such as particular notions of the good, the beautiful and the just.[43] Would this were always the case! But what Tester laments, I would celebrate.

I have discussed civil society in terms of the association of citizens – social self-organization – between households and state and aside from the market. By stressing the civility in civil society, I have made plain that civil association is conducted within a framework of law and convention; in a word, it is legitimate. Interestingly similar thinking informs Rose's recent distinction between a civil and an uncivil economy made in the context of discussions about the transformation in Eastern Europe following the collapse of state socialism. Rose argues that 'Democracy presupposes a civil society, a recognition by the state that individuals, informal groups and formal institutions should be free to pursue their interests and ideals independent of the state in most spheres of life.'[44] He believes that great advances have been made towards a civil society in Eastern Europe, but whilst the command economy has been abandoned it is not yet clear what will replace it. One possibility is a civil economy – the Western norm – with legal concepts of private property, contracts, profit and loss accounts, joint stock companies, etc. Another is an uncivil economy outside the law.

Within an uncivil economy individuals and firms can buy and sell on terms freely accepted by both parties, as in the private sector in a market economy; taking a 'bootleg' taxi is an example of this. Uncivil transactions sometimes involve the willing trade in illegal goods and services, such as gambling, prostitution or drugs. The uncivil economy also includes the unwilling trade in illegal services, as when mobs extort protection money from wealthy people.[45]

In short, a civil economy operates within a framework of law and fair dealing, an uncivil economy does not. Rose here throws an interesting light on what others have called second or black economies. They are inappropriate ways for citizens to treat each other.

CIVIL RELIGION AND POLITICAL RELIGION

Myths, stories, images, icons, celebrations and rites play a part in the imagining of national community from generation to generation. They are key features of both civil and political religion.

The idea of a civil religion is prefigured in classical writings, in Augustine and doubtless in other places too. The term 'civil religion', however, originated with Rousseau. It rests upon a distinction between the 'religion of man', which is a private matter between the individual and God, and the 'religion of the citizen', which is a public matter of the individual's relation to society and government. There is, according to Rousseau, 'a purely civil confession of faith of which the Sovereign should fix the articles, not exactly as religious dogmas, but as social sentiments without which a man cannot be a good citizen or a faithful subject'.[46] Civil religion should bind all members to society, tell them their duties, even move them to fight for their society where necessary. Rousseau's formulations clearly influenced Durkheim, but the term 'civil religion' found contemporary currency only with Bellah's work on the United States.[47] In his original essay, Bellah neglected to define civil religion. This omission was remedied by J. A. Coleman as follows: civil religion is 'a set of beliefs, rites and symbols which relates a man's role as citizen and his society's place in space, time and history to the conditions of ultimate existence and meaning'.[48] To this I would add that civil religions must set out the proper relationship between (civil) society and the state in securing a society's place in space, time and history.

The term 'political religion' was coined by Apter in the context of the politics of modernization and nation-building especially in Africa, but it is Christel Lane's use of the term in her work on the Soviet Union which I wish to develop because she differentiates, on two counts, between 'civil religion' and 'political region'.[49] First, civil religion connects the political order to a transcendent power, such as God, drawn from the religion(s) of the society concerned, whereas political religion simply presents a sacralization of the existing political order. Second, civil religion confines itself to the political order, whereas political religion claims authority over all social life. This twin distinction breaks down, however, when applied to cases like the United States as described by Herberg in 1955.[50] There (and then) the civil religion connected the political order to a transcendent God, but it also extended far beyond the democratic constitution to celebration of free enterprise and the American way of life. Lane's distinction between civil and political religion needs to be reworked.

Rousseau contrasted his civil state to the state of nature. Later theorists divided the civil state into civil society and the state. This distinction, much discussed again in the 1980s, provides us with a clearer way of distinguishing civil and political religion than Lane's. Society is the prime mover of civil religion; the state the prime mover of political religion. The collective representations in a civil religion are genuinely representative of society as a whole, or at least of many sections of it; of course politicians who control the apparatus of the state exploit them, but they also ignore them at their peril. By contrast, the collective representations of a political religion are superimposed on society by those who control the state. The one is historically rooted; the other is politically contrived. Alternatively, with civil religions it is ultimately the state which heeds society; with political religions it is ultimately society which submits to the state. Both have a critical potential, but in the one the roles of critic and criticized are the reverse of the other. In sum, when Lane concludes that 'Civil religion is celebrated in societies where the individual is dominant, and political religion evolves where society is primary', I would argue that civil religion is celebrated where civil society is strong, and political religion where the (party-)state seeks to impose itself.[51]

Although I reject absence of a reference to a transcendent God as a distinguishing characteristic of political religion, I agree with Lane that those political religions which make no reference to gods are still political *religions*. The conception of religion which we share is the Durkheimian one. Where many sociological definitions of religion depend upon a distinction between the supernatural and the natural, Durkheim's hinges on a distinction between the sacred and the profane. Things, persons, representations sacred are set apart from things, persons, representations mundane. They are treated with awe, reverence, special respect. Though often supposedly of divine origin, they are, in reality, social constructions; thus in acknowledging the authority the sacred has over them, men and women acknowledge their individual dependence on society. For Durkheim, the unbelieving son of a rabbi, no avowedly secular system of values and norms could easily secure the respect due to a system believed to contain the word of God. Nevertheless, those who would establish secular ideologies could still be expected to try to vest elements of their systems with sacredness, thereby placing them, in so far as they succeeded, beyond criticism. Within this perspective, there need be no surprise, for example, that Stalin's 1936 constitution for the Soviet Union made several references to the sacred.

Integral to Durkheim's theory of religion is a theory of ritual which emphasizes that ritual regulates our contact with the sacred and prevents us from profaning it. Rites, ceremonies, also celebrate values and help fix them in the minds of each new generation of celebrants. Even the stylized words, acts, music, dance or whatever of the ritual remind those who participate, and those who witness, that the occasion is extraordinary – set apart from ordinary life. On return to the routines of mundane life, recall of the experience is also recall of the values celebrated. Civil and political religions include political rituals, or what Lane, following Goodin, calls 'the rites of rulers'.[52] Civil religions, because they represent the whole of society or at least most sections of it, afford political legitimacy. Political religions only do so where the whole of society, or at least most sections of it, willingly accedes to them.

I will illustrate the difference by comparing Bellah on the United States with Lane on the Soviet Union. Bellah's famous account of civil religion in America, published in 1967, centres on America's self-understanding of her obligation to carry out God's will in earth.[53] It refers to a covenant between God and nation, to America as the new Israel and Americans as a chosen people, and to an understanding of American history in which the Revolution represents Exodus, the Civil War death, sacrifice and rebirth – and the Cold War a Manichean conflict between righteousness and evil. In the course of his essay, Bellah alludes to: statements from the founding fathers, the Declaration of Independence, presidential inaugural addresses from Washington's to Kennedy's, the Gettysburg Address and other pronouncements; symbols and monuments (I would say sacred places) such as the motto of the

United States ('In God We Trust'), the Lincoln Memorial and the
Arlington National Cemetery; and celebrations and rituals such as
Thanksgiving Day, Memorial Day, Veterans Day, saluting the flag
and ceremonies in schools. Bellah acknowledged that there had
always been a danger that the high moral content of American civil
religion would degenerate into national self-idolatry, and in subsequent writings he referred ever more astringently to the 'broken
covenant'.[54] Even so, his account of civil religion in America is
about shared representations of 'we the people' – even if subsequently questions could be asked about if, when and how they have
been shared with blacks and Hispanics.

Lane's account of political religion in the Soviet Union, published in 1981, examines the sacralization of the October Revolution, the Great Patriotic War and the heroic achievements of
labour, and the accompanying symbols and rites, such as October
parades, visits (pilgrimages?) to the Lenin Mausoleum, the placing
of Lenin photographs (icons?) in every public office, war mem-
orials and remembrances and Labour Days. She also carefully
examines references to the motherland and to Soviet endeavour in
familial life-cycle rituals, rituals of initiation into social and political
collectives, labour ritual, the calendar of holidays and their ritual,
ritual of the military-patriotic tradition and the mass political holidays of the revolutionary tradition. She quotes Sally Falk Moore's
comment that ritual 'communicates the non-negotiability (the
unquestionability), the sacredness of certain interpretations of
social life', and notes how it is used in the Soviet Union to legitimize and put beyond question the existing political order.[55] That it
failed in 1991 only confirms that it was a political religion without
believers. Anyone doubting that it was a political religion, as distinct from a civil religion rooted in civil society, has only to note
how little of it survives in Russia today.

The political culture of a society will vary according to whether
the predominance of either civil or political religion aligns with the
predominance of either a civic or an ethnic nation. A four-cell
matrix (figure 1) illustrates the possibilities. The illustrations are
crude in so far as the provision of examples in a four-cell matrix
takes no account of the presentation above of both civic and ethnic
nations and civil and political religions as ideal-types, but they do
capture something about differences of political culture. To take
the least familiar case, there is a difference in the prevailing conception of nation in the successor republics to Czechoslovakia. In the
Czech Republic, the larger component of the old Czechoslovakia

Figure 6.1 Determinants of political culture

	Civil religion	Political religion
Civic nation	USA Britain French Fifth Republic Czech Republic	Soviet Union French Third Republic
Ethnic nation	Poland after 1980–81 Federal Republic of Germany Slovakia	People's Republic of China German Third Reich Japan after 1867

and the location of its capital, Prague, there remains a notion that the Czech nation can and should embrace considerable cultural differences. It is symbolized in the retention of the Czechoslovak flag whose colours represented all its peoples. In Slovakia, which was and is smaller in size and population, there is a notion that Slovaks can at last express their own national identity; this could lead to difficulties for the Hungarian minority.

Civic nations are unconcerned about ethnic purity and unlikely to contemplate ethnic cleansing, but where their political culture aligns civic nation and political religion there is a limit, sometimes a very oppressive limit, to their political pluralism.

CONCLUSION

I have lauded civility in terms of interpersonal and inter-group respect, citizen association and the pluralist accommodation of difference. If one thinks of the mixed bag of civic virtues, however, it is easy to see that civility is nowhere assured. On the contrary, the incivilities of crimes against the person and property, tax evasion, indifference to – or worse corruption of – the political process, pollution of the environment, disfigurement of public space and individualist and apathetic dissociation from others are all readily evident in different proportions and configurations in most societies. In some cases an underclass is denied the very material and cultural means to be civil.

Weitman has argued that the establishment of civil societies in postcommunist Eastern Europe will be a protracted affair because the 'social and cultural infrastructures without which formal liberties ... have little chance of being enshrined into actual liberties' have either never existed there or were destroyed by 'the totalitarian State under the old regime'.[56] His list includes independence of spirit, self-reliance, organizational skills and habits of co-operation, a synergetic rather than zero-sum attitude to others, a pragmatic willingness to find a *modus vivendi*, an ethic of responsibility, a willingness to horse-trade and find honour in compromise, an avoidance of intransigent last stands and respect for rules and mistrust of those who cynically bend or ignore them. Just to elaborate such a list is to indicate how big the task is. Too many politicians, self-deluding or not, have supposed that a quick transition to liberal democracy and a market economy is possible in Eastern Europe – though, interestingly, President Havel of the Czech Republic has recently indicated that he is not one of them.[57]

In Western societies the realization of civil society is a never-ending project. In some cases, it may not be a particularly formidable project; in others there is much to be done. Thatcherite neo-liberalism in Britain, for example, did great damage to civil society, which even elements of the new right are now ready to concede.[58] Yet if repair there is daunting, it is nothing compared with that needed in America to combat crime or that needed in Italy to overcome half a century of political and business corruption. In all cases, however, civility is not a virtue we can afford to surrender or a practice we can afford to disregard.

NOTES

This essay is derived from a paper presented to the 'Democracy in Contest' Research Seminar at the Central European University, Prague, in April 1993. The seminar was one of a series supported by the ESRC East–West II Research Programme. I am grateful to colleagues who have commented on the draft, then and subsequently, and to ESRC.

1 E. Gellner, *Nations and Nationalism*, Blackwell, Oxford, 1983,
2 For Weber on nation, see M. Weber, *Economy and Society*, University of California Press, Berkeley, Cal., 1978, pp. 395–8, 921–6, and D. Beetham, *Max Weber and The Theory of Modern Politics*, Allen and Unwin, London, 1974. The quotation is from Weber's comments at the 1912 meeting of the German Sociological Association as translated in Beetham, p. 122.
3 B. Anderson, *Imagined Communities*, 2nd edn, Verso, London, 1991, p. 6.
4 Anderson, *Imagined Communities*, p. 7.
5 Anderson, *Imagined Communities*, p. 7.
6 Anderson, *Imagined Communities*, p. 7.

7 E. Gellner, *Thought and Change*, Weidenfeld and Nicolson, London, 1964, p. 169.

8 Anderson, *Imagined Communities*, p. 6.

9 M. Hroch, 'From National Movement to the Fully-formed Nation: The Nation-Building Process in Europe', *New Left Review*, no. 198, 1993.

10 A. D. Smith, *The Ethnic Origins of Nations*, Blackwell, Oxford, 1986.

11 Gellner, *Nations and Nationalism*, pp. 44–5.

12 Anderson, *Imagined Communities*, p. 135.

13 A. Giddens, *The Nation-State and Violence*, Polity, Cambridge, 1985, pp. 116, 119.

14 D. McCrone, *Understanding Scotland: The Sociology of a Stateless Nation*, Routledge, London, 1991. On the ethnic structure of Yugoslavia according to the 1971 census, see J. Krejci and V. Velimsky, *Ethnic and Political Nations in Europe*, Croom Helm, London, 1981, table 10.1, p. 146.

15 L. Colley, *Britons: Forging the Nation 1707–1837*, Yale University Press, New Haven, Conn., 1992.

16 H. Kohn, *The Idea of Nationalism*, Macmillan, New York, 1944, and *Nationalism: Its Meaning and History*, Van Nostrand, Princeton, N.J., 1955. See also E. Kamenka, 'Political Nationalism', in E. Kamenka, ed., *Nationalism*, Edward Arnold, London, 1973.

17 A. D. Smith, *National Identity*, Penguin, London, 1991, pp. 80–1.

18 Smith, *National Identity*, p. 82.

19 Smith, *National Identity*, p. 82.

20 Smith, *National Identity*, p. 82.

21 Smith, *National Identity*, pp. 82–3.

22 Hroch, 'From National Movement to the Fully-formed Nation', p. 12.

23 C. G. A. Bryant, 'Civil Society and Pluralism: A Conceptual Analysis', *Sisyphus: Social Studies*, vol. 1, 1992. K. Kumar reviews the same range of writings on 'civil society' in 'Civil Society: An Inquiry into the Usefulness of an Historical Term', *British Journal of Sociology*, vol. 44, 1993. I think the concept is valuable, and he does not. For our exchange of views in the *British Journal of Sociology*, see C. G. A. Bryant, 'Social Self-Organisation, Civility and Sociology: A Comment on Kumar's "Civil Society"', vol. 44, 1993, K. Kumar, 'Civil Society Again: A Reply to Christopher Bryant's "Social Self-Organisation . . .", vol. 45, 1994, and C. G. A. Bryant, 'A Further Comment on Kumar's "Civil Society"', vol. 45, 1994.

24 A. W. Gouldner, 'Civil Society in Capitalism and Socialism', in his *The Two Marxisms: Contradictions and Anomalies in the Development of Theory*, Macmillan, London, 1980; L. Schneider, ed., *The Scottish Moralists on Human Nature and Society*, University of Chicago Press, Chicago, 1967.

25 A. de Tocqueville, *Democracy in America*, Harper & Row, New York, 1966.

26 Tocqueville, *Democracy in America*, vol. 1, p. 233.

27 Tocqueville, *Democracy in America*, vol. 2, p. 662.

28 Gouldner, 'Civil Society in Capitalism and Socialism', pp. 364, 370.

29 Gouldner, 'Civil Society in Capitalism and Socialism', p. 371.

30 J. Keane, *Democracy and Civil Society*, Verso, London, 1988, and ed., *Civil*

Society and the State, Verso, London, 1988.

31 A. Arato, 'Civil Society Against the State: Poland 1980–81', *Telos*, no. 47, 1981.

32 J. Frentzel-Zagórska, 'Civil Society in Poland and Hungary', *Soviet Studies*, vol. 42, 1990.

33 J. Habermas, *The Structural Transformation of the Public Sphere: An Inquiry into a Category of Bourgeois Society*, Polity, Cambridge, 1989.

34 N. Fraser, 'Rethinking the Public Sphere: A Contribution to the Critique of Actually Existing Democracy', paper presented to XII World Congress of Sociology, Madrid, July 1990.

35 I have discussed variants of both plural societies and (political) pluralism in Bryant, 'Civil Society and Pluralism', pp. 114–17.

36 R. Brubaker, *Citizenship and Nationhood in France and Germany*, Blackwell, Oxford, 1992.

37 Brubaker, *Citizenship and Nationhood*, pp. 138ff.

38 Brubaker, *Citizenship and Nationhood*, pp. 75ff.

39 K. Tester, *Civil Society*, Routledge, London, 1992.

40 Tester, *Civil Society*, pp. 146–7.

41 Tester, *Civil Society*, p. 147.

42 E. Goffman, *Interaction Ritual: Essays on Face-to-Face Behavior*, Doubleday, New York, 1967; G. W. H. Smith, 'A Simmelian Reading of Goffman', PhD thesis, University of Salford, 1989, p. 499.

43 A. MacIntyre, *Secularization and Moral Change*, Oxford University Press, Oxford, 1967.

44 R. Rose, 'Towards a Civil Economy', Studies in Public Policy, no. 200, University of Strathclyde Centre for the Study of Public Policy, Glasgow, 1992, p. 3.

45 Rose, 'Towards a Civil Economy', pp. 7–8.

46 J.-J. Rousseau, *The Social Contract*, Dent, London, 1963, p. 114.

47 E. Durkheim, *The Elementary Forms of the Religious Life*, Allen and Unwin, 1915; R. N. Bellah, 'Civil Religion in America', *Daedalus*, vol. 96, 1967.

48 J. A. Coleman, 'Civil Religion', *Sociological Quarterly*, vol. 31, 1974, p. 70.

49 D. Apter, 'Political Religion in the New Nations', in C. Geertz, ed., *Old Nations and New States*, Free Press, New York, 1963, and *The Politics of Modernization*, University of Chicago Press, Chicago, Ill., 1965, ch. 8; C. Lane, *The Rites of Rulers: Ritual in Industrial Society – the Soviet Case*, Cambridge University Press, Cambridge, 1981.

50 W. Herberg, *Protestant, Catholic, Jew*, Doubleday, New York, 1955.

51 Lane, *The Rites of Rulers*, p. 44.

52 R. E. Goodin, 'The Rites of Rulers', *British Journal of Sociology*, vol. 29, 1978.

53 Bellah, 'Civil Religion in America'.

54 R. N. Bellah, *The Broken Covenant*, Seabury, New York, 1975, and 'Religion and Legitimation in the American Republic', in T. Robbins and D. Anthony, eds, *In Gods We Trust*, Transaction, New Jersey, 1981.

55 Unpublished paper by S. F. Moore (1974), quoted in Lane, *The Rites of Rulers*, p. 32.

56 S. Weitman, 'Thinking the Revolutions of 1989', *British Journal of Sociology*, vol. 43, 1992, p. 17.

57 V. Havel, 'The Post-Communist Nightmare', *New York Review of Books*, vol. 41, 1993.
58 C. G. A. Bryant, 'Civil Society and Incivility in Thatcherite Britain', in P. Ploszajski, ed., *Philosophy of Social Choice*, IFiS Publishers, Warsaw, 1990. On the second thoughts of the new right, see D. G. Green, *Reinventing Civil Society*, I. E. A. Health and Welfare Unit, London, 1993 and the 'immanent critique' of the new right in J. Gray, *Beyond the New Right*, Routledge, London, 1993.

7

Philosophers' Models on the Carpathian Lowlands

Chris Hann

Civil society was not a prominent concept in the literature when I took undergraduate courses on communist government and the economic development of Eastern Europe in the early 1970s. My teachers at Oxford introduced us to standard models of centrally planned economies, but also to the already burgeoning literature on the reform of socialist economic systems.[1] Similarly in politics, we were exposed to simple models of totalitarianism, but also to a number of significant modifications, such as elements of pluralism and interest-group competition in socialist conditions.[2] In spite of this encouragement from stimulating teachers to think critically about entrenched Western models of 'the Soviet bloc' and the 'Iron Curtain regimes', the material that I could find in English conveyed rather little about how life was lived in different socialist countries. I switched to social anthropology as a graduate student with the hope that this subject's focus on 'everyday life' and 'culture' would offer the kind of understanding that was signally missing in the Soviet and East European Studies literature of the time. Thanks to the prevailing climate of *détente* and the generous terms of the exchange scheme administered by the British Council, I was able to spend the years 1975–7 in Hungary. An initial year of familiariz-ation and language work in Budapest was followed by a year's fieldwork in the rural community of Tázlár, some 80 miles south-east of the capital. You will search in vain for the concept of civil society in my account of this research.[3] The main purpose of the present chapter is therefore to investigate the usefulness of this term in this particular ethnographic context, where fieldwork has been periodically renewed through to the demise of socialist institutions in the early 1990s.

If I had made my first trip to Hungary a decade later it is likely that civil society would have been a central concept of the research; or if not, I would have had to explain the reasons at my PhD defence! Somehow in the course of the 1980s civil society came to occupy the high ground of international intellectual debate. It was not just an Eastern European phenomenon, for the concept has been deployed in cases as diverse as postcolonial African states and the Kemalist Republic in Turkey.[4] By the 1990s civil society was no longer the preserve of an elite of political philosophers and historians. It was regularly used to add a certain *gravitas* to the prose of politicians and journalists in a bewildering variety of circumstances. On a recent visit to the United States I was told that this is nowadays the vital concept to insinuate into all social science research proposals – particularly if you are looking for support from an organization such as USAID.

Alas, you can almost hear the purists sigh. The concomitant of this popularization and internationalization of civil society must surely be the simplification and debasement of the original idea. But what was the original idea? Part of the reason, perhaps, for its massively successful dissemination is the lack of any general agreement on this point. From Hegelian Marxists to the Scottish moralists, you can invest the concept of civil society with almost any pedigree you like. Ernest Gellner, for one, has admitted that 'the history of this concept is a muddle'. But this does not prevent him from finding civil society more 'concrete sociologically' than notions such as democratization; it is helpful 'in understanding what happened in the Soviet world ... (and) a useful slogan for escaping from the Soviet morass'.[5]

It is obvious that political struggles in Eastern Europe have helped to explain the recent popularity of a Hegelian approach in which civil society is sharply contrasted to the state. Gellner seems to have been among the earlier Western commentators on the region to take up the term in this way.[6] In a 1984 article in *The Times Literary Supplement* he suggested that socialism had become 'the new version of Byzantine caesaro-papism'. The Czech case was identified as the most pitiful: 'the civil society is apathetic, broken and dispirited. It barely resists at all. Its members largely accommodate themselves by means of an inner immigration'.[7] The absence of civil society in Poland (the main focus of this article) was documented by the author's failure, in the course of four days' wandering in the High Tatras, to meet a single party of mountaineers. Gellner deduced that the only possible explanation for this strange absence must be repression of civil society by the state: 'Freelance mountain climbing must be out. Perhaps it would inevitably be a cover for other things.'[8] Gellner was here reproducing – with his usual verve and wit – the kind of stereotyped images of Eastern Europe that dominated Western perceptions of East European societies throughout the Cold War period.[9] By this time any number of East European 'dissident' intellectuals were also invoking the concept of civil society to denote the heroic underdog in a 'zero sum' struggle with the totalitarian state.[10] Instead of questioning such models and subjecting them to serious ethnographic scrutiny, Gellner gives them his unconditional endorsement. Most other Western commentators on the 1989 revolutions and their aftermath have done likewise.

This is surely too simplistic a model for examining state–society relations in the late twentieth century. As far as Eastern Europe is concerned, such a model has numerous drawbacks. For example, it fails to draw attention to the many constructive interventions of states in the lives of their citizens in the socialist period. It also leaves little room to explore the immense differences that existed in state–society relations in different parts of the region – for example, between Poland and East Germany, or between Hungary and Romania. In short, in my view, the triumphalism of the early 1990s that has accompanied some imagined victory of civil society over communism is testimony to the abiding power of totalitarian models, but it does not reflect any improvement in our understanding of the region. I suggest a simple remedy. Concepts coming from the traditions of political philosophy should be explored not through anecdotal evidence at high altitude, but through sustained fieldwork engagement throughout the region, as emphasized in modern social anthropology. For the rest of this chapter I therefore descend to the village of Tázlár on the Great Hungarian Plain. Following the conventions employed in my monograph I divide this discussion of civil society into three parts: politics, economics and social morality.[11]

POLITICS

If civil society was not yet in the air during my fieldwork in 1975–7, there was another phrase that performed some similar rhetorical functions. I refer to 'human rights', then one of the trademarks of President Jimmy Carter's foreign policy. The Budapest daily paper to which I subscribed ran frequent articles that were critical of this policy, particularly in the context of the Charta 77 movement in Czechoslovakia. None of this coverage had even the faintest echo in the village. The range of issues associated with a free civil society, such as the conditions for pluralism and constitutional government, were not issues that the villagers themselves ever articulated. Only the word 'democracy' was used regularly, often with ironic intent (that is, to imply that the substance of participatory, representative government was missing), though sometimes simply as a non-evaluative shorthand for the communist regime under which they had lived since the 1940s.

Villagers were not completely apathetic about politics and what has been termed the 'public sphere' by Habermas.[12] A common definition of civil society focuses on the range of 'intermediate associations' between the state on the one hand and families and households on the other. In this sense I think that it can be a useful concept for the analysis of what was most unsatisfactory about local political systems under socialism. My analysis of political institutions and other associations in Tázlár in the mid-1970s would therefore have benefited from the concept of civil society.[13] In brief, I found that civil society in this sense (where it may be used synonymously with 'public sphere') had been very substantially eroded by pressures originating outside the village. The Communist Party was the only local political organization. It had very few members, and even some of these were not members from conviction: for example, a teacher might join to improve his or her promotion prospects, whilst a headteacher would *de rigeur* join the party, but perhaps leave it just as soon as (s)he retired. Even the appointment during my fieldwork of a young agronomist as a full-time salaried secretary did nothing to raise the profile of the Communist Party in village life (the fact that he was not a Tázlár native but commuted to the village from a nearby town certainly did not help).

At higher levels the party was closely identified with the state itself, an identification recognized in the social science literature with the concept of the 'party-state'. In theory, local government was based on the same Leninist doctrines as those applied to Communist Party organization, but 'democratic centralism' did not seem to leave villagers with much sense that they were represented in government at any level. Local elections, like national parliamentary elections, were arranged through approved lists without competition. The Patriotic People's Front, which supervised the

162 *Chris Hann*

drawing up of these lists, was a body controlled by the local council chairman and a few other Communist Party members.

None of this was a surprise to me, though I was slightly surprised in the 'reforming', 'liberal' Hungarian climate of the 1970s to find that similar controls were rigorously enforced outside the sphere of politics in the narrower sense. Thus church groups were strictly monitored and unable to initiate any activities outside the religious sphere, narrowly defined. Not even in sport were villagers effectively brought together, either to play or to cheer on a local football team. The socialist Culture House had responsibility for organizing a variety of clubs and associations, but few of these existed on any regular basis. Indeed, those who initiated their own cultural activities in the upper hamlet of the village met with resentment and obstruction from the administrators of the Culture House in what seemed to me to be the best example of the unwillingness of the authorities at this time to tolerate any form of organization 'from below'.

There was just one possible forum in which villagers could come together to make their views known: their agricultural cooperatives. This village, like many others in this part of Hungary, had experienced a distinctive form of collectivization. Most villagers, though nominally members of a cooperative, did not play any significant part in collective farming. However, almost all had a direct interest in how the cooperatives were managed, and most relied upon the larger unit for assistance in their own household-based production process, as they did with marketing.[14] By the time of my fieldwork, as a result of a series of mergers, there was just one cooperative in Tázlár. It had a leadership of well-educated outsiders whose policies, influenced by ideological pressures at the national level in the mid-1970s, were threatening the perceived interests of many ordinary members by seeking to extend the acreage under collective cultivation. Yet these cooperatives had impeccable democratic constitutions to ensure that their externally appointed leaders were accountable to the members. I spent a lot of time in 1977 observing how, in spite of such a constitution, local wishes were ignored or breached. One key group was the 'executive committee', a body that met fairly regularly. By influencing nominations for this body, and then through establishing good personal relations with these 'delegates', asserting their own higher political or educational credentials when appropriate, the cooperative leaders were able to manage this committee without great difficulty. But there were more serious problems with the 'general meetings' of all members that had to be held at least once a year. At one meeting that I witnessed in 1977, some villagers were quite prepared to speak up and to make trouble for their leaders and other visiting dignitaries on the platform. But the eventual outcome was simply that the leaders ignored these views from below and carried on with their previously agreed policies regardless. The abandonment of even the fiction of the cooperative's democratic, self-governing character was quite shameless. I attributed this to the pressure applied from 'the party outside', which had succeeded in stifling the only remaining means of expression for what I might now in retrospect identify as the local civil society.

Such was my 'snapshot' view of Tázlár during the 1970s. But a diachronic perspective on the succeeding years suggests a slightly different picture. Ostensibly the modernizing outsiders who led the cooperative at the time of my initial fieldwork were able to win easy victories over the members, thanks to blatant manipulation of meetings and the support of 'the party outside'. But in fact their 1977 'victories' were achieved at considerable cost. Within a short time the outside appointees had departed, the chairman falling prey to a serious nervous disorder. The new chairman, again an outsider imposed upon the members by Communist Party officials based outside the village, was unable to improve the atmosphere of distrust. However, in 1982 he in turn was replaced by the chief agronomist, a man from a neighbouring village who was widely respected both for his knowledge of farming and his personal integrity. He was not a member of the Communist Party and seems to have been chosen by popular acclaim rather than 'the party outside'. Over the next decade, under this chairman's leadership, the cooperative prospered in an atmosphere of stability. Small farmers were fully supported, new schemes were launched to integrate small-scale and large-scale production techniques, and sideline activities developed by the cooperative created many new jobs that were low paid but highly valued nonetheless, especially by village women.[15]

The other significant development of the early 1980s occurred at the village council. Its long-serving communist chairman received a suspended gaol sentence after being convicted of attempting to extort money and other goods from farmers during the implementation of rural electrification schemes. He was succeeded by the local headmaster, who also held the post of director at the Culture House (rechristened the General Culture Centre in 1985). This man, though a long-time Communist Party member, also enjoyed the confidence and respect of most villagers.

Against this background of recent changes, it is perhaps less surprising that the 'revolutions of 1989' left no dramatic mark in Tázlár. The Communist Party (which changed its name to the Hungarian Socialist Party in 1989) collapsed almost totally (it now numbers only two or three members, compared to a few dozen at its peak). Two new parties were formed, of which the larger was the Independent Smallholders Party. This had been the most popular political party in Hungary in the 1940s, but after 1990 there were fierce disputes throughout the country over the best way to develop the rediscovered legacy from the pre-communist period. The local organization in Tázlár was highly unstable almost from its inception. Three years later it still retains a core of some 20 members, but it appears to be hardly any more active or representative of villagers than the Communist Party had been before the demise of communism. The only other political party to establish a branch in Tázlár has been the Christian Democratic People's Party, with about a dozen active members. However, this group too has immense difficulty in convening even the occasional committee meeting. The members are almost all elderly churchgoers, apart from one younger teacher who serves as its secretary.

The parliamentary and local elections of 1990 provided the first major opportunities for new forms of organization in the village. In the former, a Smallholder candidate, a well-respected vet with a practice in the nearby market town, won a clear majority of local votes. Local elections held some months later proved to be much more controversial.[16] The mayoral contest was acrimonious. It was eventually won by the veteran executive secretary of the out-going communist council, who resigned from the Communist Party and, running as an Independent, beat off a strong challenge from another Independent, a local entrepreneur whose campaign featured leaflets and manifestos that promised all kinds of dynamic initiatives under his leadership. But he was not trusted; too many villagers were suspicious of the way he had made his money and was continuously developing his various business interests. The headmaster, the retiring council chairman, chose not to run for mayor but, having resigned from the Communist Party, he was easily elected as an ordinary councillor. The eventual composition of the 'first freely elected' council was not very different from what it had been in the 1980s (when competitive elections had already been introduced, albeit under the aegis of the Patriotic People's Front).

Talking to people about the new council's activities over the last few years, most people seem to see very little change. Most meetings are attended only by the councillors themselves. Although there are some specialist committees dealing with issues of vital concern to the villagers, such as land distribution, these have not generated much interest and participation. They frequently have to be postponed for lack of a quorum. The mayoress herself and several councillors feel that they have, if anything, less room for autonomous decision-taking than the former communist council, particularly in view of tight financial pressures. Even though changes in local government have been designed to weaken the powers exercised at county level in the socialist period, the mayoress finds that it remains essential to cultivate personal networks with an array of external officials. Decisions taken at village level must still be ratified by state controllers before implementation (this control is now enforced by sending the minute books to a 'commissioner of the republic' in a provincial city for confirmation).

This impression of *plus ça change, plus c'est la même chose* is confirmed by my investigations of the transformation of the village cooperative in the 1990s. By 1992 it had ceased agricultural production on a collective basis, many assets had been privatized (a process initiated in the mid-1980s) and 'shares' had been distributed to members according to a complex formula to assess their contribution to the cooperative's past performance.[17] In August 1992 I was able to attend a meeting to approve a new constitution for this cooperative, at which the continuities with earlier styles of management were all too apparent. The leadership was able, just as it had been 15 years earlier, to manipulate the proceedings to suit a platform that now had two legal advisers in the places occupied by visiting Communist Party dignitaries in the past. At several points these lawyers were called upon to provide 'expert' support for the wishes of the leadership, and in effect to overrule potentially troublesome suggestions from the body of the hall. The meeting dragged on for several hours longer than planned, but the mutton and wine commensality that followed could not conceal the fact that the new cooperative was no more satisfactory an agent of self-organization than the old cooperative had been under communism.

In short, I find little evidence to support the notion that a more effective civil society (in the sense of public sphere) has been able to develop in Hungary in recent years. A theatrical group in the upper

hamlet remains active, but is still complaining that it does not get
sufficient support from the administrators of the General Culture
Centre. Sports life is still moribund, and there has been no general
renaissance in any of the churches represented in the village. In the
central arenas of the council and the cooperative important changes
were introduced gradually in the course of the 1980s and these have
continued after the demise of communism. But there have been no
sharp changes in practice, and most villagers do not seem to feel any
closer to these institutions after four years of 'freedom' than they
did during 40 years of communism.

I think this picture corresponds to that obtaining in many other
contemporary East European villages.[18] One possible explanation
is the argument that communism was so successful in destroying
the old civil society that it will take many decades or generations
to rebuild it. This implies that a robust civil society existed in rural
Hungary before the communist period, which is precisely what
some analysts have attempted to show. For example, Elémer
Hankiss has recently attempted to quantify the differences.[19] But
what do such calculations really tell us about the conditions of life
in pre-communist rural Hungary? It is of course difficult to gener-
alize and there is no space in this chapter for details and nuances.
But those segments of the rural population of the interwar period
discussed by Illyés or Pálóczi-Horváth, who were subjected to
every imaginable form of exploitation, economic, political and
sexual, might not have been too impressed to be told, on the basis
of statistics recording a large number of clubs and associations, that
pre-socialist Hungary had a thriving civil society.[20] Concerted programmes to end the extremes of inequality and create a modern
form of citizenship that would extend to the whole population
were not effectively mounted until after 1945.

Tázlár is a particularly interesting setting for examining the
evolution of civil society in the generations before 1945. This area
was not repopulated until late in the nineteenth century, and the
resulting community was thus a very direct product of the uneven
capitalist development experienced by the country as a whole. Most
immigrants were very poor peasants who settled in isolated farm-
houses (Hungarian: *tanya*) on plots of poor quality, sandy soil. It is
clear that they did form associations, for example to manage pasture
land for the use of all the farmers of the community, though it is
difficult today to reconstruct how these operated. It is also clear
that, even in this settlement that was relatively free of large estates
and feudal encumbrances, the system of local government was con-

trolled by the wealthier farmers. Associations linked to the churches seem also to have been dominated by the more prestigious families. In any case it is doubtful if such societies can really be seen as the organizations of a free civil society, given the very close links which united the Roman Catholic Church in particular to the conservative Horthy state. Similar doubts might be expressed concerning other organizations that would conventionally be identified with a civil society in a Western context, such as the Boy Scouts and the Levente youth movement. And this state was, of course, one that ruthlessly denied communists the right to free association.

I would suggest that for the majority of citizens in the pre-communist period Hungarian society did not in fact offer much space for self-organization. It would be anachronistic to apply a model that opposes 'society' to 'state': certainly people themselves would not have used this dichotomy in the way that many of them did come to use it under socialism. But it might be realistic to suggest that rural Hungarians during and after the Depression years were less concerned about constraints on the freedom of their civil society than they were about exacting more decisive interventions on their behalf from the state. For example, nothing seems to have come of land claims submitted by Tázlár dwellers in the course of land reform committee meetings after the First World War, in the course of which a large estate owner was able to frustrate the aspirations of poorer farmers. On the other hand, public funds were released for urgently needed housing construction in the village centre in the 1930s, in a remarkable project that far exceeded the scope of public-sector housing construction in the village throughout the communist period.

ECONOMICS

Although the communist state was not active in rural housing construction, in its later decades the housing stock was nonetheless quite dramatically improved through private investments. In Tázlár, as elsewhere in Hungary, the 1970s and 1980s were a boom period. The revenues from small-scale farming were for the most part spent in consumption, and above all in privately owned housing. At the same time there were some villagers who invested in new workshops, in tractors and other machinery, as a sign of their accumulation orientation. As I tried to show in my mono-

graph, the relative lack of interest shown by villagers in the public
sphere must be related to their time-consuming and exhausting
private economic activities. Many analysts have commented on
the macro-level contrasts that developed, for example between
Hungary and Poland during this period. In Poland there was very
little opportunity to divert citizens' energies into private accumulation and consumption. There was therefore greater scope for
developing an alternative political society to that of communist
orthodoxy.[21] In Hungary the pattern documented in the preced-ing
section seemed for a long time to hold at the macro level as
well: civil society was unable to develop as a zone of free political
space between households and government because its members
were too busy in the spheres of commodity production and
exchange.[22]

   But is this political dimension the only or the most important
dimension of civil society? For Marx, civil society is identified more
strongly with the economic spheres. But you do not have to be a
Marxist to argue that it is Hungary, rather than Poland, that carried
the development of civil society further in the communist period:
not in terms of autonomous political space, evidently, but in laying
the economic foundations for a robust citizenry based on extensive
entrepreneurship and private property rights, the preconditions
for effective democratic politics. It is appropriate at this point to
follow Szelenyi on a brief excursion into semantics.[23] Civil society
in German is *burgerliche Gesellschaft*, for which 'bourgeois society'
might be a more appropriate translation than 'civil society'. In a
curious manner the ever-widening scope of socialist economic reform measures in communist Hungary after 1968 encouraged
the development of a more bourgeois social structure. This is the
phenomenon studied by Szelenyi.[24] His results suggest some direct
continuities (through the familial transmission of cultural capital)
between the new rich and those whose families had already em-
barked on an 'embourgeoisement trajectory' before the socialist
period. The Hungarian term *'polgár'* has about the same meaning as
the German *Burger*; thus it combines the meaning of the French
citoyen and *bourgeois*.[25] The concept of *polgárosodás* has a consequent ambiguity, and its meaning can shift over time, as Szelenyi
shows. But it is the economic dimension that he emphasizes in his
book, arguing that socialist embourgeoisement has engineered a
'silent revolution from below' that, by implication, has far more
radical effects on the structures of power than the more attractive,

romantic but ultimately hopeless political route to a *bürgerliche Gesellschaft* in the Polish manner.[26]

Szelenyi's work draws upon a number of earlier theorists, notably the Hungarian sociologist Ferenc Erdei. It was Erdei who developed the concept of *polgárosodás* in his acute analyses of the backward condition of Hungarian society before 1945. He argued that a bourgeois structure had remained embryonic; especially in the countryside, much of the population remained caught up in feudal dependencies. Influenced also by Lenin, Erdei was the minister of agriculture who launched the Hungarian collectivization drive in 1949, and he continued to defend this policy until his death in 1971. However, the later efflorescence of small farming and the prosperity achieved under late socialism also owed much to the flexible manner in which he argued for the implementation of socialist principles: he had deeper sympathies with Chayanovian models of 'vertical integration' than with Stalinist levelling through the obliteration of the traditional household economy. As a result of these policies the immense poverty of rural Hungary in the first half of the twentieth century was largely overcome within a single generation after collectivization. Ironically, the ingredients for unobstructed *polgárosodás*, diagnosed by Erdei as sorely missing in the pre-communist period, were finally supplied through the stimulus given to the rural sector in the latter decades of communism.

These small-scale farmers remained in a political sense atomized, fragmented as peasants have generally been throughout history. As noted above, they did not organize cohesively in the local political context. Yet in pursuit of their economic objectives they were phenomenally successful. The symbiosis of large and small in collectivized Hungarian agriculture gave the managers of large-scale farms common interests with small-scale producers. The agrarian lobby was therefore able to operate with the overwhelming support of the rural population. And in the occasional moments when this lobby did not work effectively, for example when ideological objections to high rural earnings were raised by urban communists, 'market forces' were able to secure the outcomes desired by the farmers. Thus when prices were held down shortly before the period of my fieldwork in the 1970s, small-scale producers responded rationally enough by cutting back on their production.[27] The authorities were not prepared to accept disruptions in supplies and soon adjusted their guaranteed prices upwards. This episode illustrates the power of the mass of small-scale producers to influence government policy via direct economic action in the period when they had no political party or trade union to represent their interests.

It is instructive to contrast the successes achieved by the small-scale producers in the 1970s with their economic predicament in recent years, when the Independent Smallholders Party has been a partner in the coalition government. In spite of this and the formation of many other organizations ostensibly concerned with the promotion of their interests, the real incomes of farmers have plummeted. Land is being privatized on a massive scale in line with postcommunist ideologies, but demand is low or non-existent because the prospects for the agricultural sector are seen to be so gloomy. Villagers feel their state has abandoned them. Those who were successful entrepreneurs in agriculture in the 1970s and 1980s are now looking at other sectors – any other sector seems preferable to farming – or giving up their small business activities altogether. As rural unemployment rises inexorably, housebuilding programmes have slowed and the era of *polgárosodás* in this second, economic sense is apparently over for good.

MORALITY

It is important to consider how these spheres of politics and economics have interacted in different ways in different parts of Eastern Europe, but it is also essential everywhere to add another dimension. The concept of civil society must also direct our attention to the study of values, to the study of moralities in society. This too has been of major concern in the Hungarian literature on *polgárosodás*. Although the primary associations of the term, certainly in the village, would be material and economic, for many urban and intellectual groups it is also strongly associated with the spread of 'bourgeois' educational and moral standards or, in other English terms all derived from the same root, the spread of civilization, civic consciousness and civility.

It is quite clear that the values of the many commentators and dissident East European intellectuals who have presented civil society in a simple adversarial relationship with the socialist state are the values of Western bourgeois (or liberal) individualism. It is less clear that these values are or have ever been espoused in the same way and to the same degree by East European villagers. Superficially there are of course points of contact. The peasant who has his land appropriated in the course of collectivization is easily recruited to the private property rights tradition of John Locke. But even when Hungarian villagers did hold the land as parcels of private real estate, as most of them did in Tázlár, this was a comparatively recent development and it should not be misinterpreted. It did not mean absolute rights for private individuals: the rights were thought by villagers to be held by families rather than by their individual members. Even in areas of scattered settlement such as Tázlár, villagers acknowledged the 'moral economy' of their community, which constrained the behaviour of individual members. Thus the 'individualism' of the pre-socialist community was qualified by a broad moral tradition, within which the constraints and responsibilities systematically inculcated by the various churches were probably the most significant factor.

The imposition of communism was clearly an intervention that was rejected by the mass of the peasantry: the collectivism of communist morality had nothing in common, so it seemed, with the moral economy of the village. Communism, so this argument goes, destroyed the fabric of the traditional society. But this collectivist system, paradoxically, then proceeded to encourage individualism and self-exploitation. The consequent emergence of dynamic entrepreneurs and development of limited private property rights in the era of 'market socialism' is then presented in terms of corruption and *anomie*. Communism, rather than weave elements of individualism back into a system of collective morality, only further undermined its own claims to moral legitimation through the encouragement of the new, 'anything goes' *polgárosodás*. The moral consequences are typically represented as especially dire when sudden wealth is bestowed upon previously poor villagers. I came across such attitudes frequently during my years in Budapest.

My own analysis is quite different. First, the extent to which the market socialist economy stimulated only selfishness should not be exaggerated. Private housebuilding relied on a family's ability to recruit labour through traditional mutual aid groups that were also marked by extensive festive socializing, More generally, economic activities that depended on networks of kin and friends should not simply be written off as pathological deviations from a very artificial ideal type of Western economic interaction. What Sik terms 'network capital' is important in all societies.[28] Rather than associate all such networking with the problems of coping with crises in an economy of perpetual shortage, the reciprocal exchanges of labour characteristic of rural Hungary in the past continued to promote the integration of households in the socialist period.

Judgemental approaches to values, especially rural values, are not new in the social science literature. Discussions concerning the absence of values in Eastern Europe under socialism bear a certain resemblance to earlier debates in the anthropological literature about 'amoral familism' in rural Italy.[29] For example, Janine Wedel's recent work on Poland suggests that, even in urban situations, loyalties to networks and 'social circles' are as incompatible with the development of a new market economy as they were with the old communist principles.[30] This reminds me of Banfield's contentions concerning entrenched cultural barriers to progress and 'modernization' in the Italian South. Critics of such views have pointed out that, as soon as realistic new economic opportunities have been made available, the apparent barriers tend to melt away. It is therefore a mistake to reify value systems as 'obstacles to progress'. It is much worse to judge them, whether implicitly or explicitly, by a certain Western configuration in which notions of public or civic responsibility, civility, civilization and citizenship are collapsed together.

I do not wish to argue that values are unimportant. On the contrary, I think that shifting the controversies over civil society in the direction of 'civility' and 'civilization', not to mention 'citizenship', will help us to draw up a very different 'balance sheet' for communism and also a very different prognosis of postcommunist dilemmas.

It is easy to list the problems of the former period. Abuse of alcohol was the factor I emphasized most strongly in my account of Tázlár in the 1970s. It seemed to be increasing, particularly through the uncontrolled and illegal distillation of spirits. Sexual immorality was also reputed to be increasing in the village, more especially in the outlying *tanya* areas where it was easy for unmarried couples to live together undisturbed (relationships popularly known as *vad házasság*, literally 'wild marriage'). Older people would often comment negatively on the effects of television, on the reprehensible recreational interests of young people and on their frequent failure to observe traditional etiquette by offering respectful greetings to their elders. Such points would seem to epitomize a decline in civility. Yet the socialist system also provided all village children with a far better education than they had received in the past, and politeness codes have always been rigorously enforced in schools and other public arenas. The provision of electricity and a public water supply has greatly improved the quality of everyday life for all residents of the centre and many *tanya* dwellers as well. All residents have benefited from modern health care services. Those who have done well out of the opportunities created in agriculture have gained access to a range of consumer goods that their parents could never even have dreamed of. Not all of this wealth has been used for short-term consumer gratification and status competition. Some of it has been used to take families on holiday for the first time, whether by private car or through an organized Ibusz tour, thereby expanding cultural horizons, particularly of the young. Some young people from Tázlár have been able to travel in groups to remote parts of the former Soviet Union, while others have been able to arrange private exchanges with acquaintances in Switzerland. Villagers have certainly not shared in all of these benefits equally, but it is important to make clear that the record of socialism in rural Hungary was neither unremitted stagnation nor the mindless squandering of new wealth.

In broad outline the picture is one that may resemble the transformations of rural communities in many other parts of the world over the same period. Certainly the 'diseases of civilization' can be observed in similar ways in some parts of Western Europe, and the tendency for old people to deplore the morals of the young is, if not universal, certainly very widespread. There are of course some other aspects of moral behaviour in rural Hungary that must be seen as more specific, local products. Some of these go back a long way: for example, high suicide and alcoholism rates existed in pre-socialist Hungary and were not the creations of socialism. But in other cases it would seem that substantial changes are directly related to socialist institutions. The destruction of 'civil society' in the sense of public sphere, as noted above, is one area in which change for the worse may have taken place: villagers did not come together socially in as many contexts as they had done in the past. But, quite apart from the fact that the reasons for this were as much economic as political, as noted above, even this example needs further qualification. It is also the case that the need to police the village has declined substantially in the socialist period. Before the 1940s a police station manned by some five or six *csendör* was considered essential for the maintenance of public order. In the 1970s just one policeman lived in Tázlár, and even he was seldom required for duty within the boundaries of the village. People did not seem to feel that there were any problems of public order, not even in the remoter *tanya* areas; and so perhaps this should be entered in the positive column of socialism's balance sheet as a contribution to civility.

There may nevertheless be good reasons why intellectuals such as Elémer Hankiss should view the socialist period as entirely destructive of civility and civilization.[31] A significant gulf between town and countryside has long played a part in political and ideological debates in Hungary. It is possible that the socialist period contributed to a deterioration in the relationship between villagers and better-educated professional elites based in towns and cities. When intellectuals complain that socialism was prejudicial to the 'values of civil society', what they really mean is that large numbers of people became less willing than they had been previously to display deference to the cultural superiority of their elites. I think these tensions were accentuated by the incentives supplied to small farmers in the last decades of socialism. Farmers who had always been cynical about the world of bureaucrats could afford to become more openly contemptuous as their incomes exceeded those of the pen-pushers for the first time; and as I observed at cooperative general meetings, the lawyers who sit on the platform today have no more respect from the audience than the communist *nomenklatura* of old.

Rather than see such behaviour as evidence of the amoral or immoral character of socialism, I think it is preferable to link it to an older morality that the later socialist period did much to strengthen. This older morality was composed of diverse strands. One of these, as noted, emphasized the 'private' ownership of land, and in this context it is easy to see how socialist policies, particularly the appropriation of land, were perceived to be deeply antagonistic. This explains how it is possible for politicians and economists who link the present shift to a full market economy with a call for a system of pure private property rights to gain support from the ideologists of parties whose main base is in the countryside, and from villagers themselves.[32] Some villagers (but far fewer than expected, thanks to the gloomy prospects for agriculture in the present conjuncture) have shown a strong interest in re-establishing their property rights over land taken from them in the course of collectivization.[33]

But there is another, at least equally important element in traditional peasant culture in Hungary, that asserts hard work as the basis of value and 'mastery'.[34] An affinity between the values of the peasantry and Marxist notions of the 'labour theory of value' has been widely reported.[35] Hungarian economic reforms after 1968 meant that, following the disruption caused to traditional patterns of ownership in the earlier decades of communism, for millions of small-scale farmers there was now an unusually direct link between the labour invested by themselves and their families in farming activities, and their consequent economic rewards. Of course not everything depended upon the time and intensity of labour: in Tázlár, for example, a fortunate inheritance and superior skills could generate superior returns for some wine-producers, and this was considered legitimate. But on the whole, it was 'honest physical labour' that commanded greatest respect and was seen to bring its just reward. The obverse of this morality was the frequency with which complaints were made about those whose earnings were seen as unwarranted by this criterion, for example the excessive 'tips' expected by more and more professionals. Accusations of embezzlement, as we have noted, brought down a communist council chairman in the 1980s. They were frequently levelled against cooperative officials, who were often held in general contempt ('living off the fruits of our labour'). Such people were only able to stave off complaints if they were known to work on their own farms in their spare time, as all cooperative leaders in Tázlár have done in recent years. Even now, however, they are regularly condemned for being coy about their precise salaries and for paying themselves performance-related bonuses that, following the logic of the old peasant morality, no amount of ingenuity with paperwork and marketing ploys can ever justify.

These values are not a helpful basis for successful transition to a new market economy, and the villagers' commitment to the values of honest labour in the above sense is of course deeply inimical to much of what is going on in Hungary today. My point is that the villagers' lack of respect for white-collar elites is based on deep moral principles rather than the lack of them. The villagers do not observe the niceties of civil discourse at cooperative meetings. On the contrary, they are blunt and rude. But they know perfectly well that nothing they say is likely to affect the outcome of such proceedings. As a matter of taste, most people probably prefer the discourse of today's leaders to that of the elites of the socialist period: rural Hungarians do clearly respond more enthusiastically to the religious and nationalist imagery that is now prominent in the public sphere than they ever responded to the symbology of communism. There was much that made villagers cynical in both the earlier and the later phases of communist rule. The repression of the 1950s set the tone for relations of antagonism. By the 1980s

villagers reserved their vituperation for those new elites whose
wealth was thought to derive from 'speculation', insurance frauds
and the like (as in the case of the mayoral candidate, reported
above). Moral criteria were applied to the economic opportunities
available: hard work was not enough to justify profits if they
were thought to derive from traffic in drugs, for example. But in
Hungary in the 1990s it is blatantly obvious to everyone that the
most disreputable activities are the most profitable. The transition
to market economy has been associated with an agricultural crisis
in which traditional peasant virtues bring only heavy economic
losses. Some villagers have felt morally obliged to buy back their
patrimony, out of respect for their forebears; and they have worked
hard on the precious plots, as of old, only to find that the land
absorbs their lifetime's savings in a single unsuccessful season.
Simultaneously, the villagers see that the 'transition' is a nice earner
for many white-collar elites.

In the popular mind, then, the transition to the new slogans of
'market economy' and 'civil society' is associated with windfall
profits for the few, particularly people operating various forms of
cartel known as *mafia*. In Tázlár as throughout Eastern Europe,
crimes against property have increased in the last few years. In
some areas there have been efforts to establish a kind of 'neighbourhood watch' scheme. If eventually such an organization emerges in
the village it might be hailed as an example of the self-organization
of civil society. But you can see that such self-organization has only
been made necessary by the decline in public order that might also
be considered an essential part of living in a civilized society. There
is a fine line between a neighbourhood watch scheme and a vigilante
group.[36]

Space does not allow me to illustrate here the many ways in
which the welfare state built up in Hungary under communism is
now being scaled down, in line with similar developments in Western countries such as Britain. Some of the benefits that all Tázlár
residents had enjoyed as citizens in the socialist period are now
being eliminated.[37] Farmers whose income flows have always been
irregular, and who may have no reliable income at all in the new
economic circumstances, are unable to pay the new high premiums
required for health insurance. So far the educational system has
remained largely intact; but whereas in the communist past almost
all village children proceeded to some form of secondary school
(following the eight-grade primary school) and employment was
guaranteed to all school leavers, nowadays many teenagers must

face unemployment and years of painful dependency on their families. At the other end of the age spectrum, rural pensions remain desperately low. Elderly villagers have been especially active in opposing the dissolution of cooperatives: in Tázlár and elsewhere they see this collective institution as virtually the sole bulwark of security in their very uncertain lives.

Sik has argued that the transition to market economy has been accompanied by increased mobilization of network capital, as people search for the best possible guidance for 'grabbing the postcommunist cake'.[38] This analysis may be plausible in most urban contexts, though even here I wonder how far it is characteristic of the former blue-collar workforce, the new unemployed. Certainly, few, if any, villagers of Tázlár stand any chance of benefiting significantly from the new property relationships. Most are more worried about survival strategies, in the course of which previous networks may remain important; but I have the impression that reciprocal labour relationships may be declining along with the decline in housebuilding and agricultural activity, and that at least some households may be forced into greater isolation, that is, they are moving into a situation where they have fewer opportunities for informal association and sociability than existed under communism.

In summary, the villagers of the *tanya* settlement of Tázlár have little acquaintance with 'civility' in the Western bourgeois sense and have been reluctant to show deference to allegedly more civilized elites. This sort of behaviour has been linked by some observers to a general crisis of values under socialism. But I argue that important elements of socialist ideology had profound resonances in the countryside, and that these should not be dismissed. Some elements in the 'populist' ideological traditions of rural Hungary can be made to fit with the new ideological blueprints of right-wing politicians and free marketeers. But other elements, I would say on balance of greater significance, align the villagers with the moral imperatives that were operationalized in the later socialist period, in which hard work by individuals and families (with high levels of reciprocity between them) were seen to obtain their just reward. This unlikely affinity gained surprising confirmation in the national elections of May 1994, when the Hungarian Socialist Party polled strongly in rural areas, including Tázlár.

Contrary to the usual stereotypes of this region, the communist decades extended rights of citizenship very effectively throughout the population in states that had previously excluded most of their subjects from such rights. None of the terms we have been considering – civility, civilization, citizenship, civil society – has figured either in socialist discourse or in local discourse in Tázlár. But if we are going to explore these themes here or elsewhere in contemporary Eastern Europe, it is essential first to understand the 'objective' improvements which communism brought about in the living conditions of the rural population. Second, it is no less important to grasp how the more subjective, moral issues have been perceived over recent decades. Put the two together and you may be able to understand why, for many villagers themselves, the moral achievements of communism have only become clear retrospectively, against the backcloth of the present agricultural crisis and elites that do not seem to care.

CONCLUSIONS

When old concepts in philosophy are reinvented after a long silence you must expect them to undergo a certain coarsening, and sometimes more radical distortion. I think both have occurred in the case of civil society, particularly when the term is opposed crudely to the totalitarian state. There is some irony in the fact that the conservative Ernest Gellner's use of the term owes more to Hegel and Gramsci than to other possible lineages. But this adaptation makes sense when you see how he applies it to recent history in Eastern Europe. Gellner is not concerned with the history of the concept. Rather, he has taken over the simplistic models of dissident intellectuals and Western totalitarian theorists, with all their shortcomings. The concept of society itself is now widely regarded as obsolete, but even if we do not reject this concept it must be doubted whether civil society can ever exist as a singular, unified agent.[39]

Yet clearly Gellner is right to note that civil society has become a powerful slogan. It ought to be possible to investigate ethnographically how this has come about, for example, the conditions of intellectual production, and the interests of various parties as concepts and information are exchanged. 'Zero sum game' models that pit civil society against the state may be simplistic, but they have been widely disseminated among all sections of the population in the former socialist countries as well as in the West. (Perhaps the part played in this by external power relations, and by institutions such as Radio Free Europe, should not be overlooked.) In other words, the models of some intellectuals can be treated as 'folk models', and the twin concepts of totalitarianism and civil society can be seen by anthropologists as central ideas that constitute social life in Eastern Europe. But Ernest Gellner does not usually privilege ideas to this extent. When he claims that civil society is 'concrete sociologically', I take him to mean that he wishes to approach it not as a folk concept but as a term of analysis, for understanding and explaining socialist societies and their eventual collapse. In this sense he leaves me unconvinced.

Perhaps it is, after all, important to look more carefully at the contexts in which ideas have been developed, and in the case of civil society some possible uses have more to commend them than others. In this chapter I have tried to distinguish three dimensions in which the concept might be 'operationalized' in positive analysis, and I illustrated each of these with reference to the Hungarian village of Tázlár. In the first, civil society is taken as 'a space or arena between the household and the state, other than the market, which affords possibilities of concerted action and social self-organization'.[40] In this aspect of its deployment, I agree with Krishan Kumar that the concept of civil society adds little to Habermas's concept of the 'public sphere', and the latter is preferable in as much as it has fewer confusing connotations.[41] Civil society in this sense was acutely missing in Tázlár in the mid-1980s. But so what? It is almost equally elusive in both the pre-socialist and the post-socialist village as well. If one looks outside the village, there would appear to be many more possibilities for 'social self-organization' in the 1990s than at any time over the previous half century in this part of Central Europe. But this appearance could be deceptive, and if you ask farmers when the state took notice of their interests, they would probably say that things were much better under socialism than when the Smallholders Party came to share power in an allegedly free government after 1990. A political scientist might even concede that the shady lobbies of Kádár's socialism permitted more effective interest articulation than has been accomplished either before or since as far as the rural population is concerned.

The second aspect of civil society considered in this chapter was the economic. Exploiting an important linguistic ambiguity that Hungarian shares with German, and building on the insights of generations of Hungarian social scientists, I argued that the later socialist period witnessed considerable progress towards civil society in the sense of a more bourgeois economic and social structure. The reformed socialist economy, sometimes known as 'market socialism', brought special benefits to small-scale farmers. It is clear that the prosperity achieved by many has had far-reaching political effects. Thanks to the economic revolution, the absence of civil society in the first, political sense, was of little concern to the great majority of Hungarians. Idealized images of the public sphere in bourgeois society do not impress villagers who have unprecedented opportunities in the economic sphere; and perhaps Szelenyi is right to point out that this was, after all, what came first in Western European civil societies as well.[42]

The most important theme for further anthropological research must be the third aspect identified in this chapter: the culture of 'civility', and questions of values that remain of central concern throughout the region in the 1990s. Intellectuals have frequently bemoaned the lack of values in late socialist Hungary; but to judge, for example, from rises in virtually every type of crime, many things have only become worse in recent years. Equally, those who admired the role played by Solidarity and the church as the pillars of a strong civil society in Poland can draw little comfort from the *anomie* of recent years in that country. If anything, it would seem that the ultimate problems of 'civility' and 'civilization' have become even more intractable throughout Eastern Europe since the demise of communism. There is no sign of improvement in the longer term, though the 1994 election results suggest that some Hungarian villagers are now realizing an important affinity between the values of 'reformist' communism as implemented among them in the 1970s and 1980s and the traditional values of the peasant community.

In the late twentieth century it is anachronistic to emphasize that philosophical tradition in which civil society is identified with a 'pure market economy' and stands sharply opposed to the state. In Eastern Europe such a model of civil society has been prominent as a surrogate for and successor to totalitarian theory, but anthropological work shows that such models have always been misleading. Indeed, to adapt Karl Kraus's verdict on another body of intellectual ideas that originated in Central Europe a century ago, I think that this version of civil society 'is itself that spiritual disease of which it considers itself to be the cure'.

NOTES

1 For example, A. Nove and D. Nuti, eds, *Socialist Economics*, Penguin, London, 1972.

2 For example, H. Skilling and F. Griffiths, eds, *Interest Groups in Soviet Politics*, Princeton University Press, Princeton, N.J., 1971.

3 C. Hann, *Tázlár: A Village in Hungary*, Cambridge University Press, Cambridge, 1980.

4 J.-F. Bayart, *The State in Africa*, Longman, London, 1993; S. Mardin, *Religion and Social Change in Turkey*, State University of New York Press, Albany, 1989, and 'Civil Society and Islam', in this volume.

5 E. Gellner, 'Review of C. Kukathas, et al, eds, *The Transition from Socialism. State and Civil Society in the USSR*', *Soviet Studies*, vol. 44, 1992, pp. 353, 355.

6 Credit (if credit is due) for being the first Western commentator to use civil society in this way should go to Andrew Arato, for his 'Civil Society Against the State: Poland 1980–1', *Telos*, no. 47, 1981. Of course, such commentators were in close contact with local intellectuals who took up the term in the same period, notably Adam Michnik and Vaclav Havel.

7 E. Gellner (under the pseudonym Philip Peters), 'The State of Poland', *Times Literary Supplement*, no. 4246, 1984, p. 916.

8 Gellner, 'The State of Poland', p. 916.

9 See C. Hann, 'Gellner on Malinowski: Words and Things in Central Europe', in J. A. Hall and I. C. Jarvie, eds, *The Social Philosophy of Ernest Gellner*, Editions Rodopi, Amsterdam, forthcoming.

10 C. Hann, ed., *Market Economy and Civil Society in Hungary*, Frank Cass, London, 1990.

11 Hann, *Tázlár*.

12 J. Habermas, *The Structural Transformation of the Public Sphere: An Inquiry into a Category of Bourgeois Society*, Polity, Cambridge, 1989.

13 Hann, *Tázlár*, ch. 5.

14 For further details, see Hann, *Tázlár*.

15 C. Hann, 'Property relations in the new Eastern Europe: the case of specialist cooperatives in Hungary', in H. de Soto and D. Anderson, eds, *The Curtain Rises*, Humanities Press, New Jersey, 1993.

16 C. Hann, 'Civil Society at the Grass Roots: A Reactionary View', in P. Lewis, ed., *Democracy and Civil Society in Eastern Europe*, Macmillan/St Martin's Press, London, 1992.

17 C. Hann, 'From comrades to lawyers: continuity and change in local political culture in rural Hungary', *Anthropological Journal on European Cultures*, vol. 2, 1993.

18 For an example, see P. Skalnik, '"Socialism is Dead" and very much alive in Slovakia: political inertia in a Tatra village', in C. Hann, ed., *Socialism: Ideals, Ideologies, and Local Practice*, Routledge, London, 1993.

19 E. Hankiss, *East European Alternatives*, Oxford University Press, Oxford, 1990, pp. 33–4.

20 G. Illyés, *People of the Puszta*, Chatto and Windus, London, 1971; G. Pálóczi-Horváth, *In Darkest Hungary*, Gollancz, London, 1944.

21 I. Szelenyi, 'Eastern Europe in an Epoch of Transition: towards a socialist mixed economy?', in V. Nee and D. Stark, eds, *Remaking the Economic Institutions of Socialism*, Stanford University Press, Stanford, Cal., 1989; Z. Pelczynski, 'Solidarity and the Rebirth of Civil Society', in J. Keane, ed., *Civil*

Society and the State, Verso, London, 1988.
22 However, by the second half of the 1980s a plethora of new organizations had appeared in Budapest. Many of these played an important part in preparing the way for the exit from the one-party state, long before the terms of this exit were finally settled by external fiat in 1989.
23 I. Szelenyi, *Socialist Entrepreneurs*, Polity Press, Cambridge, 1988.
24 Szelenyi, *Socialist Entrepreneurs*.
25 Szelenyi, *Socialist Entrepreneurs*, p. 51.
26 Szelenyi, *Socialist Entrepreneurs*, p. xv.
27 N. Swain, 'The Evolution of Hungary's Agricultural System since 1967', in P. Hare et al., eds, *Hungary: a Decade of Economic Reform*, George Allen and Unwin, London, 1981.
28 E. Sik, 'Network Capital in Capitalist, Communist and Post-Communist Societies', paper presented at the 13th Sunbelt Social Network Conference, Tampa, Florida, 1993.
29 E. Banfield, *The Moral Basis of a Backward Society*, Free Press, Glencoe, 1958.
30 J. Wedel, ed., *The Unplanned Society*, Columbia University Press, New York, 1992.
31 Hankiss, *East European Alternatives*.
32 For example, J. Kornai, *The Political Economy of Communism*, Princeton University Press, Princeton, N.J., 1992.
33 C. Hann, 'From Production to Property: decollectivisation and the family–land relationship in contemporary Hungary', *Man*, vol. 28, 1993.
34 M. Lampland, 'Pigs, party secretaries and private lives in Hungary', *American Ethnologist*, vol. 18, 1991.
35 S. Gudeman, *The Demise of a Rural Economy*, Routledge, London, 1978.
36 R. Abrams, 'Sungusungu: village vigilante groups in Tanzania', *African Affairs*, vol. 86, 1987.
37 See Hann, 'Property relations in the new Eastern Europe'.
38 Sik, 'Network Capital in Capitalist, Communist and Post-Communist Societies'.
39 T. Ingold, ed., 'The Concept of Society is Theoretically Obsolete', Manchester, Group for Debates in Anthropological Theory, 1991. Solidarity in Poland is frequently cited to show that societal unity was possible; but fieldworkers in Poland were always aware of how incomplete the alleged unity was (e.g. C. Hann, *A Village without Solidarity*, Yale University Press, New Haven, Conn., 1985); this awareness became widespread as soon as the movement was called upon to assume democratic responsibilities after 1989.
40 C. G. A. Bryant, 'Social Self-Organisation, Civility and Sociology: A Comment on Kumar's "Civil Society"', *British Journal of Sociology*, vol. 44, 1993.
41 K. Kumar, 'Civil Society: An Inquiry into the Usefulness of an Historical Term', *British Journal of Sociology*, vol. 44, 1993, and 'Civil Society Again: A reply to Christopher Bryant's "Social Self-Organisation . . ."', *British Journal of Sociology*, vol. 45, 1994.
42 Szelenyi, 'Eastern Europe in an Epoch of Transition'.

8

Post-Marxism, No Friend of Civil Society

Hudson Meadwell

In this chapter, I assess the role that the concept of civil society has played in post-Marxism. I will make two general arguments. The first claim is that post-Marxism, in ways to be discussed in this chapter, has become organized around republican values. The second, and related, argument is that the post-Marxist concept of civil society privileges conformity over diversity. Civil society, in post-Marxist discourse, is not structured by differences that must be politically mediated; instead a teleological disposition towards agreement is assumed to be the deep structure of civil society. I will approach these issues through a discussion of the treatment of new social movements. This exercise should shed some light on the renewed interest in civil society in post-Marxist discourse, since new social movements and civil societies are intertwined parts of new thinking within the left in the West. I will rest my case on a discussion of one central set of arguments best articulated by Cohen and Arato.[1] Since they draw so heavily on the work of Habermas, the chapter will also examine his arguments at certain points in the discussion.

Republicanism is a set of attitudes towards community and the individual, and towards the moral and political economy of community. These attitudes typically involve ontological, moral and political commitments. Politically speaking, republicans favour small communities because smallness permits direct democracy and eliminates the need for political representation. Smallness also makes face-to-face interaction a larger subset of all interaction, and this is valued because it is conducive to transparency in interaction and to solidarity. Republican moral economy juxtaposes virtue and commerce. Its archetype is the Greek household economy, but more generally, the argument is that economic activity must be subordinated to the telos of group life. Republicans grant ontological priority to the community as well.

It is my claim that these republican conventions, while modified in some important ways, are recognizable in and central to post-Marxist discourse, and that they influence post-Marxist attitudes towards civil society. Republicanism is, moreover, an important constitutive feature of new social movements and not simply an external interpretation of them. Once this dimension of post-Marxist discourse is identified, the interpretation summarized above is given coherence. In other words, 'republican' is a more revealing description of this discourse and practice than other terms sometimes used to identify them, such as 'left-libertarian' or 'communitarian', and it is more specific than 'post-Marxist', which is too general to pick up the distinctiveness of this perspective on late modernity.

Some elements of this complex of republican attitudes were present in Marx's work, perhaps most visibly in the first volume of *Capital* where he drew on Aristotelian categories of economic analysis in introducing the distinction between use-value and exchange-value.[2] Arendt has even suggested that Marx's vision of communism reproduced the political and social conditions of the Athenian city-state and, more recently, a number of commentators have examined the Aristotelian background to Marx's moral economy.[3] Post-Marxists have reworked these features of Marx's legacy basically by abandoning the preoccupation with the economy of capitalism. The distinction between use- and exchange-value is refashioned and the terms of the new argument are embedded in a framework that has the advantage, they claim, of avoiding the economic reductionism of Marx. Yet despite these changes, republicanism continues to be important to their arguments. This claim can be developed through an examination of the treatment of civil society.

CIVIL SOCIETY AND THE LIFEWORLD

Cohen and Arato's conception of civil society is post-Marxist, they argue, because they do not identify civil and bourgeois society and because they abandon the goal of total revolution.[4] Like most other theorists of civil society, they distinguish civil society from the state. They go on to differentiate the economy from civil society, a move that distinguishes their work from both Marx and liberals such as Gellner.[5] Civil society has a special relationship to the lifeworld; the associations of economic and political society are not structured by this relationship and therefore are set outside civil society. Their approach is rooted in the work of Habermas. This inspiration is most obvious in their definition of the institutions of civil society: 'institutions that must be coordinated communicatively appear under the heading of civil society.'[6] By this move, they locate civil society in the lifeworld, and in picking out communication as the distinctive marker of civil society, they draw on the constitutive features of the lifeworld that distinguish it from political and economic subsystems. The lifeworld is unlike these systems because it alone is constituted by mutuality and reciprocity. In short, 'solidarity is not a steering resource like power and money.'[7] The connection between lifeworld and civil society is closely drawn, and defence of the lifeworld is also defence of civil society.[8] The debt here to Habermas is so deep that we need to turn to his work to unpack some of their arguments.

Habermas straightforwardly links communication and solidarity: 'communicative action is a switching station for the energies of social solidarity.'[9] More importantly, it is Habermas, of course, who establishes the distinction between system and lifeworld. His separation of system and lifeworld draws together three elements. The first is a reworked version of the distinction between exchange and use-value. To this starting-point, he joins two other dualisms: the hermeneutic reworking of the Kantian distinction between the transcendental and empirical self and Durkheim's distinction between the sacred and the profane.

Habermas's attitude is that there is something more dignified about the lifeworld, that the lifeworld is a world of meaning and the system is a space characterized by instrumental relations between humans and between humans and nature. Hermeneutics is required to understand the lifeworld, it is not needed to understand the imperatives of the system and its subsystems. This is an old argument about modernity, refashioned to some extent by Habermas through his use of the language of system and life world and the way he uses hermeneutics to mark off the distinctiveness of the lifeworld. In the first place, his attitude plays on the juxtaposition between virtue and commerce, and on the relationships between economies and communities in the modern world, once economic relationships are organized in markets that have a dynamic which is not subordinated to the needs of the community.

Habermas, however, distinguishes his approach to these questions from historical materialism. Marx, he argued in *Theory and Practice*, fused interaction and labour under the rubric of social praxis.[10] The result was the conflation of communicative action with instrumental action, the identification of a science of man with natural science and a monistic theory of value. The separation between system and lifeworld is not really presupposed in Marx's economic concepts. Habermas thus seeks to establish this separation through the theory of communicative action. His approach is like Marx's because he intends to recover a potential for reason encapsulated in the forms of social reproduction. However, 'looked at philosophically, this potential is to be reclaimed without ontological backing, without recourse to Aristotle – that is, without falling back behind Kant.'[11]

The central move in the hermeneutic language game, reworked by Habermas to yield this distinction between system and lifeworld, is a reading of the Kantian dualism between the empirical self and the transcendental self. This distinction establishes the grounds for the debate about the *Geisteswissenschaften*. The proponents of hermeneutics insist on the necessity of understanding in the human sciences, usually pointing to constitutively distinctive features of humans to support their positions, and they locate these features in the lifeworld. Their argument builds on this dualism in Kant, which they read as a contrast between the natural and the social worlds, between science and moral choice. While Habermas argues that his discourse ethics gives up Kant's dichotomy between an intelligible and a phenomenal world, a dualism which reworks this dichotomy continues to be expressed in his work.

The hermeneutic tradition also plays on this Kantian dualism in another important way. Kant's argument establishes a limit to knowledge because, in distinguishing the phenomenal and the noumenal worlds, he argues that things in themselves cannot be known. This price he pays in order to argue for the constitutive importance of the categories and the moral autonomy of agents. In the hermeneutic tradition, this limit becomes a thesis about language and lifeworlds. There are some things about lifeworlds which cannot be said because lifeworlds have a prelinguistic, preconceptual dimension. This is the Kantian thesis about limits, expressed in the terms of language and not with regard to experience. And this argument about the pre-conceptual, pre-reflexive background of the lifeworld is taken up by Habermas.

The reworking of Kant through the hermeneutic tradition provides for Habermas an important part of the contrast between system and lifeworld, for the system is a naturalized world in which there is no distinction to be made between this ineffable background and foreground. It is a world not of freedom, but of necessity, a world that is thus devalued when set alongside the lifeworld, which is a world of meaning, of autonomy and of moral choice. By contrast, the system is steered by the mechanisms of money and power, generalized media of exchange in which persons are constructed as means and not as ends. Relations between individuals are instrumental, and systemic imperatives do not flow from principles, but from strategic necessities. These media are universal, and not marked by the particular, but the space they structure is not a moral space.

Habermas does not want to go back behind Kant because pre-Kantian philosophy is 'First Philosophy', hence foundationalist, and Habermas claims that his work is not foundationalist.[12] Yet Habermas does not rework Marx so thoroughly that the Aristotelian elements of Marx are expunged, and thus he commits himself to arguments that are pre-Kantian and pre-modern. The distinction between system and lifeworld is a conceptual reworking of Marx's terms of exchange and use-value (and these are Aristotelian in inspiration to begin with) set in part, as the above suggests, within hermeneutics; the arguments behind these two sets of dualisms are not that different, once the economic thrust of Marx's terms are modified. Republicanism thus is introduced into Habermas's analysis via *both* Marx and hermeneutics. The latter only reinforces the republican moment, it is no counterweight to it, and thus Habermas is carried along, seemingly against his will, back before Kant.

Cohen and Arato are dependent on the work of Habermas, and their arguments reproduce all of these features. The result is a form of Marxism (post-Marxism) that is more thoroughly republican that Marx ever was. Cohen and Arato do claim, however, that their concept of civil society is 'posttraditional'. By this description, they mean that 'a modernized rationalized lifeworld involves a communicative opening-up of the sacred core of traditions, norms and authority to processes of questioning . . . Communicative action involves a linguistically mediated, intersubjective process through which actors . . . coordinate their interaction by negotiating definitions of the situation and coming to an agreement.'[13] This argument, once again, is indebted to Habermas. More importantly, for the purposes of this chapter at least, their argument is directly taken from Habermas's interpretation of Durkheim. Habermas's incorporation and modification of Durkheim provides the final element for his separation of system and lifeworld.

Habermas gives Durkheim a linguistic twist by arguing that Durkheim's treatment of the sacred is not sensitive to the linguistic mediation of consensus in modernity: '... The authority of the holy is gradually replaced by the authority of an achieved consensus ... the *spellbinding* power of the holy is sublimated into the *binding/bonding* force of criticizable validity claims.'[14] This modifies Durkheim but merely relocates the boundary between the sacred and the profane, although in sublimated form. This appropriation of Durkheim has consequences for his discussion of new social movements. There is a privileged place in Habermas's work for these movements because they are pure expressions of communicative action unspoiled by the attractions of money and power. For their purity to be preserved, however, contact with the profane must be avoided. This is the reason for Habermas's interest in discourse as a means of reaching distortion-free agreement. Discourse is true to the lifeworld and its institutions.

The genealogy of this argument is of some interest: Cohen and Arato, Habermas, Durkheim. Durkheim's argument is that the sacred is constitutive of society and the deep structure of the social, invariant across counterfactual conditions. His sociology rests on a transcendental deduction that drastically modifies the structure of transcendental arguments. Durkheim brings in ontological commitments that are inconsistent with the structure of transcendental arguments as established by Kant.[15] In drawing on Durkheim, therefore, Habermas once again reinforces the pre-Kantian roots of the system/lifeworld distinction.

The foundations of Durkheim's sociology provide an ontology congenial to republicans. His critique of utilitarianism builds on this ontology, and the language of that criticism is the language of republicans. Even when the division of labour was an important part of social life, he argued, society did not become a 'jumble of juxtaposed atoms' between which contact was only transient and external. 'Rather the members are united by ties which extend deeper and far beyond the short moments during which the exchange is made.'[16] The cooperation between individuals that was present in exchange was not the product of the exchange but presupposed society itself. Utilitarians 'reverse the natural order of facts and nothing is more deceiving than this inversion.'[17] To be sure, Durkheim modelled his sociology on the natural sciences, thus violating hermeneutics. This feature of Durkheim's sociology is the reason why Habermas wants to rework Durkheim. Durkheim's distinction between the sacred and the profane, once set within a linguistic framework, fits nicely with Habermas's hermeneutics.

Habermas's work turns on the distinction between system and lifeworld. This distinction draws together three sets of dualisms. The first is Aristotelian in origin: exchange and use-value. The second is taken from Durkheim: the profane and the sacred. The third is the hermeneutic reworking of the Kantian distinction between the empirical and the transcendental self. These sets of distinctions overlay one another and together point in the same direction. Each of the traditions that generates these dualisms is republican. I conclude that the work of Habermas and of Cohen and Arato is republican.

Post-Marxists turn out to be pre-Kantians in part, and Marxism reduces to republicanism, when the economic core of Marx's work is removed and the distinction between virtue and commerce, and use and exchange-value, is maintained in different conceptual form. There is a set of core illiberal attitudes that Marxists and republicans share, and the virtue of this strand of post-Marxism is to make them dramatically visible against a Marxist background.

These moves within post-Marxism do have clear consequences. The conceptual role of virtue changes. Where in republican thought and in Marxism, one function of virtue was to mark off the distinctiveness and the problems of the modern economy, it now functions much more as the fulcrum of a critique of politics in the developed West. With this shift in emphasis, the modern economy and its corrupting effects on human nature drops out as an object of criticism and as a site for radical mobilization. To the extent that the economy remains part of the story, it is positive, as a source of discretionary resources (time and money) that afford the constituencies of some of the new social movements the opportunity for participation. Republican virtues no longer provide a claim for fundamental economic transformation and have only marginal consequences for economic organization. The requirements of efficiency and market rationality take priority and must be satisfied before the demands of reciprocity and solidarity are met.[18]

There is very little remaining that is radical in this admission, or in the reordering of the relationship between virtue and commerce that it produces. A radical critique that is worth its name, even one that is self-consciously 'self-limiting', must therefore shift its ground, and this is one reason why politics has been taken up. Republicanism contains a normative model of political life that can underwrite a critique of the systems of interest-representation of liberal democracy. A shift to politics then becomes a way to attempt to renew a radical critique, although one along republican lines.

In defining civil society so that it no longer includes the economy, however, these post-Marxists effectively eliminate economic power and economic position as a basis for political change. They also have removed the institutions of interest-representation of liberal democracy from the ambit of civil society. These are governed by the steering media of systems – power and money – and cannot stably transmit demands that challenge the organizing logic of the economy and polity. All that is left, then, to mount a challenge are the resources of the lifeworld within civil society. These are the only uncorrupted resources and this is the only pristine site available for resistance. New social movements require this uncontaminated seed-bed and, if civil society were defined to include the economy, this requirement would not be satisfied. Only a certain kind of civil society can nurture these movements. A civil society that included the modern economy would leave room only for 'old' movements, whether Marxist or liberal. It would not create the space that these 'new' forms need.

REPUBLICAN CIVIL SOCIETY AND
NEW SOCIAL MOVEMENTS

My argument about new social movements and civil society in post-Marxism can be summarized: (1) New social movements function theoretically as a substitute for the proletariat; (2) At least some of these movements rest, sociologically speaking, on the new middle class; they are dependent, to this extent, on material affluence and thus on the success of capitalism; (3) The critique provided by these movements is directed much less at the capitalist economy and much more at political and cultural practices and institutions; (4) New social movements are islands of republican practices and institutions that, to be sustained, must be embedded in a certain sort of civil society; (5) This state of affairs is a second-best option; the preferred state of affairs would establish the identity of state and civil society, but this is considered infeasible in late modernity; (6)

This ordering of preferences produces the political strategy of 'self-limiting radicalism'; (7) The post-Marxist argument about new social movements and civil society draws on hermeneutics as a methodological device; (8) The substantive and methodological presuppositions of these positions are rooted in *republicanism*; (9) As a consequence, this discourse is illiberal and, to some extent, pre-modern.

The focus of new social movements includes the ecological externalities created by industrialism, the linkages between industrialism and other practices (militarism), the invasive practices that stabilize late capitalism (bureaucratization, corporatism), or other cultural practices only tangentially related, if at all, to the capitalist economy (patriarchy, sexism). Capitalism, at least its intrinsic features as a system of production and exchange, has virtually disappeared as an object of critique in this strand of post-Marxism. These are the new social movements built, not on the ruins of capitalism, but on some of its successes, and the carriers of criticism and change in this new world. New collective carriers of change have been identified, and the working class has been abandoned. The working class has become the enemy, the harbinger of industrialism in a postindustrial age. Thus this move also provides a solution to the Gramscian problem of 'organic intellectuals'. There is now no need to worry about relations between bourgeois leaders and working-class followers. The concerns of these new social movements are not the material questions of economic production and distribution, but the forging of new collective identities and political cultures that are not based on class.

New social movements are themselves republics: small communities governed by non-hierarchical participation, authenticity in interpersonal relations, a shared sense of the good and the willingness to sacrifice for the group. This, at least, is the normative model that distinguishes these movements from other forms of politics and organizations in their environments. They are republican islands in a sea of profane institutions and practices.

This is the reason why the theory and practice of new social movements make such a fetish of identity-formation. Any other paths to change will be infected by the steering mechanisms of the system. Identity-formation thus combines the ontological and political commitments of republicanism: the priority accorded to a shared lifeworld, which must be presupposed before the individuation of persons becomes possible, underlies the argument about identity-formation, and the republican attitude towards the contaminating effects of participation in representative institutions is also duplicated in the focus on collective identity. There is a strong dose of the politics of perfection in these attitudes toward identity, and this suggests that the politics of identity-formation is at times also meant to be the nucleus of a more radical politics which is looking for a means of bootstrapping itself out of the constraints of the system, so as to challenge it much more fundamentally than the rhetoric of self-limiting radicalism would suggest.

All of this, when set against a Marxist backdrop, is the result of and represents an enormous crisis of confidence within the European left. Post-Marxism abandons Marx, to fall back on republicanism. While Cohen and Arato attempt to present the situation in a more positive light, beginning their book by referring to 'the threshold of yet another great transformation of the self-understanding of modern societies', the lessons for Marxism are essentially negative.[19] This post-Marxist alternative has no power to change the world – it is too hemmed in by capitalism and liberalism. All that is left for the left are new social movements as vehicles for defensive resistance. It is difficult to retrieve from the separation of system and lifeworld much that is more positive, although Cohen and Arato do try.

This separation therefore has two faces in post-Marxism. It marks, first of all, the way in which Marxism is refashioned along republican lines. Second, it functions to define the claim about the distinctiveness of *new* social movements and their relationship to political institutions. New social movements, according to Cohen and Arato, are caught between system and lifeworld imperatives. To the extent that they cross the threshold of formal organization, they become structured by power and money. To the degree that they remain authentic to the lifeworld, they become politically marginalized. A successful reconciliation of these oppositions would mean that these movements have avoided the dilemmas of the old left. Indeed, they would have escaped the structures of the modern world altogether. These are not new dilemmas in processes of political mobilization; they are captured in classic models of mobilization in the developed West,[20] but it is clear that some of the participants in new social movements, especially the ecological movements, thought they could be managed, if not solved.[21] Cohen and Arato also want to have it both ways. They argue that these movements can incorporate the competing demands of expressive and instrumental action. In order to manage these tensions, movements must be structured by strong collective identities that are expressions of solidarity; otherwise, they quickly will become thoroughly stratified by money and power. Yet these identities cannot be so strong that they produce a politics of zealotry.

CIVIL SOCIETY AND DIVERSITY

A series of problems, systematically ignored in the work of Cohen and Arato, arises from this argument about identities and civil society. The root problem is that there are multiple new social movements, each structured by a different collective identity. On the face of it, there is not *one* movement organized to decolonize the lifeworld and civil society and to roll back the penetration of the lifeworld by system imperatives; there are, instead, several movements. Whatever their differences at the level of collective identity, however, these movements are taken by Cohen and Arato to be fundamentally expressions of a single shared orientation. This position must be their real presupposition; otherwise we could reasonably expect that different identities, and the solidarity that is assumed to be associated with each identity, could combine to cause conflict between movements. Solidarity, instead, is presupposed to extend to the social movement sector as a whole. All of these movements, by definition, are expressions of communicative action and these authors presuppose that communicative action is constituted by understanding, and reaching understanding is, in turn, a process of reaching agreement. In this rosy picture, 'Solidary individuals are consciously rooted in the same or significantly overlapping lifeworlds, and this guarantees consensus about important matters . . .'[22] Consensus, not over procedural or institutional arrangements that might address the political problems produced by diversity within a political community, but consensus over the content of the lifeworld, is assumed to be present. Civil society, then, is constituted by identity rather than difference, by unity rather than diversity. In the end in this line of argument, there is only one new social movement (internally differentiated), one collective identity and one lifeworld that nests within it sub-lifeworlds that differ only at the margins. Perhaps this is the reason why civil and political society can be separated in this discourse. Since there are no differences to speak of, there is no politics in civil society.

The upshot of their arguments is that the purpose and value of civil society is not the creation of institutions for the management of diversity, since diversity is not characteristic of civil society. Instead they emphasize the presence of deep consensus. Diversity, in fact, is inimical to their preferred state of affairs, since it would threaten solidarity. This point of view looks to 'manage' difference by excluding it. Their civil society is built, not on toleration, but on conformity. They assume that the deep structure of civil society is agreement. Civil society allows that latent structure to become manifest in associational life. Here again is why identity-formation is so important. This is the process through which essentially identical selves are formed. Republicans have to be educated into republican practices and they have to be reminded about what they have been taught. These processes of socialization and education, so central to republicanism, are incorporated in this discourse under the conceptual rubric of 'identity-formation'.

This argument has little to do with diversity, whatever its claims. I want to address this issue of diversity and difference, especially given that Habermas acknowledges heterogeneity in new social movements and also asserts that these movements are constituted by practices of communicative action, and hence are an approximation of his ideal speech situation.

More specifically, I consider some of the consequences of difference and disagreement for Habermas's treatment of social action. In clarifying the place of personal diversity in the ideal speech situation, we can get clear on the limitations of his universal pragmatics and any derivative account that builds on his work. I claim that there are two distinguishable sources of failure in the ideal speech situation – distortion and diversity – and that Habermas systematically ignores the latter. In Habermas's universal pragmatics, distortion is the most fundamental barrier to understanding. However, the ideal speech situation also fails when distortion-free difference is introduced into its structure. It is this phenomenon of understanding *and* disagreement that I want to explore.

Habermas's conflation of understanding and agreement makes anomalous a situation in which individuals understand each other (in Habermas's sense), but do not agree with each other. This situation is unstable according to Habermas; the direction of discourse is towards the closure of this gap between understanding and agreement. 'The goal of coming to an understanding is to bring about an agreement.'[23] 'Reaching understanding,' he also has argued, 'is considered to be a process of reaching agreement.'[24] The anomaly of this situation trades, however, on the presupposition that understanding and agreement are constitutively related and only unnaturally held apart.

Habermas presents three conditions which make possible the hermeneutic experience of the ideal speech situation. These validity claims are that: (1) the propositional content of communication is true; (2) the speech act is right with respect to the existing normative context; and (3) the intention of the speaker is meant as expressed.[25] These are conditions which produce agreement through understanding: 'Agreement is based on recognition of the corresponding validity claims of comprehensibility, truth, truthfulness (or sincerity), and rightness.'[26] In order to treat difference as a principle on the same footing as Habermas's other principles of the ideal speech situation, I introduce two other conditions. There is a fourth condition: (4) '... for all possible participants, there is a symmetrical distribution of chances to choose and to apply speech-acts.'[27] This is the condition of nonexclusion. Because these conditions are 'general' and 'universal', a fifth and final condition should be unpacked as a separate postulate. This is a condition which (5) admits diversity among interlocutors. These new conditions are correlated but still distinguishable. The principle of nonexclusion can hold over interchangeable or different individuals. The principle of difference does not depend on nonexclusion, although the consequences of difference can vary with the presence or absence of exclusion. Inclusion is justified by an interest in equal access to participation; exclusion, however, not only fails to satisfy this interest but can also restrict diversity, depending on the systematic pattern (if any) of exclusion. An ideal speech situation is constituted by these five conditions.

This ideal speech situation is defined now to eliminate sources of distortion (ignorance, bias, lying, coercion) and to admit difference. Either distortion or difference can cause disagreement. These causes are independent because differences can occur in the absence of distortion. Otherwise, the elimination of distortion always produces agreement, which implies that the only source of disagreement is distortion.

Of these two causes which produce disagreement – distortion and difference – the latter is more central. For disagreement can arise directly out of difference without distortion, and indirectly out of motivated distortion caused by difference. So the condition of diversity collects both the direct and indirect consequences of difference and the other conditions specify distortion-effects independent of distortion motivated by difference. This raises a problem, however. Non-distorted communication need not yield agreement. The consequence of this juxtaposition of non-distortion and disagreement is that there is no ideal speech situation which satisfies truth, sincerity, rightness, nonexclusion and diversity.

There are some ways of avoiding this dilemma. One is to argue that agreement is not a feature of the ideal speech situation while continuing to hold that diversity is a condition. Thus disagreement can co-occur with the five conditions. In this case, the speech situation is only distortion-free. This argument is not open to Habermas because agreement is constitutively related to understanding and thus, as already argued, to the ideal speech situation.

Another way of eliminating the dilemma is just to exclude diversity from the conditions which constitute the ideal speech situation. This eliminates the grounds for disagreement other than distortion. Yet this seems to deny this speech situation a great deal of its robustness and interest because it implies that the only sources of disagreement are distortions in communication. Habermas instead embeds his universal pragmatics in an evolutionary theory. By entering into debate, one is disposed towards agreement. This telos of speech will direct and regulate differences, and individual changes will in some way converge. This seems to say that disagreement disappears as differences are effaced. Agreement is process-dependent and rests, critically, on the supposed presence of a teleological disposition in speech.

We could say also that the ideal speech situation is a set of validity claims which presupposes agreement, holding when agreement is present. Indeed, the evolutionary argument might be read in this way: the argument about the ideal speech situation holds only for those individuals who stand at some appropriate stage of cognitive development. But this kind of argument has rather serious problems which must be resolved before it is convincing. It, too, buys into a teleological point of view, combined with a unilinear model of development which assumes one endpoint towards which individuals converge. Further, such a position is tacitly exclusionary, thus violating condition (4), because it marks off a privileged place for those interlocutors who are appropriately developed.

The dilemma might also be dissolved if differences were not always associated with disagreement. Differences may be present, but against the background of shared conventions, rules, presuppositions (however this shared background is theorized). Or individuals may agree about how their differences are to be regulated within social life. And, of course, some differences may not engage individuals in actual disagreement because differences have been socially segregated in some fashion. The latter two possibilities are issues of constitutional choice. The first, on the other hand, opens up the possibility that the shared background is a result of tacit or unconscious habit or tradition, rather than open, rational interaction. And if the background is a consequence of choice, rather than socialization, then this situation is another instance of constitutional choice. The ideal speech situation, however, is not set up to suggest how differences are to be constitutionally regulated. These proposed resolutions to the dilemma canvassed in this paragraph take us beyond the ideal speech situation.

Another solution to the problems produced by the structure of the ideal speech situation lies in the precondition of comprehensibility.[28] This can be used as a screening mechanism to restrict the kinds of diversity which are present in the ideal speech situation. If it is assumed that some minimum, non-trivial level of agreement is constitutive of comprehensibility, this restriction on diversity is justified because the precondition could not otherwise be met. Under this interpretation, however, comprehensibility is doing more work than Habermas's universal pragmatics can consistently take on board. Agreement has become the foundation for the ideal speech situation, rather than its outcome.

The stumbling block for Habermas is that he wants agreement in the presence of what many take to be central to late modernity-pluralism. The agreement that he seeks is more likely to be found in his image of pre-modern contexts, where pluralism is weak or absent, and diversity is constrained by tradition. But agreement in these circumstances, if it is present, does not meet the requirements of the ideal speech situation. The postmodern move is no more attractive to Habermas because of its celebration of difference. He is trapped between the pre- and the postmodern, and has not yet shown how modernity can be completed.

NOTES

I would like to thank James Booth, John A. Hall, Phil Oxhorn and Jim Tully for our conversations about these issues, and John A. Hall for his comments on this chapter.

1 J. L. Cohen and A. Arato, *Civil Society and Political Theory*, MIT Press, Cambridge, Mass., 1992. This book has been called by a commentator 'one of

the most significant treatises in the realm of political theory to have been published in the last two decades'. R. Wolin, 'Review of Cohen and Arato', *Theory and Society*, vol. 22, 1993.

2 S. Meikle, 'Aristotle and the Political Economy of the Polis', *Journal of Hellenic Studies*, vol. 99, 1979.

3 H. Arendt, *Between Past and Future*, Viking, New York, 1968, p. 19; W. J. Booth, *Households: On the Moral Architecture of the Economy*, Cornell University Press, Ithaca, New York, 1993; A. Gilbert, *Democratic Individuality*, Cambridge University Press, New York, 1990, pp. 263–304; G. E. McCarthy, ed., *Marx and Aristotle*, Rowman and Littlefield, Savage, Maryland, 1992.

4 Cohen and Arato, *Civil Society and Political Theory*, p. 71.

5 See the chapter by Ernest Gellner in this volume.

6 Cohen and Arato, *Civil Society and Political Theory*, p. 480. See also p. 429.

7 Cohen and Arato, *Civil Society and Political Theory*, p. 472.

8 Cohen and Arato, *Civil Society and Political Theory*, pp. 471–4.

9 J. Habermas, *The Theory of Communicative Action*, vol. 2, trans. T. McCarthy, Polity Press, Cambridge, 1987, p. 57.

10 J. Habermas, *Theory and Practice*, trans. J. Viertel, Beacon Press, Boston, 1973, p. 168.

11 J. Habermas, 'Reply to my critics', in J. Thompson and D. Held, eds, *Habermas: Critical Debates*, MIT Press, Cambridge, 1982, p. 221.

12 H. Meadwell, 'The foundations of Habermas's universal pragmatics', *Theory and Society*, vol. 23, 1994.

13 Cohen and Arato, *Civil Society and Political Theory*, p. 435.

14 Habermas, *The Theory of Communicative Action*, vol. 2, p. 77 (emphasis in original).

15 H. Meadwell, 'Communitarian Foundations', typescript, 1994.

16 E. Durkheim, *The Division of Labour in Society*, trans. G. Simpson, Free Press, New York, 1964, p. 227.

17 Durkheim, *The Division of Labour in Society*, p. 280.

18 Cohen and Arato, *Civil Society and Political Theory*, pp. 416, 417.

19 Cohen and Arato, *Civil Society and Political Theory*, p. 1.

20 A. Downs, *An Economic Theory of Democracy*, Harper and Row, New York, 1957; A. Przeworski, *Capitalism and Social Democracy*, Cambridge University Press, New York, 1985.

21 H. Kitschelt, *The Logics of Party Formation*, Cornell University Press, Ithaca, New York, 1989; C. Offe, 'Reflections on the Institutional Self-Transformation of Movement Politics: A Tentative Stage Model', in R. Dalton and M. Kuechler, eds, *Challenging the Political Order*, Oxford University Press, New York, 1990.

22 Cohen and Arato, *Civil Society and Political Theory*, p. 472.

23 J. Habermas, *Communication and the Evolution of Society*, Beacon Press, Boston, 1979, p. 3.

24 J. Habermas, *The Theory of Communicative Action*, vol. 1, Beacon Press, Boston, 1984, p. 286.

25 Habermas, *The Theory of Communicative Action*, vol. 1, p. 99.
26 Habermas, *Communication and the Evolution of Society*, p. 3.
27 Cited in J. Thompson, 'Universal pragmatics', in Thompson and Held, *Habermas: Critical Debates*, p. 123.
28 Habermas, *The Theory of Communicative Action*, vol. 1, p. 98.

9

Animadversions upon Civil Society and Civic Virtue in the Last Decade of the Twentieth Century

Adam B. Seligman

Some time ago, in the city of Cluj-Napota (or Kolosvar, or Klausenberg – depending if one is Romanian, Hungarian or German), I learnt how limited was my understanding of the realities of contemporary Eastern Europe. After attending sabbath services at the local synagogue, I asked whether the local Jews were German or Hungarian. My question was not understood, so I imagined that my Yiddish was at fault. I repeated the question (now more sure of my grammar), and received the reply that 'Yidn Sind Yidn' (Jews are Jews). Pondering this on my way home, past election slogans proclaiming that only the return of the king could unite all of Romania, I realized just how distant contemporary accounts of collective membership and identity in Eastern Europe are from those principles of civil society, individualism and legal autonomy that we associate with citizenship in the West.

In Eastern Europe, the abjuration of universal identities, commitments and what may be termed Kantian desiderata in favour of a renewed saliency of local, ethnic, religious and sometimes national particularisms calls into question our ideas of citizenship. Given this state of affairs and the very pressing need felt in Eastern and East Central Europe to reclaim or re-articulate some model of citizenship, it may be well worth our while to return to two 'early modern' strands of political thought to help us understand the terms of current problems. For the very different, yet not wholly distinct strands of political thought that I have in mind, those of civil society and civic virtue, bear great relevance to the current situation and may help us to understand the 'stakes' that adhere to different ideas of citizenship currently being propounded. Debate about the nature of citizenship is, it must be stressed, as troubled in the West as in the East, as is obvious from argument about multiculturalism, communitarianism and republicanism.

By 'stakes' I am referring to that normative vision of society that is represented by the modern idea of citizenship. Our current conceptions of citizenship as the formalized and legally ascertained rights and duties incumbent upon individuals in their relations within society – conceived of as a nation-state – are, to a great extent, rooted in the noted traditions of civic virtue and civil society. These two traditions represent, however, contrasting models of citizenship, and so also of the social good. Further, many of the current debates over citizenship in the West as in the East – whether of a highly principled nature (the liberal-communitarian debate) or of immediate practicality (over multiculturalism, language instruction in schools in some North Atlantic communities, the status of Russian minorities in the Baltic states or indeed over the status of ethnic minorities throughout Eastern and East Central Europe) – are rooted in principles that derive from these two political traditions. I shall argue that these principles are ultimately irreconcilable.

Now, to some extent, this insight is not terribly new. In fact Benjamin Constant's 1819 speech given at the Athénée Royal 'De la liberté des anciens comparée a celle des modernes' is precisely an explication of some salient differences between the traditions of civic virtue and civil society – though not expressly presented in those terms.[1] Given the tenacity of current debates in political theory and the challenges facing societies in both Eastern Europe and the West at the end of the twentieth century, it may be prudent to review this territory again, to isolate those areas of convergence and, of perhaps greater importance, of divergence in these two traditions – within whose contrasting desiderata our own ideas of the social good are so deeply rooted.

VIRTUE AND CIVILITY COMPARED

Both civil society and civic virtue are, as is all political theory, concerned with the defining relations between the individual and the social, and of positing this relationship in normative as well as descriptive terms. Both are firmly rooted in the intellectual traditions of Western Europe, in the doctrines of natural law and in

the political philosophies and images of ancient Greece and republican Rome. Both played a considerable role in the early modern era
when, with the breakdown of the feudal order and of the universal
Catholic Church, a new basis was sought for the organization of
society.[2] Both continued in different and often interwoven forms
in the eighteenth and, albeit to a lesser extent, in the nineteenth
centuries among very different thinkers, making it impossible to
give a full history of these terms in this paper. What is possible is
the abstraction of some of the core analytic ideas of the respective
traditions, particularly towards notions of the social good. Both are
after all concerned with providing the foundations of what could be
termed a 'moral community' as the base of social life. In both
traditions the idea of 'virtue' is seen as central to the existence of
this moral community. Similarly, both are concerned with the
forces of 'corruption' threatening this moral community. These
forces are posited, moreover, in strikingly similar terms, of luxury,
envy, avarice and what we would term the growing differentiation
of society – and, by the end of the eighteenth century, by the
growth of the market and ties of purely instrumental exchange
between social actors. Similarities notwithstanding, there are important differences, both historical and analytical, between the two
traditions.

Civil society was more an Anglo-American tradition, albeit its
greatest thinkers, Francis Hutcheson, John Millar, Hugh Blair,
Adam Ferguson and Adam Smith, were leaders of the Scottish
Enlightenment. By contrast, the tradition of civic virtue would
seem more continental in nature, with our immediate associations
running from Machiavelli through Jean-Jacques Rousseau (though
the importance of civic virtue in England among 'neo-
Harringtonians' and as an influence on colonial culture in the
decades of independence is critical).[3] The civic virtue tradition was
furthermore more immediately rooted in the political philosophy
of ancient Greece and Rome, and in this sense more 'backward
looking'. Taking the ancient city-state as a model of republican
virtue, it sought, and in some sense still seeks, to return to the
definition of citizenship embodied in the Athenian polis or Roman
republic. It thus insists on a definition of man as citizen where,
following Aristotle, man's (and now presumably woman's) telos
was to be found in and only in the sphere of political activity.

This concept of man as the 'complete citizen' or what can be
alternatively rendered as the 'totalization' of man as citizen was far
from that tradition of social thought that we associate with the idea

of civil society, at least as it developed in the eighteenth century among the Scottish moralists.[4] While recognizing the virtue of ancient republican government, these thinkers were more sensitive to the irremediable nature of historical change and their thought was, consequently, more attuned to positing a new foundation for reciprocity, mutuality and cooperation (and so, ultimately for virtue) and less with a return to a form of social organization whose efficacy in the support of virtue in eighteenth-century commercial society was increasingly in doubt.

In some sense, these latter assumptions of the Scottish moralists would seem to have been vindicated by the passage of time. For by the last third of the eighteenth century and more definitely in the early nineteenth century, the civil society tradition begins to take the place of the civic virtue tradition. This becomes clearer as the nineteenth century progresses and the ideas of civil society are in some sense institutionalized within the growing struggles over citizenship.

These historical differences can however, serve as no more than an introduction to what are the crucial differences between the two traditions. And our interest, fed as it is more by current concerns and less by a purely theoretical interest in the history of ideas, must thus focus on what are the crucial analytic differences between these two traditions in their vision of human endeavour within society.

These differences turn on what are essentially different definitions of virtue, or, in somewhat broader terms, different conceptions of the moral order. In more sociological terms these can be expressed as different conceptions of solidarity where the moral sense is a function of public or of private morality respectively. We need only recall Durkheim's analysis and comparison of repressive and restitutive law as characteristic of mechanical and organic solidarity to apprehend the immediate parallels with the very different moral visions represented by these two political traditions.[5]

In the civic virtue tradition from Aristotle (man's telos in polis) through Machiavelli, the neo-Harringtonian (fear of corruption in the eighteenth century), Rousseau (surrender of all natural liberty to community) and even into Hannah Arendt's philosophical vision (where human realization can only be in the participatory light of the public realm) the moral idea is a *public* one.[6] It is defined by the 'conscience collective' or, to use Rousseau's famous expression, by the general will.[7] Morality, or the stuff of virtue, is less a private attribute and more a public or communal enterprise. It is

realized by the active and continual participation of collective
members in communal affairs and can, following Machiavelli, be
abstracted and removed from all elements of private morality.[8]
Moreover, Rousseau defines 'virtue' succinctly as the 'conformity
of the particular wills with the general will'.[9] This is of course
congruent with the overall moral vision wherein what is regulated
and subjected to authority is not only man's 'actions' but his 'will'
as well.[10] Of course the sovereign authority in question is not that
of the despot but of the community – that community constituted,
as Rousseau explains in *The Social Contract*, by 'the total alienation
of each associate together with all his rights to the community'.[11]
That community where 'each of us puts his person and all his
power in common under the supreme direction of the general will,
and, in our corporate capacity, we receive each member as an
indivisible part of the whole' (emphasis mine) is not only a model of
that type of solidarity which Durkheim termed mechanical, but is,
in essence, a model of citizenship which most closely approximates
the ideal society in the civic virtue tradition.[12]

A community then of a totally unmediated relation between the
parts and the whole, where 'private interests' and 'partial associations' are condemned and where the relation 'of the members to
one another' are 'as unimportant' and the relation of the member
'to the body as a whole' are 'as important as possible'.[13] A moral
community where what is moral is precisely the community. Now
to be sure, once we have abandoned a transcendent morality (and if
we remain unenticed by utilitarian theory) we have few choices but
to follow Durkheim's strictures on the communal nature of all
morality. I note this only for the purpose of keeping a crucial
distinction in mind – that between community as the source of
morality (a sociological truism) and the notion of community as
morality. The latter idea is at the heart of the civic virtue tradition
where a community of virtue is one where the social good is defined
solely by the subjugation of the private self to the public realm.

We are now entering somewhat tricky ground, for the boundaries, indeed the very definition of the public and private, are not
only continually changing but, in the eighteenth century, were only
beginning to emerge as a distinction worthy of thought.[14] Thus
before turning to further distinctive characteristics of the civic
virtue tradition, it may be wise to contrast its very public character
with that of the civil society tradition as exemplified by the Scottish
moralists. In the civil society tradition, the moral basis of society
becomes more and more a *private* ideal. This private idea (and ideal)

of virtue stands in such marked contrast to the public character of virtue in the former tradition as to exemplify, as noted, a fundamentally different model of citizenship and of the social good. In fact, the move from virtue as an attribute of the public sphere to one of private morality was a crucial development in the making of modern liberal-individualism and its models of order. It is as such worth our attention.

The tradition of civil society is, as I have argued elsewhere, first and foremost an ethical edifice.[15] From Shaftesbury's *Characteristics of Men, Manners, Opinions, Times* (1711) through Francis Hutcheson's *Inquiry Into the Origins of Beauty and Virtue* (1725), Adam Ferguson's *An Essay on the History of Civil Society* (1767) and until the 1790 edition of Adam Smith's *The Theory of Moral Sentiments*, it is concerned with positing the moral sense or a 'universal determination to benevolence in mankind' as a fundamental given of human nature.[16] It was this moral sense which assured mutuality, compassion and empathy, that is, a basis for human interaction beyond the calculus of pure exchange. In Adam Ferguson's words:

> What comes from a fellow-creature is received with peculiar emotion; and every language abounds with terms that express somewhat in the transactions of men, different from success and disappointment. The bosom kindles in company, while the point of interest in view has nothing to inflame; and a matter frivolous in itself, becomes important, when it serves to bring to light the intentions and character of men. . . . the value of a favour is not measured when sentiments of kindness are perceived; and the term misfortune has but a feeble meaning, when compared to that of insult and wrong.[17]

Kindness, like insult and wrong, exists beyond the province of meagre interest and achieves its full meaning only in the complex web of human interaction. It is, ultimately, these sentiments that, for the thinkers of the civil society tradition, kept society *civil*.

Now to be sure, the definition and conceptualization of this moral sense was different among the different thinkers of the Scottish Enlightenment. Shaftesbury's 'natural affection' which discerns 'the amicable and the admirable' is not the same as Ferguson's 'moral sentiment' or 'principle of affection to mankind'.[18] Nor were either of these as developed philosophically as Adam Smith's principle of 'sympathy and approbation' which for him provided the driving force of 'all the toil and bustle of the world . . . the end of avarice and ambition, of the pursuit of wealth'.[19] However, they are (with the partial exception of Smith, to be discussed later) strikingly similar in positing an innate moral sense whose existence is both independent of reason and a function of individual moral psychology.[20] The 'conscience' that the thinkers of eighteenth-century Edinburgh and Glasgow were struggling towards was one of individual mores rather than public commitments. It was rooted in the individual self rather than in a social being. If for Rousseau the moral sense in the form of the general will can be said to arise *sui generis* out of society, for the thinkers of the civil society tradition it also exists *sui generis*, beyond reduction to other interests, reasons and passions.[21] Yet in struggling to posit an autonomous grounding to moral facts, they had recourse not to the social but to the individual self as guarantor of the moral order.

Of course the idea of civil society maintained elements of the civic virtue tradition, notably, the communal locus of individual life. The ideas of 'vanity' for Ferguson, or 'approbation' for Smith, play this role and provide the basis for natural sympathy and moral affections upon which moral community is predicated.[22] Both build on the social nature of our existence and on our individual validation in and through the eyes of others. They link us to the social whole as we become who we are through the other's perception of us, a sort of Meadian social self *avant la lettre*. Yet, crucially here the communal or social 'Other' is internalized in the self which remains inviolate, though not abstracted from community. This however is very different – if not diametrically opposed – to the classical tradition which saw the individual as only human within the polis and through activity in the public realm (and which, in ancient Rome, even saw the intimate activity of procreation as a fulfilment of civic duties) or from Rousseau's ideal where only the replacement of the individual personality by a 'corporate and collective body' with its own communal identity, life and will can guarantee civic virtue and human realization.[23]

Interestingly both models seek to protect moral and communal ties against corrupting influences, against, in Rousseau's terms, the 'cheapening of virtue'. But whereas the former achieves this by rooting communal virtues in individual selves, the second seeks to achieve this by restricting individual virtue to the public realm.[24] A good example of this difference can be found in the question posed to the Edinburgh Belles Lettres Society in the early 1760s: 'Whether the Character of Cato or that of Atticus is most excellent?', i.e., public or private man. From this of course followed the true residency of virtue, which for the literati of Edinburgh society was to be found in Atticus' role as a virtuous individual, an impartial and sympathetic observer of the public realm.[25]

This emphasis on private morality as a guarantee of public welfare was a common feature of eighteenth-century thinking on civil society, especially in Scotland where it was propounded by such thinkers as Hugh Blair and the Moderate Preachers, enjoined in such publications as the *Edinburgh Magazine* or the *Caledonian Mercury* and debated in such societies as the Mirror Club and the Parthenon Society.[26] Thus it was precisely in those social organizations of the public realm – where civil society is today, somewhat nostalgically, seen to reside – that argument was most forcefully presented for the necessary foundation of public order on private morality.

In slightly different terms, 'sociability' can be said to replace 'virtue' as the foundation of moral community. This is at one and the same time a more differentiated and sophisticated theory of the moral community which rests on a different conception of the social enterprise. Most strikingly, the idea of conscience as the internal impartial spectator takes the place, in Smith's supremely sophisticated psychology, of the general will, as virtue is defined as that which is approved by the impartial spectator. Indeed this juxtaposition of the internal, impartial spectator as against the idea of the general will is, I would claim, the very heart of the issue at hand and adds both a historical specificity and analytic sophistication to our prior contrast of private and public conceptions of virtue. For while subjection to the general will is a rational act that guarantees (public) virtue by the suppression of all partial (private) interest through the creation of a new 'corps collectif', the idea of the impartial observer is but an individual psychological mechanism through which, for Smith, the workings of mutual sympathy progressed.[27]

Smith, it should be noted, did not share with Hutcheson, Ferguson and others the idea that 'sympathy' or 'mutual sympathy' was a particular type of emotion, irreducible to any other – a psychological datum as it were. Rather, he saw sympathy as a function of that practical virtue termed 'propriety' which was assessed by the 'impartial spectator'. Without entering here into Smith's complex and subtle psychology of interactive emotions, it is sufficient to point out that 'propriety' (and so the workings of sympathy) turn on the idea of the impartial spectator – conceived as impartial, informed and sharing in the common standards of the community. Through assuming the position of the impartial spectator we judge both our own conduct and that of others. In Smith's words:

> We endeavour to examine our own conduct as we imagine any other fair and impartial spectator would examine it. If, upon placing ourselves in his situation, we thoroughly enter into all the passions and motives which influenced it, we approve of it, by sympathy with the approbation of this supposed equitable judge. If otherwise, we enter into his disapprobation and condemn it.[28]

This exercise aids us in bringing our own passions in line with propriety, tempering the intensity of our own felt experience to fit common standards; an independent moral standpoint detached from any given social morality is thereby created.

The idea of propriety, as a standard to judge both our own actions and those of others is, for Smith rooted in 'the eyes of a 3d party', that impartial spectator 'the great inmate of the breast' who 'judges impartially' between conflicting interests.[29] As Smith advises us when assessing our interests in opposition to those of our fellows:

> Before we can make any proper comparison of those opposite interests, we must change our position. We must view them, neither from our own place nor yet from his, neither with our own eyes nor yet with his, but from the place and with the eyes of a third person, who has no particular connexion with either, and who judges with impartiality between us.[30]

As convincingly argued by Knud Haakonssen, it is the continual search for this neutral third party position, for the standards of this impartial spectator, that makes social life possible, in that is provides the foundation for a morality higher than the changing whims of any given set of social mores.[31]

With this insight Smith breaks with both the preceding tradition of civil society with its naive anthropology and notions of an innate sympathy as well as with any attachment to collective norms and mores – what may perhaps be termed today, in the language of republican citizenship, the 'latent community' upon which the civic virtue tradition is based. For in revising the sixth (1790) edition of *The Theory of Moral Sentiments*, Smith abandoned his idea of a harmonious society in which public opinion can be seen as a guide to moral action and proposed in its stead a psychological mechanism for the development of an internal conscience. As the 'man within the breast' takes the place of the man outside as the source of virtue, a new foundation is posited for the pursuit of the social good. In the move from the first to the sixth edition of *The Theory of Moral Sentiments*, the impartial spectator is internalized, removed from any facile identification with public opinion, and virtue casts off its moorings in the public sphere.[32] While men are, in this reading, still social beings, what permits sociability is not the dissolution of self in any general will but the constitution of self through that higher morality imparted by the impartial, internal spectator – higher that is than the mere motive of recognition and approval on the part of 'high society', a motive that Smith was to view with increasing apprehension through the closing decades of the eighteenth century.[33]

Here then, I submit, we have a very different model of virtue, of social mutuality and of the common good than that presented in the different thinkers whom we associate with the traditions of civic virtue. In that tradition, the public good is one which overrides all private goods and rests, ultimately, on the overcoming of self-interest for public concerns. This however is not simple public-spiritedness, but a vision of humankind which sees in the public arena the only possibility to realize and fulfil the self-identity of the private citizen. By contrast, the ethical idea in the civil society tradition is a private one, realized within the hearts, minds and acts of exchange of individual social actors. To be sure, after Hume's critique of the Scottish Enlightenment view of reason, it became increasingly difficult to continue to posit an innate propensity towards mutuality and sympathy among humans, for all that this notion had served Shaftesbury, Hutcheson and Ferguson so well.[34] In the works of Adam Smith however, a new prop is added to the armature of civil society which was not only more sophisticated and supple, but served to ground interactive sympathy in individual virtue (specifically, by the final edition of *The Theory of Moral Sentiments*, in that of self-command).[35] These differences between the two traditions of political thought are outlined schematically in table 1.

From these fundamental distinctions on what may be termed the nature of virtue other distinctions follow. They are I believe of less analytic importance and of less relevance to current concerns than the prior distinctions noted and so we shall summarize them rather than submit them to analysis.

Table 9.1

	Civil Society	Civic Virtue
Realm of Virtue	private	public
Definition of Virtue	moral sentiments; natural sympathy, attention and approbation	shared community
Mechanisms of Virtue	impartial spectator	*volonté générale*
Model of Self	divided (and so) reflexive (relatively differentiated)	constituted by 'conscience collective' (relatively undifferentiated)
Orientation of Self	inward	outward

Attitude towards the 'Distinction of Talents'

The civil society tradition has a more moderate – or perhaps more ambivalent – attitude towards the processes of social differentiation. On the one hand, it sees it as leading towards civility and the civilizing process; this is as true of Ferguson as of Smith. On the other hand, when differentiation was great and combined with extensive territory (and so the loss of face-to-face interaction characteristic of a small community), it is viewed as a source of corruption. In Ferguson's telling words:

> Under the distinction of callings by which the members of polished society are separated from each other, every individual is supposed to possess his species of talent, or his peculiar skill, ... and society is made to consist of parts, of which none is animated with the spirit that ought to prevail in the conduct of nation ... [In brief and] in proportion as territory is extended, its parts lose their relative importance to the whole. Its inhabitants cease to perceive their connection with the state and are seldom united in the execution of any national, or of any factious designs ... It is even remarkable, that the enlargement of territory, by rendering the individual of less consequence to the public, and less able to intrude with his counsel actually tends to reduce national affairs within a narrow compass, as well as to diminish the numbers who are consulted in legislation or in other matters of government.[36]

Within the civic virtue tradition and especially with Rousseau, the distinction of talents as a function of life in society is also seen as the cause of inequality and the loss of virtue.[37] We should note too that the tradition of civic virtue is in fact predicated on the idea of the city, a 'closed' society or community of non-anonymous individuals for whom mutual trust and responsibility presupposes mutual acquaintance.[38]

Source of Corruption

This, of course has been viewed very differently by different thinkers, especially within the older civic virtue tradition. Corruption was also held to follow from external factors, notably in eighteenth-century England and America.[39] In its most classical form, this external force took the form of *fortuna* whose influence on human affairs could be mitigated only by the possession or pursuit of *virtu*.[40] In the civil society tradition there is a greater appreciation of internal corrupting influences – internal to society and, even more, internal to the individual. This is perhaps most evident in Adam Smith's increasing ambivalence to wealth and to 'our disposition to admire, and consequently to imitate, the rich and the great' which is for him 'the great and most universal cause of the corruption of our moral sentiments'.[41] Thus the problem of *fortuna* (and/together in the eighteenth century of external influences) gives way to the problem of market ties, the pursuit of particular interests and, more interestingly with Adam Smith, to the corruption of individual conscience. Although the concern with particular interests, cupidity, and with the problem of wealth is also present in the civic virtue tradition, especially with Rousseau, note an important difference: the problem exists at analytically different levels in the two traditions. For Rousseau it is constitutive of our very being in society and can only be overcome by the pursuit of virtue through submission to the general will. In Rousseau's words: 'all the inequality which now prevails owes its strength and growth to the development of our faculties and the advance of the human mind, and becomes at last permanent and legitimate by the establishment of property and laws.'[42] In the civil society tradition, the problem of particular interests is more 'tactical', it only becomes a problem when it takes an extreme form, and covetousness is only a threat when it is unmediated by conscience and the workings of the internal, impartial spectator. Particularity, privateness and the individual have, as noted, a validity in this tradition that they lack in Rousseau and in the whole tradition of civic virtue of which he is a part.

THE STAKES

With an eye to current concerns in both the West and the East, we must now inquire into the moral basis of social solidarity in both traditions. What keeps society civil and/or virtuous? The ramifications of this question on the current debates between universalists and communitarians, advocates of liberal or republican versions of citizenship and, more crucially, over the current situation in Eastern and East Central Europe should be clear.

The debate over liberal or republican versions of citizenship is, in many respects nothing but a contemporary reformulation of the contrasting visions of citizenship, of the individual and of the public good contained in the two traditions of political thought we have been discussing. Liberal (or what Charles Taylor has called 'procedural') theory views society as an assortment of morally autonomous individuals, each with his and her own concept of the good life, with the function of society being limited to ensuring the legal equality of these individuals through a procedurally just or fair process of democratic decision-making in the public sphere.[43] It is concerned with insuring the continued operation of universally valid principles of justice or right rather than with imposing any particular moral vision on the individual social actors who make up society.

Republican versions of citizenship posit, by contrast, a conception of society as a 'moral community' engaged in the pursuit of a common good, whose ontological status is prior to that of any individual member. In this reading the terms of selfhood no less than those of community are transformed as, following Sandel's critique of Rawls, there can exist no 'radically situated' or 'unencumbered' self free from the morally binding and constituting ties of a particular community.[44] Even without further explication, it is not difficult to hear the (slightly modified) echoes of Smith and Rousseau resonating in these different positions across two hundred years.

However, what is debated in highly principled terms in Harvard, McGill or Princeton is, in other parts of the world, a subject for less civil and studied debate. Throughout Eastern and East Central

Europe, in Hungary, Slovakia, the Baltic states, the Czech Republic
and elsewhere, the emergent civic polities are all struggling to define
new principles of social organization and solidarity along a fault
line of what can roughly be termed the principles of either a
'demos' or an 'ethnos', principles that draw on either of the two
models we have been analysing.[45]

As tellingly argued in an article by Yoav Peled on the terms of
citizenship in contemporary Israel, any given polity may be defined
not solely by its acceptance of one or the other of these models but,
especially in ethnically heterogeneous societies, by a mixture of
both – and so by differential definitions of the terms of mutuality
and solidarity as well as by the obligations and rights of citizenship
of different ethnic groups within society.[46]

Of great importance to this debate (regardless of whether it is
carried out in the West, East or Middle East) is thus those terms of
solidarity or membership which inhere to the different models of
political theory and so of citizenship represented by the traditions
under discussion. This of course draws on the different conceptions
of self and society represented by both traditions. And if, for
the liberal-individualist or universalist tradition which emerges
out of the idea of civil society, the model of solidarity is one of
acts of exchange between morally autonomous individuals, for
the communitarian or republican tradition it is one rooted, most
often, in primordial or ascriptive criteria. This is even so in Sandel's
description of individuals 'as members of *this* family or community or nation or people, as bearers of *this* history, as sons and
daughters of *that* revolution, as citizens of *this* republic' (emphases
mine).[47]

This is the real problem not only with the idea of republican
citizenship, but with all traditions of political thought rooted in the
traditions of civic virtue, especially when viewed as an ongoing
concern disconnected from military exploits – courage being seen,
not surprisingly, as an essential component of civic virtue. For
despite its very strong affective elements, seemingly cogent solutions to some of the pervasive problems of citizenship as we know
it today and strong appeal both in the past and the present, it is
virtually impossible to articulate a model of civic virtue free from
primordial referents. Indeed, the development of universal principles of citizenship following the French Revolution, partial and
halting though it was, goes some way in explaining the gradual
replacement of this strand of social thought by ideas stemming
from the tradition of civil society.

Not surprisingly, the consistent articulation of a model of solidarity based solely on the principles of political virtue posed a continual problem to thinkers working within this tradition. In the early modern period, this was evinced in that problematic interrelation of 'providence' and *fortuna*, 'grace' and *virtu*, explored most fully by Pocock, who stressed the pervasive difficulty of explaining how *virtu* could succeed unaided by prophetic grace.[48] Counterfactually, we may note that the only example of 'institutionalized' *virtu* is in eighteenth-century America where it was aided by a secularized and nationalized grace.[49] This is a crucial point, for if we remove the affective commitment engendered by either revolutionary upheavals or foreign wars, and if we accept the existence of highly differentiated societies where the non-mediated existence of the citizen in the polis is no longer possible and if we discount the totalitarian implications of a public will, what remains to provide basis for virtue? The fact that this problem was only solved – and that only partially in eighteenth-century America is of great importance. The absence of ascriptive or primordial ties within that ideological community owed much to pre-existing Puritan traditions of the community of believers, that is, to some secularized idea of a community of grace.[50] How *virtu* can be institutionalized without such a referent remains an open but critical question – ultimately, I would claim, undoing the ideal of civic virtue.

Here of course, a necessary clarification must be made. This is only an insurmountable problem when we normatively reject a primordially defined basis for the political community, that is, when virtue is to be effected solely by the participation in shared political institutions. Indeed, among contemporaries, the only one to posit this utopian ideal was Arendt, all others, including contemporary accounts of republican citizenship, maintaining ascriptive components of civic virtue tradition – the early modern version of which, for Rousseau and others, was of course that of a small community of shared history and social interaction.[51] Why or whether this need be so is another matter, ultimately depending on one's own philosophical anthropology. Yet historically and theoretically the construction of a binding 'tradition' and so of a community, moral or otherwise, existing over time, without some referent to primordial 'givens' has proved a fruitless enterprise.[52] Again, the partial exception is the United States, and more particularly eighteenth-century America, where the primordial element was replaced, though only partially, with a 'transcendent' grounding of political institutions in a polity of grace and in the traditions of the community of saints. Without either of these principles as supports of virtue the constitution of a moral community based solely on the principles of participatory politics has proved to be untenable.

Interestingly enough, the idea of civil society as it developed in the second half of the eighteenth century in Scotland arose out of a need to posit a model of solidarity and mutuality freed from primordial attributes. The failure of the Jacobite uprisings of 1715 and 1745 and the memories of the battle of Culloden in 1746 were all telling reminders of the inadequacy of existing national (or ethnic) solidarities as foundations for political identity in the increasingly differentiated and interlocking commercial economies of eighteenth-century Scotland and England.[53] Thus, from Ferguson to Smith we find that new 'universal' and increasingly 'individualistically' defined basis for the construction of communal life which formed the basis of liberal-individualistic principles of citizenship.

The models of solidarity and mutuality contained in this ideal carried with them, however, a set of contradictions that were somewhat different in nature from those studied of the civic virtue tradition. Ultimately, as we know, the idea of civil society came to rest on the notion of the autonomous and moral individual as standing at the foundation of the social order.[54] This idea of the moral individual became of course the basis of liberal political beliefs and, as such, was institutionalized within liberal-democratic polities. In the process of institutionalization the earlier and rather labile concepts of mutuality – and, by implication civic equality – between individuals were replaced with formal, legal and, to different extent in different countries, economic guarantees. These are, in effect, the attributes of citizenship as developed by T. H. Marshall, extending and formalizing the mutuality of the autonomous individual in different realms of shared, public life.[55] Current concerns over entitlements can be viewed as the continuation of this process in different realms.

The developmental logic of this process is paradoxical. For the more the relations between individuals are defined by abstract, legalistic and formal criteria, the less the public realm can be defined by a shared solidarity based on concrete ties of history, ideas, love, care and friendship.[56] As the public space of interaction is increasingly defined by the workings of an abstract and 'instrumental' rationality, the less the concrete concerns for mutuality and trust are realized – or perhaps seen to be realized – in the public realm. One consequence of this is the increased difficulty of re-presenting social life in terms of the public sphere and, especially in the United States, the positing of, sometimes private, sometimes simply particular, entities and interests as public concerns – as in fact, defining the public good. In fact, I would claim that the whole emphasis on multiculturalism, on the maintenance of group solidarities in contrast with the prior ideology of the 'melting pot' (based of course on the ideology of the individual as moral absolute), are all part of this dynamic. In short, as a shared public sphere recedes from the affective grasp of the citizenry through its very formalization and increased institutionalization, the particular and often the private is posited in its stead as an alternative mode of symbolizing society. The renaissance of arguments based on 'republican' conceptions of citizenship by Sandel, MacIntyre and others is of course rooted in the self-same dynamic as these, somewhat less, theoretically principled developments.

VIRTUE AND CIVILITY IN CLUJ

Let me return to the story with which I began, bearing in mind these points:

1 the deep concern of both traditions to posit an alternative to capitalist market relations as the basis of moral community;
2 the importance of both traditions as precursors of our ideas of citizenship;
3 the current debates in the West over the terms and meanings of citizenship;
4 the dual challenge facing the countries of Eastern and East Central Europe in the construction of both capitalist market relations and some form of participatory democracy, that is, some form of citizenship.

Given the problems attendant on the institutionalization of the civil society version of solidarity in the liberal ideal of citizenship (problems which themselves have fuelled the debates noted in point 3), would it not seem feasible to posit the idea of civic virtue as a viable option for the emerging democracies of East Central Europe? Can the current saliency of local, ethnic and particular identities not be seen as an attempt (sometimes misdirected, oftentimes violent, but legitimate nonetheless) to rearticulate the civic virtue tradition, to provide precisely that basis of local solidarity upon which virtue can emerge and in so doing short-circuit, as it were, the pitfalls of universal-instrumental reason experienced in the West?

My answer to this is negative. The 1989 removal of King Lazar of Serbia's bones after six hundred years and their trip throughout all the monasteries of Serbia as confirmation of Serbian collective identity presents a rather grim illustration of the problems attendant on such a programme.[57] These problems are rooted in the historical development of the region: its lack of pluralistic structures and autonomous elites, the multi-ethnic nature of the states formed in the interwar years, its traditions of social reform movements as components of national struggles, rule by semi-autocratic or dictatorial elites rooted in one ethnic majority and, most importantly, the fact that the concept of the nation came before the establishment of national institutions and of state structures oriented on liberal principles.[58] This led to the development of national ideologies which, in the words of Gyorgy Csepeli, 'had to refer more actively to elements of ethnocentric heritage such as descent, cultural values and norms'.[59] Ethnic exclusiveness and the lack of salient traditions of common political institutions would seem to make the viable institutionalization of participatory citizenship along civic virtue lines highly problematic.

This theme brings us back to eighteenth-century New England and to the role of 'internalized grace', as opposed to ascriptively defined community as the basis for virtue. For if political participation alone is not sufficient for virtue, how can an idea of virtue free of primordial referents be articulated – especially given the nature of national and ethnic identification in the region? Here it may be relevant to recall Istvan Bibo's insights on the relation between Hungarians and Jews during the Second World War.[60] He points out that many Jews were indeed saved or hidden by Hungarians, often at great personal risk. Yet, according to Bibo, people took this risk when they knew the individuals, when some personal connection existed between them and the Jews threatened with deportation and murder. It was therefore on the particular basis of personal ties, not as citizens or as members of the 'Community of Reason', that such action was taken. Just how insufficient such a basis of community has proved, for Jews and other minorities throughout the region, need not be explicated.

We are thus left with a problem and no solution in sight. More concretely we are left with the problem of how to articulate citizenship in terms of participation in the public realm without stressing primordial, ascriptive elements of communal identity. How could we even begin to discuss a 'latent community' – that favourite expression of the Western republican citizenship tradition – of the Danube nations without Jews? In slightly different terms, we are left with the problem of the maintenance of virtue, but through the conceptual and institutional venues as presented in the civil society tradition. How then to provide a definition of virtue which, while maintaining the moral suasion of the civic virtue tradition, would root it in individual selves and in the organizational mechanisms of interaction that we have come to associate with the tradition of civil society?

Posed in such stark terms the problem does seem an intractable one. And perhaps it is grossly negligent even to presuppose the existence of the internalized conscience, of the individual self as *value* in those regions of Europe for which I have taken Cluj as metaphor. After all, the multi-ethnic, less-than-liberal and non-democratic Austro-Hungarian monarchy did provide a 'workable' framework for social interaction, albeit one where the ethical, legal and social value of the individual was of negligible importance. The Catholic organicist heritage of Habsburg Austria denied, as J. C. Nyiri has demonstrated, validity to liberal individualist beliefs not only in the legal and social arenas but also in the philosophical arena.[61] Neither 'individual rationality [nor] the sovereign self-determining person were taken for granted, or indeed glorified.'[62] We are a far cry from Adam Smith and the stoicism of self-command and propriety – both tied to individual conscience rather than to historical structures or public opinion.

Given such traditions, the search for a synthesis, especially one predicated on the idea of the moral individual, may in its very nature be futile. Perhaps, rather, what must be sought is a different model of community, one rooted in neither primordial/ascriptive criteria nor in the presumptions of 'methodological individualism'. Such a model would, presumably, both recognize the continuing saliency of existing, ascriptively defined collective traditions but also seek some sort of consociational framework for their respective programmes and social desiderata. Such a framework would of course have to be based on a shared recognition of human integrity and the profitability of civil or civic interaction and exchange.

Any understanding of the problems as well as the possibilities inherent to such an attempt cannot be found at the level of theory, but only in the realm of ongoing historical practice. And here perhaps it is fitting to return to Cluj where, despite its lack of civility, citizenship and moral individualism, there does seem to be under way an attempt to create secular, modern 'covenanted communities' – along the lines of the French Republican organizations of the end of the nineteenth century.[63] I have in mind the fascinating story of a Romanian priest who is attempting to construct a multimedia, multilingual broadcast station in Transylvania (Romanian, German, Hungarian). To do so however, he must bribe the whole of parliament.[64] This story, I submit, exemplifies both the hopeful possibilities for the future (a real universalism based on a commonality of what remains distinct ethnic, linguistic cultures) together with lack of political frameworks which define democratic action and within which such a communality can exist. We cannot of course know which will have upper hand, but the possible permutations of virtue and civility are many and far from circumscribed by the models of Western European and North Atlantic societies.

NOTES

1 B. Constant, *Political Writings*, ed. B. Fontana, Cambridge University Press, Cambridge, 1988.
2 The importance of civic virtue in medieval Venice and Florence exemplifies this point, in that it developed philosophically in autonomous cities, free from feudal hierarchy. General perspectives on the development of civic humanist thought can be found in Q. Skinner, *The Foundations of Modern Political Thought*, vol. 1, Cambridge University Press, Cambridge, 1978.
3 This latter theme has been developed most dramatically by J. G. A. Pocock, *The Machiavellian Moment*, Princeton University Press, Princeton, N.J., 1975. For a contrasting reading of political thought in this period see I. Kramnick, *Republicanism and Bourgeois Radicalism: Political Ideology in Late Eighteenth Century England and America*, Cornell University Press, Ithaca, N.Y., 1990.
4 On this theme see N. Bobbio, *The Future of Democracy*, University of Minnesota Press, Minneapolis, Minn., 1987, p. 31.
5 E. Durkheim, *The Division of Labour in Society*, Free Press, New York, 1933.
6 H. Arendt, *The Human Condition*, University of Chicago Press, Chicago, Ill., 1958.
7 Here I am using the term 'conscience collective' as Durkheim did in his earlier works – to describe the type of moral community constituted in societies characterized by mechanic solidarity. Some, notably Talcott Parsons, have argued that over time Durkheim changed his conception of the conscience collective, to make it an attribute of all societies, including modern ones in which of course the content of the conscience collective was radically different. On this idea see T. Parsons, *The Structure of Social Action*, Free Press, New York, 1968, vol. 1, p. 320. For a different view which stresses the continuities

between Rousseau and Durkheim and the parallels between the idea of the *volonté générale* and conscience collective see S. Lukes, *Emile Durkheim: His Life and Work*, Stanford University Press, Stanford, Cal., 1985, p. 283.

8 The importance of active participation of the citizenry for the pursuit of virtue is developed in Rousseau's *Social Contract*. See J.-J. Rousseau, *The Social Contract and Discourses*, trans. and ed. G. D. H. Cole, Dent, London, 1973, p. 265.

9 J.-J. Rousseau, *A Discourse on Political Economy*, in Rousseau, *The Social Contract and Discourses*, p. 140.

10 Rousseau, *Discourse on Political Economy*, p. 139.

11 Rousseau, *Social Contract*, p. 191.

12 Rousseau, *Social Contract*, p. 191.

13 Rousseau, *Social Contract*, pp. 203, 227.

14 See for example C. Maier, ed., *Changing Boundaries of the Political*, Cambridge University Press, Cambridge, 1987.

15 A. Seligman, *The Idea of Civil Society*, Free Press, New York, 1992.

16 The case of John Locke is of course somewhat different as he posits a transcendent matrix to ethical behaviour. On this see J. Dunn, *The Political Theory of John Locke*, Harvard University Press, Cambridge, 1969. Hume, as is well know, fatally attacked this conception in what Alasdair MacIntyre has termed 'the subversion of the Scottish Enlightenment from within'. See A. MacIntyre, *Whose Justice, Which Rationality?*, University of Notre Dame Press, Notre Dame, Ind., 1988. Kant's attempt to reply to Hume, which ended with the positing of a purely private morality marked in effect the end of the idea of civil society as it was conceived in the eighteenth century and is, therefore, beyond the scope of our present inquiry. On these developments, see Seligman, *The Idea of Civil Society*, pp. 15–58.

17 A. Ferguson, *An Essay on the History of Civil Society*, 5th edn, T. Cadell, London, 1782, p. 53.

18 Shaftesbury, *Characteristics of Men, Manners, Opinions, Times*, 6th edn, London, 1736, especially vol. 2, 'An Inquiry Concerning Virtue and Merit', pp. 117–21. Ferguson, *An Essay on the History of Civil Society*, pp. 52–66.

19 A. Smith, *The Theory of Moral Sentiments*, Liberty Classics, Indianapolis, Ind., 1982, p. 50.

20 It would be useful to compare this with Rousseau's idea of *volonté générale* to see just how much that latter conception rested on a 'reasoned' set of decisions by the participants involved. See for example, Rousseau, 'The General Society of the Human Race', included in the 'Geneva manuscript' of *The Social Contract*, p. 174.

21 Durkheim's view is not that distant from Rousseau's general will: 'The general will must be respected, not because it is stronger but because it is general. If there is to be justice among individuals, there must be something outside them, a being sui generis, which acts as arbiter and determines the law. This something is society, which owes its moral supremacy, not to its physical supremacy, but to its nature, which is superior to that of individuals'. E. Durkheim, *Montesquieu and Rousseau*, University of Michigan Press, Ann

Arbor, Mich., 1965, p. 103.

22 Ferguson, *An Essay on the History of Civil Society*, p. 52.

23 See P. Brown, *The Body and Society: Men, Women and Sexual Renunciation in Early Christianity*, Columbia University Press, New York, 1988, pp. 6–32; Rousseau, *Social Contract*, p. 192.

24 J.-J. Rousseau, *A Discourse on the Moral Effects of Arts and Sciences*, in Rousseau, *The Social Contract and Discourses*, p. 24.

25 J. Dwyer, *Virtuous Discourse: Sensibility and Community in Late Eighteenth Century Scotland*, John Donald Publishers, Edinburgh, 1987, p. 98.

26 Dwyer, *Virtuous Discourse*, pp. 10–38, 95–116.

27 Rousseau, *Social Contract*, p. 192. Compare this with the passage of Durkheim quoted above (in note 21) on the role of society in inducing moral agency. What Durkheim posits as a teleological being, existing beyond individual conscience (or consciousness – as the distinction does not exist in the French) Smith posits as a psychological mechanism working within the individual.

28 Smith, *The Theory of Moral Sentiments*, p. 110.

29 Smith, *The Theory of Moral Sentiments*, p. 134.

30 Smith, *The Theory of Moral Sentiments*, p. 135.

31 K. Haakonssen, *The Science of a Legislator: The Natural Jurisprudence of David Hume and Adam Smith*, Cambridge University Press, Cambridge, 1981, pp. 54–61.

32 On the sociological background to this move in Smith see Dwyer, *Virtuous Discourse*, pp. 168–85.

33 Dwyer, *Virtuous Discourse*, pp. 173–180.

34 MacIntyre, *Whose Justice, Which Rationality?*, pp. 218–325.

35 Smith, *The Theory of Moral Sentiments*, pp. 237–62.

36 Ferguson, *An Essay on the History of Civil Society*, p. 188.

37 See for example his *Discourse on the Moral Effects of the Arts and Sciences*.

38 L. Strauss, *Natural Right and History*, University of Chicago Press, Chicago, Ill., 1973, pp. 130–5.

39 On the theme of corruption in eighteenth-century America see not only Pocock, *Machiavellian Moment*, but also B. Bailyn, *The Ideological Origins of the American Revolution*, Harvard University Press, Cambridge, Mass., 1982.

40 Pocock, *Machiavellian Moment*, pp. 31–48.

41 Smith, *The Theory of Moral Sentiments*, pp. 61, 64.

42 Rousseau, *A Discourse on the Origins of Inequality*, p. 116.

43 C. Taylor, 'Cross Purposes: The Liberal-Communitarian Debate', in N. Rosenblum, ed., *Liberalism and the Moral Life*, Harvard University Press, Cambridge, Mass., 1989. The 'foundation text' of this view is of course J. Rawls, *A Theory of Justice*, Harvard University Press, Cambridge, Mass., 1971. Description of its implications on citizenship can be found in M. Waters, 'Citizenship and the Constitution of Structured Inequality', *International Journal of Comparative Sociology*, vol. 30, 1989.

44 M. Sandel, *Liberalism and the Limits of Justice*, Cambridge University Press, Cambridge, 1982, and 'The Procedural Republic and the Unencumbered Self', *Political Theory*, vol. 17, 1984.

45 One of the interesting arenas where this conflict is being carried out is in the assessment of the interwar regimes within the different polities of Eastern and East Central Europe. The re-interment of the remains of the interwar Regent of Hungary, Admiral Horthy, in 1993 and the protest against the honour thus accorded him by more democratic forces in society is just one of many contemporary examples of this continuing struggle. I will refrain from noting the more violent and well-known conflicts currently being waged throughout the former Soviet empire and countries of East Central Europe. Some further perspectives on this can be found in Z. Butorova, 'Two Years After November 17 1989: The Hard Birth of Democracy in Slovakia', in P. Gerlich and P. Glass, eds, *Zwischen den Zeiten*, VWGO, Vienna, 1992, and Z. and M. Butorova, 'Wariness towards the Jews as an Expression of Post-Communist Panic', Proceedings from the International Seminar on Anti-Semitism in Post-Totalitarian Europe, Prague, 1992.

46 Y. Peled, 'Ethnic Democracy and the Legal Construction of Citizenship: Arab Citizens of the Jewish State', *American Political Science Review*, vol. 86, 1992.

47 Sandel, *Liberalism and the Limits of Justice*, p. 179.

48 Pocock, *Machiavellian Moment*.

49 On different aspects of this theme see: Pocock, *Machiavellian Moment*, pp. 506–52: E. L. Tuveson, *Redeemer Nation: The Idea of America's Millennial Role*, University of Chicago Press, Chicago, Ill., 1968; N. O. Hatch, *The Sacred Cause of Liberty*, Yale University Press, New Haven, Conn., 1977; and R. Block, *Visionary Republic: Millennial Themes in American Thought 1765–1800*, Cambridge University Press, Cambridge, 1985.

50 On the sociological background to this development see A. Seligman, *Innerworldly Individualism: Charismatic Community and Its Institutionalization*, Transaction Press, New Brunswick, 1994.

51 Arendt, *Human Condition*, pp. 248–325.

52 On the importance and dynamics of tradition see E. Shils, *Tradition*, University of Chicago Press, Chicago, Ill., 1981.

53 On this dynamic, see L. Colley, *Britons: Forging the Nation 1707–1837*, Yale University Press, New Haven, Conn., 1992, pp. 101–28.

54 Hegel and Marx of course rejected this outcome, but in so doing also rejected the ideal of civil society as an ethical ideal and, in their different ways, went quite beyond it.

55 T. H. Marshall, *Class, Citizenship and Social Development*, Greenwood Press, Westport, Conn., 1973.

56 A. Giddens, *The Consequences of Modernity*, Stanford University Press, Stanford, Cal., 1990. On this general theme see A. Seligman, 'The Representation of Society and the Privatization of Charisma', *Praxis International*, vol. 13, 1993.

57 See R. Salecl, 'Nationalism, Anti-Semitism and Anti-Feminism in Eastern Europe', New School for Social Research, The East and Central Europe Program, Working Papers Series, no. 11, 1992, pp. 5–6.

58 For discussion of the political implications of these developmental features see G. Schöpflin, 'The Political Traditions of Eastern Europe', *Daedalus*, vol. 119,

1990, and J. Sźucs, 'Three Historical Regions of Europe', in J. Keane, ed., *Civil Society and the State*, Verso, London, 1988.

59 G. Csepeli, 'Competing Patterns of National Identity in Post-Communist Hungary', *Media, Culture and Society*, vol. 13, 1991.

60 I. Bibo, 'The Jewish Question in Hungary', in his *Democracy, Revolution, Self Determination: Selected Writings*, Social Science Monographs, Boulder, Colo., 1991.

61 J. C. Nyiri, 'Fin-de-Siècle Austrian Philosophy: Qualities Without a Man', in G. Ranki, ed., *Hungary and European Philosophy*, Akademiai Kiado, Budapest, 1989.

62 Nyiri, 'Fin-de-Siècle Austrian Philosophy', p. 361.

63 K. Auspitz, *The Radical Bourgeoisie: The Lingue de l'Enseignement and the Origins of the Third Republic*, Cambridge University Press, Cambridge, 1982.

64 Personal communication related to me in Cluj by the editors of the Romanian journal *Korunk*.

10

Modernity, Late Development and Civil Society

Nicos Mouzelis

BASIC DEFINITIONS

From a sociological point of view, modernity can be regarded as the social situation that became dominant in Western Europe after the English Industrial and the French Revolutions. It entailed an unprecedented social mobilization of human and non-human resources as the pronounced localism of the traditional post-medieval community was broken up and superseded by the creation of national arenas on the economic, political and cultural levels.

As loyalties and orientations shifted from the local periphery to the national centre, the creation of such broad arenas meant that the bulk of the population began to be exposed to national markets, national educational systems and, above all, the rapidly proliferating administrative networks of the nation-state.[1] This does not mean, of course, that modernization is a uniform process. Bringing the majority of the people into the national centre can take a variety of forms, not all of them beneficial to the lower classes. The process of inclusion can be achieved in such a way that the huge resources generated by modernization benefit only a small minority. The greater part of the population, although drawn into the centre, remains debarred from economic prosperity and from the political and civil freedoms that are a potential concomitant of modernization.

In other words, if by modernity or modernization we mean the type of social mobilization/inclusion the French and the English Industrial Revolutions brought about, the 'drawing-in' process can entail radically different relationships between the citizens and the national centre. It is in this context that the concept of civil society becomes relevant.

Like all key concepts in the social sciences, 'civil society' has a variety of meanings. For the purposes of this paper I think it is useful to limit the notion to the issues of autonomy and freedom that, *in the context of modernity or modernization*, mark the relationships between state and some non-state groups and institutions.[2] This definition helps us to explore the ways in which people were, or are, brought into the centre. So when the process of modernization brings about an extensive downward spread of civic and political rights, so that the lower classes are accommodated in a relatively autonomous manner, we usually consider this to be related to a strong civil society; whereas in cases where such rights are not broadly spread, that is, in cases where the masses are brought in heteronomously and in authoritarian fashion, we usually speak of a weak civil society.

It may of course be argued that civil society has existed also in pre- or non-modern settings, when the majority of the population remained firmly outside the central political process. So for instance in pre-industrial England a relatively strong land-owning class managed to stop the absolutist tendencies of the monarchical state, and in that sense one can talk about a strong civil society before the large-scale mobilization that industrial capitalism later brought about. It seems to me, however, that to stretch the civil society notion to cover also the non-state groups and institutions that exist in all state societies (from traditional chiefdoms to dynastic empires) weakens the concept's analytical utility.

In this paper, therefore, the term civil society is used rather restrictively. It refers to all social groups and institutions which, *in conditions of modernity*, lie between primordial kinship groups or institutions on the one hand, and state groups and institutions on the other. By 'conditions of modernity' I mean social settings where not only are the public and private spheres clearly differentiated,[3] but there is also a large-scale mobilization of the population and its autonomous or heteronomous inclusion into the national, economic, political and cultural arenas.[4] In accordance with the above definition, a strong civil society entails:

1 the existence of rule-of-law conditions that effectively protect citizens from state arbitrariness;

2 the existence of strongly organized non-state interest groups, capable of checking eventual abuses of power by those who control the means of administration and coercion;
3 the existence of a balanced pluralism among civil society interests so that none can establish absolute dominance. (In that sense, situations where a plutocracy or excessively strong and authoritarian trade unions[5] predominate can legitimately be said to lead to a weak civil society.)

A final point on definitions is this: should political parties be considered as part of the state or as part of civil society? There are theorists in favour of either side of the question, as well as others who distinguish between the state, civil society and political society and locate the parties in the political society category. As will become obvious in what follows, for the purposes of this paper I have found it best to more or less follow the third position: political parties, particularly in democratic parliamentary contexts, will be considered as the major organizational means for articulating civil society interests with the state.

Having outlined the concepts of modernity and civil society, I shall now explore the impact late capitalist industrialization has had on the state–civil society relationship, and focus particularly on late-developing societies with relatively long traditions of parliamentary democratic institutions.[6]

To start with, in ideal-typical terms one can say that in north-western Europe the modernization process (that is, the inclusion of the mass of the population into the nation-state) was effectuated in such a way that civil, political and social rights (which in the pre-industrial era were confined to those at the top of the social pyramid) spread widely among the lower strata. This broader diffusion of basic rights was achieved either from above (by elites competing among themselves for the political support of the underprivileged) or from below (via the economic and political organization of urban and rural workers). It is true that the process was both very slow and uneven. In many cases, though by no means all, the popular struggle for the acquisition of rights began on the political level, for instance with efforts to obtain the right to vote or to form associations; later it shifted to attempts to set up a welfare state; and today it takes the form of popular movements demanding improvements in the quality of life (for example, the ecology movement) and further democratization in not only the political but also the economic and cultural spheres (for example, movements for sexual equality, for the abolition of racial discrimination, for workers' participation in management, etc.).

In the late-developing societies of the semi-periphery, on the other hand, despite the relatively early introduction of liberal-democratic political institutions and the adoption of social welfare policies, the process of inclusion in almost all cases took a more vertical, authoritarian turn. The distribution of political, civil and socioeconomic rights was more uneven and restricted. The lower classes, although brought into the national centre, were left out as far as basic rights were concerned, rights guaranteeing them a reasonable share in the distribution of political power, wealth and social prestige.

In order to examine what the above broad differences mean in terms of the state–civil society relationships, it is important to say a few words about the role of the state in late-developing countries.

THE ROLE OF THE STATE IN LATE DEVELOPMENT

A good starting-point for this investigation is Gerschenkron's famous thesis that the later a country enters the developmental race, the more it requires guidance from above – mainly from the state or other centralized state-controlled institutions.[7] Although Gerschenkron's generalization was formulated with reference to the process of industrialization in Europe, it can easily be extended to the rest of the world. What should be added to this very plausible hypothesis, however, is that certain states are much more capable than others of drawing up and implementing development strategies; and *that it is in fact the actual structure of the state that is most crucial for understanding why late developers with comparable starting-points and resources have performed so unevenly within the world economy.*

The few countries that began their industrialization relatively late but nevertheless approached (for example, South Korea, Taiwan) or even became part of (Norway, Finland, New Zealand, Australia) the so-called first or developed world all share three basic features of development:

1 successful agricultural modernization, resulting in not only increased productivity but also in a certain rural egalitarianism capable of creating an important home market for industrial goods;

2 strong linkages between the primary and secondary sectors, and more generally the creation of an industrial sector with, sooner or later, its own niche in the world market and competitive in certain limited areas;
3 a relatively effective and interventionist state apparatus playing a crucial role in the modernization of agriculture as well as in its effective articulation with industry.

In the cases of relative failure (the majority), on the other hand, the state either did not manage to break up traditionally organized big landed estates (as in Latin America), or if it did (as in the interwar Balkans), it neglected to provide the resulting smallholders with the kind of assistance that is essential for successful modernization. The inevitable result in both instances could be only feeble development of the domestic market, and weak or permanently negative linkage between industry and agriculture.[8]

One of the most important effects of such unsuccessful economic development is its impact on the state. The failure to modernize agriculture and to articulate it profitably with industry usually leads to an over-inflated state apparatus and to an accentuation of its clientelistically corrupt features. The partial commercialization of agriculture frees human and non-human resources from the primary sector, but instead of channelling them into productive agricultural or industrial investments, leaves them to orient themselves primarily towards the service sector. This means that in all these countries the tertiary sector (both public and private) acquires enormous and on the whole highly parasitic dimensions, well before a thorough agricultural modernization and/or the large-scale development of capitalist industry.

It must be emphasized that the more the state fails to channel resources into effectively modernizing agriculture and developing industry, the more it acquires anti-developmental features that become major obstacles to balanced growth. People leave the countryside *en masse* – pushed by commercialization processes linked to the integration of latecomers into the world market, and pulled by the attractions of city life – but, given a nonexistent or highly restrictive capitalist industrial sector, find themselves unemployed or in low-productivity jobs in the rapidly growing private and public service sectors.

Particularly in countries that quite early on had adopted democratic parliamentary institutions, there is irresistible pressure to use the public bureaucracy as a means for absorbing excess labour, irrespective of productivity considerations. For politicians competing for votes, the wholesale creation of state jobs for the faithful becomes the major means of accumulating and consolidating or augmenting political capital; and the logic of acquiring such political capital for generating political profits systematically prevails over any other developmental considerations.[9] This means that, in the great majority of cases, late developers experience a highly incapacitating vicious circle: the state's failure to initiate and maintain balanced growth prevents the rationalization both of itself and of the overall economy.

Barrington Moore has argued that failure among the early developers to modernize agriculture usually led to a revolutionary mobilization of the peasantry, as both landlords and the state tried to squeeze from the direct producers resources that a non-modernized agriculture was quite unable to provide.[10] In contrast to this, the failure of late developers to modernize agriculture need not conduce to a revolutionary situation, since massive urbanization operates as a safety valve. At the same time, a massive influx of former agricultural producers into cities with weak or nonexistent industrialization, particularly in a context of parliamentary competitive politics, unavoidably leads to an over-inflation of the state apparatuses – and this, in turn, instead of helping becomes the major obstacle to development.

Several late-developing countries have, of course, managed to industrialize at some point. But theirs is the kind of industrialization that not only is led from above, but which entirely follows the logic of political domination rather than that of economic capital accumulation. So demands for economic rationalization and for the advancement of civil society interests are systematically subordinated to demands for the consolidation and expansion of party and state interests.[11]

Even though the advancement of state and civil society interests is not always contradictory, accumulation of either political or economic capital, particularly in late development, does tend to be mutually inimical. The logic of building up political clienteles more often than not undermines the logic of the market and of economic rationalization.

To give a concrete example: many semi-peripheral states during the interwar import-substitution phase of industrialization created lame-duck industries that survived long after the end of the 1929

Depression because of the persistence of high tariff walls. The logic of economic rationalization dictates that, after an initial period of protection, such industries should be gradually exposed to the rigours and disciplines of international competition.[12] But the logic of building up political capital resulted in policies that perpetuated the greenhouse conditions under which these enterprises thrived – and so created an indigenous, state-dependent industrial bourgeoisie, the survival and prosperity of which hinged less on entrepreneurial skills than on the ability to associate with powerful political patrons.

Moreover, to continue with our example, after the import-substitution process had reached a serious impasse in the 1950s and early 1960s, and when the changing international division of labour presented favourable conditions for foreign-led industrialization, there again the state failed to articulate with multinational capital in such a way as to result in balanced growth. Foreign-led industrialization, whether focused on exports or internal markets, did not spread its dynamism to the rest of the economy. It remained an island in a sea of backward-looking units of familial, small artisanal enterprises, or of state-protected and highly inefficient industrial concerns. A similar situation obtained in agriculture, where foreign or indigenously-owned modern agribusinesses co-exist with a plethora of tiny, family-run peasant units, or with huge old estates of the hacienda/latifundium type.

This situation of restricted capitalist development[13] in both industry and agriculture creates enormous productivity differentials between the more advanced and backward sectors, which lead to an under-utilization – or rather to an economically irrational utilization – of a country's human and non-human resources. This irrational utilization takes the form of large-scale unemployment, huge income and wealth inequalities and chronic balance-of-payments difficulties.

In sum, in most semi-peripheral countries the state resembles a colossus with feet of clay, a shapeless monster incapable of reacting intelligently to a rapidly changing international context. Whenever there has been a major crisis or challenge – like the need to modernize agriculture at the turn of the century, the need for effective and selective import-substitution industrialization after the 1929 world economic crisis or the need for a shift to export-oriented industrialization in the 1960s and 1970s – at every one of these critical turning-points the rigid, overpoliticized and particularistic orientations of the state have made it act in ways that further consolidate these countries' semi-peripheral position in the world economy and polity.

STATE–CIVIL SOCIETY LINKAGES:
THE POLITICAL DIMENSION

Having discussed the notions of modernity and civil society, as well as the crucial role of the state in late development, I now wish to focus more systematically on what (in the context of this paper) constitutes the major civil society problematic. This is the state–civil society linkages that prevail in late-developing societies and, more than anything else, shape what kind of autonomy those brought into the national arena achieve or fail to achieve.

Speaking again in ideal-typical terms, political inclusion of the lower classes in the course of modernization takes place in three distinct ways:

1 in what, for lack of a better term, I have elsewhere designated the *integrative mode*, which prevailed in several northwest European polities, and is marked by a relatively autonomous horizontal inclusion of the people in the national political arena;[14]
2 the *incorporative-clientelistic mode*, which brings people into the centre via their insertion into personalistic, highly particularistic patron-client networks – such networks cutting across and undermining more horizontal forms of political organization like trade unions or parties primarily based on universalistic criteria of recruitment;
3 the *incorporative-populistic mode*, which mobilizes and introduces newcomers into active politics via neither vertically organized clientelistic networks nor horizontally organized interest groups, but rather via the masses' attachment to a leader whose charisma becomes the major source of legitimation, and whose plebiscitarian organization (if any) becomes the main link between civil-society interests and the public sphere.

For reasons to be explained below, in late-developing semi-peripheral societies the integrative mode of political inclusion tends to be displaced or peripheralized by the more incorporative clientelistic and/or populistic modes – the latter bringing people into the national political arena in a more vertical, heteronomous manner.

Peripheralization of the Integrative Mode

An obvious reason for the failure to establish autonomous, legal-bureaucratic types of political integration in late development has to do with the pre-independence heritage of the countries concerned. As Max Weber, Otto Hintze and many other social thinkers have pointed out,[15] in several parts of pre-industrial Western Europe a fine balance was achieved between the monarch's centralizing administration and various *corps intermédiaires*. This balance, in conjunction with other favourable conditions, has over the past two centuries led to well-functioning democratic parliamentary regimes, which are characterized by a strong civil society able to check political/state arbitrariness. If one takes into account the remarkable distinctiveness of such a balance,[16] it becomes obvious that countries which acquired independence only in the nineteenth century or later, and did not share in the Western European pluralistic heritage, were at a great disadvantage right from the start.

To give a concrete example: until the early nineteenth century the Balkan and southern cone Latin American societies were subjugated parts of huge patrimonial empires, Ottoman and Iberian respectively. As such, these societies never experienced the West European type of absolutism with its unique balance between monarchy and aristocracy which, from very early on, resulted in the rule of law, and autonomous *corps intermédiaires* between the crown and the people. Instead, the Ottoman state (before its decline) approached very closely to the extreme of patrimonial rule that Weber called *sultanism* – a system characterized by the total subservience of the nobility and high state officials to a despotic ruler.[17] A similar type of extreme, highly despotic patrimonial rule can be said to have prevailed in colonial Latin America, where the absence of political feudalism allowed the Iberian rulers to set up a highly despotic state, intolerant of autonomous interest groups and associations.[18]

Not only does the state in late-developing societies carry a negative legacy, but their post-independence trajectories have further consolidated the pre-independence despotic features. In view of the state's enormous growth prior to the development of capitalist industry; and considering that the belated large-scale industrialization was achieved only under state tutelage; as well as, finally, the restricted type of capitalism that has eventually come to prevail in the semi-periphery; given all this, it is not surprising that the majority of civil society organizations operate not so much as safeguards against state despotism, than as administrative extensions of the state's highly corrupt and particularistic apparatuses. This is true for instance of various working-class organizations (such as trade unions) which, in contrast to the Western case, were not constituted in opposition to the state, but created by the state elites themselves with a view to cementing their control of the means of domination.[19]

This difference between the centre and the periphery/semi-periphery in respect of the articulation of state and civil society interests is made quite clear by comparing present-day corporatism in the two cases. In the First World, the collaboration of capital, labour and the state is not coerced, but based on the three partners seeking to co-ordinate policies and reach agreement from a position of relative autonomy. In the Third World, what are called corporatist agreements are based less on genuine collaboration and more on overt or covert state coercion.

In other words, corporatist arrangements prevailing in most late-developing countries fall somewhere between the democratic/pluralistic corporatism of, for example, the Scandinavian countries and, at the other extreme, the fascist legal-compulsory corporatism of Mussolini's Italy and Franco's Spain. Democratic corporatism entails a strong civil society; fascist corporatism (where labour rights are formally abolished) an almost nonexistent civil society; and authoritarian corporatism (where trade union rights are weakened *de facto* rather than *de jure*) a weak civil society.

Clientelism

Given the structural difficulties of institutionalizing integrative modes of inclusion in late-developing countries, the bringing-in process, as already mentioned, takes a more incorporative authoritarian form. One such form, which denotes strong continuity with the past, is the activation/extension of already existing clientelistic networks. In other words, in this case political inclusion – for instance, the transition from restrictive, oligarchic to broader forms of political participation – takes place via the extension and centralization of already available patronage networks and organizations.

Greece provides a good example of this type of political modernization.[20] During the second half of the nineteenth century the Greek polity (like that of several other Balkan and Latin American societies) was characterized by oligarchic parliamentarism. Despite the introduction of universal male suffrage, a handful of notable families (the so-called *tzakia*) were able by clientelistic or more coercive means to control the peasant vote more or less automatically. This type of *de facto* (rather than *de jure*) restrictive parliamentary system was broken in 1909 by a military intervention. This became the catalyst for a series of reforms that dramatically accelerated the bringing-in process. This process was effected by a new party (Venizelos's Liberal Party), which provided the organizational context for the emergence of new political elites on both the local/regional and national levels. However, despite Venizelos's repeated attempts to combat clientelism and the political corruption its practices entail, and to create a Western-type legal-bureaucratic political organization, he failed to overcome the opposition of powerful local notables and had to be content with a less radical form of political modernization.[21]

This consisted of transforming the club-of-notables oligarchic parties into more broadly based clientelistic parties with a more centralized party hierarchy. So for instance, whereas during the oligarchic period local potentates could easily change parties while retaining their clienteles, in the twentieth century such automatic transfers of personnel and votes from one party to another (implying captive clienteles) became much more difficult. This less oligarchic type of clientelism persisted in Greece until the 1967 military coup, which abolished parliamentary rule for a seven-year period.[22]

Populism

Another way of bringing the lower classes into the national political arena during rapid late modernization is through populistic mechanisms of inclusion. Here traditional, oligarchic clientelism is not merely extended and transformed but, to a large extent, replaced by a different type of political mobilization/inclusion that bypasses or undermines strong organizational intermediaries of both the clientelistic and the legal-bureaucratic type.

As Weber has pointed out, in ideal-typical terms, the populist incorporative mode entails plebiscitarian organizational structures. It entails organizational forms easily malleable by a charismatic leader who is able to bypass 'intermediaries' and appeal directly to the 'people'. In other words, while the local bosses of clientelistic parties, despite their post-oligarchic more centralized organization, retain a considerable degree of autonomy *vis-à-vis* the national leadership (an autonomy based on their ability to control their client voters through kinship or other personalized networks), this autonomy tends to disappear in the populistic case. Here the party cadres derive their authority from above, from the leader's charisma, rather than from below.[23]

Moving to a more concrete level of analysis, we must distinguish between Greece's transition from oligarchic to broader forms of political participation, which took place through predominantly clientelistic means, and the societies in the northern part of the Balkan peninsula, where the process of inclusion took a more populistic form. Given the greater egalitarianism among peasants, as well as weak land-owners and weak urban middle classes, the break-up of oligarchic parliamentarism and the broadening of political participation was marked by the development of mass peasant parties which, at least initially, were based less on traditional patron–client networks than on the direct appeal of charismatic leaders to the peasant masses.[24]

In the Latin American semi-periphery, on the other hand, the land-owners were much stronger and therefore more capable of clientelistically controlling their subordinates in the countryside. However, given higher levels of urbanization and industrialization than in the northern Balkans, oligarchic parliamentarism was broken up via urban rather than rural populism. The rapidly growing urban middle classes were able to cut back the oligarchic controls that a small number of land-owning/exporter families were exercising over the state, and entered active politics by mobilizing the urban masses and by building up populist organizations to operate as counterweights to the land-owners' persisting economic power.[25]

Populism in Latin America, especially during the interwar period, cannot of course be accounted for entirely in terms of the oligarchic/post-oligarchic political transition. An explanation of its relative frequency in the early post-oligarchic period must also consider economic factors, such as the post-1929 shift from the export of primary products to import-substitution industrialization. This switch created very favourable conditions for the development of policies based on anti-imperialist rhetoric and on carrot-and-stick inclusionary social measures – such as granting social benefits to the working class, while simultaneously undermining the autonomy of the trade union organizations.[26]

When in the early postwar years the initial model of import-substitution industrialization came to a halt, industrialization had to be deepened with the help of foreign capital. This drastically impeded the reproduction of populistic modes of incorporation, so that inclusion took on more clientelistic and/or authoritarian forms. Concerning the latter, although the rise of bureaucratic-authoritarian military regimes during the 1960s and 1970s in the more developed regions of Latin America was not directly due to the requirements of industrial deepening, there can be no doubt that an *elective affinity* exists between foreign-led industrialization and bureaucratic authoritarianism, just as there was a similar logical compatibility between import-substitution industrialization and populism.[27]

What all of the above suggests is that – unlike the typical West European trajectory, and contrary to what neo-evolutionist modernization theories have suggested – incorporative mechanisms of inclusion (clientelistic or populistic) are not peripheralized as late-developing societies achieve greater industrialization and urbanization. They tend to persist and even to dominate in a variety of combinations, as political elites struggle to accommodate the sudden and massive entrance of the lower classes into the national political arena in a social context of growing social inequalities.[28] The fact that incorporative modes (in conditions of mass politics) are not as effective as the integrative ones for supporting a well-functioning parliamentary democratic system brings more authoritarian solutions the moment clientelistic and/or populistic organizational arrangements appear to get out of hand. This does not mean that authoritarianism (in the form of military dictatorships, for instance) can be institutionalized permanently. Given the present pro-democracy international climate, the relatively long and persistent democratic traditions of several semi-peripheral societies, and the fact that bureaucratic-authoritarian regimes do not as a rule succeed in building up a mass base and/or strong organizational roots, what happens instead is: *either* a pendulum situation, where open/democratic and closed/dictatorial solutions keep alternating as civilian and military elites struggle to cope with the growing contradictions of late development (e.g. Argentina); *or* a more stable authoritarian rule, where incorporative modes of inclusion are backed by a strong dose of covert authoritarianism leading to a system of 'guided democracy' (e.g. Brazil).[29]

Finally, as far as the state–civil society problematic is concerned, the above points suggest that whereas integrative modes of political inclusion result in a relatively strong civil society (a civil society capable of checking both state despotism and the misrepresentation of private civil society interests via populist mobilization), incorporative modes weaken civil society. In the clientelistic case this weakening is due to the fact that patron–client forms of representation cater for the interests of only a minority of clients, completely ignoring those who are unwilling or unable to find patrons. In the populistic case, particularly when populist leaders come to control the state apparatus, their plebiscitarian style of leadership undermines intermediary bodies, and therefore civil society loses its ability to check state arbitrariness from above, or mob rule from below.[30]

STATE–CIVIL SOCIETY LINKAGES: THE CULTURAL DIMENSION

Edward Shils has correctly pointed out that:

> one component of civil society which was neglected in practically all discussions in the nineteenth century was the nation or nationality. Nation and nationality were thought to be characteristic of the type of society which was being superseded by civil society. *Nevertheless, as civil societies came to be increasingly realized in the course of the nineteenth century, the nation or nationality provided the cohesion which would otherwise have been lacking in those civil societies.*[31] (italics mine)

Nationality or nationalism providing the cohesion of civil society does make sense because modernization, as already argued, entails a bringing-in process that leads to the destruction of localism and the switch of loyalties from the local community to the nation-state. From this perspective Ernest Gellner is quite right when he sees nationalism as an almost unavoidable consequence of modernity.[32] Once a person's identification with the traditional community weakens, identification with a broader whole becomes almost inevitable.[33]

As there are different kinds of modernization, so there are different kinds of nationalism. In the Anglo-Saxon West, to speak again in ideal-typical terms, the transformation of subject into citizen, and the gradual integration of the latter into the mechanism of the national market, public administration and educational system, went hand in hand with the formation of national identities. As peasants or artisans became increasingly involved in the rapidly proliferating mechanisms of the nation-state, they gradually began to see themselves less as members of particular localities and more as French, Dutch, Swiss, etc.

On the other hand, in countries that acquired their political independence relatively late (which is most of the late-developing countries), the subject's identification with the national community takes place in a context where the nation-state is not yet present, or exists merely as a project yet to be realized. This means that in these countries, and/or in those that started to industrialize a century or more after the West, nationalism initially developed as an ideology, and only later took the form of the actual integration of individuals into the country's economic, political and educational mechanisms.

In the Balkans, for example, nationalist ideas developed when these countries were still a subjected part of the Ottoman empire, and were introduced mainly by the merchants and intellectuals who had strong links with diaspora centres in the West, and were themselves influenced by Enlightenment ideas and the dramatic events of the French Revolution.[34]

It is true that in both Western Europe and the late-developing countries one sees what Benedict Anderson calls *imagined communities* – in the sense that in both cases the identification with the national whole lacks the concreteness, directness and personalized character of the almost exclusive identification with the local, traditional community.[35] But there are also fundamental differences. In the Western case, the identification with the 'imagined whole' takes place in a context where there are already highly structured economic, political and educational-cultural arenas. In the case of latecomers (to political independence as well as to industrialization), such *national* arenas are either nonexistent or exist in only embryonic form.

The above difference is fundamental. It frequently decides what kind of nationalist ideology will prevail, by shaping the cultural linkages that the citizens, as members of civil society, establish with the nation-state. Oversimplifying again, in northwestern Europe the nationalist discourse had to take into account the already existing socio-political realities, whereas in the case of latecomers (at least at the stage where nationalism exists only as an ideology) there is not such restriction, and the nationalist imagination is free to take quite wild or utopian forms. Of course, such lack of realism is corrected once the countries have achieved their political independence and their elites have to deal with the difficult circumstances which, as a rule, dictate a simultaneous tackling of the problems of nation-building and economic development.[36]

For all that, in most latecomer societies the linkages between cultural-ideological and socio-political integration into the nation-state are not as strongly, or rather not as positively and organically articulated as in the West. This is due not only to the fact that the cultural-ideological inclusion precedes the socio-political one; but also because in the nation-states of the periphery the bringing-in process (as already mentioned) takes a more heteronomous form: civil, political and social rights are not spread as widely as in the Anglo-Saxon West. Therefore, lower-class citizens are both 'in' (in the sense of being implicated in state mechanisms) and 'out' (in the sense of not substantially benefiting from the fruits of modernization and development).

Given the above differences, what is specific about the ways in which citizens identify with the state in late development? Or rather, what is specific about the way in which civil society links with the state on the *cultural* level? I shall refer to three major features, all of which are, in a way, cultural manifestations of the weakness of civil society in late development.

Incorporative Ideologies

As many social scientists have pointed out, most late-developing societies suffer from a marked split between two mutually antagonistic political cultures, which results in two different conceptions of what is, or should be, the core national identity. The one points to a more traditionally oriented, indigenously based, inward-looking political orientation hostile to Western values and the institutional arrangements of modernity (seen as Westernization). The other is a modernizing, outward-looking orientation that tries to catch up with the West by adopting Western institutions and values as rapidly as possible. Although different groups or parties tend to opt for one or the other of these two orientations, in actuality there are different mixtures of the traditionalist and modern discourses, rearranged in a variety of combinations.

The more inward-looking discourses can be linked with, or rather can be seen to have a certain affinity with, the populist and clientelistic modes of inclusion we have already discussed. As a rule, populism generates a much more cohesive and comprehensive discourse than clientelism in order to explain and legitimize the

prevailing relations of domination. Very crudely put, it is a discourse emphasizing the glorification of 'the people', the denigration
of a supposedly conspiratorial establishment and its foreign masters
(who can then be blamed for all the country's misfortunes) and,
finally, a romantic search for an anti-Western route of development
that will safeguard the indigenous culture and, more generally, the
'national essence' ('Greekness', 'Argentinidad', etc.).[37]

By contrast, the clientelistic discourse lacks the internal consist-
ency and ideological sophistication of populist rhetoric. It is
usually reduced to what Juan Linz has called *mentalities*: a set of
political orientations that have very little connection with a legit-
imizing discourse, or are linked up with it only by an *ad hoc*
assortment of ideas.[38] In ideal-typical terms, clientelistic bosses either do not trouble at all to hide their particularistic practices (and
frequently pride themselves on being able to use the state apparatus
for helping their families, friends or villagers); or they try to conceal
or justify their particularistic practices, by means of diverse discourses far removed from the actual, day-to-day political practices
and exchanges. Such discourses can take a variety of forms, from
highly abstract and vacuous diatribes on justice, freedom and
progress, to anti-communist rhetoric or the glorification of the
traditional cultural heritage.

Formalism

If we now see how ideological themes (that is, second-order discourses) link up with actual political practices (first-order discourses), what is most striking in the national and political culture
of semi-peripheral societies is the huge gulf between the ideological
rhetoric (whether modernizing, clientelistic or populist) and actual
practices, or rather what Bourdieu calls the political *habitus*: the
more or less unconscious dispositions that are at the root of the
complex political games being played.[39]

Of course, some gap between 'theory' and 'practice', between
first- and second-order discursive practices, is an unavoidable feature of any polity: but the gap is particularly wide in political
systems where vocabularies imported from the West are used to
conceal and/or legitimize institutional arrangements that are a far
cry from the political modernity seen in Western European parliamentary regimes. So a typical political debate in late-developing countries takes one of two forms: it is either a highly abstract

and abstruse legalistic discussion on concepts such as freedom or democracy (or issues of national sovereignty conceived xenophobically and manicheistically) – concepts and issues that are far removed from the everyday concerns of the citizen. Alternatively, it takes the opposite form of intense competition and feuds on a purely personal level, in which case the focus shifts from the formalistic to the personalistic/particularistic, completely leaving out substantive issues, the solution of which could well improve the quality of everyday life. Whether deliberately or not, this formalistic/personalistic combination operates as an extremely effective smoke screen, hiding chronically unresolved vital problems bedevilling daily existence. In Weber's terminology, *formal rationality*, combined with an obsession with the strictly personal, completely displaces *substantive rationality*.[40]

Ambivalent Attitudes to the National Community

The above type of formalism is closely related to another fundamental cultural feature of the civil society–state linkages in late development: this is a highly ambivalent, almost schizophrenic attitude towards the national whole, the Fatherland.

On the one hand, citizens unreservedly and in highly patriotic manner support the national ideals, to the extent of being ready to give their lives for them in case of war. On the other hand, the same citizens have no qualms whatsoever in robbing the state, either indirectly by evading taxes or directly by wasting or appropriating taxpayers' money, destroying the environment or fanatically promoting sectional interests that are detrimental to the interests of the majority of the population. The contradiction between this strong support of the national ideals and the total lack of civic spirit does not necessarily imply institutionalized hypocrisy. It rather indicates a more or less unconscious refusal to see the connections between different types of national interest; or perhaps the interconnections are made on the rhetorical level but not on the level of actual dispositions and first-order political practices.

A similar ambivalence *vis-à-vis* the Fatherland can also be seen concerning the constitution of national identities. On the one hand, children are taught to view their country and themselves as national members in highly idealized terms (unique achievements, cultural superiority, etc.); on the other, via the same or different routes of socialization, they acquire strong feelings of inferiority *vis-à-vis* the

West and a highly deprecatory attitude towards their own country (nothing works, everybody is a crook, etc.). These two contradictory facets of the national identity seem to operate in quite separate compartments, never merging into some more balanced and realistic view of the nation and its people, which could provide a more accurate map of a nation's strong and weak points, or where the real problems are located, and where one should look for their solutions.

This schizophrenic attitude is less marked in countries where the cultural inclusion into the nation-state did not precede but went hand in hand with economic and political inclusion. It is also milder in countries where the majority of citizens feel less excluded from areas related to the distribution of power, wealth and prestige. This means it is less common in countries with a strong civil society and a developed welfare state.

CONCLUDING REMARKS

In summary of the above we can say that civil society–state linkages on the cultural level operate in a manner not conducive to the balanced growth of late developers. Just as the state in most of the late-developing countries acquires an orientation that is anti-developmental, the same can be said about a country's political national culture. On the level of both rulers and ruled, there is a culture which – via clientelistic/populistic ideologies, mechanisms of formalistic – displacement and ambivalent attitudes to the national community discourages the development of an adequate knowledge of the actual state of affairs and the formulation of effective policies. Instead, where there is a tendency to ignore the linkages between 'national crises' and routine economic and political practices, all responsibility for ongoing difficulties or impasses is automatically shifted inwards or outwards: the led accuse their leaders, and both put the ultimate blame on imperialism and/or the omnipotent machinations of various indigenous and foreign 'establishments'.

I do not mean by this to imply that there is no connection between imperialism (in its various forms) and dependent development. I only wish to point out that, contrary to dependency and world-systems theory, I do not believe that foreign exploitation or domination, whether deliberate or unintentional, is the only or even the major explanation of the semi-periphery's past and present misfortunes.[41] I would rather put the main emphasis *on the anti-*

developmental character of the state and its mutually reinforcing
links with an equally anti-developmental nationalism.

The final consequence of all this is that the majority of late
developers find themselves in a double bind: on the one hand, they
have to develop in a context where balanced growth can only come
from above, from effective state intervention; on the other, the state
– or rather the state–civil society linkages on the political and
cultural level – constitute the major anti-developmental forces
within society.

POSTSCRIPT: THE EAST ASIAN CONTRAST

As a postscript to the present analysis it might be useful to consider
to what extent the anti-developmental character of state–civil society linkages is an inevitable consequence of 'late-late' development[42] – at least for countries other than Canada, Australia and
New Zealand with their West European socio-cultural traditions.
Although late-late development and the state's anti-development
orientation seem to go together, Taiwan and South Korea are striking exceptions to this rule.

Both of these countries had an inter-war history very different from that of the Balkan and Latin American societies. Occupied by Japan at the time and ruthlessly exploited, they were
also subjected to a number of changes that later, in the postwar
years, proved themselves highly beneficial in terms of balanced
economic growth. Among these changes was the break-up of
the local land-owning elites, which facilitated the post-liberation
agrarian reforms and resulted in rapidly increasing agricultural
productivity.

Another legacy of the Japanese was the development of considerable social overhead capital and of industrialization. Although these
were initiated by the occupiers for their own purposes and advantage, they provided a solid foundation for industrial development
after the Second World War. Especially after 1960, and massively
assisted by the United States, progress was astounding, particularly
in industrial exports. Last but not least, the Japanese left behind
them a strongly authoritarian state fully committed to economic
planning and flexible, very selective and successful interventions in
the economy as a whole.

While multinational capital was instrumental in the late-late industrialization of Taiwan and South Korea, as it had been in Latin
America, the Asian states were better at directing this financing

where it was needed most. Ensuring that export-oriented industrialization combined properly with a balanced overall growth, these two countries experienced few serious bottlenecks. In consequence, the profits from their rapid growth (especially since the 1970s) were well dispersed over rural and urban areas, and while even today wages are still relatively low, Taiwan and South Korea have nothing like the marginalization that continues to be dominant in the Latin American societies.[43] It is not particularly surprising therefore that the *dirigiste* state controls the trade unions,[44] and closely scrutinizes the movement of indigenous and multinational capital. What is truly remarkable is that it managed to do this without stifling private initiative.

In the past ten years both countries have had to face up to new and difficult challenges, namely popular pressure for more democratization, growing trade union opposition and higher labour costs, increasing competition from other export-oriented semi-peripheral countries, etc. However, given their state structures, it is highly unlikely that either of them is going to revert to the typical features of underdevelopment shown by the majority of late-late developers.[45]

In the light of the above, what are the factors responsible for the qualitatively different developmental performance of the Southeast Asian cases?

I think the answer lies in a combination of exceptional external and internal circumstances, which facilitated the disruption of the typical anti-developmental linkages between the state, civil society and national culture. With reference to, first, the external conditions, there is no doubt that the huge American aid received by both Korea and Taiwan, particularly during the 1950s and early 1960s, was a great help, both directly and indirectly. Directly, the foreign funds enabled these economies to overcome some of the typical bottlenecks that late development entails (such as severe balance-of-payments difficulties);[46] indirectly, the Americans considered both countries as links in the United States security orbit and used the aid factor for pushing the Korean and Taiwanese governments to implement extensive reforms. This relates to a second important dimension: both countries, as divided parts of larger national units, were facing an immediate and severe communist challenge, and their politico-military elites saw balanced development as a means of both legitimation and survival.

This extremely favourable external situation was coupled with – from the point of view of balanced development – an equally favourable internal one. Here the most striking factor is that, in both Korea and Taiwan, those who controlled the state apparatus managed to insulate themselves against pressures emanating from civil society's privileged as well as underprivileged strata. As already mentioned, the demise of the big estates went in tandem with the repression of working-class organization (trade unions as well as left-wing parties). This drastic weakening of civil society forces left ample room for manoeuvre by those controlling the means of administration/domination. Such elbow room is something Latin American satellites have never known, not even when their countries were under dictatorial rule.

Of course, neither external favourable circumstances nor state autonomy from civil society are guaranteed to lead to balanced and effective socio economic growth. There is nothing to prevent state elites from using favourable internal or external circumstances to promote the growth not of a balanced economy but of their own bank accounts, or to increase their socio-political capital. *A very weak civil society may be used either developmentally or antidevelopmentally by those who control the means of domination.* What is interesting about Korea and Taiwan is that political repression and the ensuing weakening of civil society were not accompanied by the growing socioeconomic inequalities that are such a typical feature of most authoritarian capitalist regimes. It was rather that in these two cases political repression was linked to relative social equity – or, to put it differently, political inequalities ran parallel with a type of development that spread the fruits of growth to the bottom of the social pyramid. How is that to be explained?

I think here the nature of the national political culture is highly relevant. The important and multi-faceted Japanese influence (via colonization, geographical proximity, cultural diffusion, the post colonial collaboration between Japanese and indigenous capital, etc.), successfully linked nationalism with development – not only on the level of rhetoric but also on that of actual dispositions and practices. In other words, favourable internal and external structural conditions in these two countries matched up with appropriate cultural influences. These influences enabled the elites (economic, political, military, cultural) to establish strong links between nationalism and development on the level of *habitus*.

Finally, one can say that the combination of all the above pro-developmental factors is so rare that it does not only qualify but actually reinforces our general tenet of the anti-developmental linkages of state, civil society and nationalism in late development. On the one hand, once a successful developmental project is institutionalized, it then becomes a model to imitate – particularly for those geographically proximate countries that share similar cultural and historical experiences. In that sense it will not be surprising if the Korean and Taiwanese model of balanced but authoritarian development should spread to Malaysia, the Philippines, Indonesia and even China.

Perhaps the day has come for us to shift our theoretical orientations and preoccupations. We might spend less time and energy exploring the connections between modernity and Western values, and more on those between late modernity (or post-modernity) and 'Eastern' values.

NOTES

1 It should also be stressed that Western European 'modernization' did not only entail the destruction of localism but also – at the other extreme – that of the transnational, European cultural and diplomatic space with which the *ancien régime* upper class identified. For an early sociological analysis of the modernization process see R. Bendix, *Nation-building and Citizenship*, Action Books, New York, 1969.

2 Civil-society organizations and interests are typically viewed as occupying the space between state and kinship institutions. See for example R. Tester, *Civil Society*, Routledge, London, 1992.

3 Tester, *Civil Society*, p. 14.

4 Bendix, *Nation-building and Citizenship*.

5 This was the case in Argentina, for instance, during the post-Peron era. See H. Spalding, *Organized Labor in Latin America*, Harper, New York, 1977 and R. J. Alexander, *Labor Relations in Argentina, Brazil and Chile*, McGraw Hill, New York, 1962.

6 I have in mind here mainly Latin American societies (particularly those of the southern cone region), as well as most Balkan societies. All of these became independent at the beginning of the nineteenth century, in the course of that century adopted democratic parliamentary forms of rule, and experienced large-scale industrialization after the 1929 Depression. For convenience, I shall use the term 'parliamentary semi-periphery', or 'semi-periphery', *tout court*, when referring to these societies. For an examination of the long-term political developments in the parliamentary semi-periphery see N. Mouzelis, *Politics in the Semi-Periphery: Early Parliamentarism and Late Industrialization in the Balkans and Latin America*, Macmillan, London, 1986.

7 A. Gerschenkron, *Economic Backwardness in Historical Perspective*, Praeger, London, 1962.

8 D. Senghaas, *The European Experience: A Historical Critique of Development*

Theory, Berg, Leamington Spa, 1985, and U. Manzel, 'The Experience of Small European Countries with Late Development: Lessons from History', paper presented at the International Symposium on the Functions of Law in the Development of Welfare Societies, Oslo, 1990.

9 For statistics on the monstrous size of state apparatuses in the parliamentary semi-periphery see Mouzelis, *Politics in the Semi-Periphery*, pp. 10–15.

10 B. Moore, *The Social Origins of Dictatorship and Democracy*, Beacon Press, Boston, 1966.

11 Mouzelis, *Politics in the Semi-Periphery*, pp. 199–206.

12 This happened to a large extent in the case of European latecomers. See Senghaas, *The European Experience*.

13 For the term of 'restricted capitalism' see J. Taylor, *From Modernization to Mode of Production: A Critique of the Sociologies of Development and Underdevelopment*, Macmillan, London, 1979.

14 Mouzelis, *Politics in the Semi-Periphery*, pp. 73ff.

15 M. Weber, *The City*, Macmillan, London, 1958, and O. Hintze, 'The Preconditions of Representative Government in the Context of World History', in F. Gilbert, ed., *The Historical Essays of Otto Hintze*, Oxford University Press, Oxford, 1975.

16 P. Anderson, *Lineages of the Absolutist State*, New Left Books, London, 1974.

17 M. Weber, *Economy and Society*, ed. G. Roth and C. Wittich, University of California Press, Berkeley, Cal., 1978, pp. 231–2.

18 C. Veliz, *The Centralist Tradition in Latin America*, Princeton University Press, Princeton, N.J., 1980, and M. Sagatti, *Spanish Bureaucratic Patrimonialism in America*, Politics of Modernization Series no. 1, University of California, 1966.

19 For all the above points see Mouzelis, *Politics in the Semi-Periphery*.

20 N. Mouzelis, *Modern Greece: Facets of Underdevelopment*, Macmillan, London, 1978.

21 G. Mavrogordatos, *Stillborn Republic: Social Coalitions and Party Strategies in Greece 1922–1936*, University of California Press, Berkeley, Cal., 1983, ch. 3.

22 N. Mouzalis, *Modern Greece*, chs 6 and 7.

23 N. Mouzelis, 'On the Concept of Populism: Populist and Clientelist Modes of Incorporation in Semiperipheral Politics', *Politics and Society*, vol. 14, 1985.

24 D. Bell, *The Agrarian Movement in Bulgaria*, unpublished PhD thesis, Princeton, 1970 B. Peselz, *Peasant Movements in South-Eastern Europe*, unpublished PhD thesis, Georgetown University, 1950; and N. Mouzelis, 'Greek and Bulgarian Peasants: Aspects of their Sociopolitical Organization during the Interwar Period', *Comparative Studies in Society and History*, vol. 18, 1976.

25 Mouzelis, *Politics in the Semi-Periphery*, pp. 62–72.

26 For the debate on the linkages between import-substitution industrialization and populism see J. Malloy, *Authoritarianism and Populism in Latin America*, University of Pittsburgh Press, Pittsburgh, Penn., 1977.

27 For the initial theory on the rise of bureaucratic authoritarianism see G. O'Donnell, *Modernization and Bureaucratic Authoritarianism*, University of

California Press, Berkeley, Cal., 1973; for the long debate on O'Donnell's theory, see D. Collier, *The New Authoritarianism in Latin America*, Princeton University Press, Princeton, N.J., 1979.

28 N. Mouzelis, 'Class and Clientelist Politics: The Case of Greece', *Sociological Review*, vol. 26, 1978.

29 For a development of this point see Mouzelis, *Politics in the Semi-Periphery*, pp. 97–184, and N. Mouzelis, 'Regime Instability and the State in the Parliamentary Semi-periphery', in C. Thomas and P. Saravanamutha, eds, *State and Instability in the Third World*, Macmillan, London, 1989. For the democratization trends in Latin America and southern Europe see G. O'Donnell, P. Schmitter and L. Whitehead, eds, *Transitions from Authoritarian Rule: Prospects for Democracy*, John Hopkins University Press, Baltimore, Md., 1985.

30 Populism in its extreme form seriously undermines civil society, and so has a strong affinity with W. Kornhauser's concept of mass society; see his *The Politics of Mass Society*, Free Press, Glencoe, Ill., 1959.

31 E. Shils, 'The Virtue of Civil Society', *Government and Opposition*, vol. 26, 1991.

32 Gellner, *Nations and Nationalism*, Basil Blackwell, Oxford, 1983.

33 It goes without saying that the 'need' for broader identification should not be teleologically transformed into 'cause'. The *specific* form taken by a person's identification with the national whole will depend on a variety of historical developments that cannot be derived armchair-fashion by a theory of needs or of functional requirements.

34 P. Kitromilidis, *The French Revolution and South-Eastern Europe*, Diaton, Athens, 1990 (in Greek).

35 B. Anderson, *Imagined Communities*, New Left Books, London, 1983.

36 On the issue of the sequence of crises in development, see L. Binder et al., *Crises and Sequences in Political Development*, Princeton University Press, Princeton, N.J., 1971.

37 For the concept of populism and the various debates on contrasting definitions and theories see M. Canovan, *Populism*, Junction Books, London, 1981; E. Laclau, *Politics and Ideology in Marxist Theory*, New Left Books, London, 1977; N. Mouzelis, 'Ideology and Class Politics', *New Left Review*, no. 112, 1978; Mouzelis, 'On the Concept of Populism', and Mouzelis, *Politics in the Semi-Periphery*.

38 J. Linz, 'Notes towards a Typology of Authoritarian Regimes', paper presented at the Annual Meeting of the American Political Science Association, 1972.

39 P. Bourdieu, *The Logic of Practice*, Polity Press, Cambridge, 1990.

40 For a concrete example of this type of displacement mechanism see Mouzelis, 'Ideology and Class Politics', pp. 134–49.

41 From this perspective, I think that Wallerstein and his followers are wrong when they stress that world-market mechanisms constitute the main reason for underdevelopment or dependent development. It is misleading to argue, for instance, that relations between central, semi-peripheral and peripheral nations have a zero-sum quality, in the sense that a few countries moving from the

periphery to the centre makes it more difficult for other peripheral countries to do likewise.

In fact, if one looks at the growing inequalities between central, semi-peripheral and peripheral countries, if my analysis is correct, it is not at all obvious that they are due to the dynamics of the world capitalist market. It might well be that the major reason for the tripartite periphery/semi-periphery/centre structure not being pear-shaped (that is, not having a narrow bottom and broad middle) has less to do with the world market than with the internal organization of peripheral states.

If the profoundly anti-developmental character of most Third World state apparatuses and their nationalist/cultural orientations are taken into consideration, neither more favourable world-market mechanisms nor less exploitative centre–periphery relations will enable peripheral countries to move up. So if the tripartite stratification of present-day states in terms of wealth, for instance, has a 'Brazilian' rather than a 'Swedish' profile, this might be due less to the nature of the world economy than to how the state in the periphery articulates with civil society. Another way of putting this is to say that the highly unequal distribution of wealth on a world scale might be due not so much to the shortsightedness or selfishness of the core, but rather to an inter-state system within which the majority of members are systematically prevented by their administrative structures and cultural/nationalist orientations from taking advantage of the developmental opportunities the changing world economy is constantly generating.

42 The 'late-late' label is used in development theory to make a distinction between the (compared to England) relatively late Western European industrializers (e.g. Germany) and those societies that experienced *large-scale* industrialization only after 1929. See on this point A. Hirschman, *A Bias for Hope*, Yale University Press, New Haven, Conn., 1970, ch. 3.

43 D. Morawetz, *Twenty-five Years of European Development 1950–1975*, World Bank, Washington, D.C., 1977.

44 R. Wade, 'State Intervention in Outward-looking Development: 1950–1975', in G. White and R. Wade, eds, *Developmental States in East Asia*, Institute of Development Studies, Brighton, 1985. See also R. Wade, *Governing the Market*, Princeton University Press, Princeton, N.J., 1990, and F. C. Deyo, ed., *The Political Economy of the New Asian Industrialism*, Cornell University Press, Ithaca, N.Y., 1987.

45 S. Haggard, *Pathways from the Periphery*, Cornell University Press, Ithaca, N.Y., 1990.

46 Haggard, *Pathways from the Periphery*, p. 84, points out that in the case of Taiwan, 'of a total current account deficit of $1.3 billion between 1951 and 1962, aid financed $1.1.' The level of American aid to South Korea was equally high.

11

From Controlled Inclusion to Coerced Marginalization: The Struggle for Civil Society in Latin America

Philip Oxhorn

Renewed interest in civil society has coincided with the resurgence of political democracy throughout the world. Most researchers generally agree that a 'civil society' of some sort is inextricably intertwined with the fate of democratic political regimes. In Latin America, the historical weakness of civil society is often seen as an important factor in explaining the fragility of political democracy in the region. I will argue that while this has been true in the past, it may not be true in the future. Specifically, as processes of *controlled inclusion* have given way to processes of *coerced marginalization*, new interests and needs have led to the beginnings of civil society in areas where it was absent.

The possibility that civil society may be emerging in Latin America is often obscured by the narrow way in which the concept is used to understand Latin American politics. On one extreme, the emergence of various grass-roots organizations over the past several decades has contributed to a naive optimism concerning the emergence of Latin American civil society among some researchers.[1] Such authors take for granted the capacity of these positive tendencies to transform existing structures of domination. As a result, they are at loss when attempting to account for the decline in the influence of these tendencies once democratic transitions are under way. The 'resurrection' of civil society during democratic transitions[2] invariably gives way to the 'eclipsing' of civil society as relatively small groups of elites come to control democratic politics in an increasingly undemocratic fashion.[3]

Such an outcome is consistent with conclusions drawn by another set of scholars at the opposite extreme. For these people, the unique historical and cultural experiences of Latin America preclude the emergence of civil societies. These authors generally associate the development of civil society with the spread of modern market relations and capitalism.[4] Latin America's Iberian colonial heritage and the 'late' and/or dependent nature of its economic development have distorted the region's development in ways which are inimical to the values and patterns of social relations which characterize the civil societies of Western Europe and North America.

The problem with this latter approach is its implicit historical determinism. Latin America seems to be condemned to a vicious circle of political instability, underdevelopment and authoritarianism in its various guises. This approach cannot provide an adequate descriptive account of the emergence of significant associational life in most Latin American countries since the 1960s. Prescriptively, it offers little insight concerning possible remedies for the weakness of civil society in developing countries.

Both extremes reflect a common problem: an inadequate theoretical analysis of *how* civil societies emerge. It will be argued here that socioeconomic and political changes in the region over the past 30 years are propitious for the emergence of civil societies similar to those found in Western Europe. The associational life which appeared to flourish during the 1970s and into the 1980s is a result of this context and reflects the incipient emergence of civil society in many countries. In contrast to Western Europe, however, there is also the potential for 'democratizing' civil society which is paradoxically the result of the authoritarian experience itself. Whether or not incipient civil societies will continue to grow (let alone become more democratic) will be dependent, I argue, on the role played by political parties in relation to both civil society and the state.

DEFINING CIVIL SOCIETY: A COLLECTIVIST PERSPECTIVE

Civil society is a rich social fabric formed by a multiplicity of territorially and functionally based units. The strength of civil society is measured by the peaceful coexistence of these units and by their collective capacity simultaneously to *resist subordination* to the state and to *demand inclusion* into national political structures. The public character of these societal units allows them to justify and act in open pursuit of their collective interests in competition with one another. Strong civil societies are thus synonymous with a high level of 'institutionalized social pluralism'.[5]

Two implications of this collectivist perspective are worth highlighting. First, it presupposes that individual units possess a high degree of autonomy in defining their collective interests. Such autonomy helps ensure the effective representation of all the principal interests in any given society. It avoids or lessens the tendency in capitalist societies for the interests of dominant actors and social classes to subordinate completely the interests of other less powerful actors and social classes. Because they are self-constituted, the units of civil society serve as a foundation for political democracy. Schmitter's distinction between 'societal' and 'state' corporatism illustrates this point well.[6] Societal corporatism is characterized by strong centralized labour movements with deep roots in civil society. The strength of such labour movements within civil society allows them to define and pursue their own interests in relations with representatives of capital and the state. While having to accept important constraints on their ability to pursue their interests freely, they have won impressive concessions. These include the most comprehensive social welfare institutions among Western democracies, high levels of employment and various other rights and privileges for the working class. In contrast, state corporatism has been characteristic of authoritarian regimes in developing countries such as Mexico and Brazil. Corporatist institutions are used to control working-class demands and mobilization. Hierarchical labour institutions lacking effective roots in civil society are created by the state to maintain political stability and promote economic growth in the absence of comprehensive social welfare institutions or measures to address growing income inequality.

The importance of such autonomy is not limited to relations with the state. Autonomy in the definition of the group's interests is also essential in its relations with other actors, particularly political parties. Where political parties come to completely dominate civil society, they simultaneously weaken it and limit the societal pluralism which is responsible for the close association between strong civil societies and political democracy.

The second implication of this collectivist perspective relates to causality: the dual dynamic of *resistance* and *inclusion* characteristic of civil societies demonstrates that political democracy is often the result rather than the cause of a civil society. Historically, civil society emerges with the process of struggle among self-constituted units competing over jurisdiction and in the pursuit of collective interests. The strength of civil society is reflected in the dispersion of political power throughout entire polities. Ultimately, this contributes to the advent of stable democratic regimes supported by already strong, vibrant civil societies whose component elements struggled for democracy in the first place. Conversely, as we shall see, it is the weakness of civil society that contributed to the institutionalization of authoritarian structures in most of Latin America.

In sum, this collectivist perspective stresses the importance of socioeconomic change and the emergence of new collective actors in creating civil societies. It is this collectivist and organizational dynamic which is central to understanding the prospects for civil society in Latin America. Collective struggle and a *lack* of consensus must be recognized as important catalysts for the emergence of civil society.

It should be noted that civil societies are characterized by varying levels of citizen participation. A *democratic* civil society will be defined as one in which there is a maximum amount of direct citizen participation in the decision-making processes which affect their lives. This necessarily requires a multiplicity of relatively small, participatory and democratically structured organizations. As will be discussed below, the nature of socioeconomic processes and political repression in Latin America over the past several decades has contributed to the widespread emergence of these kinds of organizations.

THE HISTORICAL UNDERDEVELOPMENT
OF CIVIL SOCIETIES

If Latin American civil societies are analysed from a collectivist perspective, the historical factors responsible for their weakness become apparent. They revolve around certain aspects of Latin America's colonial legacy and the region's subsequent pattern of socioeconomic development. Together, these factors have contributed to an extreme geographic and social concentration of power resources which has stifled the emergence of vibrant civil societies. The colonial heritage has had a lasting impact on the evolution of national civil societies in most of Latin America.[7] The patterns of colonial trade and administration were highly centralizing influences, concentrating economic, political and social resources in a few major cities and ports throughout the region. After independence, these same cities came to dominate the national political, economic and social scenes in most countries. Competing power centres did not emerge in Latin America, as they did in Western Europe, to contribute to the institutionalization of social pluralism. The cities which had acted as the centralizing link between the colonial power and the territory retained their grip on national politics after independence. These cities became national capitals and colonial administrators generally were the first rulers of the new countries.

As the main link to the international economy, these principal cities served as the conduit for the export of primary products and the importation of manufactured goods and capital. Once the process of urbanization set in, the concentration of economic resources acted as a magnet for attracting rural migrants. It is in these cities that industry tended to concentrate. Throughout Latin America, as the rural population began to fall, these same cities soon dwarfed other cities in terms of population.

In Latin America, the rural oligarchy often lives in the capital and is closely linked to the urban elite. Whereas in north-west Europe, cities were islands in the feudal sea, in Latin America the shared interests of those connected to the export economy dominated urban life. This contributed to a further concentration of resources and power, as well as the blurring of identities which were important in forming variegated civil societies in Western Europe.

Economic development has followed a model of import-substituting industrialization. Dependency on imports of technology, capital and intermediate goods exacerbates income concentration. This is a result of the tendency to mimic production patterns found in industrialized countries as a function of the needs of international capital rather than national development.[8] Industrialization only provides for the partial inclusion of those relatively skilled workers associated with the modern, technologically advanced sectors of the economy.[9] The rest of society is excluded from political and economic power.

Social forces (such as rapid expansion of the working class) which might otherwise have generated stronger civil societies were contained through limited processes of *controlled inclusion*. For example, sustained economic growth allowed for the doubling of per capita GDP in the region between 1960 and 1980, as people moved from low-productivity jobs (largely in the rural sector) to higher-productivity employment in the cities. This resulted in upward social mobility for approximately one quarter of the economically active population, particularly among the young.[10] Many people had realistic expectations for social mobility during most of this period.

These expectations contributed to the institutionalization of rigid hierarchical patterns of controlled political participation. The clearest example of this is state corporatism in countries such as Brazil and Mexico. More generally, political elites of all stripes were able to use the resources at their disposal to build popular support through clientelism and populist appeals. The autonomy of collective actors was sacrificed or subordinated to the narrow interests of political elites. While this often resulted in important gains for those in the populist coalition (leading some analysts to focus mistakenly on populism's progressive reformist tendencies[11]), in the longer term, the costs have been quite great. Aside from hindering the emergence of strong civil societies, populism has ultimately undermined most of its short-term gains. By contributing to periodic economic crises, through inflationary fiscal policies, real gains in worker incomes have been eroded. Reforms which were perceived as 'progressive' in one period (say the 1930s and 1940s) became rigid ceilings for further reforms in later periods (such as the 1960s and 1970s). Where pressures for further reforms could not be contained, the result was a violent imposition of authoritarian rule. Where these pressures were contained, as in authoritarian Mexico or democratic Venezuela, the outcome has not been significantly different in terms of worsening socioeconomic inequality.[12]

Fundamentally, populism and clientelism prey upon the economic and political vulnerability of the 'popular sectors'[13] by offering them important but limited responses to immediate needs. In taking advantage of their weakness relative to other actors, populism ultimately reinforces the subordinate position of popular sectors within society. It ignores the structural causes of popular-sector problems, while making them dependent upon the elite actor responsible for the initial assistance.

In sum, whereas societal pluralism characterizes civil society in Western Europe, in Latin America the pattern seems to be more one of concentration of economic and political power resources. There is a blurring of important potential sources of societal cleavage and a concomitant accentuation of others as a result of the extreme inequality between the major sectors and classes in society. Many potentially self-defined units are incapable of acting autonomously in the definition and defence of their interests and ideals.

Somewhat paradoxically, the problem of autonomy has increased with the consolidation of strong political party systems under democratic regimes. As a 'political class' is created within political parties, partisan interests begin to penetrate all spheres of society. Political parties competing for control of the state define the interests that social organizations express and defend. Rather than act as a damper or brake in moderating polarizing tendencies at the national party level, social organizations controlled by parties magnify them throughout society. Political crises at the national party level easily become societal crises, and the resultant polarization (which in effect represents the stratified nature of these societies) can threaten regime stability. Unlike the situation in Western Europe, where a close association between societal organizations and political parties is not viewed as problematic (and is often an important resource for Social Democratic and Labour parties in particular), in the underdeveloped civil societies of many Latin American countries this association can magnify contradictions and threaten the stability of democratic regimes.

Given the strength of its competitive party system and long experience with political democracy, Chile best exemplifies what could be described as the absorption of civil society by political parties. A myriad of well-organized and mobilized societal units belied a relatively weak civil society due to the dominance of an institutionalized political party system dating back to the latter part of the nineteenth century. Political parties came to be the principal arena for the constitution of new social actors, leading to a situation in which all other societal interests were subordinated to increasingly narrow partisan concerns. As political parties became polarized around inflexible ideological positions during the 1960s and early 1970s, their political polarization was amplified throughout society by the various social organizations which the parties had created. Ultimately, the parties lost control of the polarization process they had started and societal stalemate was broken by military intervention.[14]

FROM CONTROLLED INCLUSION TO COERCED MARGINALIZATION

Processes of controlled inclusion generally prevailed in the region for over a generation, beginning in the 1930s and 1940s in most of the now more industrialized countries. By the late 1960s, important changes were beginning to take place in a number of countries as more exclusionary processes became increasingly dominant. Economic and political instability converged to reverse many fundamental features of the previous period. While the experiences of particular countries varied greatly, the region as a whole underwent fundamental changes which have generated tendencies toward a new phenomenon: *coerced marginalization.*

Coerced marginalization is characterized by the extreme political and economic exclusion of the popular sectors. It is marginalization in the most fundamental sense: subordinate classes are denied basic citizenship and economic rights as a result of state policies. Its coercive nature similarly reflects the convergence of economic and political factors. Coerced marginalization in Latin America is the result of the failure of the existing development model. It emerges when elites in control of the state (especially the military) perceive that the politicization of the popular sectors is a key factor in the demise of that model and an obstacle to the consolidation of a new one.

The 1964 military coup in Brazil was the first dramatic sign that processes of controlled inclusion were breaking down. This was the first of the so-called 'bureaucratic-authoritarian' regimes in Latin America and was followed by similar regimes in Argentina (1966 and 1976), Chile (1973) and Uruguay (1973). These regimes were essentially responses to the perceived excesses of populism and growing signs of economic stagnation. Military institutions assumed control over political systems for indefinite periods in order to force a complete break with the political abuses of the past and to re-establish an institutional foundation for renewed economic growth.

Fundamentally, bureaucratic-authoritarian regimes reflected the belief that controlled inclusion had gone too far and had to be reversed. Policies were adopted which were designed specifically to neutralize the political influence of the popular sectors. Political party activity was either banned outright or, as in the case of Brazil, tightly curtailed. The left and other representatives of the popular sectors (such as labour and peasant leaders) became targets for unprecedented levels of repression. The political space for popular-sector participation contracted sharply as the state's repressive capacity expanded dramatically.

The increasing predominance of exclusionary politics in the 1960s and 1970s reflected the exhaustion of the old development model centred on import-substituting industrialization and the inability of populist policies of inclusion to solve the structural causes of more immediate problems which they sought to alleviate. The viability of the industrialization model required growing domestic markets. Ultimately, this led to growing demands by the lower classes which Latin American economies were increasingly strained to meet.[15] By the 1970s, for example, the capacity of education to provide an avenue for social mobility was nearing exhaustion as the creation of new high-paying employment opportunities failed to keep pace with the expansion of educational levels in the workforce. This led to frustration as new generations of young people were unable to realize the level of social mobility which earlier generations had enjoyed. High levels of income concentration, capital flight and speculative investments further constrained the growth of productive employment. Protectionism, as well as the patronage and corruption associated with controlled inclusion,[16] exacerbated problems of inefficiency and waste. Upward social mobility was barely sufficient to allow for a gradual decrease in the relative level of poverty, while the actual number of people living in poverty increased by 16 per cent during the 1970s alone.[17]

These developmental problems culminated in the debt crisis and regional recession of the 1980s. As the region's per capita GDP declined by almost 10 per cent during the 1980s, the already disadvantaged and least organized were affected disproportionately. Open unemployment for the region as a whole rose from an average of 6 per cent of the urban EAP in 1974 to 14 per cent in 1984. The relative level of poverty again began to rise. By 1989, 183 million people lived in poverty – 71 million more than in 1970.[18]

The predominant response to this economic crisis reflects the emergence of a neo-liberal policy consensus among policy-makers (both within and outside the region) concerning the need for market-based, outward-oriented economic policies. Central elements of this consensus include fiscal discipline, trade liberalization, competitive exchange rates and the desirability of attracting direct foreign investment.[19] Regardless of their success in generating sustained economic growth, an immediate consequence of their implementation has been greater socioeconomic exclusion.[20] As policies intended to create more open, outward-oriented economies are being implemented, there has been a clear trade-off with increases in poverty.[21] The need for generating economic growth with higher levels of social equity has been de-emphasized, despite a growing recognition that long-term development is dependent on greater investment in human resources. Public expenditures generally remain regressive in Latin America. Education, health care and other programmes designed to contribute to human resource development have not been immune from the efforts of budget-cutters to trim the size of the state. Programmes which remain are generally targeted to alleviate specific problems for the poorest segments of society and do little to eliminate the causes of inequality.[22]

The privatization of services formally provided by the state has exacerbated the exclusionary effects of the neo-liberal model. In selling off state enterprises which provide the infrastructure for development (energy, transportation, communications, etc.), concentration of economic resources is reinforced as such services become more oriented towards satisfying the demand of the wealthiest economic actors. Similarly, the privatization of key social services such as social security, health care and housing favours the middle and upper classes which have the incomes necessary to pay profitable prices. But perhaps the most dramatic change has come in the area of education: rather than help promote social mobility, education has become '... a mechanism for the reproduction of social inequality and the introduction of new elitist forms in society'.[23]

In sum, crucial mechanisms for neutralizing pressures which might have otherwise led to the emergence of more vibrant civil societies have been undermined over the course of the past two decades. Processes of coerced marginalization have replaced the processes of controlled inclusion dominant since the 1930s. This has continued as a consequence of the new neo-liberal, outward-oriented development model. The return of political democracy in most of the region has lowered the level of political violence associated with coerced marginalization and restored important citizenship rights. State policies, however, continue to exacerbate economic exclusion in ways which are incompatible with earlier mechanisms of controlled inclusion. The dramatic and rapid nature of socioeconomic change has created new popular-sector needs and interests which the state is typically unwilling or unable to meet.

Expansion of the state's repressive capacity and its efforts to penetrate society violently have amplified the popular sectors' need collectively to *resist subordination* to the state as a matter of self-defence. Similarly, democratic accountability, participation and the re-establishment of citizenship rights can be understood as mechanisms for collective self-defence. The fact that state policies have caused the popular sectors' economic and political marginalization suggests the popular sectors' growing collective interest in organizing to *demand inclusion* into national politics as one way to reverse or at least stop these processes of coerced marginalization.

THE POPULAR SECTORS AND THE STRUGGLE FOR CIVIL SOCIETY

In response to varying degrees of coerced marginalization over the past two decades, community-based organizations among the popular sectors have emerged throughout Latin America.[24] Such organizations range from handicraft workshops and soup kitchens, to cultural, youth and women's groups, to organizations which are dedicated to the defence of human rights and the struggle for transitions from authoritarian to democratic regimes. Although there are important differences from case to case, certain general patterns can be identified. Fundamentally, the popular organizations represent collective responses to the socioeconomic and political exclusion which the popular sectors have had to confront. They are new collective actors which simultaneously seek to *resist subordination* to the state and *demand inclusion* into national political structures.

While popular organizations can be found throughout the region, they are most significant in countries with authoritarian regimes. Such regimes highlight the political exclusion of the popular sectors which is associated with coerced marginalization and leave few alternatives to self-help for alleviating pressing needs. Moreover, repression in these countries shifts the locus of political activity to non-party arenas by effectively proscribing traditional political party activity. These non-party arenas typically will be at the grass-roots level, where their suppression is more difficult. This is due to greater possibilities for concealing such activity and for either sheltering or replacing leaders than at the intermediate and elite levels.

Repression under authoritarian regimes may also indirectly favour the expansion of local rather than functionally based organizations. Labour organizations are by far the most important functionally based organizations. These organizations (along with political parties) were typically the most heavily repressed by authoritarian regimes over the past two decades. The conditions necessary for viable union organization and which make labour leaders more vulnerable do not exist in the same way at the local level. Labour leaders tend to be easily identifiable. The success of the organization depends on the organizers' ability to bring in as many potential members as possible in order to increase the effectiveness of collective bargaining and the ultimate threat of a strike. By contrast, local organizations do not require the participation of even a majority of the community to be minimally effective in meeting the needs of their members. The atomization of groups is not as detrimental an impediment to effective organization. Leaders are not as visible as in the more confined and monitored space of a firm or factory.

More generally, an indirect result of authoritarian regimes is a 're-territorialization' of political activity at the grass-roots level. The policies of deliberate atomization, the destruction of networks of representation and the emphasis on centralized and technocratic policy-making which have characterized authoritarian regimes in Latin America contribute to the development of organizations based on narrowly circumscribed territorial domains.[25] The combination of efforts to depoliticize society with the limits to the state's repressive capacity leaves space for territorially differentiated political activities that largely escape the control of the authoritarian regime.[26]

Popular organizations under these circumstances resist further penetration of society by the state in a variety of ways. Human rights groups are perhaps the most obvious. In denouncing abuses of human rights, keeping records of abuses and helping defend the rights of victims, human rights groups challenge the state's use of its coercive apparatus. Through education and consciousness-raising activities, these groups help undermine the legitimacy of authoritarian regimes and encourage other groups to express their dissent. *Las Madres de la Plaza de Mayo* in Argentina, for example, stood up to the military regime when apparently no one else would, and spurred other opposition groups to voice their dissent publicly.[27]

More generally, popular organizations represent a model for the alleviation of societal problems contrary to the one being imposed by those in control of the state. They are collective solutions to problems such as hunger, unemployment and inadequate housing. They stand in sharp contrast to the individualistic, market-oriented approaches to these problems being promoted by the state. This self-help dynamic also distinguishes popular organizations from less autonomous forms of popular-sector mobilization associated with controlled inclusion.

The logic of these organizations can not be reduced merely to economic or political needs. Popular organizations typically engage in a variety of activities and pursue multiple objectives. These relate to the full spectrum of popular-sector interests stemming from the social, political and economic situations of their members as people belonging to marginalized groups in highly segmented, unequal societies. New identities emerge within popular organizations that exhibit many of the characteristics which Jean Cohen identifies with the 'self-limiting radicalism' of new social movements in Western Europe.[28] Popular organizations generally favour structural reform rather than revolution. They champion political participation, pluralism and political democracy. Popular organizations have formed an important element in the broad social fronts which mobilized to pressure reluctant elites to expand partial processes of democratization in Latin America. As a result, popular organizations helped to push such transition processes further than would otherwise have been the case.[29]

The impact of coerced marginalization on the emergence of civil society becomes clear when examining the evolution of popular-sector organizational activity in Chile during the military regime, which lasted from September 1973 to March 1990. By 1987, 220,000 people – 16 per cent of all the urban poor in Santiago – were members of popular organizations.[30] There were literally thousands of popular organizations dealing with the protection of human rights, problems of inadequate housing, hunger, unemployment and inadequate health care. There were also women's and youth groups, cultural groups and coordinating bodies working with numerous popular organizations. Fundamentally, these organizations represented a collective response to the economic, political, social and cultural exclusion imposed on the popular sectors by the military regime.[31] As such, they represented an important element in the strengthening of Chilean civil society.

This development of civil society was not automatic. Organizations among the popular sectors emerged almost immediately after the 1973 military coup, but they were viewed only as short-term responses to a situation of emergency and funnelled resources from various support institutions, particularly the Catholic Church,[32] to the victims of repression and their families. There was no autonomous organization by the popular sectors. This began to change in 1978, as the military regime tried to institutionalize itself through the introduction of a neo-liberal economic model and various changes to state institutions, culminating in a new constitution in 1980. As the socioeconomic dislocations caused by this effort at institutionalization mounted, alternatives open to the popular sectors narrowed. Popular organizations began to evolve in order to cope with rising levels of unemployment, increased poverty and declining social welfare services.

This evolution was aided by support institutions which sought to increase the capacity of the popular sectors to organize themselves. There was a new emphasis on teaching the urban poor about the importance of organizing and how to organize. Stress was placed on the need for collective action and solidarity. Support institutions also endeavoured to respect the autonomous decision-making processes of popular organizations. A certain level of self-sufficiency was necessary because resources were never enough to satisfy the organization's needs. Handicraft workshops and groups working with the unemployed, for example, assumed more responsibility for creating economic opportunities and managing their own affairs. Collective kitchens had to find ways to augment the diminishing contributions they were receiving so that their members could eat.

At the same time, there was a change of perceptions within the popular organizations. Members began to recognize the severe limitations created by their dependence on support institutions. Autonomy to define and defend their own interests became increasingly important to them. Members of popular organizations also started associating their problems with the need for political change. Popular organizations became the locus for resistance to the military regime. They represented an alternative to the authoritarian and individualist model for social relations that was being imposed by the military.

By the mid-1980s, the survival of popular organizations had become dependent upon their ability to produce and reproduce a new popular collective identity among their members. At its core, this identity reflected a commitment to finding collective solutions for overcoming the myriad of obstacles which affected the popular sector's limited life chances and consumption possibilities. Central values of participation and community shaped the collective identity. Emphasis was placed on the importance of consensus, organizational autonomy and the greatest amount of democratization at all levels, including the political regime and local communities. The importance of participation, particularly through the establishment of democratic procedures and self-help (rather than possible substantive policy outcomes under a democratic regime) suggested that due to this identity, popular organizations could be a pillar of support for a democratic regime.

This collective identity, in turn, served as a basis for new forms of popular-sector collective action at levels that reached beyond the specific communities in which each popular organization was located. It provided for the definition of interests and demands on the part of the popular sectors in their interactions with other political actors. Ultimately, these interests and demands were to be represented by a new collective actor at the national level, a *Unitary Poor People's Command* (CUP).[33]

Until now, the discussion of coerced marginalization has focused on the violent expulsion of groups previously given certain economic and political rights through processes of controlled inclusion associated with import-substituting industrialization. Coerced marginalization is also present in countries with different development models and no history of controlled inclusion. In these cases, deliberate state policies of repression and economic transformation have also resulted in an extreme exacerbation of the socioeconomic and political exclusion of the popular sectors. This has been particularly true, for example, in El Salvador since the mid-1980s.[34] There, similar processes of coerced marginalization over the past decade have contributed to the strengthening of civil society. Although the scale of violence was greater in El Salvador, the same concerns motivated disadvantaged groups to organize: the defence of human rights, the resolution of pressing economic needs and the establishment of popular cultural identities. By looking at popular organizations in El Salvador, it becomes clear that the impact of coerced marginalization on the emergence of civil society is not limited to any particular level of socioeconomic development or development model. At the same time, the contrast between Chile (where controlled inclusion went further than perhaps any other country in the region) and El Salvador (where the popular sectors have struggled for decades for even minimal inclusion) will highlight some of the obstacles to the further development of civil societies in Latin America.

An important factor in the emergence of popular organizations in El Salvador was the sheer magnitude of the political violence. This created both political and economic needs which popular organizations were created to meet. By 1989, tens of thousands of people had been killed in a country whose population was just over five million. A quarter of the population had been displaced. The economy was put into a tailspin with dramatic effects on the poor: per capita GDP was reduced to its 1975 level, the real minimum wage was just 35.6 per cent of its 1980 level and over 55 per cent of the all families lived in poverty, according to official statistics.[35] In areas under guerrilla control, government services were minimal at best,[36] and the endemic nature of repression led to a generalized distrust of authorities among the poor.

Unlike Chile, where the historical strength of political parties conditioned popular-sector organizational activity in fundamental ways, the absence of even minimal processes of controlled inclusion in El Salvador tied the fate of popular organizations more closely to the guerrilla movement. Popular organizations were generally sympathetic to the Farabundo Martí National Liberation Front (FMLN) and supported it in numerous ways, but they retained an important level of autonomy.[37] Just as the banning of political parties by the Chilean military regime and the regime's efforts at institutionalization led to the growth of popular organizations, a turning-point in the development of popular organizations in El Salvador was an intensification of the war and a change in FMLN strategy in the mid-1980s. The FMLN abandoned its strategy of organizing large forces to maintain control over extensive territories. Instead, it opted for a strategy of 'defensive war' based on small mobile units which would conduct a classic guerrilla war. As popular organizations began to address the growing concerns of their members, the FMLN was forced to re-evaluate the role of civilian organizations and recognize their independent role. The new strategy also taxed the Salvadoran military's resources, creating additional space for popular-sector organizing.

As with Chile (and most other cases of extensive popular organizations), the Catholic Church has played an important role in facilitating autonomous popular-sector organizational activity. Through the spread of grass-roots Christian base communities, the church has increased the capacity of the urban and rural poor to organize themselves. In particular, the church has stressed the importance of solidarity and collective action for dealing with immediate socioeconomic problems, as well as alternative conceptions of human rights.

Popular organizations resist penetration by the state and demand inclusion into national political processes by struggling to preserve their organizational autonomy and emphasizing the importance of collective self-help initiatives. Unlike Chilean popular organizations, however, Salvadoran organizations have successfully developed into regional, even national, actors. For example, in 1984, various rural cooperatives formed a peak organization, the Confederation of Cooperative Associations of El Salvador (COACES). In 1985, COACES was able to mobilize over 20,000 people in a march through San Salvador to celebrate its first anniversary and demand the passage of a law on cooperatives which it had presented to the legislative assembly.[38] It now represents approximately 400 rural cooperatives with 75,000 members, and even sits on the Forum for Economic and Social Concertation.[39]

Similarly, 55 community councils in the provinces of Morazán and San Miguel formed the Association for Community Development of Morazán and San Miguel (PADECOMSM) in April 1988.[40] These councils had been created in the mid-1980s to deal with problems of health care, education and a deteriorating economic situation. Their participative and self-help qualities were transferred to the new peak organization. PADECOMSM stresses principles of maximum participation, accountability and consensus in selecting leaders and determining policy at all levels, from the grass roots through to its executive council. Local and regional development are promoted in order to minimize PADECOMSM's dependence on outside assistance and provide resources for expanding services to the local population. For example, it has established the Agricultural School of San Fernando to increase local agricultural production by training local producers and to improve the diet of the poor. The school plans to become self-financing through the sales of agricultural produce and livestock from its experimental farms.

The resurgence of rural organizations was preceded by renewed organizational activities among the urban popular sectors.[41] In the early 1980s, for example, various community development organizations were beginning to emerge. In May 1988, a number of these organizations formed the Salvadoran Communal Movement (MCS). By mid-1993, it represented approximately 200 communities with 86,000 people.

Like its rural counterparts, the MCS is committed to promoting community development through solidarity and self-help initiatives. Maintaining the MCS's autonomy is a primary concern, and it pursues a variety of activities designed to minimize dependence upon outside actors. The MCS is a relatively complex organization with secretariats for education, the promotion of organizational activities within communities, local economic development, women's and youth organizations, health, ecology and human rights. Already, it has constructed low-cost housing in several communities and initiated a School for Communal Leaders. Future plans include a vocational education school, sponsorship of a national literacy programme and developing a proposal for municipal reform.

Despite the massive militarization of society in El Salvador, its popular organizations appear to be stronger than Chile's. Whereas the CUP largely failed to establish itself as a legitimate interlocutor for the popular sectors in Chile, organizations such as the MCS, PADECOMSM and COACES have achieved a level of organization that transcends individual communities and can attempt to influence national political processes. Paradoxically, Chile's lower levels of violence and long experience with popular participation prior to 1973 did not seem to create a more conducive environment for popular-sector organizational activity compared to El Salvador, with its much higher levels of violence and history of only limited political participation.

Perhaps equally important, Chilean popular organizations found themselves competing with strong, institutionalized political parties for the allegiance of the popular sectors. In El Salvador, political parties are much weaker and the FMLN as a guerrilla organization had a very different relationship with popular organizations. After the FMLN adopted a strategy of defensive war, the guerrilla movement and popular organizations played complementary but clearly distinct roles. The ability of the FMLN to wage an insurrectionary war depended upon support from the organized popular sectors. Similarly, the strength of popular organizations allowed popular sectors to survive the ravages of civil war. Popular organizations in El Salvador were able to achieve a level of autonomy and institutionalization which their Chilean counterparts found difficult, if not impossible. I will return to these issues shortly. But first, it is important to discuss one more aspect of this particular kind of organizational activity: its contribution to the democratization of civil society.

At the grass-roots level of society, local organizations have historically tended to be egalitarian and participatory.[42] Their importance as forums for the practice and learning of norms and behaviours appropriate for political democracy has been commented upon as far back as Tocqueville.[43] This has been no less true of the popular organizations which have emerged throughout Latin America in recent years, whose democratic nature has been stressed.[44] Popular organizations, regardless of their purposes or goals, tend to be democratically organized and emphasize the importance of each member's participation in the group. An alternative identity as a 'neighbour' (*vecino*) begins to emerge and popular organizations often seek to demonstrate and develop an alternative democratic lifestyle.[45]

While a general definition of political democracy would be incomplete if it focused only on participation, participation is the principal defining quality of democracy at the level of civil society. The myriad of organizations which characterize the base level of civil society provide the most abundant and effective mechanisms for direct citizen participation. It is at this level, as opposed to the level of the political regime in modern nation-states, that the ideal of direct democracy is most feasible. The ideal of a 'democratic civil society' is virtually synonymous with that of a 'participatory society' or 'participatory democracy'.

A variety of factors account for the democratic qualities of popular organizations. The small size and face-to-face contact which are characteristic of popular-level organizations tend to generate equal status and decision-making processes based on consensus within the organization. The continual direct interaction of members often generates greater empathy among them, as individuals make others' interests their own.[46]

Organizations also tend to be more democratic internally in the *absence* of material benefits to membership.[47] The presence of material benefits provides a relatively unambiguous measure of the value of belonging to an organization. When members join organizations in order to contribute to the achievement of worthwhile goals, members generally demand institutionalized means for influencing the definition of purposes and the tactics used to achieve them. Where membership is motivated more by the satisfaction of belonging and interacting in a group, organizational democracy is an important aspect of such satisfaction. It is also a by-product of the social ties among members which precede their membership in the organization.

Poverty seems to have contributed to the formation of a sense of community throughout poorer areas of Latin America, and this further strengthens the democratic qualities of popular organizations.[48] For example, solidarity and mutual self-help seem to characterize many aspects of life in the shantytowns of major Latin American cities, even in the absence of popular organizations.[49] People know each other quite well and are in constant contact with one another. Neighbours baby-sit each other's children and share in each other's and community celebrations. The members of these communities frequently help mitigate family crises by pooling their limited resources to help meet family emergencies resulting from a sudden illness, injury or death. Limited barter economies may emerge as an alternative for individuals to help make ends meet collectively when employment is scarce.

Often, the democratic qualities of popular organizations reflect a deliberate decision by the organization's members to offer a symbolic challenge to an undemocratic government. When traditional channels for political participation are closed, the constitution of democratic spaces within society becomes an important way of voicing dissent. It can help to undermine the legitimacy of authoritarian regimes by demonstrating the possibility of more democratic alternatives. The organizations which formed the PADECOMSM in El Salvador, for example, abandoned traditional organizational structures which were deemed to be too centralized and hierarchical in the late 1980s to create an alternative which is more participatory and democratic.[50] In Chile, the young co-founder of a cultural organization explained that:

> In the organization you live the society that you want to construct. It is the starting-point where you build society . . . What one lives now [in the organization] is what one wants to live tomorrow – democracy, participation are lived within organizations. Criticisms are accepted, people accept their errors as knowledge – they take responsibility for them and learn from them . . . The organization is for people to develop and grow, to search for new roads. It is liberating . . . in every sense, helping its members to liberate themselves.[51]

Similarly, another young Chilean who co-founded a shantytown self-defence organization added: 'We are fighting for the real participation of the people in the decisions which involve them. We have to realize this [in our organizations] . . . We are fighting for respect.'[52]

With the eclipsing of authoritarian regimes, the struggle for civil society in Latin America is now entering its most decisive phase. The struggle will either continue, as popular organizations help redefine the nature of popular-sector incorporation, or wither away as new processes of controlled inclusion emerge to reinforce old patterns of socioeconomic and political stratification. Paradoxically, popular organizations face a major challenge in adapting their experiences to the more propitious environment which democratic regimes seem to offer. This is because of the fundamental role that repression and political exclusion played in their emergence. To date, it seems that civil society is 'losing': once elections are called, there is a generalized demobilization of society as political activity is channelled through political parties. This helps explain why – in every case – the political influence of popular organizations declines once a democratic regime has been installed.

Political parties and their relationship with popular organizations provide a central axis around which the fate of civil society will revolve. Whether it be under an authoritarian regime or in a democratic political system, important conflicts seem inevitably to emerge between popular organizations and political parties as the former become more established. Political parties were traditionally a primary mechanism for the controlled inclusion of the popular sectors and its negative consequences for the emergence of vibrant civil societies. They continue to be the principal mechanism for inclusion under the democratic regimes that have emerged in Latin America in recent years. Even where parties are weak, such as in Brazil, their very weakness tends to reinforce the clientelism and populist tendencies which have historically circumscribed the development of civil society. When party systems are strong, as in Chile, or dominated by a single hegemonic party, as in the Mexican case, the sheer strength of political parties seems to smother the potential for civil society's emergence.

Tensions between popular organizations and political parties result from a number of causes. The presence of multiple parties competing for popular-sector support is divisive and fragments popular organizations. There is also a clash between the participatory and democratic organizational style characteristic of popular organizations and the more hierarchical style of political parties, which places less emphasis on aspects of internal democracy and participation in favour of representation. This is reflected in the 'process' orientation of popular organizations. These organizations exist as a source of solidarity, friendship and other collective values among members who form a community. In contrast, political parties are more 'result' oriented and frequently reorganize to be more efficacious in achieving results – often at the expense of popular-organization autonomy.

These tensions are not inevitable. Democratic party structures can help ameliorate many of these problems. To avoid confrontation, political parties could adopt some of the participatory values expressed by popular organizations if they wish to interact with them. Rigid, hierarchically organized political party structures, which have an insulated national party elite who manage party affairs in a highly centralized fashion, are most likely to generate conflicts between parties and popular organizations. Party structures would have to decentralize in order to allow for a maximum amount of participation by grass-roots members in the party's decision-making processes. Such decision-making processes would need to be characterized by a two-way flow of information and an interchange of ideas between different levels of the party. Democratic lines of accountability would be required to link the party's elite or national levels with local branches.

Moreover, parties would have to be willing to accept that such organizations maintain a certain level of autonomy from party structures. Pluralism tends to characterize popular organizations with memberships who belong to a variety of political parties or no party at all. The surest way to exacerbate tensions between political parties and popular organizations would be for the political parties to attempt to 'capture' these organizations and subordinate the organizations' interests to their own. Instead, parties could attempt to work with, not control, these organizations.

There are promising tendencies in this direction. The Workers' Party in Brazil and the so-called Renovated Left in Chile offer examples of progressive parties which see the popular sectors as a potentially important social base.[53] They reject a rigid Marxist-Leninist project based on the primacy of the working class or proletariat. Instead, these parties find inspiration for an alternative project (a more democratic and participatory society) in the organizational style associated with popular organizations.

With the possible exception of Chile, however, it is still not clear how far these tendencies can go in transforming entire political systems. Despite the socioeconomic and political dislocations of the past several decades, populism and clientelism are still dominant characteristics of Latin American politics which have not given way with the recent wave of democratization.[54] Rather than a cultural problem, as many have suggested, the problem reflects the continued weakness of civil society in most of Latin America. While authoritarianism and economic 'shocks' have gone a long way to reversing its historic underdevelopment, historical processes which took hundreds of years in Western Europe cannot be telescoped into several decades in Latin America. At most, popular-sector organizations encompass 10 to 15 per cent of all members of the popular sectors. While this is significant, much more remains to be achieved.

Moreover, the very nature of dependent development, with its characteristically high levels of social inequality and poverty, creates special problems for the emergence of strong civil societies. The majority in these countries lack (and will lack for the foreseeable future) the resources easily to resist cooptation and manipulation by self-interested elites. This has always been the trump card of clientelism and populism: the ability to make appeals to people's pressing material needs in exchange for their support. While today's populists lack resources compared to their predecessors, the needs of the popular sectors have become even more acute.

The experience of El Salvador is interesting in this regard. El Salvador lacks any experience with effective political democracy, and former guerrilla groups are just beginning to grapple with the problems of turning themselves into political parties. Clientelism and populism were never effective mechanisms for achieving even the controlled inclusion of the popular sectors. Popular organizations are still strong, especially in relation to most political parties which compete to represent popular-sector interests. Political parties are much more dependent on the continued support of popular organizations than is the case elsewhere, and popular organizations have acquired a level of legitimacy and institutionalization that will make it difficult for other political actors to either ignore or manipulate them.

Increasingly, comparative studies of democratic consolidation in Latin America have emphasized the necessity of creating strong, institutionalized political parties in a region notorious for their weakness.[55] While this is certainly important for the future of democracy, I have argued here that traditional political parties are also part of the problem because of the ways in which they undermine the emergent civil society. Political parties are important, but they must be of a particular type if civil society is to be strengthened. The alternative is increasingly tenuous democratic regimes founded on new forms of controlled inclusion rather than the vibrant civil societies characteristic of consolidated democracies in the West.

Civil society ultimately reflects a much more equitable distribution of power than is typical of most Latin American societies. The dislocations of the last two decades have undermined previous patterns of domination, but it is far from clear that a fundamentally different balance has been struck among the various actors competing for political influence. Popular organizations can help disperse power within Latin American societies, and simultaneously contribute to the democratization of those societies. But the task is daunting and far from complete. Cooperation with other actors is essential. Political parties, in particular, can play an important role in fostering what are arguably among the most positive tendencies to emerge within the region in a long time. Perhaps the true challenge facing Latin America is to create institutionalized political party systems which can open up multiple new opportunities for democratic participation, rather than close them off.

NOTES

I would like to thank John A. Hall and Carmen Sorger for their comments on earlier drafts of this chapter.

1 For example, see T. Evers, 'Identity: the Hidden Side of New Social Movements in Latin America', in D. Slater, ed., *New Social Movements and the State in Latin America*, CEDLA, Amsterdam, 1985; O. Fals Borda, 'Social Movements and Political Power in Latin America', in A. Escobar and S. Alvarez, eds, *The Making of Social Movements in Latin America*, Westview, Boulder, Colo., 1992.

2 G. O'Donnell and P. Schmitter, *Transitions from Authoritarian Rule: Tentative Conclusions about Uncertain Democracies*, Johns Hopkins University Press, Baltimore, Md., 1986.

3 G. Ducatenzeiler and P. Oxhorn, 'Democracia, autoritarismo y el problema de la gobernabilidad en América Latina', *Desarrollo Economico*, vol. 34, 1994.

4 For example, see A. Seligman, *The Idea of Civil Society*, Free Press, New York, 1992; E. Gellner, 'Civil Society in Historical Context', *International Social*

Science Journal, no. 129, 1991; E. Shils, 'The Virtue of Civil Society', *Government and Opposition*, vol. 26, 1991; and N. Mouzelis in this volume.

5 See P. Schmitter, 'An Introduction to Southern European Transitions from Authoritarian Rule', in G. O'Donnell, P. Schmitter and L. Whitehead, eds, *Transitions from Authoritarian Rule: Southern Europe*, Johns Hopkins University Press, Baltimore, Md., 1986, p. 6.

6 P. Schmitter, 'Still the Century of Corporatism?', *The Review of Politics*, vol. 36, 1974.

7 S. Stein and B. Stein, *The Colonial Heritage of Latin America*, Oxford University Press, New York, 1970.

8 F. Cardoso and E. Falleto, *Dependency and Development in Latin America*, University of California Press, Berkeley, Cal., 1979.

9 The extreme social stratification associated with this particular pattern of development is analysed in A. Portes, 'Latin American Class Structures: Their Composition and Change during the Last Decades', *Latin American Research Review*, vol. 20, 1985.

10 This mobility was closely linked to increasing levels of education among workers. See CEPAL, *Transformación Ocupacional y Crisis Social en America Latina*, United Nations Comisión Económica para America Latina y el Caribe, Santiago, 1989.

11 For example, see T. Di Tella, 'Populism and Reform in Latin America', in C. Veliz, ed., *Obstacles to Change in Latin America*, Oxford University Press, Oxford, 1965, and M. Coniff, ed., *Latin American Populism in Comparative Perspective*, University of New Mexico Press, Albuquerque, 1982.

12 S. Eckstein, *The Poverty of Revolution*, Princeton University Press, Princeton, N.J., 1988; T. Karl, 'Petroleum and Political Pacts: The Transition to Democracy in Venezuela', in O'Donnell, Schmitter and Whitehead, *Transitions from Authoritarian Rule: Southern Europe*. Growing inequality has placed Venezuela's democratic regime under increasing strain. There have been two military coup attempts and popular disillusionment with existing democratic institutions only seems to be growing.

13 The 'popular sectors' are the disadvantaged groups in highly segmented, unequal societies. They are characterized by their limited life chances and consumption possibilities. In urban areas, the popular sectors include both organized and unorganized workers in the formal economy, the unemployed who are seeking employment, people working in the informal economy and the lumpenproletariat who are largely outside the formal and informal economies. The peasantry, including small land-owners, subsistence farmers and rural wage labourers, are also part of the popular sectors. P. Oxhorn, *Organizing Civil Society*, Pennsylvania State University Press, University Park, forthcoming.

14 It should be noted that political parties did not 'create' the demands which served as the basis for mobilizing the popular sectors. While the parties may have been responsible for raising expectations and for a lack of political moderation on the part of the popular sectors, the popular sectors' demands reflected needs that were the result of Chile's economic underdevelopment.

Ironically, the collapse of Chile's democratic regime is perhaps the best example of how limited populist reforms are for improving the long-term position of the popular sectors.

15 The following is based largely on CEPAL, *Transformación Ocupacional.*

16 Ironically, the most pernicious aspects of controlled inclusion are the most durable. Mexico began to deal with these problems only in the 1980s and Brazil has yet to come to grips with them. Even Argentina, despite the massive repression associated with the so-called 'dirty war' of the late 1970s, has only been able effectively to address problems of a bloated and inefficient public sector since the election of a Peronist president in 1989.

17 CEPAL, *Transformación Ocupacional,* p. 55.

18 CEPAL, *Magnitud de la Pobreza en America Latina en los Años Ochenta,* United Nations Comisión Económica para America Latina y el Caribe and Programa de las Naciones Unidas Para el Desarrollo, Santiago, 1990.

19 J. Williamson, ed., *Latin American Adjustment: How Much Has Happened?,* Institute for International Economics, Washington, D.C., 1990.

20 Even their implementation tends to be the result of the continued political exclusion of most of the population. Democratic governments in almost every case have sought to isolate policy-makers from social pressures of any kind, undermining the long-term prospects for democratic consolidation in much of the region. See Ducatenzeiler and Oxhorn, 'Democracia, autoritarismo y el problema de la gobernabilidad'.

21 World Bank, *World Development Report,* Oxford University Press, New York, 1990, p. 55.

22 World Bank, *World Development Report,* p. 37; CEPAL, 'Equidad, Transformación Social y Democracia en America Latina', United Nations Comisión Economica para America Latina y el Caribe, Santiago, 1988, mimeo.

23 CEPAL, 'Equidad, Transformación Social y Democracia en America Latina', p. 12.

24 A. Escobar and S. Alvarez, eds, *The Making of Social Movements in Latin America,* Westview, Boulder, Colo., 1992; S. Eckstein, ed., *Power and Popular Protest,* University of California Press, Berkeley, Cal., 1989; J. Jacquette, ed., *The Women's Movement in Latin America,* Unwin Hyman, Boston, Mass., 1989; F. Calderon, ed., *Los movimientos sociales ante la crisis,* Universidad de las Naciones Unidas, Buenos Aires, 1986.

25 See O'Donnell and Schmitter, *Tentative Conclusions.*

26 Unlike Soviet-style communist or European fascist states, Latin American states generally lack the repressive capacity to silence all sources of dissent, even if this is their goal. There are high costs associated with sustained repression at such unprecedented levels in terms of both international and domestic opposition. Such territorially based organizations might be viewed as less of a threat by the regime, given the greater immediate capacity of organized labour to wreak havoc on the economy and the left's explicit objective of taking state power. Moreover, the state's repressive capacity is frequently undermined by widespread corruption and inefficiency associated with controlled inclusion. In extreme cases, such as in many Central American coun-

tries and Peru, the state's repressive apparatus has been so weakened that revolutionary groups have been able to erect substantial military structures within the national territories.

27 See M. Navarro, 'The Personal is Political: Las Madres de la Plaza de Mayo', in Eckstein, *Power and Popular Protest*.

28 J. Cohen, 'Strategy or Identity: New Theoretical Paradigms and Contemporary Social Movements', *Social Research*, vol. 52, 1985.

29 O'Donnell and Schmitter, *Tentative Conclusions*.

30 This experience is examined in much greater depth in Oxhorn, *Organizing Civil Society*.

31 It should be noted that with the loss of its privileges, the organized working class found itself in the same basic situation as other members of the popular sectors. While there were important struggles over the restoration of those privileges, they generally did not create significant divisions within the popular sectors.

32 The Catholic Church has played a crucial role in supporting popular organizations throughout Latin America. The emergence of liberation theology and other progressive church tendencies in Latin America have led the church to promote human rights and grass-roots organizing in many countries since the mid-1960s. The church has also used its position in these predominately Catholic societies to help shelter popular organizations from repression by allowing them to meet on church properties.

33 The movement was ultimately undermined by political party interference in its activities. It ceased to exist in 1988 after political parties forced the movement's leaders to conform to the opposition's strategy for ensuring a transition to democracy. The opposition ultimately succeeded in securing a transition to democracy, but the popular social movement remains disarticulated above the level of individual grass-roots organizations. See Oxhorn, *Organizing Civil Society*. I return to the problematic relationship between political parties and popular organizations below.

34 Research for this section was carried out in San Salvador during July and August 1993. It was made possible by a grant from the Fonds pour la Formation de Chercheurs et l'Aide à la Recherche of Quebec.

35 It is worth noting that neo-liberal economic reforms introduced since mid-1989 by El Salvador's conservative president Alfredo Cristiani have exacerbated many of these negative economic trends for the poor. By mid-1990, for example, 63 per cent of all families were living in poverty, and unemployment had increased by over 45 per cent compared to the level of a year earlier. See L. Binford, 'El desarrollo comunitario en las zonas conflictivas orientales', *Estudios Centroamericanos*, vol. 47, 1992, p. 602n.

36 For example, a 1990 study of 44 communities in the FMLN-controlled northern part of the Morazán found that 41 of these communities had received no economic or social assistance from the government for the last five years. See Binford, 'El desarrollo comunitario', p. 588.

37 M. Lungo, *La Lucha de las masas en El Salvador*, UCA Editores, San Salvador, 1987, and Binford, 'El desarrollo comunitario'.

38 Lungo, *La Lucha de las masas*, pp. 76–7.
39 This body was set up as part of the current peace process in order to establish a societal consensus on social and economic issues.
40 The following is based largely on Binford, 'El desarrollo comunitario'.
41 Lungo, *La Lucha de las masas*, and Binford, 'El desarrollo comunitario'.
42 See M. Castells, *The City and the Grassroots*, University of California Press, Berkeley, Cal., 1983.
43 J. S. Mill, *Utilitarianism, Liberty, Representative Government. Selections from Auguste Comte and Positivism*, H. B. Acton, ed., Dent, London, 1972, and A. de Tocqueville, *Democracy in America*, trans. G. Lawrence, Anchor Books, New York, 1969.
44 For a general survey of different country cases, see the sources listed in n. 24. I talk at greater length about democratizing civil society in general and the specific case of Chile in Oxhorn, *Organizing Civil Society*.
45 T. Tovar, 'Barrios, Ciudad, Democracia y Política', in E. Ballon, ed., *Movimientos Sociales y Democracia*, DESCO, Lima, 1986.
46 J. Mansbridge, *Beyond Adversary Democracy*, Basic Books, New York, 1980.
47 J. Wilson, *Political Organizations*, Basic Books, New York, 1973.
48 M. Taylor, *Community, Anarchy and Liberty*, Cambridge University Press, Cambridge, 1982.
49 For example, one study estimated that more than 70 per cent of the adults in domestic households in Santiago shantytowns are actively involved in mutual assistance networks based on trust and reciprocity. See C. Hardy and L. Razeto, *Nuevos actores y prácticas populares*, Centro de Estudios del Desarrollo, Santiago, Documento de Trabajo no. 47, 1984.
50 Binford, 'El desarrollo comunitario'.
51 Personal interview, Santiago, Chile, 1986.
52 Personal interview, Santiago, Chile, 1986.
53 On the Brazilian Workers' Party, see M. Keck, *The Workers' Party and Democratization in Brazil*, Yale University Press, New Haven, Conn., 1992. On the renovated left in Chile, see M. Garretón et al, *La Renovación socialista*, Ediciones Valentin Letelier, Santiago, 1987.
54 For example, see R. Gay, 'Popular Incorporation and Prospects for Democracy: Some Implications of the Brazilian Case', *Theory and Society*, vol. 19, 1990, and F. Hagopian, 'After Regime Change: Authoritarian Legacies, Political Representation, and the Democratic Future of South America', *World Politics*, vol. 45, 1993.
55 See Hagopian, 'After Regime Change'; F. Hagopian, 'Democracy by Undemocratic Means? Elites, Political Pacts, and Regime Transition in Brazil', *Comparative Political Studies*, vol. 23, 1990; and Ducatenzeiler and Oxhorn, 'Democracia, autoritarismo y el problema de la gobernabilidad'.

12

Civil Society and Islam

Şerif Mardin

Civil society is a Western dream, a historical aspiration; it is also, in the concrete form this dream has taken, part of the social history of Western Europe. The dream suffered a number of ups and downs as it was crystallizing, and Karl Polanyi is one of the many authors to give us the down side of the picture.[1] The dream itself, the ability to dream the dream, is the expression of a unique premiss concerning the components of a social system, a premiss which also assumed more precise outlines within modern European history. That postulate is the idea that social relations are both sustained and energized by autonomous, secular collectives with legal personality operating within a frame of rationalized self-referential law. In the first part of my paper, I consider the interaction of civil society as a 'virtual' society and civil society as a set of concrete institutions that has promoted the concept of civil society as a central social value in the West.

By 'dream' I mean, in this first instance, that there exists, buried in the background of Western social history, a view of human agency to which the modern history of Western Europe added a structural dimension. Richard Bernstein traces this concern for agency to dominant themes of Western history going back to ancient Greece and to the philosophy of Aristotle in particular. These themes have been embodied in recurrent concepts such as those of praxis or action. The more general framework that Bernstein associates with this view of agency is that of pragmatism, a pragmatism which sees man as an 'active manipulator advancing new hypotheses, actively testing them, always open to ongoing criticism and reconstructing himself and his environment'.[2]

Another explanation of 'dream' or of 'virtual' society would be to point out that political legitimacy – that extraordinarily difficult, slippery concept – is best understood as the objectification of the *telos*, the dream of a society; a *telos* which is latent and which in fact can only be reconstructed after the flight of the Owl of Minerva but one which we may approximate by looking at the long-range transformation of a society. What I have in mind is not Braudel's *longue durée* which is a very French invention of a French historian, but the shape of a dialectic of emergence and unfolding, an eye of the observer which follows the ontological connotations of transformation.

A characteristic of the history of the transformation of the Western dream into a reality is that this metamorphosis is limited to the West. Civil society, for instance, does not translate into Islamic terms. Civility, which is a latent content of civil society, does, but these two are not interchangeable terms. Well-intentioned students of the Middle East have showed a reluctance to make this distinction which I highlight in the second part of my paper.

The persistence of what I call the Western dream may be underlined by showing that theories of civil society which one finds in Locke arise in a different form in Hegel and, in our time, in Habermas's theories of communicative action oriented to understanding. There is here a continuity which merits investigation.[3] The point of view I will try to set out is that rationalized law as it developed in the West enabled this diffuse concept of social agency to acquire a mooring, a structural base.

In this attempt to establish the foundation of a comparative approach to civil society in the Islamic 'East' and the 'West', I take an approach somewhat different from that of a recent book, Janet Abu Lughod's *Before European Hegemony*, in the sense that I rely strongly on Weber's *The City* to draw a contrast with the Islamic city.[4] The following brief outline of the development of civil society in the Western setting is the first frame against which I would like to test the relevance of civil society for Muslim culture and more specifically for the history of the Ottoman Empire and modern Turkey. The history of the medieval Western town occupies a central place here because the kernel of the concept of an autonomous sphere of activity, the core constituent of civil society, may be traced to its development. The emergence of the modern nation-state, seen in the perspective of the law that framed it, enters into this argument. The second frame I shall use is that of the comparability of the *telos* – or 'dream' – of each society.

THE EMERGENCE OF CIVIL SOCIETY

It is not useless to start the comparison I have in mind by retracing some of the steps of Western urban history, since each one of the thresholds of this history adds another characteristic layer to our present understanding of civil society as a concept. It is the status and role of merchants and of towns as recipients of charters providing the town and activity of the merchants with special legally legitimated protection that enabled the medieval town as an entity to become a field of power, enabling the town merchant oligarchy to prosper and city governments to develop within its walls.[5] These developments and the three-cornered competition of monarchy, nobility and town enabled modern capitalism to develop with the unique force it acquired in modern times. The acceptance of the changed legal status of a serf who had left the demesne of the lord and had lived in the town for a year, in so far as it was accepted by the lord himself, shows the early development of a certain fixity in the understanding of the very concept of law as early as the Middle Ages.[6] In this sense, the contrast with Weber's 'Kadi justice', or with what is still studied as 'judge-made' law, is instructive.[7] In addition, the type of auto-limitation of the ruling class implied by this state of affairs would have seemed quite peculiar to an Otto man. By contrast, a well-established argument in the history of Western law establishes the limitations of the will of the sovereign implicit in the medieval concept of the rule of law,[8] in a somewhat more extensive and intensive sense than that encountered in the Islamic area.

While, on the one hand the competition between monarchy, nobility and merchant class enabled the leading town-dwellers to expand their legally protected sphere of action, it also created a community of interests between the town and the monarchy.[9] European law provided the added advantage of corporate personality which allowed the commercial firm a special level of survival. Even the medieval revival of Aristotle had an aspect which was used for the rationalization of commercial undertakings.[10]

Urban developments in Europe, it is true, showed a variety of patterns. In France, from the time of Philip Augustus (1165–1223) onward, it was clear that the relations between monarchy and town would be more centralizing than in Italy or Germany.[11] The history of the assertion of the monarchical principle in England showed similar outlines. But the contrast between the civil self-governing tradition of the medieval town and the earlier military tradition of Roman urbanism is evident.[12]

All of this does not mean that in the Middle Ages, within the town itself, principles of freedom as we know them in our modern democratic system prevailed or that the individual automatically accorded respect to authority exercised by the urban elite. On the contrary:

> The bourgeois context did nothing to free the individual from this kind of pressure but seems rather to have intensified it. Since everyone knew that the preservation of the local civic liberties hung upon the continuance of orderly behaviour, all emotional resources were drawn to secure this end. The merchant controlled his staff of apprentices and servants by the help of some of the overtones that were to be found in the ideas of lordship and paternity.[13]

However, in the long run the medieval kernel was transformed to bring out the features of what today we call civil society and the liberties we associate with this concept.

The urban movement lost its original force in the fourteenth century. The monarchs who expanded the boundaries of centralization, forcing the frame of an emerging state on medieval institutions, understood the need for more liberal trade policies and knew that craft protectionism and corporate particularism had to be curbed. An example of what this meant institutionally may be given for the town of Bristol.

> Authority once understood as an outgrowth of civic medieval brotherhood had become by the renaissance majestic sovereignty descending from God and monarch. Gone were many of the collective political celebrations accompanying holy day festivities, which had been the great moment of civic pageantry in late medieval Bristol.[14]

Despite the eclipse of power of the town, the bourgeoisie within the town found itself at the centre of an economy of greater scale, and therefore its potential power grew rather than waned. But more important was the increasingly well-established idea that political rights and obligations stemmed from property.[15] The concept of civil society itself seems, according to the *Oxford English Dictionary*, to be a late sixteenth-century development, but it is still, at that time, coequal with the idea of good government as had always been the case and as one would expect with the rise of the powers of the state.[16] However, monarchical authority was already in the process of being eroded by new philosophical skirmishes whose promotion of the ideas of property fitted well with the ideology of townsmen. The townsmen's dream, systematized, was in the process of becoming the foundation of political legitimation.

First, there was a successful attack on the idea of the monarch as patriarch, and in particular on the *Patriarcha* (1680) of Robert Filmer, its key proponent. This was followed by a greatly elaborated version of rights of property as the key element in the constitution of civil society, the latter still defined as a society of good government. If C. S. Macpherson's stress on Locke's statement that 'the only men who are assumed to incorporate themselves in any commonwealth by express compact are those who have some property, or have the expectation of some property in land' has been challenged,[17] it, nevertheless, seems unusually in tune with the ideas of Locke's time. The final philosophical anchoring of the idea of property was the concept of contract; a type of contract which implied a 'dignifying of the legal order of the English polity' but which had consequences which went well beyond it.[18] *Late* European contractarian theory in contrast with the earlier tacit contract was increasingly taking the form of a concrete legal obligation, a sense which was the substance of the libertarian, American interpretation of Locke.[19]

But we have to go back to another picture of the actual arrangements prevailing in England in that eighteenth century to complete our overview of the total social condition prevailing at the time.

> In the England of my period . . . such activities as police, fire protection, the conduct of the Mint, postal services, the construction and maintenance of roads, canals, harbours, light houses, education, the provisioning of the army, the operation of jails, the servicing and accounting of the national debt, street cleaning, regulation of domestic industry and trade were in large part or entirely farmed out or abandoned to private profit enterprise, to individual charitable initiative or to ancient guilds.[20]

This may have been the economic picture but it cannot be evaluated without a glance at its twin, at law.

> The one element of constitutional continuity in seventeenth-century England was the acceptance by King and Parliament of a political rule of law. Law was the touchstone of politics. No matter how men might differ as to what the law said or what it might be made to mean,

all were committed to a legal standard in the conduct of their political affairs. This is not to suggest that both King and Parliament adhered without exception to the substance of the law; yet for each there was an unbroken reliance upon its structure, its arguments, its procedure and its forms. The common law provided a constant conceptual framework for political action. Throughout the century virtually every important controversy was formulated and every position justified in legal language and common law paradigms.[21]

Further, a key social value which we have to take as a package together with Locke's ideas about contract, was his conception about *knowledge*, a conception that became widely shared by the Enlightenment. This belief which further promoted the strength of a 'virtual' city now 'enshrining' human agency was that:

> The primary category of human experience was cognition. It was in knowing that man became properly human, even transcended human experience, and it was as a knower that he was necessarily an individual. To be saved a man needed to attain not emotional prostration before a hidden God but a knowledge of the truth of religious propositions. Even the incidence of divine grace was to be determined not by emotional conviction but by the purely naturalistic process of believing statements to be true.[22]

Locke had thus conflated both the 'virtual', ideological and the 'material' aspect of civil society. Civil society was subsumed under the even wider umbrella of natural law, taking in all components of Locke's package. 'Freedom of information' had been tacked onto the definition of property. Civil rights were equated with civil society.

The first radical anti-religious use of the new concept of man as a knower was to surface in Bayle's *Dictionnaire historique et critique* (1695–7) in France.

> One of the fundamentals of Bayle's exposition is his so-called scepticism, namely his view that we are unable to attain absolute certainty and truth. No philosophical system, as he pointed out in his *Dictionnaire Historique et Critique* can give us the absolute truth or pretend to do so; each gives only a portion of the truth.[23]

A new trend was also emerging which gradually undermined the idea of civil society as simply that of good government and that was what Hannah Arendt has entitled the 'rise of the social', the interdependence of the twin forces of manufacture/labour and state which came with the growth of modern capitalism.[24] The connection between the new, structurally enhanced role of what Adam Smith called[c] the mercantile system' and the more marked importance, under the circumstances, of civil society as an autonomous sphere separate from government appears in the theories of Adam Ferguson. Ferguson understood that a 'government of laws' – a theme promoted by none other than Montesquieu – suffered from important limitations in so far as civil liberties were concerned. Ferguson thus recognized that the medieval observance of law by the prince had degenerated into the application of the positive public law of the nation-state.

> The centralized political-legal arrangements of civil society ... can help to restrict political abuses and secure citizens' civil liberties and 'rights of property and station'. But centralized government based on the rule of law cannot alone guarantee the civil freedoms of citizens since those who exercise power directly are apt constantly to abuse it. Hence the dilemma: modern civil society requires for its survival a sovereign, centralized constitutional state which, together with commerce and manufacturing breaks 'the bands of society' and threatens citizens' civil liberties and capacity for independent association, thus undermining a *sine qua non* of life in a civil society.
>   Ferguson's attempted resolution of this dilemma is brief and tentative but nevertheless of great interest to a contemporary history of the modernization of the concept of civil society. His key normative principle is the creation and strengthening of citizens' associations – whether in courts of law (juries), the military (citizen's militia) or in civil society at large ... man ... acts best when in social groups.[25]

Ferguson's new approach also underlined the dependence of civil society on the state, that is, civil society had become *part* of the definition of equilibrium in the modern state.[26] In Paine, Ferguson's formula becomes 'co-operative forms of social life which are self-reliant and independent of state institutions'. With Hegel the distinction between the two realms becomes even clearer:

> civil society [*Burgerliche Gesellschaft*] is conceived not as a natural condition of freedom but as a historically produced sphere of ethical life [*sittlichkeit*] 'positioned' between the simple world of the patriarchal household and the universal state. It includes the market economy, social classes, corporations and institutions concerned with the administration of welfare ... and civil law. Civil society is a mosaic of private individuals, classes, groups and institutions whose transactions are regulated by civil law.[27]

But the adjustment is on the other foot, so to speak: in contrast to Paine, Hegel considers that there is no necessary identity or harmony among the various elements of civil society from which derives his reassertion of the role of the state.

In our modern thinking, the concept of civil society has kept its often latent association with all the preliminaries that entered in its formation. It has been questioned whether the attempted re construction of a blueprint of society according to the original dream that propelled it ahead was wise. Yet, set in the form of an ideal counterpoise to the state, civil society with its components of an autonomous sphere of social activity, its reinvigorated defence of the rule of civil law in opposition to public law (that is, *raison d'Etat*), its respect of individual cognition, has been the foundation of rule of modern democratic theory. Quite clearly, the promotion by the state of the interests of civil society in the eighteenth century was the latest pattern of the relations between the state and civil society but this promotion and the control it established over civil society did not mean that civil society would not eventually act as a counterpoise to the state by infiltrating it.[28] This had become the typical relation between state and civil society at the time when the French Prime Minister Guizot launched his motto: 'enrichissez-vous'. Marx proceeded from this point onwards.

IDEAS AND INSTITUTIONS IN ISLAM

I have attempted to present this short history of the idea of civil society in order to compare the intricacy of the steps by which the concept and its applications were constructed and the layering in the history of Western civil society with arrangements we find in the Islamic cultural area and in particular with that of the Ottoman Empire. We may begin with identifying the Muslim 'dream' of society.

The Muslim dream was one which appeared at three levels. The most profound level of the dream was the idea that the Muslim would only bow to the political obligations set by the Qur'an. The second level was that he would accept as an equivalent the Qur'anic verisimilitude of the Qur'an's commentators. Third, because neither of these systems were able to assert themselves unequivocally, the Muslim dream shifted to the ideal of a social equilibrium created under the aegis of a just prince.

Two distinguishing characteristics of this dream should be highlighted. First, it relied on the charismatic authority of a leader to fill
the cracks of a compromised, unrealized system of justice, a feature
which in Europe was minimized by the rationalization of legal
practice and the self-referential aspect of law.[29] Secondly, though it
was filled with its own rich, humanistic content, the dream, once
anchored in Islam precluded the adoption of a concept concerning
the gradual perfectibility of man through man's making of his own
history. The dream of a just prince was therefore linked with primal
time, with a yearning for a return of a golden age. A further comment on this centrality of justice in the Muslim realm would underline the Muslim's idiosyncratic reading of 'freedom' as 'justice'.
When the concept of freedom was introduced into the Ottoman
Empire in the first half of the nineteenth century no Turkish
equivalent was found. A neologism *serbestiyyet* had therefore to be
invented: compassion, respect for the individual as an emanation
from one of the divine attributes and respect for justice seen as the
harmonizing of rival claims[30] were elements of Islamic/Ottoman
civilization; 'freedom' was not.[31]

As to the structural component of Islamic society, while the
'mosaic' of institutions mentioned in the case of Hegel consisted of
voluntary associations, the 'mosaic' of the Islamic city was somewhat different. The Islamic town was founded on segmented units,
described as 'sections' by Muslim historians; these may have existed
at an early stage of medieval history in Europe, but they were
erased by the hegemony of the bourgeois. A further development in
this erasing of segmentation in the West was the formation of the
(eventually) secular legitimation mechanism of consultative legally
constituted communal collectivities whose existence was further
promoted by sectarian opposition to the religious establishment and its Roman bureaucracy, principally as an outcome of the
Reformation.[32]

The Islamic components of towns were religious communities[33]
and groups belonging to different legal schools, guilds, fraternities,
lineage groups and ethnic communities.[34] The historian Makrizi[35]
pointed to this arrangement in the title of his book on urbanism
which was entitled *The Sections*.[36] A summary of typical arrangements taken up by him may be seen in the description of the state
of affairs in Moroccan towns before 1912:

Before 1912 there were no municipalities nor municipal life in
Morocco in the sense those words have had in European countries

since the Middle Ages, a sense inherited from Roman tradition. The towns had no finances of their own, the expense of public service was met in large measure by the revenue of religious foundations . . . and buildings or improvements were dependent on the good will of the Prince.[37]

In the somewhat different sense of the control of the market by discontented artisans or resentful merchants, various groups did play an important role in Islamic municipal life.[38] But a distinction has to be made here once more. It was not so much that the governing powers in towns of the Islamic world were hostile to mercantile interests as such, simply that they were indifferent to them. 'Merchants did not directly enjoy the exercise of power nor could they benefit from the constraints on government policy which protect the interest of many such groups in some of the more delicately constituted societies of the modern industrial world.'[39] The difference between the structural elements of the Islamic city and those of the West may also be recaptured in the role of the Muslim 'doctors of Islamic law', the *ulama*, who, in the absence of a structure comparable to that of the church in the West did not muster as much strength as had the Catholic Church and, later, the protestant groups, in taking up cudgels against central political authority. The status of *ulama* in towns was structurally more ambiguous compared to that of priests and their links with the central political authorities more ubiquitous.[40] It is true that the *ulama* were often leaders of populist outbreaks against the unjust ruler. In that sense they constituted a structural counterpoise to the political hegemon. Elsewhere I have described this role of the *ulama* as a possible equivalent, equilibrating forces similar to those created by Western civil society.[41] But these outbreaks were episodic, diffuse, and this pattern of populistic pre-political outbreaks has been inherited by modern Islamic 'fundamentalism'.[42] A modern contention, taking this theme of a balanced urban life further, namely, that there existed an equilibrium in Middle East society underpinned by a contract with the rulers and by the threat of popular rebellions, is an idea that has been developed by Edmund Burke III.[43] Burke applies to Islamic society a concept first developed by E. P. Thompson in order to shed light on bread riots in England in the eighteenth century, namely that bread riots occurred when a tacit contract entered into between the ruler and the people regarding sustenance was broken by a rise in the price of bread.[44] But two features which make the Middle East and the

Ottoman context stand out with its own characteristics clearly separate its social conditions from those of Western society. Most obviously, in the West the *tacit* contract lived in the more general frame of a more clearly *enforceable* legal contract.[45] Just as important for municipal developments and the representation of corporate rights was the fact that Islam only recognized the physical person – not corporations as endowed with legal personality and rights,[46] an aspect which takes on increasing importance as urban interests are collectively organized.

Raymond has described the legal frame of urban life as a 'doctrine empirique mais claire'[47] but here 'empirique' is an adjective of the utmost importance as compared to the Western system in the sense that Western law was a legally enforceable contract. A legally enforceable contract in the sense of an engagement of the sultan to maintain *under public law* a privilege granted by him was, at the least, tenuous. Emperor Frederick II's miller confronted and stopped the sovereign in an encounter for which there do not seem to be strictly equivalent examples in the Ottoman Empire, although comparable stories of sultans being brought to heel by their religious obligations were circulated. Clearly a comparison of the rights of citizens in the Islamic town and in eighteenth-century England fails. I shall try to show that this is due to an insufficient understanding of the limited extent to which the normal apparatus of positivistic social history can apply to the study of Islamic society.

Not only did the modalities of the enforcement of law differ from the West but the tradition of medieval freedoms now operated in tandem with what I have called 'philosophical skirmishing' and what is also described as the 'rise of scepticism'.

Regardless of the more liberal statements concerning the dissemination of knowledge in the Qur'an, in practice, the traditional Islamic attitude towards knowledge was that knowledge was not for consumption by the masses. Possibly, even more important was the idea that truth was not a relative matter in the sense in which Bayle understood it to be. The gradual restriction of the interpretive canon of Islamic law and the decline of the quality of teaching and discussion in schools was another aspect of this constriction.[48] Finally, the Islamic cultura arena came somewhat late (in the eighteenth century) into the revolution caused by printing and the subsequent development of vernacular languages. Islamic society also lagged behind the West in the uses to which liberalism put knowledge through the intermediary of salons and literary and scientific associations.[49]

There exists, of course, another, more positive, way of examining the social structure of Islam: to look at it from the internal perspective of its social history before going on to a study of the logical implications for society of its ontology. From this vantage point, Islamic town economy and the activity of rich merchants may be understood as embedded in the 'lifeworld' created by a religious discourse. This lifeworld of Islam had a dynamic of its own, recursive in its reference to a golden age of Islam but progressive in the sense of gradually mobilizing an increasing number of Muslims for the elaboration of an Islamic ideal in modern times.[50] In this perspective, modern Muslim 'fundamentalism' is no projection of a confrontation with the West, nor of the 'identity crisis' of our times, but the end product of a Muslim historical continuity and its special discursive formations. In a wider sense, students of Islam will have to stop looking at social change in Islam in structuralist terms and fasten on its aspect of discourse.[51] This would have been intelligible to individuals in Western societies in early medieval times but was completely changed by the very evolution of civil society. What we are dealing with in our exercise in comparison are two different trajectories of social change.

What I mean by 'discourse' can be gathered from a study carried out many years ago in the Turkish town of Edremit by Lloyd and Margaret Fallers, anthropologists from the University of Chicago. The Fallerses lived in this town for a year and described their findings in an important paper.[52] The main theme of this paper was the gender division of labour. According their study, there existed two autonomous spheres of economic activity in Edremit. There were 'men's occupations': professions, farming, bureaucratic roles, trade and petty trade, artisanal activities. But there also existed an institutionalized women's sphere of occupations: tailoring, weaving, embroidering, with overlaps with the men's 'sector' in money-lending and investment in land. But the most important aspect of this differentiation between the men's and the women's economy was that the women were organized into women's groups that consulted each other regarding economic decisions and that each gender had complete, independent control of its activities, that the women were in as full control of their own sphere as men were. The women's sphere drew total incomes comparable to that of men and wealth possibly exceeding that of men. In a sense then, here were economic practices embedded in the separation of sexes structured by Islamic norms. The 'discourse' of Islam 'determined' the structure of activity.

Again, using a venue which focuses on political activity. as 'embedded' in the lifeworld of Islam, we can see the role of the *ulama* in a different perspective. This has been argued by Carl F. Petry:

> How then is the intermediate role of these figures to be defined? In this case the impact of arbitrary rule can be linked to the possibility of communal transcendence, the capacity of individuals to cope with iniquity by rising above it as a group. The role of revered persons provided the clearest example of how a non-corporate society found cohesion in its faith and solace from its oppressors. A wide gulf separated a prayer leader in the Imperial court or a Friday prayer in Al Azhar from a lowly mosque intendent or a devout ascetic in a poor quarter. But their manifestation of piety joined them together and won them public esteem.[53]

The ontological argument which comes to complement the one about the dangers of taking Western structural approaches as universals would be that there did indeed exist in Islamic society a potential for the development of 'freedom' which took its strength from the embeddedness of social practices in revelation, that is, that for the Muslim, freedom was what Richard Khuri has characterized as the freedom to follow a path leading to transcendence, a dream of a different nature that had its institutional roots in Sufism or Islamic mysticism.[54]

THE OTTOMAN EMPIRE

Any study of the Ottoman Empire has to begin by underlining a set of a structural premises which placed their stamp on Ottoman society. First, the Ottomans considered themselves to be the torchbearers of Islam, the successors to earlier Islamic empires. Second, this very allegiance to Islam is mitigated by their use of a type of 'administrative law' the origins of which went back to Genghis Khan's *Yasa* and which was of secular inspiration.[55] This secular component of Ottoman government may explain why between the end of the eighteenth century and the reign of Sultan Abdulhamid II (1876–1909) the Ottoman Empire was the first Islamic polity to undertake a systematic effort of modernization with increasingly secular content. The differences between the Ottoman realm and

European monarchies, a difference not easily discernible before the Renaissance, become accentuated as one moves towards the formation of the nation-state in the West and comparison becomes an even more complex matter as the Ottoman state begins to take over Western institutions.

I underline the difficulty of seizing on earlier differences because superficially the following description of the relations between Louis XIV and his subjects is not clearly dissimilar to those of the sultan with his subject. In France, the units with which contractual engagements were taken consisted of:

> provinces, cities, ecclesiastical foundations, social classes and even economic groups such as trade guilds. These contracts left to each group its own liberties and privileges and no one saw anything out of the way in their existence side by side with submission to the king. Provinces, cities, foundation groups, orders and estates were all faithful subjects of the king but with their own privileges.[56]

The difference only stands out when we remember that in the Western context 'liberties', 'orders' and 'estates' were all legally enforceable structures.[57] The whole point of the Western concept of 'oriental despotism' was that there existed no 'oriental' equivalent of the legal force of contract in the West.

In so far as the status of the town is concerned, Soraiya Faruqhi's rush to the defence of Ottoman towns – comparing the status of Ottoman cities of the seventeenth century to the abolition by the centralized state of independent cities[58] – does not square with the perpetuation of the earlier liberties of towns in modified form in the Western *Standestaat*. Faruqhi's statement also erases the continuity of the Western 'dream' of civil society into modern times which I have underlined here. The real Ottoman situation in Istanbul sees mosques as the focus of spatial configuration, the pashas as contributors to urbanism, the founders of mosques as elements of the ruling 'military' class, deportees treated as a unit of urbanization and non-Muslim districts as units of urban structure.[59] A similar description underlining differences from Western town government is found in the late Jean Pierre Thieck's desciption of eighteenth-century Aleppo in his *Passion de L'Orient*.[60] Possibly, the most important difference between the West and the Ottoman Empire consisted in the Ottoman sultan's wide-ranging policies of forced deportation, partly a means of enriching the professional and economic demographic 'mix' of the towns but which towns did not have much choice in accepting or rejecting.[61] Local notables may have established *de facto* control over towns at the time when Ottoman central control was weakening but the state lay in wait to re-establish its grip over urban centres.

One of the main changes in the structure of the Ottoman Empire in modern times was that the servants of the sultan increased their power *vis-à-vis* their master for reasons that were related to the impact of the modernized West on the Ottoman Empire. Ottoman servants of the state lost battles against the West. They tried to find out what it was that made the West militarily superior, and they had to redraw their institutions to face that challenge. The redrawing was done on the model of enlightened despotism and the Western practice of Cameralism[62] which made Ottoman bureaucrats more powerful as a class, that is, the functionaries now made up a unified entity endowed with its own internal dynamic. Indirectly, the forces at work here were the same as those described by Poggi during the bureaucratization of the political institutions of the West.[63] It is true that there were sultans sympathetic to modernization: Selim III (1789–1807) and Mahmud II (1808–39) were leaders of reform but the situation in the Ottoman Empire in the stretch between 1773 and 1839 shows more clearly the mark of an awakened, patriotic bureaucracy increasingly quizzical about its own rights and admiring of the operation of civil society in the West, possibly because it enabled them to think of their own lives and property as protected – which was not the case under the Ottoman *ancien régime*. The reforms promoted by these bureaucrats still bore the stamp of the main Western school of modernization – which had worked through enlightened despots to promote its ideas of government rationalization. In this sense, the Ottoman bureaucrats still had both feet in the Ottoman view of a social collectivity made up of subjects rather than citizens. Indeed, during the second stage of the reform movement, initiated in 1839, the Ottoman bureaucratic elite, while promoting a government of laws and facilitating economic enterprise, had not as yet given its own citizens the type of liberty that one associates with the growth of civil society in the West. This provided a third group of bureaucrats of the 1860s, having one foot in the development of Ottoman journalism and a closer connection to Western ideas of constitutionalism, with a weapon to fight their predecessors of the 1830s. Surprisingly, the promotion of constitutionalism by this bureaucratic Ottoman intelligentsia of the 1860s now linked its own stand with an idealized Islamic polity it accused its predecessors of having forgotten, and here we have to look at some of the justification for this attitude.⁶⁴

While this group, known as the Young Ottomans, worked for the adoption of a form of Western constitutionalism, it also claimed that these Western institutions were no different from those which were enjoined by Islamic culture and also had existed to a degree in the Ottoman Empire at its nadir. It spoke of representative government as a requisite of Islamic law. It alluded to a Golden Age of Ottoman society. While it is clear that the Young Ottomans' view of this golden age could not be demonstrated in fact, what they referred to were certain equilibrating features of Ottoman society about which they were more clearly on target.⁶⁵ There indeed existed in the Ottoman capital and its larger cities a sophisticated cultural network. The day-to-day activities of the urban population were well served by a price and product control mechanism established by the state but filled by personnel from the religious institution. The collective recollection of an age in which Ottoman society had been relatively in good shape, namely the eighteenth and early nineteenth centuries, was lively.⁶⁶

During the nineteenth century, as a consequence of the turn to the West of the reforming Ottoman bureaucracy, a mix of what Braudel would have described as the 'material' culture of the West and the Western-oriented cultural aspirations of both the liberal *and* the conservative bourgeoisie took hold of the Ottoman capital and its elites. This change was in full swing in the 1870s and 1880s.⁶⁷

Islamic culture was left as a residue; it continued to be the culture of the folk. The Ottoman elite's juggling act of keeping abreast of two cultures, one Western, one 'native', was made even more difficult by the attempt of Ottoman statesmen to conciliate the leadership of the Christian peoples of the empire (Serbs, Bulgarians, Greeks and Armenians). These people had a somewhat better understanding of the West through their contacts with it and were on the way to create their own – sometimes fairly literal and wooden – versions of Western civil society.

By the end of the nineteenth century, a new Ottoman elite emerged, stamped by the positivist views it had acquired in the new higher educational institutions of the empire. These schools had been created with the purpose of training competent bureaucrats with military, administrative and medical skills. The activist graduates of the schools – as well as many dropouts – are collectively known as the Young Turks. Through their estrangement from what they considered the backward ways of the folk, the once strong linkage between upper-class bureaucratic culture and folk culture now almost completely disappeared.[68] Finally, around 1910, the Young Turk elite brought out its own view of a Western-inspired civil society in the form of the French doctrine of solidarism.[69]

This was a programme that kept some of the features of the older Ottoman/Islamic culture in the sense of its affirmation of a sense of community responsibility and idealized conception of civil intercourse as free of conflict. Solidarism as an ideology was taken over by the more clearly secular – Jacobin – founding fathers of the Turkish Republic who made it the ideological foundation of republican society in 1923. Possibly it is this conservative element in solidarism and the role of Atatürk as the awaited just prince that allowed these republican luminaries to have their case heard at the popular level between 1923 and 1950. But solidarism without Western economic institutions had no roots. Both the earlier and later versions of solidarism were thus marked by the government's attempts to create a local class of entrepreneurs, a fairly successful undertaking which rebounded when the recipients of the government's incentives began to see themselves as an autonomous group and worked for the establishment of a more liberal political regime from the 1930s onward.

An altogether different situation has arisen since the instauration, between 1946 and 1950, of multiparty government in Turkey. The educational apparatus of the single-party Republic of the years 1923–46 was meant to mobilize rural populations. The system was taken over by the new administration of Turkey after 1950, and a backward glance at its performance shows a clear success in achieving the mobilizing goal of the early republic. The irony of history is that with the development the new Turkish democracy this success has reverberated into the political sphere. The educational mobilization of the masses has projected what was left of Islamic civic culture and civility into the front stage of Turkish social life. But this culture is not today what it was two centuries ago. The remaining, somewhat disparate elements of Islamic/Ottoman civic culture have now acquired a new and idiosyncratic momentum in a media-regulated populistic 'lifeworld'. In this sense, a new/old Islamic/Ottoman aspiration has in our time been legitimated in the Turkish media and in everyday life. Although its clientele is not clearly aware of it, this movement will not bring back the Islam of the seventh century. Nevertheless, its anchor is a new popular culture, and this culture needs to be examined with as much care as any collective aspiration. It is, after all, the dream of the Muslim come to life. It demands to be studied from a perspective which will accept as a dream both Islamic collective memory and the tracks traced by modern postindustrial society.

To summarize the experience of the Ottoman Empire, we may say that the 'dream' of Ottoman society was never given the structural moorings that would have enabled it to produce its own native and original social system; the encounter with the West made it something fragmented and incomplete. What remained of the dream was the Islamic religious ideal now disjoined from its total *telos*. Today, the autonomy of collectivities and the conception of rights that evolved in the West is slowly being worked into the fabric of Turkish society, helped by the successful multipartyism of the past 40 years. The understanding that features of Western society which in reality are part of the Western dream of civil society may be required for prosperity is increasingly understood. The difficulty consists in making Turkish society dream the Western dream in an era when, even in the West, dreams have lost their original connection with the growth of capitalism and when the primordialist dreams of lumpen fascists are everywhere replacing the dream of civil society. Consequently, it is not extraordinary to see Islamic collective memory slowly emerging as a force in Turkey, but what this other dream means in the frame of contemporary social life is still an enigma.

CONCLUSION

Through the introduction of bits and pieces of the social frame of Western civil society, many modern Muslim states are beginning to acquire a skeleton of institutions similar to those I have described for the West.[70] Yet the *dream* of Western societies has not become the dream of Muslim societies and this incongruity is part of the difficulty the latter experience. Orientalists, secular Jacobins, Marxist and ex-Marxisant scholars, as well as *bien pensant* deconstructionists, will have to look at countries in the Islamic culture area which do not have the Western historical background of civil society as, nevertheless, operating with the collective memory of a total culture which once provided a 'civilized' life of a tone different from that of the West but sufficiently attractive in its own terms to have left a positive trace. Seemingly incommensurable dimensions of social life can be bridged but only by studying the 'other' with the same depth as one studies one's self. This approach may shed more light on the enigma of the Muslim future than simple-minded defences or orientalist disparagement of Muslim culture.

NOTES

1 K. Polanyi, *The Great Transformation*, Beacon Press, Boston, Mass., 1957. The history I relate does not differentiate clearly enough between 'primary actors' and the people. What I attempt to isolate is the 'life' of institutions.

2 G. Ritzer, *Contemporary Sociological Theory*, 3rd edn, McGraw Hill, New York, 1992, p. 454, commenting on R. Bernstein, *Praxis and Action: Contemporary Philosophies of Human Activity*, University of Pennsylvania Press, Philadelphia, 1971. A number of contemporary philosophers have underlined the difference between this Aristotelian notion of practical rationality and its modern offshoot as an oppressive, cagelike rationality linked to a surrender to the demands of modern technology. I do not bring this point into my discussion since I believe that there is no necessary connection between this outcome and the elements of the dream I reconstruct. I would describe civil society as a set of equilibrating social mechanisms which can be studies of their own, without bringing consideration of these more recent and ominous developments into the picture.

3 See M. Kelly, 'The Gadamer/Habermas Debate Revisited: The Question of Ethics', in D. Rasmussen, ed., *Universalism vs Communitarianism*, MIT Press, Cambridge, Mass., 1990, pp. 139ff.

4 J. Abu Lughod, *Before European Hegemony*, Oxford University Press, New York, 1989, and her critique of existing theories about the Islamic city in 'The Islamic City: Historic Myth, Islamic Essence and Contemporary Relevance', *International Journal of Middle East Studies*, vol. 19, 1987. See also D. Eickelman, 'Is There an Islamic City? The Making of a Quarter in a Moroccan Town', *International Journal of Middle East Studies*, vol. 5, 1974.

5 M. Weber, *The City*, Free Press, New York, 1958.

6 E. Ennen, *The Medieval Town*, trans. N. Fryde, North Holland Publishing Company, Amsterdam, 1979, p. 89; F. Rörig, *The Medieval Town*, University of California Press, Berkeley, Cal., 1967, *passim*.

7 For 'judge-made' law, see A. A. Shiller, 'Jurist's Law', *Columbia Law Review*, vol. 58, 1958, p. 1230.

8 See H. J. Berman, *Law and Revolution: The Formation of the Western Legal Tradition*, Harvard University Press, Cambridge, Mass., 1983.

9 Rörig, *The Medieval Town*, p. 48.

10 A. J. Gourevitch, *Les Catégories de la Culture Mediévale*, Gallimard, Paris, 1983, pp. 279–80.

11 Rörig, *The Medieval Town*, p. 61.

12 J. H. Mundy and P. Riesenberg, *The Medieval Town*, J. Van Nostrand, Princeton, N.J., 1958, pp. 23, 24, 59.

13 S. Thrupp, *The Merchant Class of Medieval London, 1300–1500*, Chicago University Press, Chicago, Ill., 1948, p. 16.

14 D. H. Sacks, 'Celebrating Authority in Bristol', in S. Zimmerman and R. F. E. Weissman, eds, *Urban Life in the Renaissance*, University of Delaware Press, Newark, 1989, p. 13.

15 Thrupp, *The Merchant Class of Medieval London*, p. 100.

16 See J. Locke, *Two Treatises of Government*, ed., P. Laslett, Cambridge University Press, Cambridge, 1967, p. 343, and T. Hobbes, *De Cive*, ed. H. Warrender, Oxford University Press, Oxford, 1983, pp. 88–9.

17 J. Dunn, *Political Obligation in Historical Context*, Cambridge University Press, Cambridge, 1980, p. 39, referring to C. S. Macpherson, *The Political Theory of Possessive Individualism*, Oxford University Press, Oxford, 1962.

18 Dunn, *Political Obligation in Historical Context*, p. 60.

19 Dunn, *Political Obligation in Historical Context*, pp. 53–77. But we have also been made aware of the contractual element in medieval vassalage. For the way in which this concept operated as a 'productive fiction' in the course of time, see T. Szucs, 'Three Historical Regions of Europe', in J. Keane, ed., *Civil Society and the State: New European Perspectives*, Verso, London, 1988, p. 301.

20 J. Viner, 'Man's Economic Status', in D. A. Irwin, ed., *Essays on the Intellectual History of Economics*, Princeton University Press, Princeton, N.J., 1991, p. 278.

21 H. Nenner, *By Colour of Law*, University of Chicago Press, Chicago, Ill., 1977, pp. ix–xi, cited in J. C. Smith and D. N. Weisstub, eds, *The Western Idea of Law*, Butterworth, London, 1983, p. 433.

22 Dunn, *Political Obligation in Historical Context*, pp. 58–9.

23 H. Kamen, *The Rise of Toleration*, McGraw Hill, New York, 1972, p. 237.

24 H. Arendt, *The Human Condition*, Chicago University Press, Chicago, 1958, p. 38.

25 J. Keane, 'Despotism and Democracy: The Origin and Development of the Distinction between Civil Society and the State, 1750–1850', in Keane, *Civil Society and the State*, p. 43.

26 R. Bendix, J. Bendix and N. Furniss, 'Reflections on Modern Western States and Civil Societies', in *Research in Political Sociology*, vol. 3, JAI Press, Connecticut, 1987.

27 Keane, 'Despotism and Democracy', p. 48.

28 Keane, 'Despotism and Democracy, p. 59, citing Tocqueville's fear that the modern state stands over the whole of civil society as a power which is 'absolute, differentiated, regular, provident and mild' (*De la Démocratie en Amerique*, ed. F. Furet, Gallimard, Paris, 1981, vol. 2, p. 385).

29 Although an interesting parallelism is found in Europe before the self-referential development of Western law. See J. R. Strayer, *On the Medieval Origins of the Modern State*, Princeton University Press, Princeton, N.J., 1970, p. 15.

30 For the problem as posed by Aristotle, see H. V. Jaffa, 'Aristotle', in L. Strauss and J. Cropsey, eds, *The History of Political Philosophy*, 2nd edn, Chicago University Press, Chicago, Ill., 1973, pp. 112–14.

31 For the somewhat complex attitude of the Mutezilites, see S. Pines, 'Philosophy', in P. M. Holt, A. K. S. Lambton and B. Lewis, eds, *The Cambridge History of Islam*, vol. 2B, Cambridge University Press, Cambridge, 1970, pp. 790–1. Notice that the idea of justice was basically an equilibrating and conservative one. The contemporary shi'i idea of the downtrodden (*mustafizin*) as deserving special consideration is a reflection of Western ideas of class conflict.

32 M. Walzer, *The Revolution of the Saints*, Athenaeum, New York, 1973, p. 219. But the rise of deliberative bodies promoted by protestantism may be seen itself as an outcome of earlier European history.

33 I. M. Lapidus, 'Muslim Cities and Islamic Societies', in I. M. Lapidus, ed., *Middle Eastern Cities*, University of California Press, Berkeley, Cal., 1969, p. 51.

34 For ethnic communities, see J. Schacht, 'Law and Justice', in J. Schacht and C. E. Bosworth, eds, *The Legacy of Islam*, Oxford University Press, Oxford, pp. 552–3. A more general statement, made with characteristic delicacy, is that of I. M. Lapidus (*A History of Islamic Societies*, Cambridge University Press, Cambridge, 1988, p. 270):

> Whereas in the Middle East individual obligations were defined in terms of religiously commanded participation in a religiously defined community, in Europe the individual was perceived on two levels. One was in terms of the specialised roles which individuals played in occupational, corporate and office holding situations; the other was in terms of an inherent spiritual identity. Society itself came to be conceived in terms of individuals fulfilling a function, a calling, a role in a corporate, pluralistic and secular world.

See also, H. Lowry, 'Portrait of a City: the Population and Topography of Ottoman Selanik (Thessaloniki) in the Year 1478', in *Studies in Defterology: Ottoman Society in the Fifteenth and Sixteenth Centuries, Analecta Isisiana*, vol. 4, Istanbul, 1992, pp. 47–64.

35 *The Encyclopedia of Islam*, 2nd edn, vol. 6, C. E. Bosworth, E. Van Donzel, B. Lewis and C. H. Pellat, eds, E. J. Brill, Leiden, 1987, pp. 193–4.

36 During the modernization of Egypt, Ali Mubarak, the premier urbanist of Egypt, showed how little his point of view had changed as compared to that of Makrizi in so far as his own *Hitat* was simply an *enumeration* of all villages, canals, buildings, streets and other topographical features with hardly any detail about the structure of Egyptian society. See S. Fliedner, *Ali Mubarak und Seine Hitat*, Klaus Schwartz, Berlin, 1990.

37 *The Encyclopedia of Islam*, 2nd edn, vol. 1, B. Lewis, C. H. Pellat and J. Schacht, eds, E. J. Brill, Leyden, 1960, pp. 972–81.

38 M. A. Cook, 'Economic Developments', in Schacht and Bosworth, *The Legacy of Islam*, pp. 216ff. For a description of the role of a rich merchant, see N. Hanna, 'Isma'il Abu Taqiyya et le commerce international au Caire 1585–1625', in D. Panzac, ed., *Les Villes dans l'Empire Ottoman*, vol. 1, CNRS, Paris, 1991, pp. 211–19.

39 Cook, 'Economic Developments', p. 224.

40 A. Raymond, *Grandes Villes Arabes a l'Epoque Ottomane*, Sindbad, Paris, 1985, pp. 80–1, and, for 'Urban Functions', pp. 118ff.

41 See my article in *Cumhuriyet Dönemi Türkiye Ansiklopedisi,* Iletişim, Istanbul, vol. 7, 1993 (reprinted in *Türkiyede Toplumve Siyaset*, Iletişim, Istanbul, 1990, pp. 16–17), and R. Peters, 'The Battered Dervishes of Bab Zuwelyla: A Religious Riot in Eighteenth Century Cairo', in N. Levtzion and J. O. Voll, eds, *Renewal and Reform in Islam*, Syracuse University Press, N.Y., 1987, pp. 93–115.

42 In the sense of the institutionalization of 'nomadic' practices described by G. Deleuze in *A Thousand Plateaus*, Athlone Press, London, 1987, p. 159.

43 E. Burke, 'Understanding Arab Protest Movements', *Arab Studies Quarterly*, vol. 8, 1986.

44 E. P. Thompson, 'The Moral Economy of the English Crowd in the Eighteenth Century', *Past and Present*, no. 50, 1971.

45 'By the twelfth century C.E., 'The Spirit of Islam' had become essentially static ... this stagnation was inherent in the bases on which Islamic Law was founded' (F. Rahman, *Islam and Modernity*, Chicago University Press, Chicago, Ill., 1982, p. 26). Thanks to Joyce Marino for bringing this passage to my attention.

46 G. Makdisi, *The Rise of Colleges*, Edinburgh University Press, Edinburgh, 1981, p. 224.

47 Raymond, *Grandes Villes Arabes*, p. 127.

48 Makdisi, *The Rise of the Colleges*, p. 263.

49 An echo of the discussions that characterize eighteenth-century salons can be found in the Beşik taş Scientific Society which functioned in Istanbul at the beginning of the nineteenth century. See S. Mardin, *The Genesis of Young Ottoman Thought*, Princeton University Press, Princeton, 1962, p. 17.

50 Lapidus, *A History of Islamic Societies*, pp. 563ff.

51 See S. Mardin, *Religion and Social Change in Modern Turkey*, State University of New York Press, Albany, 1989.

52 L. A. and M. C. Fallers, 'Sex Roles in Edremit', in J. G. Peristiany, ed., *Mediterranean Family Structures*, Cambridge University Press, Cambridge, 1976.

53 C. F. Petry, *The Civilian Elite in Cairo in the Later Middle Ages*, Princeton University Press, Princeton, N.J., 1981, pp. 322–3.

54 R. Khuri, 'Freedom and the Arab-Muslim World', unpublished manuscript.

55 H. Inalcik, *The Ottoman Empire: The Classical Age, 1300–1600*, Weidenfeld and Nicolson, London, 1973, pp. 66–8. The introduction of administrative law was facilitated by the fact that the key institution of a 'truly' Islamic polity, the Caliphate, had been in decline since the sack of Baghdad. C. H. Fleischer (*Bureaucrat and Intellectual in the Ottoman Empire: The Historian Mustafa Ali (1541–1600)*, Princeton University Press, Princeton, N.J., 1986, p. 286) puts the matter neatly:

> the ideal of a universal Islamic empire effectively died in 1258 with the Mongol conquest of Baghdad ... subsequent universalistic claims, and indeed most political experiments were based on a nomad Central Asian

tradition of hegemony separate from but not antithetical to, the 'classical' sedentary pattern of Islamic government ... the concept of a universal caliphate was indeed a dead-letter by the fifteenth/sixteenth centuries; although the title 'caliph' was used in diplomatic correspondence throughout this period, it signified nothing more than 'Muslim sovereign'.

56 P. Goubert, *Louis XIV and Twenty Million Frenchmen*, Random House, New York, 1970, p. 52, cited by Bendix, Bendix and Furniss, 'Reflections on Modern Western States and Civil Societies', p. 9.
57 This is made particularly clear by G. Poggi, *The Development of the Modern State*, Stanford University Press, Stanford, Cal., 1978, pp. 72–3. The extent to which law became codified with time made the rights of Western 'estates' more precise and their tactic of rallying public opinion in defence of these possible. See the very clear description in W. Doyle, *The Old European Order, 1600–1800*, Oxford University Press, Oxford, 1978, p. 228.
58 S. Faruqhi, *Towns and Townsmen of Ottoman Anatolia*, Cambridge University Press, Cambridge, 1984, p. 301.
59 *Encylopedia of Islam*, 2nd edn, vol. 4, E. van Donzel, B. Lewis and C. H. Pellat, eds, E. J. Brill, Leiden, 1978, pp. 22ff, 229, 231, 239, 240.
60 Khartala, Paris, 1992, pp. 115–21.
61 Lowry, 'Portrait of a City', pp. 47–64.
62 For Cameralism see Doyle, *The Old European Order, 1660–1800*, p. 254.
63 Poggi, *The Development of the Modern State*, pp. 80–1.
64 Mardin, *The Genesis of Young Ottoman Thought*, passim.
65 S. Mardin, 'Freedom in an Ottoman Perspective', in M. Heper and A. Evin, eds, *State, Democracy and the Military: Turkey in the 1980s*, Walter de Gruyter, Berlin and New York, 1988, pp. 23–35.
66 Anyone who would like to have an idea of the content of Islamic law in the way it operated for Islamic citizens should read the ruling of a 1993 rabbinical court in Teaneck, N.J., which used a Jewish law on ruinous competition to curb the expansion of an entrepreneur in the delicatessen trade (*New York Times*, 14 February 1993, p. 41).
67 I have described that transformation fully in *The Genesis of Young Ottoman Thought*.
68 S. Mardin, 'The Just and the Unjust', *Daedalus*, vol. 120, 1991.
69 On solidarism, see J. E. S. Hayward, 'Solidarity: The Social History of an Idea in Nineteenth Century France', *International Review of Social History*, vol. 4, 1959, pp. 261–84, and 'The Official Social Philosophy of the French Third Republic: Leon Bourgeois and Solidarism', *International Review of Social History*, vol. 6, 1961, pp. 19–48.
70 For which see *The Middle East Journal*, special issue on civil society, vol. 47, 1993.

13

Civil Society and its Future

Salvador Giner

Civil society is one of the current concerns about which it seems nearly impossible to speak without at least an implicit reference to its future. The revival of interest in that area of interdependent processes which, long ago, received the generic name of 'civil society' does not only reflect a newly found curiosity about an apparently long-neglected and yet important notion. It also expresses an intense malaise about the evolution and ultimate fate of the social order in which we live. Unsatisfactory though that order is, it still seems to possess certain features that most people cherish and many fear to see gone forever. No one now defends the outright abolition of the inherited features of civil society in the confidence that their demise will be succeeded by the triumph of liberty, equality and fraternity in our midst.

This is an essay about the future of civil society. In composing it I have been aware of two things. First, that the notion itself may again fall out of fashion or even into oblivion, regardless perhaps – as happened in the past – of the continued presence into the future of what it denotes. In the second place, my observations cannot possibly ignore the fact that a number of authors have had serious doubts about the significance of the very term 'civil society'. Some of them believe that it is only a catch-all concept, a notion that has cast its net too widely, at best vaguely referring to the world outside the institutions of government and the state, at worst thoroughly empty.[1] Others, however, claim that the expression, vague and polysemic though it may often be, is a useful one. They also believe that the intense contemporary interest in civil society is entirely justified. For the problems and ideas associated with the notion of civil society, as Ernest Gellner says, 'are indeed intimately connected with the establishment of a democratic or liberal social and political order. In fact, "democracy", though acceptable as a shorthand code term for participatory and accountable government, carries with it a model which is less useful than the one suggested by "civil society".'[2] I share this view. Yet, one can share it and also confront the fact that, as a structure, civil society possesses a high degree of complexity and also not a small amount of ambiguity. As I define it below, however, it seems to me that the expression 'civil society' does refer to an identifiable social order, whose historical and current vicissitudes and changes can be quite recognizably followed, and about whose future one may, with due circumspection, speculate and even put forward a couple of plausible hypotheses.

Liberal democracy – encompassing not only political representation and participation, privacy and the autonomy of associations and private institutions, but also the free formation of all sorts of movements and parties, whether socialist, liberal, conservative, feminist, environmentalist, or of any other kind – has been closely tied to civil society throughout modern history. It may well be the case that the destiny of civil society will continue to be inextricably intertwined with that of democracy. Of course, a democratic society not grounded upon the double structure of a pluralistic civil society and a constitutional liberal polity is conceivable in the realm of abstraction and pure logic. But all societies are the outcomes of known historical realities. The institutional framework of all existing modern democracies stems from a group of specific civil societies which have developed within liberal states and market economies. (There has been a range of variations among them, often imposed by the rise of the welfare state and public enterprise, but the basic framework, shared by all, has always been respected.) A reasonable argument about the future of civil society must therefore assume that the historical bonds between it and liberal democracy will have to be maintained for either of them to endure, even if further modifications – indeed, improvements – are introduced in their mutual relationships as well as in their own respective textures and orders.

Historically, civil societies have only existed, with varying degrees of intensity, durability and success, in certain Western countries. There never was a golden age of civil society in any of them, though there was a time when, buttressed by a state zealous of its autonomy and indirectly underpinned by class inequality, it thrived practically unmolested in a few significant countries. Its features slowly and unevenly spread to others, nearly always hand in hand with the consolidation of liberal democracy in nations which had only had a sporadic or brief acquaintance with it in the past.

The end of the twentieth century has seen the growth of interest in the development of civil society in countries which either never had it, or where it had been suppressed, or where it had only led a most precarious life, often perilously confined to small and unstable enclaves. Given the intense contemporary transformation of the world and the ongoing globalization process, perhaps a fully-fledged consideration of the prospects for civil society ought also to take into account its predicament and promise (if any) in those parts of the world where it has not yet taken root or where people ardently desire its coming.[3] Yet, the task would be too large for my very limited purposes. For clarity's sake I will confine my attention only to those countries which historically saw the development of the network of relatively independent institutions that make up a civil society as well as the cultural attitudes of civility and tolerance which are an indispensable part of its civic and political culture. It is essentially their future, and not that of other possible or actually rising civil societies, that I wish to consider here. Yet, it is advisable to keep in mind that, whatever destiny awaits the civil societies of the liberal democratic universe, it is a universe which is now firmly attached to the rise of a single, interdependent world, increasingly comprising all human societies. Many of them do not possess our kind of polities. Indeed, their own institutional, cultural and political orders are frequently profoundly antipathetic to ours. Globalization will, accordingly, continue to produce its discontents as well as no little amount of friction between liberal democracies and other forms of conceiving the polity.

THE CLASSICAL STRUCTURE OF CIVIL SOCIETY

It is symptomatic of the endemic problems posed by the notion of civil society that any reflections upon the future of what it refers to must begin by establishing its meaning. The historical evolution of the concept and the theories about civil society have been traced and analysed many times. Recent scholarship has shown that both the concept and the theories of civil society are much older than the writings of John Locke and Adam Ferguson or the early growth of liberalism. It has also been shown that the relationships of civil society to other, alternative, structures and values are far more complex than it is often assumed.[4] We now possess a rather complete account of the development of the idea through time, its different meanings and the diverse theories or schools into which civil society conceptions can be marshalled.[5]

That account tells us that there is a variety of interpretations, often at loggerheads with each other. There is no such thing as *the* classical conception of civil society. There is a Lockean interpretation, but there is also a Hegelian one; and then there are Hobbesian, Marxian and Gramscian theories of it, to mention but a few among the more influential ones. They only share one thing in common: they refer to the sphere of social life which falls outside the state, though some do not see it as necessarily free from state interference. Although the recent revival of interest in civil society has increased the degree of consensus about the chief characteristics of civil society among analysts, there still remains ample room for disagreement between authors and schools.

As my own contribution needs some firm ground on which to stand, and I must circumvent the difficulty of having to face so much discrepancy, I have no option but to put forward yet another definition of civil society and to give some elementary details about its components. In doing so I do not wish to add to the debate but rather to detract from it. The following is a fairly eclectic definition. Yet, it cannot please everyone, for it incorporates inequality and conflict to a degree that tends to be ignored by some contemporary analysts of the phenomenon. My definition refers precisely to those features of modern society whose presence appears to be crucial for a proper consideration of the likely future evolution of the sphere of human activity covered by the concept 'civil society'.

Civil society is a historically evolved sphere of individual rights, freedoms and voluntary associations whose politically undisturbed competition with each other in the pursuit of their respective private concerns, interests, preferences and intentions is guaranteed by a public institution, called the state. Any mature civil society exhibits at least five prominent dimensions: individualism, privacy, market, pluralism and class.[6] They may be briefly described as follows.

1 Individualism   The main ontological assumption of liberalism is that the ultimate unit of social life is the individual, and that all political, economic and cultural institutions are no more than associations, or aggregates, of discrete individuals. A civil society is grounded on this belief. The individual is the seat of sovereign will. As such, individuals are also the sovereign components of the polity, and are defined as citizens. (Democracy, and the state, exist for protecting and fostering the rights and interests that belong to individuals in civil society, that is, independently of political life.)[7] Churches, parties, trading companies, are only aggregations of individual wills. They can be dismantled or modified by the citizens who set them up. In so far as the universe of an individualistic civil society has been successful (and there are no collectivistic civil societies) it has permitted both ontological and ideological individualism to thrive. As a seriously held belief or as important legal fiction, the assumption of individualism is the cornerstone of any civil society.

2 Privacy   Civil society is the abode of privacy in a world which has been divided into two realms: the public and the private.[8] When individual freedom is defined as a supreme good and non-interference with the life of others is considered to be a core virtue of social intercourse, privacy becomes the most characteristic achievement of a sound and strong civil society.

3 Market   If individualism and privacy are important facets of the moral justification of civil society, the market is its most salient structural feature. As civil society's organizing principle, the unhampered market allocates resources, honour, authority, as well as goods and services, through a spontaneous and ultimately anonymous process of countless contractual transactions among individuals and their associations. In a certain sense, the market is institutionless. At the economic level, from which it gets its name, the market generates equilibrium through aggregate forces of supply and demand. A similar process operates in the political, ideological, intellectual and cultural market-places. The resulting wider, generalized market is a competitive and essentially peaceful space for the production of social life.

4 Pluralism   This has two dimensions: on the one hand it entails the diffusion of power throughout society, which is then vested differently upon individual citizens, communities, associations, institutions and their diverse coalitions. They then become relatively autonomous from each other; they acquire their own spheres of competence where other entities – including the state – dare not penetrate with impunity. On the other hand, pluralism is also a culture, whereby a wide range of beliefs, conceptions and attitudes coexist freely and are equally fostered by their proponents. A substantial degree of tolerance is needed to sustain the culture of civil society. It thus indirectly legitimates the fragmentation of the social body according to individual preferences. These, in turn, tend to reflect existing patterns of class, ethnicity, belief, ideology and social closeness based on people's elective affinities. This is why civil society can be said to be the home ground of 'distinctions', the realm of 'difference' in a universe otherwise united by the imperatives of a common citizenship and equality before the law.

5 Class Social class is to a large extent the unintended consequence of citizenship. If citizenship is the political institutionalization of the sovereign individual within liberalism, and liberalism is in turn based on the competitive allocation of goods, then it follows that society must be made up of unequal people, though not perhaps of people unequal before the law, or at least not in principle. From this alone, however, it does not follow that class reproduction through time must necessarily occur.

Any serious consideration of the future of civil society cannot start from a straightforward analysis of these elementary components, as presented here in an explicit ideal-typical form. It must, rather, take into account their unavoidable transformation, indeed, deterioration, *as a result of their own inner logic* and not only as a consequence of other historical forces present in the development of modernity – though the latter also play an obvious role in the erosion of civil society arrangements. Let me then point out some of the perverse effects produced by the sheer introduction of the basic elements of any civil society into the liberal order of Western societies.

1 The limits of individualism Initially the chief difficulty in the advancement of individualism was the existence of a network of institutions inherited from the past which had to be abolished, for they were perceived as essentially inimical to individualism. The targets of early liberalism were guilds, estates, feudal privileges, as well as the ecclesiastical authority over the secular world. As soon as these powers fell, or their force was substantially attenuated, the presence of individualistically built coalitions – governments, parties, industrial and commercial enterprises – began to assert itself, often in an utterly non-individualistic manner. Though a powerful legal fiction to the contrary was maintained, it was discovered that the aggregation of interests into institutional arrangements could not easily undergo disaggregation. Vested interests endure. They do not easily bow to the proclaimed principles of universal individualism. The specific problem that ontological individualism breeds by advocating the free formation of voluntary associations is that of their collectivistic autonomy *vis-à-vis* the individuals that make them up.

2 *The utopia of privacy*   Privacy is an ideal of the liberal mind that can be approximated by being bought, or by being acquired through status, profession, power or skill. Apart from the not inconsiderable fact that there are many people who are not that keen to benefit from its blessings, privacy, by being in permanent tension with its opposite, the public life, gives rise to its own specific problem, the withdrawal from participation in public life. Citizenship, a virtue of political, rather than civil, society, demands popular involvement, lest the polity be left to the activists and the usurpers of the public sphere. An excess of privacy depoliticizes democracy.

3 *Monopoly and market*   Any social body which interferes with the market-place by imposing an extraneously determined allocation of goods and resources is bound to weaken or even destroy the social arrangements which emerge from it and which are precisely those of the civil society. 'Competitive' and 'peaceful' are, strictly speaking, contradictory terms. Permanent efforts at the restoration of market freedom (in some cases stemming from the democratic state in its role as protector of civil society) are necessary because individualists will not always extend their individualism to others. Monopolistic and oligopolistic tendencies in the economy, and oligarchic tendencies in the polity, are generated by the very logic of a mature or maturing civil society, thus leading to serious difficulties in its unhampered functioning.

4 *Asymmetric pluralism*   As in the case of the market, with which it is intimately related, pluralism always appears as a far cry from its own ideal type. The asymmetric distribution of power and influence amongst all the units that make up a pluralist order is always the norm. This is not only true of the individuals and units that compete with each other for the same goods (firms within the

economy, or parties struggling over the same sections of the electorate) but especially of those associations which confront each
other for the distribution of labour and income, as employers and
trade unions do.

5 Inequality and class A civil society is, by definition, a class
society, for it fosters an unequal distribution of goods and rewards.
Hypothetically, however, the entrenchment and reproduction of
privilege, patronage and property does not follow from the very
notion of civil society. In theory, each generation could produce
anew its own patterns of inequality. Yet, this is not so, for people
pass on to their offspring their own advantages and tend to favour
their friends, kinsmen and associates in their choices and decisions.
Morover, and contrary to T. H. Marshall's very influential position,
citizenship is not inimical to class.[9] On the contrary, citizenship
also helps the development of reproducible class positions by facilitating the consolidation of unequal advantages for the people of
the next generation, all in the name of freedom enjoyed by citizens
to transmit their own privileges to whom they wish. (That such
privileges are not any longer aristocratic or feudal in nature does
not mean they are not effective.) In addition to this, civil society,
relying as it does on 'spontaneous' contractual processes, lacks any
institutional apparatus to redress class bias. For that, people must
rely either on egalitarian social movements or on public policies,
that is, on government intervention. In classical liberal times the
state did little or nothing against class bias, and was not expected to
combat inequality of conditions. This is precisely the reason why
some notable theorists of civil society (Marx, for instance) were
able to describe the state as a mere excrescence of it, embodying
little more than the will and the interests of its ruling classes. Later,
when the state began to intervene with the purpose of attenuating
the injuries of class inequality, the fabric of civil society was not left
intact. From the standpoint of liberal orthodoxy, state intervention
in favour of civil society can only occur in the shape of deregula-
tion, denationalization and the dismantling of state agencies. State
intervention ought to exist only as withdrawal and abstention,
though government action in order to uphold the law, keep the
peace and sustain the validity of contracts freely entered into by
citizens was never questioned by the liberal conception.

Powerful and harmful though these counter-trends are for the
flourishing of a good civil society, they have never been strong

enough to be, by themselves, the causes of its obliteration. Yet, any attempt to draw up a model of what a civil society really entails must reject or at least play down certain aspects of the idealized liberal model by taking into account some of its less pleasant facets. To ignore the close relationship which binds any actual civil society to class inequality and conflict is particularly unjustified.

Civil societies had hardly begun to develop in Western Europe and North America before they stumbled upon the difficulties created by their own nascent structures. Several of them, however, as well as the bourgeois democratic state which then sheltered them, became remarkably successful, though they had to struggle continuously with the currents that stemmed directly from the endemic contradictions of the civic and liberal order. In the fullness of time such contradictions and difficulties came very clearly to the fore. It is by looking at the latter that we shall be in a better position to examine where the contemporary historical process might ultimately be taking the inherited order of civil society.

THE RISE OF THE CORPORATE ORDER

Premonitions that all was not well with civil society and that its life was more precarious than some people thought were already easy to perceive well before the Second World War. Bad omens about its fate were not confined only to countries where fascism had put a swift and violent end to its autonomy nor to those, like Russia, where, weak as it was, civil society had perished ingloriously at the first onslaught of revolution. Thus, in several advanced industrial countries a number of trends were at work which were silently eroding some of the foundations on which traditional civil society rested. These became more apparent after the Second World War, paradoxically at a time when civil society, helped by a powerful new cycle of capitalist prosperity and technological innovation, and actively protected by the victorious constitutional governments, enjoyed the benefits of powerful ideological and political reinforcements. Some of the trends working against the liberal order were prolongations of the innate dysfunctions of classical civil society; others, however, came from extraneous sources. Although such trends were varied and manifold, for clarity's sake I have grouped them under four mutually related headings, and called them, respectivelly, corporatization, state expansion, congestion and technoculture. My contention is that, taken together, they may help provide a plausible description of the future that awaits civil society.

1 Corporatization   Corporatization points to the rise of what may, with all due caution, be called a 'corporate society' in some prosperous, technologically advanced countries. Corporatization appears as a continuation of secular trends in bureaucratization, occupational specialization and the widespread proliferation of formal organizations in every field of endeavour. These organizations present a wide range of variation but are, essentially, of two kinds: they are either enterprises, firms, institutions and companies (public and private), or they are associations set up for the promotion of specific sets of collective interests and preferences, such as parties, unions, lobbies and guilds. Both kinds of organizations (or 'corporations' in the more generic sense of the word) not only tend to mediate between individuals and between classes, and between these and the state, but also between each other. Corporations now redefine the terms of social conflict, the scope of the market and the social allocation of goods, power and privilege. They distort or, at least, redirect the capacities of individuals and their associations to compete freely with each other and to form coalitions that might threaten the competence, power and ambitions of existing ones.[10]

In traditional civil society bargaining and negotiation were perfectly acceptable patterns of collective behaviour, though both the bourgeoisie and the working classes were for a long time poorly equipped for the task: the political culture of the age was, in this sphere, still too hostile to non-zero sum conceptions of power (though apparently far less so than in earlier historical periods). At any rate, negotiations were never understood as necessarily occurring between groups possessing some sort of tacitly 'official' status despite their essentially private nature. Today, by contrast, the corporatist management of labour relations, or of much of the economy, clearly challenges the traditional conception. In several countries, the institutionalization of the three-cornered relationship between government, employers and unions has entailed a major encroachment upon the market – though certainly not as great as that quietly generated by monopolies, oligopolies, cartels and powerful pressure groups – and has called forth further state intermediation, while strengthening the semi-official status of the managerial, professional and labour guilds.

The proliferation and consolidation of corporations and guild-like associations has led to the increasing displacement of other units of social life to a position where the latter – classes, communities, publics, individual citizens – must either express themselves through formally organized groups or take the often far more hazardous path of an 'alternative' movement not always capable of efficiently challenging the emerging corporate order. Although corporatization is still far from having exhausted all the available social space, the scope of corporations is much greater now than it ever was. Corporate saturation of society might not have arrived – and never will for as long as the currently strained pluralist universe effectively survives – but a situation of high corporate density is already a fact in many countries. It is not gratuitously that advanced modern society has often been described as a 'society of organizations' or 'corporations' by analysts of very different persuasions.[11] Organizational density now effectively challenges the basic tenet of civil society whereby any group of individuals can form an association of their own accord, based only on their free will and inclinations, in order to pursue their interests and try to satisfy their preferences in an environment of peaceful competition with other groups, fairly similar to them in wealth, power and influence. This might have only been part of the liberal utopia, but history shows that the notion was not groundless. Yet, today there appears to have taken place a steady decline in the possibilities opened up everywhere in advanced industrial societies for the successful establishment of associations in those areas where others already exist. The crystallization of firms, associations and corporations, as well as subsequent mergers, takeovers and syndications point towards the further development, in the decades to come, of a network of mutual dependencies and 'frozen' recognitions which makes the hypothetical fluidity of civil society as it was originally conceived increasingly problematic. The future will, most probably, further consolidate and broaden the structure of social monopolies and oligopolies which already exists in the economy, the administration, organized science and technology, the media and politics.[12]

The rules that generally characterize oligopolistic competition – diffidence, caution and agreed costs and prices – rather than market-determined ones, are bound to become those of the emerging order. This is clearly *not* to say that markets will disappear, nor that certain corporatist arrangements between bargaining groups may decline[13] (or, rather, fluctuate in their salience), nor that significant, even vast, areas of social life will continue to fall outside the bureaucratic or organizational sphere. On the contrary, the likelihood that in the future civil society will house new communal bonds and

emotionally grounded collective identitites is very high. Neo-
tribalism and other 'informal' and essentially unbureaucratic (indeed, anti-bureaucratic) manifestations of the contemporary
temper will continue to be called forth as a reaction to the anonymous, rootless and formal corporate structures that now pervade
society.[14]

2 State expansion   This has been a result of an entirely new conception of the polity that has fostered the hypertrophy of the
political and administrative apparatus sustained by a tax-paying
citizenry. It has entailed the metamorphosis of the state into a
massive regulatory and official construct. No longer a metaphor,
but a real political beast, albeit artificial, the state has penetrated
into every sphere of social life – as educator, provider of health,
police, justice and other public services, producer and consumer
of armaments, entrepreneur, investor and so on. It has thus considerably transformed the relationship which traditionally obtained
between itself and the sphere of civil society.

The process has approximated the state to the citizenry, though
not perhaps in the best and most desirable sense of the word: it has
often exposed the citizen to the predatory inclinations of the fiscal
authorities or to the prying powers of public agencies entrusted
with the surveillance of the private sphere. The state has been
increasingly involved in the life of its citizens through health and
welfare services, militarization, taxation, vigilance by police and
information agencies and such like.[15] At best this has represented an
erosion of what was once considered an inviolable sphere; at worst,
it has blurred the essential distinction and demarcation between the
public and the private, and between the state and civil society.[16]
A process that began only with some minimal and unavoidable
curbs upon the classical conception of property as *ius usum atque
abusum* now harnesses individual autonomy in this and other
matters quite systematically. Arguably, it often does so precisely in
order to protect certain freedoms and spheres of autonomy for
both individuals and associations. The rationale of public agency
interference is paradoxically the same as that which in earlier times
legally allowed official interference into areas given to privacy. In
democracies, however, the scope and intensity of protective surveillance and interference (for political, fiscal, legal, security or any
other reasons) is now much greater than it ever was. The trend,
despite vigorous reactions by civil rights groups and movements,
has not been effectively stemmed and any plausible vision of the

future must assume that there are considerable chances that the demarcation line between the state and civil society, and between the public and the private divide, may continue to undergo erosion. It is a divide that, were it to evaporate, would entail the extinction of both entities as we have known them. They would become idle notions for the analysis of society. They would only be endowed with historical interest.

3 Congestion   One of the chief causes of this particular situation is congestion. Thus there is institutional congestion due to corporate and bureaucratic density; legal congestion in the form of over-regulation; and even the contemporary state, still supposedly the defender of the fluidity and freedom of the civil society, suffers under the burden of its specific form of congestion, task overload. State overload, one of the main sources of the current crisis in the governability of advanced societies,[17] is closely related to the problems that beset civil societies. Nevertheless, by setting limits to the extent to which public agencies are capable of efficiently regulating and taking charge of private concerns and problems, the strains of government overload also help turn the tide of perennial state expansion. Vigorous reactions against state overload have already occurred, and their advocates are not only doctrinaire liberals, but also quite a few enlightened friends of a healthy public sector. By provoking such reactions, ungovernability caused by overload may paradoxically have actually helped the continued survival of civil society.

More palpably perhaps, there is congestion (in the sheer physical sense of the word) as a result of the immoderate size of the population, mass participation in formerly restricted areas of endeavour – the 'democratization' of any aspect of social life – and the rapid exhaustion of no-man's land. The connection between social congestion in all its forms (demographic, economic, cultural and political) with the environmental crisis is all too obvious. In the past, the various classical theories of civil society (whether liberal or socialist) assumed the availability of infinite resources, endless economic and industrial expansion and permanent growth, Malthus and Ricardo notwithstanding. They left much political and economic theory unprepared for what was to come. The intimate affinity between permanent material progress and the traditional conception of civil society hardly needs to be spelled out.

Congestion has changed our perception of the limits of social space. Inflationary tendencies in laws, regulations and by-laws (now not only produced by goverments, local or national, but also by international and supranational agencies) openly interfere with the 'spontaneous' development of life in civil society. Each new wave of events – increased unemployment, deindustrialization, immigration from the world periphery into its advanced prosperous core, rising crime, further pollution and destruction of the environment – generates a corresponding new wave of legislation upon a sphere which, by definition, was considered as inherently free of regulation from external bodies. For the first time, citizens feel that they cannot escape from the jurisdiction of such bodies.

Congestion leads to scarcity. Once upon a time, the ruthless Ricardian search for and opening up of virgin lands reflected a desire to flee from the pernicious externalities of capitalist and industrial growth, and not only a mere wish for the increase in profits. But the rapid diminution and exhaustion of the available virgin spaces – spaces out of the reach of regulatory constraints or negative externalities – has entirely transformed the environment into which a once-thriving, ever-expanding civil society flourished. Social congestion, Fred Hirsch pointed out, 'is a facet of social scarcity'. 'The good things of life' are now 'restricted not only by the physical limitations of producing more of them but also by absorptive limits on their use.'[18]

4 Technoculture   Of the trends which are bound to determine the fate of civil society, technoculture is the least rooted in its historical logic. The transformation in the meaning of knowledge (its frequent degradation into mere information and data gathering and control), the rise of information technology, the vast expansion of the mass media, robotization, artificial intelligence and telecommunications are the radically new traits of the age. Though it is still premature to speak of an 'information society', they have, taken together, profoundly transformed our perceptions, expectations and behaviour, as well as the political process and much of the social structure.[19] It is still an open question whether this galaxy of new technocultural elements will show itself really compatible with the inherited, albeit reformed, liberal society. For the moment it looks as though technological manipulation and control, combined with information technology, computerization and artificial intelligence, possesses an obvious affinity with corporate management as well as with the economic and political environment of the corporate society as just outlined. Thus, media and multimedia firms and corporations wholly belong to the world of the 'organizational society'. They are, by the same token, averse to the moral universe and personal freedoms fostered by certain aspects of traditional civil society, especially among its middle classes and the liberal professions, with their well-established habits of individual de-liberation based on active face-to-face discussion, often supported by much thoughtful reading of newspapers and books. Even if these practices continue to be more crucial in today's world than some pessimistic mass-culture critics would have us believe, it must be acknowledged that a powerful set of technical means for the transmission and manufacture of images and symbols now mediate between institutions, citizens and social movements. Often, the latter do not exist unless they become also media events. The dis-cussion on television of public issues and concerns may often become a travesty of a real debate between independent citizens. Civil society as a market-place has surrendered to the corporate, mass society as a showing place.

A vast and powerful technosphere – together with its cultural dimension, the emerging technoculture – has now developed and set unprecedented conditions for the whole of our cultural life, including the nature of intellectual discourse, as well as our critical perception of the world.[20] For their part, the conditions created by the development of a now wholly established mass culture are essentially different (and often hostile) to the prerequisites of a minimally autonomous body of responsible citizens.[21]

THE FUTURE

The demise of civil society has not yet taken place. Nor do we possess sufficient evidence to suggest that it will soon die. Some authors have already announced the event, however: for them a most bleak destiny awaits it, especially considering that whatever is going to substitute civil society in the future is bound to be worse, according to them.[22] By contrast, others, usually of the neo-liberal persuasion, have been notoriously busy proclaiming its return and splendid renaissance, often failing to look at several of the structural trends which may either erode or transform its fabric beyond rec-ognition, and which have already been pointed out so far in this essay.

If many of the developments identified so far militate against the future permanence of a thriving civil society, we have also encountered a number of significant processes which have acted as barriers to its demise. For instance, the injuries of class and the transgressions of ruthless capitalist and industrial practices have frequently been mitigated by social reform and public policies for resource redistribution and the protection of the underpriviledged. Thus while social democracy (or, in America, 'liberal' government policies) may have slightly eroded a few features of certain traditional civil societies, by and large, the damage this sort of public intervention has caused to them has always been far less pronounced than that produced by other forces, including those unleashed by liberalism itself. Thus, left to themselves, capitalist monopolies, economic recessions, totalitarian or demagogic and populistic politics, to give but a few examples, have been much greater foes of the open society (as embodied in the autonomy of the civil sphere) than democratic socialism, for all its interventionism, has ever been.

The subtlety of the situation is rich in paradox. The state, for example, whose unfettered expansion has posed an obvious threat to civil society, has also often become one of its safeguards, especially when some of its agencies have learnt to cooperate with voluntary associations, non-profit organizations and all sorts of philanthropic projects inspired by private citizens. For their part, vigorous citizens' rights movements have helped contain the effronteries of rulers and even combat state hypertrophy.[23]

Some guarded optimism about the prospects for democracy has been justified by all this, not to speak of the recent extension of the liberal democratic order to lands which until now were deprived of its benefits. Transitions from dictatorship to democracy in southern Europe between 1974 and 1977 strengthened the autonomy of their respective civil societies and opened the way to other, roughly similar, transitions in Latin America and elsewhere. In a number of countries, and especially in Mediterranean Europe, democratic consolidation ensued. Later on, the technobureaucratic, single-party regimes of the Soviet empire collapsed, though the difficulties encountered by the successor democratic or would-be democratic polities were much greater than in southern Europe, for civil societies had been nonexistent or much weaker there. As a Russian democrat put it in the early 1980s, before the transitions occurred: 'One of the peculiarities of the Soviet system is that an impotent society faces an omnipotent state or, to be more precise, [that there is an] absence of civil society'.[24] The vast movement for the reconstruction and democratization of those postcommunist polities in the years that came afterwards can be seen also as the result of a conscious effort to build strong and healthy civil societies and therefore to find a secure future for them.[25] All this has been strengthened by the ability of social democracy to show, as John Hall has pointed out, a capacity to become 'a just and efficient option for a nation-state within capitalist society'. The new 'consolidations of democracy open up rather than close down new historical possibilities' among which there are, practically by definition, those of civil society.[26] Yet, the prospects and possibilities for civil society are not straightforward ones. In the societies where civil society was once, as it were, naturally born, it has now undergone several of the far-reaching modifications that have been already indicated here. The chances are that further changes will take place in the future until at least the pre-industrial type of civil society (say, that of New England in America) eventually acquires a purely vestigial character.

Until now, the greatest inroads of both *étatisme* and corporatization into the fabric of civil society have taken place at the structural level, as distinct from the cultural one, but we have just seen that techno- and mass culture are also taking their toll. Nevertheless, the very needs of the modern polity and the economy, as well as the legal and ethical principles of a secular society continue to uphold the ethos of individualism and personal and associational autonomy, albeit in a novel manner. The requirements of competition, occupational recruitment and social promotion foster these attitudes within and without organizations. The shift from entrepreneurial competitiveness to the newer, occupational kind, has meant that personal qualifications and entitlements to privacy and autonomy have often been respected in significant ways by the powers that be. Why should this not be the case in the decades to come? For one thing, the corporate economy is the first to benefit from a private pool of skills, talent and expertise in all classes or, as the conservative euphemism always has it, walks of life. A defence against the class injuries of this market-like arrangement (human capital has a counterpart, the human market, as the subscribers to the 'human capital' school are well aware) is the unionization of the labour force for its own protection as well as the creation of professional associations for the consolidation of privilege. These are parallel developments with which civil society has been able to cope in the past, though it has not come out of the trial unscathed.

The civil society of the future is bound to distance itself from the now fast-receding bourgeois society and its culture, albeit not entirely from its class arrangements. My own definition of civil society incorporated class inequality as an essential component of any realistic conception of the phenomenon. Interestingly enough, a part of the culture of the old civil society, conveniently redefined, is still very useful for the maintenance of modern forms of class inequality and undemocratic power, political or otherwise. Thus there has occurred a transition from the possessive individualism of yesterday – based on private property, once the true pillar of the civil society – to *positional individualism*, based on occupation, social (not only human) capital and power within institutions and organizations. Accordingly, we must come to understand how certain components of the culture of the old bourgeois society – especially those which foster class closure and the reproduction of inequality – also underpin the now emerging societal order, especially if we wish to unravel the puzzle posed by its antinomies.[27]

The inherited liberal and pluralist framework, now recast, is not only necessary for the maintenance of inequality *and* for the fluid recruitment of qualified personnel into the positions which regularly become vacant in each corporation, but also, and very especially, for the neutralization of dissent. In this respect, the old culture of tolerance (once within the bounds of bourgeois puritanism) has reached a new extreme in the form of permissiveness and an openly acknowledged moral relativism. Its consequences for the ability of future citizens to distinguish between private and sectional interests, on the one hand, and the common interest, on the other, could eventually be dire.[28] One of those consequences, which can be felt already, is the indifference of the arrangements of the contemporary world to both permissiveness and relativism. Thus, people may now advocate the immediate implementation of the most radical and often outlandish goals. Unless they do not openly threaten the public order (including its patterns of privilege), they will be met with tolerance, indifference or, at most, with some efforts to accommodate them within the existing conventions.

Not so long ago, confronted with this phenomenon, some critics produced the theory of 'repressive tolerance' in order to explain this seeemingly intractable question.[29] The theory, unfortunately, was flawed by a rejection of those elements of the liberal creed which stem from the more universal facets of human freedom. The theorists of 'repressive tolerance' seemed to forget that the considerable degree of tolerance they themselves so much enjoyed was made possible by the development of a 'non-repressive' tolerance in their own countries, unless they believed that the totalitarian regimes which they also abhorred were unwittingly preparing the way for the future triumph of liberty and the development of a decently working civil society. Events before and after 1989 in Eastern Europe soon showed this to be highly problematic. If this be the cunning of history, it is a very low cunning indeed.

If we are to acknowledge a crisis in civil society, we must first of all establish its limits. Thus far I have shown that, rather than a breakdown, civil society has undergone several far-reaching modifications. These were, among other things, closely related to the structure of the corporate society and to the transformation of the contemporary state, fluctuations in its growth as well as the appearance of supra-state authorities. The reformed civil society of the present has become entrenched in the political realm as the ideology of pluralistic, parliamentary democracies. As such it has often been revived by people who had ceased to invoke its name long ago. Its advocates foster the survival of minimal market conditions through anti-trust laws and regulations against unfair competition. They conceive it as an essential part of the peculiar culture of compromise which characterizes our troubled times within democratic polities.

The civil society ideology now buttresses the embattled realm of citizenship. It protects the life of voluntary associations and autonomous social movements, as well as the growth of a 'non-profit', 'altruistic' or 'third' sector in the economy, deeply committed to the flourishing of a social universe capable of giving shelter to the expression of unselfish values on the part of its members, and not only to the greedy instincts of a business world made up of possessive individualists. The size of this increasingly important sector is still small if compared to the rest of the economy, but its growth, closely related to changes in the moral culture of the age, cannot be ignored: it may herald a crucial shift towards a far less production-oriented society, especially under the conditions imposed by the growing environmental crisis which we are now facing. The idea of a civil society eventually free from the shackles of a purely capitalistic conception of the polity and the economy is therefore neither a naive nor a pious one.

We may be well advised not to discard the notion of civil society in the future. The rise of new social movements, autonomous bodies, all sorts of organizations that are neither entrepreneurial nor governmental, and altruistic associations grounded on a conception of the polity as a creation for the preservation of the freedom of action of the citizenry, may unexpectedly be harbingers of a civil society stronger than that of the past. There are, of course, signs which point in a different direction: our societies are certainly not free of racism, obscurantism, political corruption, partisan arrogance and more than embryonic expressions of totalitarianism and fanaticism. These are trends that, in the past, managed to destroy entire democracies or gravely flaw the life of many of them. The fact remains, however, that, through much sacrifice, the people often reconquered or regained their lost liberal polities and rebuilt their civil societies.

Their solidity has continued to depend on the careful maintenance of the state/civil society dichotomy. The state itself would come to an end if, against a famous prediction, civil society, not the state, withered away. This follows from the very nature of the fundamental division between the two complementary spheres: in the liberal polity they had always been a function of each other, by and large mutually endorsing their respective concerns. This was essentially true even though state encroachment upon the private sphere and private control by ruling classes and powerful groups (such as castes of civil servants, *fonctionnaires* and *Beamten*) was always endemic and further blurred the necessary demarcation lines between the two halves of the traditional dual polity. At any rate, the improbability of the imminent demise of the state can be taken for granted, as I do here, only if the state itself is redefined as an identifiable sphere of public authority, officialdom and democratic political authority within a minimally democratic framework. This framework tends now to evolve towards transnational federalism. The foreseeable withering away of the 'national' state – though not of the *sphere* of the state – is therefore perfectly plausible: in some places, such as Western Europe, the early phases of the extinction process may have already begun.[30] The effective recognition of limited sovereignty by the member governments and parliaments of the European Union is only one of the more visible signs. World-state visionaries notwithstanding, the end of this hazardous road is not likely to end in a much vaster or in a single state – states can only exist in relation to one another – but in a complex, stateless network of trans-national public management bodies: agencies of large-scale imperative coordination in the fields of the environment, energy, transport, the mass media and telecommunications, health, goods distribution, peace-keeping and expeditionary forces, policing and regulatory law enforcement. If there is, then, a withering away, it looks as though it is not going to be the one envisaged by some noble dreams of the past.

No doubt events may take a different turn. What seems clear, however, is that for them to follow a discordant path from that so roughly outlined here, drastic changes both in further *étatisation* (in some areas) and 'de-statization' (in others), as well in continued corporatization would have first to take place. Yet, we do not have enough evidence that such change of course is at hand.

There have emerged unexpected innovations in the field of civil society: new civic and citizens' movements; the growth of the cooperative and the 'non-profit' sectors of the economy; a rise in the desire for participatory democracy; consumers' associations; well-established social movements, such as environmentalism, pacifism and feminism, which are no longer new. Although the contemporary effervescence brought about by their presence may not always bode well for pluralism and freedom (neo-fascist and racist agitation, for instance, or fanatical sects, as well as blind and heavy-handed responses on the part of the authorities, are unwelcome developments in the life of our democracies), a revitalization of the civil society can easily be detected: its associational texture is now richer.[31] The old civil society (in the countries where it was strong) had a powerful private sector in both economy and social structure and a significant, but small, associational and altruistic sector. This latter sector, against all the dire predictions once made by some of the ideologists of the mass society conception over several decades, is now steadily growing. It includes a motley array of very different voluntary associations and institutions, alongside others which are of a clearly neo-tribal nature, often based on ethnic, communal, belief or other affinities. Many of them, especially in the former category, are jealous defenders of their own autonomy *vis-à-vis* the powers that be. Their aggregate efforts strengthen the autonomy of the civil society.

The resulting image may give too untidy an impression of the emerging structure of civil society.[32] Some may accordingly wish to reject the picture as still holding little explanatory power. But the social world is hardly amenable to neat and simple theorizations, let alone representations. Classical civil society itself was highly complicated and all the theories that aimed at interpreting it put forward oversimplifications that were perhaps at least as gross as the lineaments of the future intimated here. Locke's, Ferguson's, Hegel's, Marx's and Gramsci's respective visions of civil society (to cite only some of the best known) considerably differed from each other, both in descriptive and normative terms, and all showed a manifest 'lack of fit' with the complex phenomenon they nevertheless so powerfully interpreted. Their analyses covered under the category 'civil society' a set of social processes similar to that proposed in this chapter. Civil society yesterday, today and, if it survives, also tomorrow, must be understood as the *sphere of that which is relatively but autonomously private within a modern polity*. The latter will remain, then, if it endures, a *dual polity*, composed on the one hand of a public component, which includes the state – or the 'neo-state' as envisaged here, as a network of public agencies – plus those elements which enter the democratic public arena: parties, citizens' movements, and such like; on the other, of a private one, made up of all other social entities, never excluding (as has always historically been the case, even in the heyday of traditional civil society) citizens and associations straddling both areas, blithely heedless of the niceties of the distinctions made by the political philosophers.

CONCLUSION

This essay has attempted to show that civil society is an essentially historical entity, having undergone, as such, continuous change. The important modifications that have affected its shape in the past, however, have not been so far so great as to justify a rejection of the notion. This seems especially so when we consider how often there have been effective 'corrections' from the path that leads away from the fundamental arrangements that keep the public/private and state/civil society divide working minimally; and even more so when we realize how many polities, at the end of the twentieth century have, often successfully, tried to reconstruct or create those two dichotomies, which their citizens saw as essential to freedom and the democratic life. On this basis, and on a careful consideration of the nature and directions of contemporary change, I have assumed that it will be not leading us in the near future into a situation out of all recognition, where the complete demise of civil society may confidently be announced.

Unfortunately for an analysis such as this, the presence, or absence, of a civil society as part of the constitution of the future order of democracy will be, in the last resort, largely a matter of opinion. If we take the minimalist position (as I do here) that the distinction between a state sphere and a private sphere (buttressed by a liberal constitution) is all that is needed for the recognition of the survival of civil society, we may be fairly confident that it has a future. If we, on the other hand, assume that certain contemporary trends (such as corporatization) are bound steadily to erode its fabric and blur all meaningful demarcation lines between public power and private autonomy, we will have no other option than that of declaring its imminent and irretrievable end. Some observers have, in fact, contended that, under the pressures of economic and other crises, contemporary capitalist societies have already been forced to give up their once crucial distinction between state and civil society.[33] This may be a rather premature opinion, inspired by a lack of awareness that such distinction was always precarious and never perfect. Civil society theorists such as Marx and Gramsci were at pains to show precisely that. Marx's idea that the state was the mere tool of the ruling classes, and that it was essentially a by-product of the civil society, subordinate to its most powerful elements, may have been an exaggeration, which overlooked the relative, albeit important autonomy of the state, but it did not ignore the structural nature of the two spheres. Gramsci's concept of hegemony, which has no doubt fared better, openly assumed the interpenetration of the two spheres, and the diffuse character of a political culture which is full of ambiguities. At any rate, neither of these two authors ignored the substantial deviations of any actual civil society from its model notion or ideal type. The chances are that the civil societies of the near future will not deviate more from that type than the bourgeois, early capitalist and industrial societies of the past did deviate from it. They will do so, of course, only in a very different manner.

Civil society, or its equivalent, may, in the future, go by another name. Yet, if the women and men of tomorrow wish to remain free citizens, capable of a decent degree of autonomy in order to carry out their own business, both public and private, they will have to continue to dwell in a universe which must be, in a fundamental sense, not dissimilar to that represented until today by civil society. That tomorrow's citizens will wish so to live will to a large extent depend on today's democrats, for whom the defence of the autonomous sphere of the civil society and the presence of strong centres of countervailing power are an essential part of a truly modern and rational conception of freedom. They ought to be aware, however, that often people of power throughout our societies no longer truly believe in its virtues and benefits, though they are forced, constitutionally as it were, to pay their public respects to it. For many of those who still proclaim the need for a flourishing civil society actively help the advent of a bleak universe in which, were they to succeed, there would be no need whatsoever for it.

NOTES

1 For instance, E. Etzioni-Halevy, *The Elite Connection*, Polity Press, Cambridge, 1993, pp. 80–1.
2 E. Gellner, 'Civil Society in Historical Context', *International Social Science Journal*, no. 129, 1991.
3 Gellner, 'Civil Society in Historical Context', refers to Eastern Europe and to the Islamic countries in their respective and difficult relationships to civil society. See also, D. Held, ed., *Prospects for Democracy*, Polity Press, Cambridge, 1993, for discussions of Eastern Europe and Sub-Saharan Africa.
4 D. Colas, *Le Glaive et le Fléau*, Grasset, Paris, 1992.
5 S. Giner, 'The Withering Away of Civil Society?', *Praxis International*, vol. 5, 1985; Colas, *Le Glaive et le Fléau*; K. Tester, *Civil Society*, Routledge, London, 1992.
6 This definition (and the following paragraphs) follow Giner, 'The Withering Away of Civil Society?', pp. 254–8.
7 M. Warren, 'Democratic Theory and Self-Transformation', *American Political Science Review*, vol. 86, 1992.
8 H. Béjar, *El ámbito íntimo*, Alianza, Madrid, 1990.
9 There is a greater affinity between citizenship and social class than T. H. Marshall assumed in his classic *Citizenship and Social Class*, Cambridge University Press, Cambridge, 1950. Class and citizenship are certainly not mutually antagonistic.
10 A. Cotta, *Le Corporatisme*, Presses Universitaires de France, Paris, 1984; R. J. Harrison, *Pluralism and Corporatism*, George Allen and Unwin, London, 1980; S. Giner and M. Pérez Yruela, *La sociedad corporativa*, C.I.S., Madrid, 1979.
11 J. K. Galbraith, *The New Industrial State*, Penguin, London, 1969; Giner and Pérez Yruela, *La sociedad corporativa*; R. Presthus, *The Organisational Society*, Knopf, New York, 1962.
12 F. Bourricaud, 'Les forteresses de l'oligopole social', in J. Lesourne and M. Godet, eds, *La Fin des habitudes*, Seghers, Paris, 1985.
13 For a critical appraisal of the assumption that corporatism (as a bargaining process) is in decline, see M. M. L. Crepaz, 'Corporatism in Decline? An Empirical Analysis of the Impact of Corporatism on Macroeconomic Performance and Industrial Disputes in 18 Industrialised Democracies', *Comparative Political Studies*, vol. 25, 1992.
14 M. Maffesoli, *Le Temps de tribus*, Meridiens Klincksieck, Paris, 1988.
15 R. M. Unger, *Knowledge and Politics*, Harvard University Press, Cambridge, Mass., 1976.

16 S. I. Benn and G. F. Gaus, eds, *Public and Private in Social Life*, Croom Helm, London, 1983; R. Sennett, *The Fall of Public Man*, Knopf, New York, 1977.

17 X. Arbós and S. Giner, *La Gobernabiladad*, Siglo XXI, Madrid, 1993; G. Pasquino, *Crisi dei partiti e governabilità*, Il Mulino, Milan, 1980.

18 F. Hirsch, *Social Limits to Growth*, Routledge and Kegan Paul, London, 1977, p. 3.

19 P. Breton and S. Proulx, *L'explosion de la communication*, Boréal, Montreal, 1989; D. Lyon, *The Information Society*, Polity, Cambridge, 1988.

20 S. Giner, *Essayos civiles*, Península, Barcelona, 1987, pp. 137–54; R. Debray, *Cours de médiologie générale*, Gallimard, Paris, 1991.

21 There has been much debate on this issue, and also a high degree of agreement. On this topic see S. Giner, *Mass Society*, Martin Robertson, Oxford, 1976, pp. 159–82.

22 Tester, *Civil Society*, p. 176.

23 R. J. Dalton and M. Kuechler, eds, *Challenging the Political Order*, Oxford University Press, New York, 1990.

24 B. Weil, 'Current Opposition in the Soviet Union', *Praxis International*, no. 1, 1981, p. 101.

25 Gellner, 'Civil Society in Historical Context', pp. 495–510; K. Z. Poznanski, ed., *Constructing Capitalism*, Westview Press, Boulder, 1992; Z. Rau, ed., *The Reemergence of Civil Society in Eastern Europe and the Soviet Union*, Westview Press, Boulder, Colo., 1991.

26 J. A. Hall, 'Consolidations of Democracy', in Held, *Prospects for Democracy*, p. 288.

27 Giner, *Essayos Civiles*, pp. 79–136; P. Bourdieu, *La Distinction*, Minuit, Paris, 1979.

28 V. Camps and S. Giner, *El interés común*, Centro de Estudios Constitucionales, Madrid, 1992.

29 R. P. Wolff, B. Moore, and H. Marcuse, *A Critique of Pure Tolerance*, Jonathan Cape, London, 1969.

30 S. Giner, 'The Rise of a European Society', *Revue européenne des sciences sociales*, vol. 31, 1993.

31 Dalton and Kuechler, *Challenging the Political Order*; Held, *Prospects for Democracy*; C. Mongardini, *Il futuro della politica*, Franco Angeli, Milan, 1990.

32 Some may see an affinity between this and what has dubiously been called a 'postmodern' world. Although this essay has carefully avoided any discussion of the future of civil society in terms of 'postmodernity', see R. R. Weiner, 'Retrieving Civil Society in a Postmodern Epoch', *Social Science Journal*, vol. 28, 1991.

33 C. Offe, *Contradictions of the Welfare State*, Hutchinson, London, 1984, p. 37.

Index

Page numbers in *italics* refer to figures or tables.